Free Methodist Studies

Free Methodist Studies:
CLASSIFICATION AND BIBLIOGRAPHY

by

Paul A. Tippey, PhD

First Fruits Press
Wilmore, Kentucky
2016

Free Methodist studies : classification and bibliography.
By Paul A. Tippey, Ph.D.

First Fruits Press, ©2016
Previously published by the Free Methodist Publishing House, 1913.

ISBN: 9781621716259 (print), 9781621716266 (digital), 9781621716273 (kindle)

Digital version at http://place.asburyseminary.edu/firstfruitspapers/71/

First Fruits Press is a digital imprint of the Asbury Theological Seminary, B.L. Fisher Library. Asbury Theological Seminary is the legal owner of the material previously published by the Pentecostal Publishing Co. and reserves the right to release new editions of this material as well as new material produced by Asbury Theological Seminary. Its publications are available for noncommercial and educational uses, such as research, teaching and private study. First Fruits Press has licensed the digital version of this work under the Creative Commons Attribution Noncommercial 3.0 United States License. To view a copy of this license, visit http://creativecommons.org/licenses/by-nc/3.0/us/.

For all other uses, contact:

First Fruits Press
B.L. Fisher Library
Asbury Theological Seminary
204 N. Lexington Ave.
Wilmore, KY 40390
http://place.asburyseminary.edu/firstfruits

Tippey, Paul A.
   Free Methodist studies : classification and bibliography / by Paul A. Tippey. -- Wilmore, Kentucky : First Fruits Press, ©2016.
      507 pages ; 21 cm.
      ISBN - 13: 9781621716259 (pbk.)
      1. Free Methodist Church of North America--Bibliography. I. Title.
BX8417.T56 2016   016.287/97

Cover design by Jon Ramsay

asburyseminary.edu
800.2ASBURY
204 North Lexington Avenue
Wilmore, Kentucky 40390

First Fruits Press
The Academic Open Press of Asbury Theological Seminary
859-858-2236
first.fruits@asburyseminary.edu
http://place.asburyseminary.edu/firstfruits

Asbury Theological Seminary
204 N. Lexington Ave., Wilmore, KY 40390
asburyseminary.edu
800-2ASBURY

Contents

Preface..2

Content by Alphabet...4

Content by Subject..165

1. Free Methodism...166

    a. Free Methodism Bibliography....................133

    b. Free Methodist Church................................304

        i. Biography...360

        ii. Church Growth.....................................371

        iii. Clergy Biography.................................374

        iv. Devotional/Christian Life....................380

        v. Discipline..382

        vi. Doctrine...383

        vii. Government..389

        viii. Handbooks, Manuals, etc..................390

    ix. History..392

    x. Holiness..396

    xi. Hymns..398

    xii. Leadership...400

    xiii. Missions..402

    xiv. Sermons...409

    c. Free Methodist Curriculum.................................415

    d. Free Methodist Periodicals..................................422

    e. Free Methodist Primary Resources.....................424

    f. Free Methodist Publishing House........................448

    g. Light and Life Press...458

2. Roberts, Benjamin Titus, 1823-1893........................496

3. Roberts, Ellen Lois Stowe..502

4. Recent Publications (last 10 years)...........................506

PREFACE

The Following bibliographic resource does not provide exhaustive coverage of all area of Free Methodism. The purpose of compiling a bibliography on Free Methodism is to identity a body of work that interprets the lives, beliefs, traditions, and labor of those within the denomination. The citations are primarily with Free Methodist subject except for those in general categories, which have reference to Free Methodism. A number of unpublished manuscripts are included. Primary and secondary works are not differentiated. Arrangement of all works is by subject.

The compiler is in debt to Dr. Robert Danielson whom reviewed a draft of the text and assisted with additional recommendations. Any mistakes or omissions are solely the responsibility of the editor. Corrections, additions and deletions for the next edition of this bibliography are welcomed and should be sent to Paul A. Tippey, Executive Director of Library Services, B. L. Fisher Library, Asbury Theological Seminary, 204 N. Lexington, Wilmore, Kentucky, USA 40390. Office: 859.858.2299 or E-mail: paul.tippey@asburyseminary.edu.

Content by Alphabet

Content by Alphabet

"(Journal, Magazine, 1932) [WorldCat.org]," n.d. http://www.worldcat.org/title/leaders-in-education-a-biographical-dictionary/oclc/42314538&referer=brief_results.

A Brief History of Holiness Movement Missions, 1899-1959. Athens, Ont.: Y.P.M.S., 1948.

Ablard, Gilbert C. "The History and Growth of the Winstanley Free Methodist Church, Wigan, Lancashire, England." Western Evangelical Seminary, 1981.

Ablard, Muriel, Christian Life Club, Joanna. Baker, Christian Life Club, and Christian Life Club. *Discovery Time: Recreation Fun, Creativity Fair, Social Event; Trailblazer; Grades 3 and 4; Year One.* Winona Lake, Ind.: Light and Life Press, 1988.

"Action." *Action.* Winona Lake, IN: for Aldersgate Publication Association by Light and Life Press, 1981.

"Activity Time." Marion Ind.: Wesley Press, 1969.

Adams, Frederick Allan. "A Case Study of the Elim Farm Project of the Filipino Free Methodist Church." Trinity Evangelical Divinity School, 1999.

Adams, Linda J. "Strengthening the Vitality of New Hope Free Methodist Church through the Natural Church Development Approach." Asbury Theological Seminary, 2000.

Adams, Paul L. "The Lessons I've Learned in Politics," 2014. http://place.asburyseminary.edu/ecommonsatschapelservices/.

Ahern, Alvin A. *Luke: Leader's Guide.* Winona Lake, Ind.: Light and Life Press, 1965.

Ahlstrom, Sydney. *A Religious History of the American People.* New Haven: Yale University Press, 1972.

"Aldersgate Dialogue Series." Winona Lake IN: Light and Life Press, n.d.

"Aldersgate Doctrinal Studies." Winona Lake IN: Light and Life Press, n.d.

"Aldersgate Graded Curriculum." Winona Lake IN: Light and Life Press, n.d.

Aldersgate Publications Association, and Aldersgate Publications Association. "Young Teen Study Guide." *Young Teen Study Guide*. Winona Lake, Ind.: Light and Life Press, n.d.

Alexander, John. *Thoughts from the Sea*. Winona Lake Ind.: Young Peoples Missionary Society, 1947.

"All-Bible Graded Series." Winona Lake IN: Light and Life Press, n.d.

Allan, David. *"From the Lumber Camp to the Ministry": The Autobiography of Rev. David Allan*. Toronto: Evangelical Publishers, 1938.

Allen, F Grace. *Fair View Mission Station*. Chicago: Woman's Foreign Missionary Society, Free Methodist Church, 1920.

Allen, Mary S. *From West to East, Or, The Old World as I Saw It: Being a Description of a Journey from California to the Holy Land and Egypt, by the Way of England, France, Switzerland and Italy*. Chicago, IL: Free Methodist Pub. House., 1898.

Allen, Ray. *A Century of the Genesee Annual Conference of the Methodist Episcopal Church, 1810--1910*. Rochester N.Y.: R. Allen, 1911.

Alma Free Methodist Church (Alma, Neb.). *A Century for Christ in the Community, 1882-1982, Alma Free Methodist Church, September 4-5, 1982*. Alma, Neb.: Journal Print, 1982.

Altopp, David P. "A Study of Sexual Attitudes, Sexual Behaviors, and the Religiosity of High School Students in Free Methodist Church Youth Groups." Southern Illinois University at Carbondale, 1981.

America, Free Methodist Church North, Maryland-Virginia Conference, Free Methodist Church of North America., and Maryland-Virginia Conference. "The News-Herald." *The News-Herald*. Reisterstown, MD: Free Methodist Church, Maryland-Virginia Conference, n.d.

America., Free Methodist Church of North. *2011 Book of Discipline*. Indianapolis, Ind.: Free Methodist Publishing House, 2012.

———. "Doctrines and Discipline." In *Doctrines and Discipline*. Winona Lake, Ind. [etc.: Free Methodist Pub. House., 1860.

———. "Doctrines et discipline de l'Eglise Méthodiste Libre de l'Amerique du Nord." Free Methodist Church of North America, n.d.

———. "Doutrinas e disciplina da Igreja Metodista Livre da AmÃ©rica do Norte." *Doutrinas e disciplina da Igreja Metodista Livre da AmÃ©rica do Norte*. S.l.: Free Methodist Church of North America], n.d.

———. "Hymns of the Living Faith.," 1964.

———. "Recent Books for Ministers." *Recent Books for Ministers*. Winona Lake, IN: Free Methodist Church of North America, 1952.

———. "The Holiness Hymnal." Cooperstown, Pa.: L.W.D. Publishing, 2011.

America., Free Methodist Church of North, Council on Social Action., Free Methodist Church of North America, and Council on Social Action. "Servanthood : A Manual." *Servanthood: A Manual*. Urbana, IL: The Council, 1982.

America., Free Methodist Church of North, Free Methodist Church of North America., Free Methodist Church of North America., and Free Methodist Church of North America. *Free Methodist Church, 1860-1978*. Sun City, Ariz.: Ecumenism Research Agency, 1967.

America., Free Methodist Church of North, Wesleyan Methodist Connection (or Church) of America., Free Methodist Church of North America, Free Methodist Church of North America., Wesleyan Methodist Connection (or Church) of America., Light and Life Press, Free Methodist Church of North America., et al. *Hymns of the Living Faith*. Winona Lake, Ind.: Light and Life Press, 1951.

America., Free Methodist Church of North, Aldersgate Publications Association., Free Methodist Church of North America, Aldersgate Publications Association, Free Methodist Church of North America., and Aldersgate Publications Association. "Discovery." *Discovery*. Winona Lake, Ind.: Light and Life Press [etc.], 1971.

America., Free Methodist Church of North, Rancho Betania., Free Methodist Church of North America, Free Methodist Church of North America., and Rancho Betania. "Rancho Betania News." *Rancho Betania News*. Nogales, AZ: Free Methodist Mexican Missions, 1991.

America., Free Methodist Church of North, Board of Bishops., Free Methodist Church of North America, and Board of Bishops. *Five Bishops Speak to the Church: Foundations, Building for the New Day*. Winona Lake, Ind.: Board of Bishops, Free Methodist Church of North America, 1988.

— — —. *Pastor's Handbook*. [Place of publication not identified]: Board of Bishops, Free Methodist Church of North America, 1998.

America., Free Methodist Church of North, Board of
Bishops., Free Methodist Church of North America,
Board of Bishops. Free Methodist Church of North
America., and Board of Bishops. *Lay Delegate's
Handbook*. [S.l.]: Free Methodist Church of North
America, 1980.

America., Free Methodist Church of North, General
Missionary Board., Free Methodist Church of North
America, General Missionary Board, Free Methodist
Church of North America., and General Missionary
Board. *Missions Heartbeat, '79*. Winona Lake, Ind.:
Free Methodist Church of North America, 1979.

America., Free Methodist Church of North, Wesleyan
Church., Lawrence R Schoenhals, Free Methodist
Church of North America., Wesleyan Church., Free
Methodist Church of North America, Wesleyan Church,
et al. *Hymns of Faith and Life*. Winona Lake, Ind.;
Marion, Ind.: Light and Life Press ; Wesley Press,
1976.

America., Free Methodist Church of North, Publication
Committee., Free Methodist Church of North America,
and Publication Committee. *The Glow of Fifty Years:
A Brief History of the Oregon Conference of the
Free Methodist Church*. [Winona Lake, Ind.?]: Free
Methodist Church of North America, 1945.

America., Free Methodist Church of North, World Ministries
Communication., Free Methodist Church of North
America, World Ministries Communication, Free
Methodist Church of North America., and World
Ministries Communication. *"Communicating Our
United World Mission for Christ": Minister's Manual*.
[Winona Lake, Ind.]: Free Methodist Church of North
America, 1972.

America., Free Methodist Church of North, Florida
    Confeence., Free Methodist Church of North America,
    and Florida Conference. "The Floridian Challenge."
    The Floridian Challenge. St. Petersburg, FL: Florida
    Conference, Free Methodist Church, 1981.

America., Free Methodist Church of North, Pacific Northwest
    Conferenc., Conference Missions Board., Free Methodist
    Church of North America, Pacific Northwest Conference,
    Conference Missions Board, Free Methodist Church
    of North America., Pacific Northwest Conferenc., and
    Conference Missions Board. "On Waves of Faith." *On
    Waves of Faith*. Seattle, WA: Conference Mission Board,
    Pacific Conference of the Free Methodist Church of North
    America], n.d.

America., Free Methodist Church of North, Central Illinois
    Conference., Free Methodist Church of North America.,
    Central Illinois Conference., Conference Committee on
    Christian Education., Free Methodist Church of North
    America, Central Illinois Conference, and Conference
    Committee on Christian Education. "Central Illinois
    Advance." *Central Illinois Advance*. Hillsboro, IL:
    Conference Committee on Christian Education, 1938.

America., Free Methodist Church of North, Central Illinois
    Conference., Free Methodist Church of North America, and
    Central Illinois Conference. "New and Views." *New and
    Views*. Mulberry Grove, IL: Y.P.M.S. of the Central Illinois
    Conference, 1935.

America., Free Methodist Church of North, East Michigan
    Conference., Free Methodist Church of North America,
    and East Michigan Conference. "The Voice of the East
    Michigan Conference, Free Methodist Church." *The Voice
    of the East Michigan Conference, Free Methodist Church*.
    Flint, MI: The Conference, n.d.

America., Free Methodist Church of North, General Conference., Free Methodist Church of North America, and General Conference. "The Convocation Daily." *The Convocation Daily*. Indianapolis, IN: The Conference, n.d.

America., Free Methodist Church of North, General Conference., Free Methodist Church of North America, and General Conference. *A Catechism of the Free Methodist Church*. Winona Lake, Ind.: Free Methodist Pub. House, 1950.

— — —. *Free Methodist Hymnal*. Chicago: Free Methodist Pub. House, 1910.

— — —. "Quadrennial Report of the General Missionary Secretary to the ... General Conference." In *Quadrennial Report of the General Missionary Secretary to the ... General Conference*. S.l.: s.n.], n.d.

America., Free Methodist Church of North, Great Plains Conference., Free Methodist Church of North America, and Great Plains Conference. "Great Plains Conference Reaper." *Great Plains Conference Reaper*. McPherson, KS: The Conference, n.d.

America., Free Methodist Church of North, Iowa Conference., Diamond Jubilee Committee., Free Methodist Church of North America, Iowa Conference, and Diamond Jubilee Committee. *Commemorating Seventy-Five Years of Progress of the Iowa Conference, Free Methodist Church: 1874-1949 Seventy-Sixth Conference and Camp Meeting, August 3-14, 1949*. [Iowa?]: [Iowa Conference?], 1949.

America., Free Methodist Church of North, Iowa Conference., Free Methodist Church of North America, and Iowa Conference. *Commemoratin One Hundred Years of Progress of the Iowa Conference, Free Methodist Church, 1874-1974*. Des Moines, Iowa: Free Methodist Church, Iowa Conference, 1974.

America., Free Methodist Church of North, Minn-I-Kota
    Conference., Free Methodist Church of North America,
    and Minn-I-Kota Conference. "Sharing." *Sharing*.
    Minneapolis, MN: The Conference, n.d.

— — —. "Super-Vision." *Super-Vision*. Wessington Springs,
    SD: Minn-I-Kota Conference of the Free Methodist
    Church, n.d.

America., Free Methodist Church of North, North Michigan
    Conference., Free Methodist Church of North America,
    and North Michigan Conference. "Annual Session."
    Annual Session. Mich.: The Conference], n.d.

America., Free Methodist Church of North, Ohio
    Conference., Free Methodist Church of North America,
    and Ohio Conference. "Leadership Link." *Leadership
    Link*. Mansfield, OH: Ohio Conference, Free Methodist
    Church, 1995.

— — —. "Ohio Conference Newsletter." *Ohio Conference
    Newsletter*. Mansfield, OH: Ohio Annual Conference,
    Free Methodist Church of North America, n.d.

America., Free Methodist Church of North, and Oregon
    Conference. "Annual Reports [of The] Oregon Annual
    Conference." *Annual Reports [of The] Oregon Annual
    Conference*. Turner, Ore.: Oregon Conference Free
    Methodist Church of North America, n.d.

America., Free Methodist Church of North, Oregon
    Conference., Free Methodist Church of North
    America, and Oregon Conference. *Connection, Oregon
    Conference: Keeping Oregon's Free Methodists
    Informed; March-April 1995*. Turner, Or.: Oregon
    Conference of the Free Methodist Church, 1995.

— — —. *Jubilee Service Honoring Golden Anniversary of the Oregon Conference of the Free Methodist Church: Wednesday Evening, 7:30 O'clock, July 11, 1945; Oregon Conference Camp Ground, Portland, Oregon*. Portland, Or.: Free Methodist Church of North America, Oregon Conference, 1945.

— — —. "Oregon Conference Connection." *Oregon Conference Connection*. OR: Free Methodist Church of North America, Oregon Conference, n.d.

America., Free Methodist Church of North, Oregon Conference., Free Methodist Church of North America, Oregon Conference, Free Methodist Church of North America., and Oregon Conference. *Leadership Orientation: Septiember 26, 1987, Salem, Oregon; "Planning for 'a New Day' in Oregon"*. Turner, Ore.: Oregon Conference, Free Methodist Church of North America, 1987.

America., Free Methodist Church of North, Pittsburgh Conference., Free Methodist Church of North America, and Pittsburg Conference. "The Pittsburgh Conference Herald." *The Pittsburgh Conference Herald*. Apollo, PA: The Conference, n.d.

America., Free Methodist Church of North, Susquehanna Conference., Free Methodist Church of North America, and Susquehanna Conference. "The Susquehanna Advance." *The Susquehanna Advance*. Syracuse, NY: The Conference, n.d.

America., Free Methodist Church of North, Texas Conference., Free Methodist Church of North America, Texas Conference, Free Methodist Church of North America., and Texas Conference. *The Texas Conference of the Free Methodist Church Its Origin and Present Churches*. [TX]: [The Conference], 1960.

America., Free Methodist Church of North, West Virginia
   Conference., Free Methodist Church of North America,
   and West Virginia Conference. "West Virginia Conference
   Echoes." *West Virginia Conference Echoes*. St.
   Morgantown, WV: Conference, 1987-, 1987.

America., Free Methodist Church of North, Conferences., and
   Free Methodist Church of North America. "Minutes of the
   Annual Conferences of the Free Methodist Church." In
   *Minutes of the Annual Conferences of the Free Methodist
   Church*. Rochester, N.Y.: "The Earnest Christian" Print,
   n.d.

America., Free Methodist Church of North, William L
   Cryderman, Free Methodist Church of North America,
   William L Cryderman, Free Methodist Church of
   North America., and William L Cryderman. "Songs for
   Renewal." Winona Lake, Ind.: Light and Life Press, 1983.

America., Free Methodist Church of North, Business
   Department., Free Methodist Church of North America,
   Business Department, and Ligth and Life Press. "Just
   Between Us." *Just between Us*., n.d.

America., Free Methodist Church of North, Commission on
   Christian Education., Free Methodist Church of North
   America, and Commission on Christian Education. *Let's
   Teach*. Winona Lake, Ind.: Light and Life Press, 1961.

America., Free Methodist Church of North, Commission on
   Christian Education., Department of Service Training.,
   Free Methodist Church of North America, Commission on
   Christian Education, and Department of Service Training.
   Better Workers for Your Church. McPherson, Kan.: Free
   Methodist Church of North America, 1953.

   — — —. *Do-It-Yourself Plans for Service Training*. McPherson,
   Kan.: Free Methodist Church of North America, 1958.

―――. *Service Training in Your Church*. McPherson, Kan.: Free Methodist Church of North America, 1955.

America., Free Methodist Church of North, Department of Christian Education., Free Methodist Church of North America., General Missionary Board., Free Methodist Church of North America., Women's Missionary Fellowship International., Free Methodist Church of North America, Department of Christian Education, General Missionary Board, and Women's Missionary Fellowship International. *All God's Children: Stories from Central Africa*. Winona Lake, Ind.: Light and Life Press, 1981.

―――. *Island Adventures: Treasures in Dominican and Pierre, a Boy from Haiti*. Winona Lake, Ind.: Light and Life Press, 1982.

America., Free Methodist Church of North, Department of Christian Education., Free Methodist Church of North America, and Commission on Christian Education. *Lay Leadership Training Handbook*. Winona Lake, Ind.: Free Methodist Church of North America, 1986.

America., Free Methodist Church of North, Department of Christian Education., Free Methodist Church of North America, Department of Christian Education, Free Methodist Church of North America., and Department of Christian Education. *What Is a Free Methodist?* Winona Lake, Ind.: Department of Christian Education, Free Methodist Church of North America, 1989.

America., Free Methodist Church of North, Tom. Fettke, Free Methodist Church of North America, Tom. Fettke, Free Methodist Church of North America., and Tom. Fettke. "The Hymnal for Worship & Celebration : Containing Scriptures from the New American Standard Bible, Revised Standard Version, the Holy Bible, New International Version, the New King James Version : By Special Arrangement with the Publisher, Hymnal of the F." Irving, Tex.: Word Music, 1989.

America., Free Methodist Church of North, and Free Methodist Church of North America. *2003 Book of Discipline*. Indianapolis, Ind.: Free Methodist Publishing House, 2004.

–––. *A Digest of Free Methodist Law; Or, Guide in the Administration of the Discipline of the Free Methodist Church* ... Chicago, Ill.: Free Methodist Pub. House, 1901.

–––. "Conference Minutes of the Free Methodist Church of North America." In *Conference Minutes of the Free Methodist Church of North America*. Winona Lake, IN: Free Methodist Pub. House, 1951.

–––. "Discovery for Juniors." *Discovery for Juniors*. Marion, Ind.: Wesley Press, for the Aldersgate Publications Association, 1971.

–––. *God Is Calling You to Minister*. Winona Lake, Ind.: Free Methodist Church of North America, 1950.

–––. "One in Love and Mission : Winona '74, One Way to a Whole World, General Conference of the Free Methodist Church, June 24-July 1, 1974, Winona Lake, Indiana." [Place of publication not identified]: [publisher not identified], 1974.

–––. *Records of the Free Methodist Church of North America,. Yearbook ... of the Free Methodist Church of North America*. Winona Lake, Ind: Free Methodist Pub. House, 1956.

–––. "Sunday School Journal." *Sunday School Journal*. Winona Lake, Ind.: Dept. of Sunday Schools, Free Methodist Headquarters, n.d.

–––. *Working Together in the 21st Century: The Misison of the Free Methodist Church Is to Make Known to All People Everywhere God's Call to Wholeness through Forgiveness and Holiness in Jesus Christ, and to Invite into Membership and to Equip for Ministry All.* Indianapolis, In: Free Methodist Communications, 1999.

———. *Y. P. M. S. and W. M. S. Conference Missionary Convention: March 15 Thru 18, 1951.* Winona Lake, Ind.? Free Methodist Church of North America, 1951.

———. "Yearbook ... of the Free Methodist Church around the World." *Yearbook ... of the Free Methodist Church around the World.* Winona Lake, Ind: Free Methodist Pub. House, 1960.

America., Free Methodist Church of North, Free Methodist Church of North America, and Free Methodist Church of North America. "Light and Life Primary." *Light and Life Primary.* Winona, Lake, Ind.: Light and Life Press, 1891.

———. *Shoes, Snakes, and Shelves: Missionary Stories from Asia.* Winona lake, Ind.: Light and Life Press, 1983.

———. "The Annual Minutes." *The Annual Minutes.* Chicago: Free Methodist Pub. House., 1879.

———. *The Y.P.M.S. Story of Winona Lake.* Winona Lake, Ind.: Light and Life Press, 1935.

America., Free Methodist Church of North, Free Methodist Church of North America, Free Methodist Church of North America., and Free Methodist Church of North America. "Minutes of the Annual Conferences." In *Minutes of the Annual Conferences.* Rochester, N.Y.: Earnest Christian Office, 1864. http://catalog.hathitrust.org/api/volumes/oclc/9064597.html.

America., Free Methodist Church of North, Free Methodist Church of North America, Free Methodist Church of North America., Free Methodist Church of North America, and Free Methodist Church of North America. "Yearbook." *Yearbook.* Winona Lake, Ind: Free Methodist Pub. House, 1971.

America., Free Methodist Church of North, Free Methodist Church of North America, Free Methodist Church of North America., Free Methodist Church of North America, Free Methodist Church of North America., Free Methodist Church of North America, and Free Methodist Church of North America. *Doctrines and Discipline of the Free Methodist Church.* Chicago, Ill.: Free Methodist Pub. House, 1915. http://ebooks.library.ualberta.ca/local/doctrinesanddisc00unknuoft.

— — —. *Doctrines and Discipline of the Free Methodist Church of North America.* Winona Lake, Ind.: Free Methodist Pub. House, 1970.

America., Free Methodist Church of North, Free Methodist Church of North America, Free Methodist Church of North America., Free Methodist Church of North America, Free Methodist Church of North America., Free Methodist Church of North America, Free Methodist Church of North America., Free Methodist Church of North America, and Free Methodist Church of North America. *The Book of Discipline, 1989. The Book of Discipline.* Winona Lake, Ind.: Free Methodist Pub. House, 1990.

America., Free Methodist Church of North, Free Methodist Church of North America, Free Methodist Church of North America., W S Kendall, Free Methodist Church of North America, and W S Kendall. *From Age to Age, My Church, a Living Witness.* Winona Lake, Ind.: Free Methodist Church of North America, 1955.

America., Free Methodist Church of North, and Department of Evangelism and Church Growth. "Reaching out in Love." *Reaching out in Love.* Indianapolis, IN: Free Methodist Church of North America, Dept. of Evangelism and Church Growth, n.d.

America., Free Methodist Church of North, Department of Evangelism and Church Growth., Free Methodist Church of North America, Department of Evangelism and Church Growth, Free Methodist Church of North America., and Department of Evangelism and Church Growth. "Reach out in Love." Winona Lake, Ind.: [Light and Life Press], 1980.

America., Free Methodist Church of North, Edward Payson Hart, Free Methodist Church of North America, Edward Payson Hart, Free Methodist Church of North America., and Edward Payson Hart. *A Digest of Free Methodist Law: Or, Guide in the Administration of the Discipline of the Free Methodist Church*. Chicago: Free Methodist Pub. House, 1908.

America., Free Methodist Church of North, Tillman. Houser, Free Methodist Church of North America, and Tillman. Houser. *Foreign Mission Statistical Reports of the Free Methodist Church, 1864-1969*. Winona Lake, IN.: General Missionary Board, 1970.

America., Free Methodist Church of North, Association of Free Methodist Educational Institutions., Free Methodist Church of North America, and Association of Free Methodist Educational Institutions. "Heart & Mind." *Heart & Mind*. Indianapolis, IN: Association of Free Methodist Educational Institutions, n.d.

America., Free Methodist Church of North, Women's Ministries International., Free Methodist Church of North America, and Women's Ministries International. *Trend Analysis: Number of Women Serving on Conference Boards and Committees, Free Methodist Church of North America, 1991-1996*. [Indianapolis, IN]: Women's Ministries International, 1997.

America., Free Methodist Church of North, Paul. Livermore, Free Methodist Church of North America, and Paul. Livermore. *Foundations of a Living Faith: The Catechism of the Free Methodist Church*. Indianapolis, IN: Light and Life Communications, 1996.

America., Free Methodist Church of North, General Council for Church in Mission., Free Methodist Church of North America, and General Council for Church in Mission. *What Is a Free Methodist?*. Winona Lake, Ind.: General Council for Church in Mission, Free Methodist Church, 1970.

America., Free Methodist Church of North, Commission on Missions., Free Methodist Church of North America, and Commission on Missions. "Report of the General Missionary Secretary." *Report of the General Missionary Secretary*. Winona Lake, Ind.? General Missionary Secretary], n.d.

America., Free Methodist Church of North, Commission on Missions., Free Methodist World Missions., General Conference of the Free Methodist Church of North America, Free Methodist World Missions, Free Methodist Church of North America, Commission on Missions, Free Methodist World Missions, North America General Conference of the Free Methodist Church., and Free Methodist World Missions. "Quinquennial Report of Free Methodist World Missions." In *Quinquennial Report of Free Methodist World Missions*. Winona Lake, Ind.: Light and Life Press, 1963.

America., Free Methodist Church of North, Department of World Missions., Free Methodist Church of North America, and Department of World Missions. "World Net." *World Net*. Winona Lake, IN: Free Methodist Church, Dept. of World Missions, 1987.

America., Free Methodist Church of North, Department of Evangelistic Outreach., Free Methodist Church of North America, and Department of Evangelistic Outreach. *Distinguished Disciples: A New World of Opportunity*. Winona Lake, IN: Free Methodist Church Headquarters, n.d.

———. *North Michigan Conference Survey: Requested by the North Michigan Conference and Conducted during the Conference Year 1967-68*. Winona Lake, Ind.: Dept. of Evangelistic Outreach, Free Methodist Church, 1969.

America., Free Methodist Church of North, General Woman's Missionary Society., General Women's Missionary Fellowship International., Free Methodist Church of North America, General Women's Missionary Society, and General Women's Missionary Fellowship International. "The Missionary Tidings." *The Missionary Tidings*. Winona Lake, Ind.: General Woman's Missionary Fellowship International of the Free Methodist Church, 1897.

America., Free Methodist Church of North, Woman's Foreign Missionary Society., Free Methodist Church of North America, and Women's Foreign Missionary Society. "Missionary Tidings." *Missionary Tidings*. Chicago, Ill.: [Woman's Foreign Missionary Society of the Free Methodist Church], 1899.

America., Free Methodist Church of North, Woman's Missionary Society., Free Methodist Church of North America, and Woman's Missionary Society. *Historical Record of Fifty Years, 1899-1949: Women's Missionary Society of Southern California Conference, Free Methodist Church*. [Place of publication not identified]: [publisher not identified], n.d.

———. *The Living Faith in Japan*. Winona Lake, Ind, 1957.

———. *Woman's Missionary Society of the Free Methodist Church, Ninth Quadrennial Meeting: Greenville, Illinois, June 11-22, 1931*. Chicago, Ill.: [Woman's Missionary Society], 1931.

America., Free Methodist Church of North, Woman's Missionary Society., Free Methodist Church of North America, and Women's Missionary Society. *The Woman's Missionary Society of the Free Methodist Church, Fifteenth Quadrennial Meeting: June 8-18, 1955, Winona Lake, Indiana.* Winona Lake, Ind.: [Woman's Missionary Society], 1955.

America., Free Methodist Church of North, Central Board of Ministerial Training., Free Methodist Church of North America, and Central Board of Ministerial Training. "Recent Books : A Quarterly Review for Ministers." *Recent Books: A Quarterly Review for Ministers.* Winona Lake, IN: Free Methodist Church of North America, Central Board of Ministerial Training, 1958.

America., Free Methodist Church of North, Clyde E Van Valin, Free Methodist Church of North America, Clyde E Van Valin, Free Methodist Church of North America., and Clyde E Van Valin. *Pastor's Handbook of the Free Methodist Church.* Winona Lake, IN: Light and Life Press, 1986.

America., Reformed Free Methodist Church of North, Reformed Free Methodist Church of North America, and Reformed Free Methodist Church of North America. *Discipline of the Reformed Free Methodist Church.* [Perryopolis, Pa.]: [Sound of the Trumpet Ministries], 1960.

American Free Methodist Mission, and American Free Methodist Mission. "Praise and Prayer : Giving Information of the Work of the American Free Methodist Mission in China." *Praise and Prayer: Giving Information of the Work of the American Free Methodist Mission in China.* Kaifeng, Honan, China: American Free Methodist Mission, n.d.

Anderson, A. *African Jungle.* Anderson Ind.: Gospel Trumpet Co., 1920.

———. *Nkosi: Story of an African Chief's Son.* Anderson In.: Warner Press, 1938.

———. *Ukanya: Life Story of an African Girl.* Anderson Ind.: Warner Press, 1931.

Anderson, Dorothy. *I Have You in My Heart: The Delights of Overseas Ministry.* Indianapolis, Ind.: Wesley Press, 1989.

———. *Man of Compassion, Carl Eric Anderson.* Essex Junction Vt.: Roscoe Printing House, 1966.

Anderson, Myrtle. *The School in the Vale: A History of Oakdale Christian High School.* [Place of publication not identified]: [publisher not identified], 1985.

Anderson, Myrtle. *Just over the Hill: My Four-Score-plus Years under God.* Gerry, NY: M. Anderson, 1988.

Andrews, E A. *A Symposium on Instrumental Music in Public Worship.* Chicago, Ill.: Free Methodist Pub. House, n.d.

Andrews, Edwin Alvia. *Musings on Self-Deception.* Chicago, Ill.: Charles Edwin Jones, 2005.

———. *Reminiscent Musings.* Spring Arbor MI: E.A. Andrews, 1926.

Andrews, Robert F. *The Web of Emptiness.* Winona Lake, IN: Light & Life Hour, n.d.

———. *When You Need a Friend.* Winona Lake, Ind.: Light and Life Media, Dept. of Communications, Free Methodist Church of North America, 1979.

Angel, Esther., and Robert C Buswell. *At Ease under Pressure: James, I, II Peter Leader's Guide.* Winona Lake, IN: Light and Life Press, 1982.

Antista, Victoria Johnson. *So It Goes in America.* Winona Lake, IN: Light and Life Press, 1988.

Archer, A C. *The Man with a Thorn in His Flesh*. [Medford Ore.]: Schmul Pub. Co., 1930.

Arksey, Leon. *A Mission Boyhood in Mozambique*. S.l.: Tornado Creek], 2011.

Arnold, Helen. *Under Southern Skies: Reminiscences in the Life of Mrs. Adelia Arnold*. Atlanta Ga.: Repairer Pub., 1924.

"Arnold's Commentary : International Sunday School Lessons." *Arnold's Commentary: International Sunday School Lessons*. Winona Lake, Ind: Light and Life Press, 1895.

Arnold's Practical Commentary on the International Sunday School Lessons Uniform Series for 1949: A Practical Help for All Who Use the Uniform Lessons in the Sunday School, or Who Desire to Do Individual Bible Study ... Winona Lake, Ind.: Light and Life Press, 1947.

"Arnold's Practical Commentary on the International Sunday School Lessons, Improved Uniform Series." *Arnold's Practical Commentary on the International Sunday School Lessons, Improved Uniform Series*. Winona Lake, Ind.: Light and Life Press, 1936.

"Arnold's Practical Sabbath School Commentary on the International Lessons." *Arnold's Practical Sabbath School Commentary on the International Lessons*. Winona Lake, Ind.: Light and Life Press, 1895.

Arthur, William. *The Tongue of Fire, Or, The True Power of Christianity*. Winona Lake, Ind.: Light and Life Press, 1900.

Asher, Mildred Graves. *Saints Alive!* New York: Vantage Press, 1955.

Association., Aldersgate Publications, and Aldersgate Publications Association. "Explorer 1." *Explorer 1*. Winona Lake, Ind.: Light and Life Press, 1975.

———. "Explorer 2." *Explorer 2*. Winona Lake, Ind.: Light and Life Press, 1975.

———. "Junior Teacher." *Junior Teacher*. Winona Lake, Ind.: Light and Life Press, n.d.

Association., Aldersgate Publications, Aldersgate Publications Association, and Aldersgate Publications Association. "Young Teen Teacher." *Young Teen Teacher*. Winona Lake, Ind.: Light and Life Press, n.d.

Association., Railroad Evangelistic, and Railroad Evangelistic Association. "The Railroad Evangelist." *The Railroad Evangelist*. [Winona Lake, Ind. [etc.: Light and Life Press [etc.]], 1938.

Atkinson, Donald. *A Study of Methods Used in the Establishment and Growth of Selected Churches in the Pacific Northwest Conference of the Free Methodist Church*, 1970.

Augustus L and Jennie D Hoffman Foundation, J Donald Frey, Helene S Clark, Brenda L Dean, Lynne M Partch, Hilary P Garrett, Michele Parker, et al. *Hoffman Foundation Wayne County History Scholarship Essays: Submitted for 1979 Scholarship Awards*. [Place of publication not identified]: [publisher not identified], 1979.

Augustus L and Jennie D Hoffman Foundation, Valerie Miller, Erin Olson, Sheila A Baynes, Mark C Sturges, Carolyn Oakley, Daniel H Russell, et al. *Hoffman Foundation Wayne County History Scholarship Essays: Submitted for 1999 Scholarship Awards*. [Place of publication not identified]: [publisher not identified], 1999.

Azusa Pacific University Graduate School of Theology, Free Methodist Center for Transformational Leadership, Karen Strand Winslow, Azusa Pacific University., Graduate School of Theology., Free Methodist Center for Transformational Leadership., Karen Strand Winslow, Azusa Pacific University., and Graduate School of Theology. "The Free Methodist Newsletter." *The Free Methodist Newsletter*. [Azusa, Calif.]: Azusa Pacific University Graduate School of Theology, 2013.

Babcock, Charles A. *Life and Labours of Chas. A. Babcock: With a Brief Sketch of Early Days in the District in Which He Was Born*. Brockville, Ont.: Standard Publishing House, 1938.

"Back Lane, United Free Methodist Church," n.d. http://www.leodis.net/display.aspx?id=2007913_164724.

Backenstoe, Martin. *Triumphant Living*. Kutztown Pa.: Kutztown Pub. Co., 1944.

Bai, Zhixin. *Ran dian yi sheng: zhang zhe shi feng shi kuang yu xin dong xiang, Xianggang Xun li hui zhang zhe shi gong yan jiu*. Xianggang: Jidu jiao zhuo yue shi tuan, 2005.

Bailey, Anne., Christian Life Club, Jo. Boyd, Christian Life Club, Christian Life Club., Anne. Bailey, Christian Life Club., Jo. Boyd, and Christian Life Club. *Trailblazer Squadron Activities; Year One, Grades 3 and 4*. Winona Lake, Ind.: Light and Life Press, 1988.

Bailey, Robert Q. *The Servant Story: Mark: Study Guide*. Winona Lake, Ind.: Pub. for Aldersgate Publications by Light and Life Press, 1980.

Baker, Frank. *Methodism and the Love-Feast*. London: Epworth Press, 1957.

Baker, H. *Sackcloth and Purple*. [Indianapolis Ind.]: [Pilgrim Pub. House], 1945.

Baker, H E. *Degrees of the Spirit*. Freeport, Pa.: Fountain Press, 1978.

———. *Sparks from the Anvil of Truth*. [East Liverpool, Ohio]: The author, 1944.

———. *Springs of Water*. Freeport, NY: Transylvania Bible School Press, n.d.

———. *The Wardrobe of Christ*. Olean, N.Y.: H.E. Baker, 1972.

———. *Travailing for Souls*. [Freeport, PA]: [Transylvania Bible School Press], 1944.

———. *Unlighted Glory*. Freeport, Pa.: Fountain Press, 1972.

———. *Where the Corn Grows Tall*. Freeport, Pa.: Fountain Press, 1980.

Baker, Merlin C, and Theological Research Exchange Network. "Concerns of Pastoral Ministry with a Biblical Perspective from the Gospel of Mark," 1982.

Baldwin, H. *Lessons for Seekers of Holiness: Containing Numerous Quotations from Wesley, Fletcher, and Other Standard Authors, and Designed to Aid such as Are Groaning after Purity of Heart in Entering upon the*. Chicago: W.B. Rose, 1907.

———. *Objections to Entire Sanctification Considered*. Pittsburgh: Published for the author, 1911.

———. *The Fisherman of Galilee a Devotional Study of the Apostle Peter,*. New York Chicago: Fleming H. Revell Co., 1923.

Baldwin, H A. *Holiness and the Human Element*. Chicago: Free Methodist Pub. House, 1919.

———. *The Coming Judgment, General and at the End of Time*. Chicago, Ill.: Free Methodist Pub. House, 1927.

———. *The Indwelling Christ*. Chicago: Free Methodist Pub. House, 1912.

Baldwin, Harmon. *The Carnal Mind; a Doctrinal and Experimental View of the Subject*. Chicago, Ill.: Free Methodist Pub. House, 1926.

Baldwin, Harmon A. *The Coming Judgment: General and at the End of Time*. Salem, Ohio: Allegheny Publications, 1987.

Ballard Free Methodist Church. *Ballard Free Methodist Church: 1986-87 Directory*. Ballard (Seattle), Wash.: Ballard Free Methodist Church, 1986.

Ballard Free Methodist Church, and Wash.) Ballard Free Methodist Church (Seattle. *Celebrating God's Family: August 6, 1989*. Seattle, Wash.: Ballard Free Methodisct Church, 1989.

Ballew, Jean., Marilyn. Sutton, Christian Life Club, Christian Life Club., Christian Life Club, Marilyn. Sutton, Christian Life Club, and Christian Life Club. *Guide Squadron Activities; Year Two, Grades 5 and 6*. Winona Lake, Ind.: Light and Life Press, 1988.

Banks, Stanley. *Saints in Work Clothes*. Winona Lake, Ind.: Light and Life Press, 1975.

Barber, Gertrude A. *Records of the Free Methodist Church, Ferndale, Sullivan County, N.Y.*, 1990.

Barker, John H J. *This Is the Will of God: A Study in the Doctrine of Entire Sanctification as a Definite Experience*. Salem, Ohio: Schmul, 1975.

Barnett, Lillian Pool. *Yorokobi no otozure*. Rosanjerusu: Rosanjerusu Furi Mesojisuto Kyokai, 1965.

Barron's Profiles of American Colleges: An in-Depth Study. Woodbury NY: Barrons' Educational Series Inc., 1971.

Bartlette, William. *Ethics, Real or Relative?: An Inquiry into the Place of Christianity in World Ethical Philosophies*. New York: Vantage Press, 1971.

Bastian, Donald N. *Along the Way*. Winona Lake, Ind.: Light and Life Press, 1977.

———. *Belonging!: Adventures in Church Membership*. Winona Lake, Ind.: Light and Life Press, 1978.

———. *Counterfeit: The Lie of Living Together Unmarried*. Toronto: Light and Life Press Canada, 1988.

———. *Cultivating Church Members: For Free Methodist Pastors Only*. Winona Lake, IN: Light and Life Press, 1978.

———. *Galatians: Leader's Guide*. Winona Lake, Ind.: Light and Life Press, 1964.

———. *Leading the Local Church: For Members of the Official Board*. Winona Lake, Ind.: Light and Life Press, n.d.

———. *Managing Tainted Money*. Winona Lake, Ind.: Light and Life Press, 1986.

———. *Sketches of Free Methodism*. Indianapolis, Ind.: Light & Life Press, 1995.

———. *Temptations and What to Do about Them*. Winona Lake, IN: Free Methodist Church, 1973.

———. *The Joy of Christian Fathering: Five First-Person Accounts*. Winona Lake, Ind.: Light and Life Press, 1980.

———. *The Mature Church Member*. Winona Lake, Ind.: Light and Life Press, 1963.

Bastian, Donald N, Free Methodist Church of North America, and Free Methodist Church of North America. *Give It a Rest*. Indianapolis, Ind.: Light and Life Communications, 2008.

Bastion, Donald N, and Leslie Ray Marston. *Thumb-Nail Sketches of Doctrinal Patterns*. Winona Lake, Ind.: Light and Life Press, 1978.

Bates, Gerald Earl. "A Study of the Processes of Conflict Resolution between a Protestant Mission and Selected National Churches Overseas," 1975.

Bates, Gerald. *Soul Afire: Life of J.W. Haley*. Winona Lake, Ind.: Light and Life Press, 1981.

Bates, Gerald., and Howard A Snyder. *Soul-Searching the Church: Free Methodism at 150 Years; Reflections on the "Search for the Free Methodist Soul."* Indianapolis, Ind.: Marston Memorial Historical Center, 2007.

Bates, Gerald., Howard A Snyder, Marston Memorial Historic Center, and Marston Memorial Historical Center. *Soul Searching the Church: Free Methodism at 150 Years*. Indianapolis, Ind.: Light & Life Communications, 2007.

Bauer, David R. *Gospel of the King: Matthew Study Guide*. Winona Lake, IN: Light and Life Press, 1986.

Baym, Nina. "A History of American Women's Western Books, 1833-1928," 2011, 63–80.

"Be Ye Holy : A Study of the Teaching of Scripture Relative to Entire Sanctification : With a Sketch of the History and the Literature of the Holiness Movement (Book, 1965) [WorldCat.org]," n.d. http://www.worldcat.org/title/be-ye-holy-a-study-of-the-teaching-of-scripture-relative-to-entire-sanctification-with-a-sketch-of-the-history-and-the-literature-of-the-holiness-movement/oclc/5428992&referer=brief_results.

Beazley, Samuel W. "Revival gems : number three, a great collection in a modest book." Chicago: Samuel W. Beazley & Son, 1929.

Beegle, B L. *Panama and the Canal Zone*. Chicago: Woman's Missionary Society, n.d.

Beers, Adelaide. *The Romance of a Consecrated Life: A Biography of Alexander Beers*. Chicago: Free Methodist Pub. House, 1922.

Benson, Mary C. *Church Library Manual,*. Winona Lake, Ind.: Light and Life Press, 1967.

"Bible Lesson Stories. 1-31, No.4." Providence, Rhode Island: Religious Press, 1930.

"Bible Stories for Threes." Kansas City MO: Beacon Hill Press, 1961.

"Bible Stories for Twos." Kansas City MO: Beacon Hill Press, 1964.

Bidwell, Dale. "Leading Lay Ministers : A Study of the Relationship between Leadership and Factors Associated with Lay Minister Job Satisfaction in the Fort Worth Free Methodist Church," 1995. http://place.asburyseminary.edu/ecommonsatsdissertations/93/.

Bilezikian, Vartran S. *Apraham Hoja of Aintap*. Winona Lake, IN: Light and Life Press, 1951.

Binney, Amos. *Binneys' Theological Compend Improved: Containing a Syncpsis of the Evidences, Doctrines, Morals and Institutions of Christianity: Designed for Bible Classes, Theological Students, and Young*. New York; Cincinnati: Methodist Book Concern, 1902.

Black, Harry. *From Newsboy to Preacher: The Story of My Life*. [Place of publication not identified]: [publisher not identified], 1932.

— — —. *Is the End of the Age at Hand*. Los Angeles, CA: H. Black, n.d.

———. *Prophecy Sermons by a Newsboy Preacher*. Redlands, Calif.: Black, n.d.

———. *Revival Sermons on Bible Prophecy*. Los Angeles, CA: Harry Black, n.d.

———. *Signs of His Coming and Other Sermons*. Los Angeles, Calif.: Mrs. H. Black, 1900.

———. *Soul Food Messages*. Los Angeles, CA: Harry Black, 1936.

———. *Sunday Morning (soul Food) Sermons*. Los Angeles, Calif.: Black, 1900.

———. *The Holy Ghost Baptism: And Seven Other Sermons on Sin, Salvation, and Holiness*. [Los Angeles, CA]: [Harry Black], n.d.

———. *The Price of a Revival and Other Sermons*. Los Angeles, CA: Harry Black, n.d.

———. *The Rich Man and Lazarus and Other Sermons*. [Los Angeles, Calif.]: [Harry Black], n.d.

Black, Harry, Prophetic News Office., Prophetic News Office, and Prophetic News Office. *The Four Horses of the Apocalypse: Evangelistic Messages on Revelation: (an Expository and Evangelistic Message for Each Chapter in the Book of Revelation). Book 1. Messages on Revelation Book 1. Messages on Revelation*. Los Angeles, Calif.: Prophetic News Office, 1940.

Black, Harry. *Satan's Masterpiece, the Antichrist: Evangelistic Messages on Revelation*. Los Angeles: Harry Black, 1953.

———. *The Four Horses of the Apocalypse: Evangelistic Messages on Revelation*. Los Angeles, CA: Harry Black, 1953.

———. *Tribulation Plagues Are Coming: Evangelistic Messages on Revelation*. Los Angeles: Harry Black, 1952.

Black, Joseph. *"The Word of the Lord Came unto Me Also."* Winona Lake, Ind.: Light and Life Press, 1950.

Blackie Buffalo and Other Stories of North American Missions. Winona Lake, Ind.: Light and Life Press, 1967.

Blews, Richard. *Master Workmen Biographies of the Deceased Bishops of the Free Methodist Church*. Winona Lake Ind.: Light and Life Press, 1939.

———. *Master Workmen Biographies of the Late Bishops of the Free Methodist Church during Her First Century, 1860-1960*. Winona Lake Ind.: Light and Life Press, 1960.

Bliss, Edwin. *The Encyclopedia of Missions: Descriptive, Historical, Biographical, Statistical*. New York; London: Funk & Wagnalls Co., 1910.

Boileau, Elmer L. *It Occurred to Me. . .* Winona Lake, Ind.: Department of Information and Stewardship, Free Methodist Church, 1950.

Bonney, Rollin Brian. "A Program of Ministry Training Opportunities for the Kentucky-Tennessee Conference of the Free Methodist Church," 1981.

"Book Review Doctors, I Salute . Emilie Conklin. 92 Pp. Winona Lake, Indiana: Light and Life Press, 1938. $1.50." *N Engl J Med New England Journal of Medicine* 221, no. 2 (1939): 84.

Bosco, Nicholas. *Rye Field to Pulpit: The Life Story of Rev. N.A. Bosko*. Picton Ontario, 1968.

Boulder Daily Camera, Charles Wendt, Paul Wilkes, and Paul C Ruby. *Focus Magazine*, 1965.

Bounds, Edward M. *Preacher and Prayer*. Winona Lake, Ind.: Light and Life Press, 1946.

Bowell, Gary. *Reflections and Thoughts on a Hymnal: The 1910 Free Methodist Hymnal*. [Place of publication not identified]: Gary E. Bowell, 2014.

Bowen Ind.), B F (Logansport, B F Bowen, and B F (Logansport Bowen Ind.). *Progressive Men and Women of Kosciusko County, Indiana and 1903 Plat Maps*. Winona Lake, Ind.: Light and Life Press, 1989.

Bowen, Elias. "Slavery in the Methodist Episcopal Church." Auburn [N.Y.] : William J. Moses, printer, 1859.

Bowen, Elias. *History of the Origin of the Free Methodist Church*. Rochester, N.Y.: B.T. Roberts, 1871.

Bownes, Leona K. "A Study of the Christian Day School Movement in the Arizona-Southern California Conference of the Free Methodist Church (Book, 1962) [WorldCat.org]." Seatlle Pacific University, 1962. http://www.worldcat.org/title/study-of-the-christian-day-school-movement-in-the-arizona-southern-california-conference-of-the-free-methodist-church/oclc/253708848&referer=brief_results.

Boyd, Myron. *Flame of a Century, What Made It Burn?: Radio Messages on John Wesley and Early Methodism*. Winona Lake Ind.: World-Wide Gospel Broadcast, 1958.

Boyd, Myron F. *A More Excellent Way: Radio Messasges on the Deeper Spiritual Life*. Winona Lake, IN: Light and Life Hour, n.d.

———. *Finding, Enjoying and Retaining God!* Winona Lake, Ind.: Light and Life Hour, 1940.

———. *Honoring the Spirit: 18 Radio Messages on Love and the Holy Spirit*. Winona Lake, Ind.: Light and Life Hour, 1953.

— — —. *Light and Life Hour, Sixteen Radio Messages: World-Wide Gospel Broadcast*. Winona Lake, Ind.: Light and Life Press, 1946.

— — —. *To Tell the World: Thirty Radio Messages*. Winona Lake, Ind.: Light and Life Hour, 1964.

Boyd, Myron F, Robert F Andrews, Spring Arbor Light and Life Seattle Light and Life Choir., Spring Arbor Light and Life Seattle Light and Life Choir., Ind.) Marston Memorial Historical Center (Winona Lake, Light and Life Hour (Radio program), Seattle Light and Life Choir, et al. "Moments of Memory." Winona Lake, Ind.: The Center, 1968.

Boyd, Myron F, Light and Life Hour., Light and Life Hour, and Light and Life Hour. *Light and Life Hour, Eighteen Radio Messages: World-Wide Gospel Broadcast*. Apollo, Pa.: West Pub. Co., 1949.

Brandt, Martin Emerson. *Henry and Emma Brandt: Memorabelia*. McPherson, KS: Brandt Family, 1980.

Branson, W T. *Hymns and Songs of Worship*. Chicago: Free Methodist Pub. House, 1892.

Brauer, Jerald. *The Westminster Dictionary of Church History*. Philadelphia: Westminster Press, 1971.

Brause, Dorsey. *Expanded Ministry to Adults: Program Guidelines*. Winona Lake, Ind.: Light and Life Press, 1979.

Bready, J Wesley. *Faith and Freedom: The Roots of Democracy*. Winona Lake, Ind.: Light and Life Press, 1952.

Bready, J Wesley, American Tract Society, and American Tract Society. *This Freedom - Whence?* Winona Lake, Ind.: Light and Life Press, 1950.

Brito B., Israel, and Israel Brito B. *Historia de la Iglesia Metodista Libre Dominicana*. Santo Domingo, D.N.: Editora Educativa Dominicana, 1975.

Brock, Lyle Walter. *The Life Story of Rev. Lyle and Doris Brock: Pioneer Pastors of the Free Methodist Church in the West Kansas Conference and the California Conference*. [Stanwood, WA]: [The Author], 1987.

Brodhead, Chloe Anna Sanford. *Our Free Methodist Missions in Africa, to April, 1907*. Pittsburgh: Aldine, 1908.

Brooks Hill Free Methodist Church. *Brooks Hill Free Methodist Church History: 80th Year Anniversary, 1894-1974*. [Portland, Or.?]: Brooks Hill Free Methodist Church, 1974.

Brooks, Philip F. "The History of Pacific Northwest Conference of the Free Methodist Church," 1969.

Brown, Arthur L, Arthur W Secord, and Edna C White. *A Handbook for Sunday School Workers*. Winona Lake, Ind.: Department of Sunday Schools, Christian Education Commission : Light and Life Press, 1946.

Brown, Arthur S. "The Local Church in a Christian Academic Community a Process for Discovering and Developing Its Identity, Mission and Ministry." Asbury Theological Seminary, 1981.

Brown, Zella. *Aldersgate: The College of the Warm Heart*. [Moose Jaw Sask.]: [publisher not identified], 1977.

Brown, Zella M. *Trail-Blazers in Livingstone Country: The Story of Ronald and Margaret Collett*. Winona Lake, Ind.: Light and Life Press, 1981.

— — —. *Trailblazers in Livingston Country / by Zella M. Brown*. Winona Lake, Ind.: Light and Life Press, 1981.

Buchanan, Jim. *The Development of Ecclesiastical Autonomy for the Free Methodist Chuch in Canada.* S.l.: s.n., 1990.

Buchanan, Robert James., Free Methodist Church in Canada., and National Task Force on a Canadian General Conference. "The Development of Ecclesiastical Autonomy for the Free Methodist Church in Canada," 1990.

Bucke, Emory. *The History of American Methodism.* New York: Abingdon Press, 1964.

Bundy, David. *Keswick: A Bibliographic Introduction to the Higher Life Movements.* Wilmore Ky.: B.L. Fisher Library Asbury Theological Seminary, 1975.

Burgess, Robert J. *Winning Others: Studies in Evangelism for Everyone.* Winona Lake, Ind.: Light and Life Press, 1900.

Burgess, Stanley. *Dictionary of Pentecostal and Charismatic Movements.* Grand Rapids Mich.: Regency Reference Library, 1988.

Burritt, Carrie T, Free Methodist Church of North America., Woman's Missionary Society., Free Methodist Church of North America. and Women's Missionary Society. *A Guide for Missionary Workers.* Winona Lake, Ind.: Womans' Missionary Society, Free Methodist Church, 1952.

Burritt, Carrie T, and Emma L Hogue. *The Story of Fifty Years.* Winona Lake, Ind.: Light and Life Press, 1935.

Burritt, Eldon Grant. *The Pupil and How to Teach Him.* Chicago: Light and Life Press, 1927.

Buswell, Robert C. *At Ease under Pressure: James, I, II Peter Study Guide.* Winona Lake, IN: Light and Life Press, 1982.

Calkins, Philip J. "A Comparative Investigation of Levels of Attainment in the Development of the Indigenous Church Principle on Latin American Free Methodist Mission Fields," 1968.

Callahan-Howell, Kathy. *Spiritual Exercises for Couch Potatoes*. Indianapolis: Light & Life Communications, 1997.

Cameron, Richard. *Methodism and Society in Historical Perspective*. New York: Abingdon, 1961.

Campbell Free Methodist Seminary. *Fourth Catalogue, 1913-1914*. Greenville, Tex.: Greenville Print. Co., 1913.

Canada, and Canada. *The Free Methodist Church Act, 1927*. Ottawa: Acland, Law Printer to the King, 1927.

Canada., Free Methodist Church in, Free Methodist Church In Canada, Free Methodist Church, and Free Methodist Church in Canada. *The Book of Discipline. The Book of Discipline*. Mississauga, Ont.: Light and Life Press Canada, 1990.

Canon, C Howard, Eugene W Cowsert, Ralph Page L, and Ralph Page L.,. *History of the Pittsburgh Conference of the Free Methodist Church: Centennial Edition, 1883-1983*. [Pittsburgh]: Pittsburgh Conference, 1983.

Carpenter, Adella. *Ellen Lois Roberts, Life and Writings. A Sketch,.* Chicago: Woman's Missionary Society, 1926.

Casberg, Jessie. *Dhatu and His Friends*. Winona Lake Indiana, 1919.

Cathey, Norma. *Sharing God's Vision: 1982-2002*. [Seattle, WA]: Vision Press, 2002.

– – –. *The First Free Methodist Church of Seattle, Washington: Centennial Year, 1880-1980*. [Place of publication not identified]: [publisher not identified], 1980.

Cathey, Norma G, Free Methodist Church of North America, Pacific Northwest Conference, Free Methodist Church of North America., and Pacific Northwest Conference. *Free Methodist Church Centennial: Pacific Northwest Conference, 1895-1995*. [Seattle, Wa.]: [Free Methodist Church of North America, Pacific Northwest Conference], 1995.

Cattell, Jaques. *American Men of Science: A Biographical Directory*. Lancaster Pa. ;New York: Science Pr.; Bowker, 1906.

———. *Leaders in Education: A Biographical Dictionary*. Lancaster Pa.: Science Press, 1948.

Centz, Herman B. *Prelude to Armageddon: Shadows on the Sundial*. Winona Lake, Ind.: Light and Life Press, 1951.

Chalker, Gideon I. *Papers*, 1904.

Chapman, Mary. *Mother Cobb, Or, Sixty Years' Walk with God*. Chicago: Arnold, 1896.

Chauke, Happyson William Matsilele., and Tillman. Houser. *H.M. Chauke Research of African Hlengwe People*, 2009.

Cheeseman, Sheila. *Eight Gates beyond*. Winona Lake, Ind.: Light and Life Press, 1981.

———. *Wee Brown Lambs*. Winona Lake, Ind.; Dept. of Evangelism and Church Growth: Free Methodist Church of North America ;, 1984.

Chesbro, S K J. *Reopening the Wells, a Sermon*. Chicago, IL: Free Methodist Pub. House, 1900.

Chesbrough, Samuel K J. *Defence of Rev. B.T. Roberts, A.M., before the Genesee Conference of the Methodist Episcopal Church at Perry, N.Y., Oct. 13-21, 1858*. Buffalo: Clapp, Matthews & Co's Steam Printing House, 1983.

"Christian-Life Greaded Bible Lessons." Winona Lake IN: Light and Life Press, 1948.

Christianity., Forum for Scriptural, and Forum for Scriptural Christianity. *Discovery: Basic Belief Studies for Free Methodists*. Indianapolis, Ind.: Light and LIfe Communications in cooperation with Bristol House, 1999.

Church, n.d.

Church (General): [vertical File], n.d.

"Church Growth in Paraguay (Book, 1988) [WorldCat.org]," n.d. http://www.worldcat.org/title/church-growth-in-paraguay/ oclc/19005181&referer=brief_results.

Church, Henry G. *Theological Education That Makes a Difference: Church Growth in the Free Methodist Church in Malawi and Zimbabwe*. Blantyre, Malawi: Christian Literature Association in Malawi, 2002.

Church, Henry. *Light Is Shining in the Africa I Know*. Winona Lake, Ind.: Light and Life Press, 1987.

Church., Wesleyan, Christian Youth Crusaders., Wesleyan Church, and Christian Youth Crusaders. *Crusaders Guide for Young Teens*. Winona Lake, Ind.: Light and Life Press, 1969.

— — —. *God and Church -- Doctrine: For Young Teens in All Local Churches*. Winona Lake, Ind.: Light and Life Press, 1970.

City Planning Department of Boulder Colorado. *2150 Pearl Street*. Boulder, Colorado: Boulder (Colo.) City Planning Department, 1986.

Clark, Elmer. *An Album of Methodist History*. New York: Abingdon-Cokesbury Press, 1952.

— — —. *The Small Sects in America*. New York: Abingdon-Cokesbury Press, 1949.

———. *Who's Who in Methodism*. Chicago: A.N. Marquis, 1952.

Clark, John Paul. "A Five Year Strategy of Church Growth for Wesley Free Methodist Church," 1990.

Clarke, Ethel. *Mary E. Chenoweth: Missionary to India*. Chicago: Woman's Foreign Missionary Society of the Free Methodist Church, 1915.

Clem, Mabeth., and Robert Q Bailey. *The Servant Story: The Gospel of Mark: Leader's Guide*. Winona Lake, Ind.: Published for the Aldersgate Publications Association by Light and Life Press, 1980.

Clemente, David Warren. "Filipino Group Life : A Contextual Study of Small Groups in Free Methodist Congregations," 2002.

Cleveland Ohio Free Methodist Church. *Year Book Reference Manual and Directory [of The] Free Methodist Church, Bridge Avenue and West 45th Street, 1913-1914*. [Cleveland, O.]: [the author], 1913.

Climenhaga, Grace Garratt. *The Call Was Clear*. Victoria, B.C.: Climenhaga, 1975.

Climenhaga, Grace Garratt., and Jean. Mercer. *The Call Was Clear: Superintendents of the Free Methodist Church in the Canadian Prairie Provinces, 1901-1995*. [Canada], 2010.

Clyde, Arlene A. "A Study of Minimum Requirements in Religious Education for Free Methodist Missionaries," 1954.

Clyde, Arlene A, Free Methodist Church of North America., Woman's Missionary Society., Free Methodist Church of North America. Woman's Missionary Society, Free Methodist Church of North America., and Woman's Missionary Society. *International Cookbook*. Winona Lake, Ind.: Light and Life Press, 1979.

Coates, Gerald., Free Methodist Church of North America., General Conference, Free Methodist Church of North America, and General Conference. *Passion of the Founders: General Conference 2003*. Indianapolis, Ind.: Free Methodist (Light and Life) Communications, 2003.

Coates, Gregory R. *Politics Strangely Warmed: Political Theology in the Wesleyan Spirit*. Eugene, Ore.: Wipf & Stock Publishers, 2015.

Cochrane, Ruth L. *Years of Beginnings: Washinton Conference, 1880-1896; Outline*, 1960.

Cockroft, Bethany, and Christian Life Club. *Trailblazer Chapel Plans; Year One*. Winona Lake, Ind.: Light and Life Press, 1988.

Cockroft, Bethany., Christian Life Club., Christian Life Club, Faith. Staneart, Christian Life Club., and Christian Life Club. *Guide Chapel Plans; Year One*. Winona Lake, Ind.: Light and Life Press, 1988.

Cockroft, Mary., and Kathi. Cottrill. *Expanded Ministry to Children: Program Guidelines*. Winona Lake, Ind.: Light and Life Press, 1984.

College, Minister's Conference of Greenville, George E Kline, Minister's Conference of Greenville College, George E Kline, Minister's Conference of Greenville College, and George E Kline. "The Wesleyan Message, Its Scriptures and Historical Bases : Addresses Delivered at the 12th Annual Ministers' Conference, Greenville College, April 10-14, 1939." Winona Lake, IN: Light and Life Press, 1940.

college., Ministers' conference of Greenville, Ill. Greenville, George E Kline, Ministers' Conference of Greenville College, George E Kline, Ministers' conference of Greenville college., Ill. Greenville, and George E Kline. *The Wesleyan Message Bearing Fruit*. Winona Lake, Ind.: Light and Life Press, 1942.

College., Ministers' Conference of Greenville, and George E Kline. *The Message Bearing Fruit,*. Winona Lake, Ind.: Light and life press, 1942.

"Colorado Free Methodism." *Colorado Free Methodism*. Howard, Colo.: A J. McKinney, 1895.

Compton, Hazel. *Through Eyes of Love: Ventures of Faith in India*. Winona Lake, Ind., 1988.

Conable, Francis. *History of the Genesee Annual Conference of the Methodist Episcopal Church: From Its Organization by Bishops Asbury and M'Kendree in 1810, to the Year 1872*. New York: Nelson & Phillips, 1876.

Conference, Free Methodist World, Frank J Kline, Free Methodist World Conference, and Frank J Kline. "Asia Fellowship Conference, April 19-28, Osaka, Japan : A Compilation of Reports, Documents, Interpretation." Winona Lake, Ind.: Continuing Committee of the Free Methodist World Fellowship, North American Division, 1960.

Conference, Greenville Ministers', and Greenville Ministers' Conference. "The Wesleyan Message : Addresses Delivered at the 12th-14th Sessions of the Ministers' Conference, Greenville College, 1939-1941." Winona Lake, Ind.: Light and Life P., 1940.

Conference., Warm Beach Family Bible, Free Methodist Church of North America., Warm Beach Family Bible Conference, Free Methodist Church of North America, Warm Beach Family Bible Conference., and Free Methodist Church of North America. "Notes." *Notes*. [S.l.]: Warm Beach Family Bible Conference., n.d.

Conklin, Emilie. *Songs in the Night,*. Winona Lake, Ind.: Printed for the author by Light and life Press, 1938.

Conklin, Emilie Chamberlin. *Religion Marches*. Winona Lake, Ind.: Printed for the author by Light and Life Press, 1939.

Conklin, Emilie. *Doctors, I Salute*. Winona Lake, Ind.: Light and Life Press, 1938.

Cook, Arnold W. "An Analysis of the Responsibilities and Training of Selected Ministers in Church Business Administration." East Tennessee State University, 1970. http://www.worldcat.org/title/analysis-of-the-responsibilities-and-training-of-selected-ministers-in-church-business-administration/oclc/25498799&referer=brief_results.

Cook, E Dean. *Chaplaincy: Being God's Presence in Closed Communities: A Free Methodist History 1935-2010*. Bloomington, IN: AuthorHouse, 2010.

― ― ―. *Salt of the Sea: A Navy Chaplain's Experience Ashore and at Sea*. [Longwood, Fla.]: Xulon Press, 2005.

Cook, Thomas. *New Testament Holiness*. London: Epworth Press, 1952.

Cooke, Sarah. *The Handmaiden of the Lord, Or, Wayside Sketches*. Chicago: Arnold, 1981.

Cooke, Sarah A Bass. *The Handmaiden of the Lord, Or, Wayside Sketches*. Chicago: Shaw Pub. Co., 1896.

― ― ―. *Wayside Sketches (abridged), Or, The Handmaiden of the Lord*. Salem, Ohio: Schmul Pub. Co., 1983.

Coolen, John, and Thunder Bay Branch of Ontario Genealogical Society. *O'Connor Free Methodist Cemetery: Grave Marker Transcriptions, OGS #5737, O'Connor Township, Thunder Bay District, Ontario*. Thunder Bay, Ont.: Ontario Genealogical Society, Thunder Bay Branch, 2009.

Coon, Arvilla. *Life and Labors of Auntie Coon*. Atlanta: Repairer Office, 1905.

Coon, H A. *Early Free Methodists*. Pueblo, Colo.: Mary Orem, n.d.

Cooper, Ralph E. "A Projected Growth Strategy for the Madras Free Methodist Church," 1976.

Copeland, John Bruce. "A Strategy for Relational Evangelism at Skyline Family Fellowship," 2000.

Cordell, Bessie Bell. *Blossoms from the Flowery Kingdom*. Winona Lake, Ind.: Light and Life Press, 1949.

Cordell, Bessie. *Precious Pearl*. Winona Lake, Ind.: Light and Life Press, 1948.

Cox, Betty Ellen. *Mwene of the Congo*. Winona Lake, Ind.: Light and Life Press, 1963.

— — —. *Simply Following: In All My Journeying God Went before*. Spring Arbor, Mich : Saltbox Press, 1998.

Crandall, Robert A. *Ministry to Persons: Organization and Administration*. Winona Lake, IN: Light and Life Press, 1981.

Cranston, Robert J. "A Workable Program of Church Growth for the Free Methodist Church of the Philippines," 1984.

Cranston, Robert., and Carolyn. Cranston. *Stars for the Baliti Tree: The Story of Free Methodist Missions in the Philippines*. Winona lake, Ind.: Published for Women's Missionary Fellowship International by Light and Life Press, 1983.

Crawford, Daniel Lee. "Finding Small Healthy Free Methodist Churches in the State of Illinois." Asbury Theological Seminary, 1993. http://place.asburyseminary.edu/ecommonsatsdissertations/75/.

Crider, Donald William. "Development and Rationale of Theological Education by Extension of the Free Methodist Church in South Africa with a Programmed Text on Pastoral Theology for Africa," 1980.

Cross, W J. *The Great Apostle and the Great Epistles* ... [Winona Lake, Indiana]: [Free Methodist Pub. House], 1939.

Cryderman, Lyn. *Glory Land: A Memoir of a Lifetime in Church.* Grand Rapids, Mich.: Zondervan, 1999.

— — —. *No Swimming on Sunday: Stories of a Lifetime in Church.* Grand Rapids, Mich.: Zondervan, 2001.

Cullum, Douglas R. "Gospel Simplicity : Rhythms of Faith and Life among Free Methodists in Victorian America," 2002.

— — —. "What Does It Mean to Be a Methodist? : An Examination of Denominational Self-Identity in John Wesley, the Methodist Episcopal Church and the Free Methodist Church," 1991.

Culumber, Terry Joe. "Church Growth Theology, Strategy, and Goals for the Department of Evangelism and Church Growth of the Free Methodist Church of North America," 1981.

Curtiss, Geo. *Manual of Methodist Episcopal Church History: Showing the Evolution of Methodism in the United States of America for the Use of Students and General Readers.* New York: Hunt & Eaton, 1893.

Dake, Vivian A. *Kindling Watch-Fires: Choice Extracts.* Waukesha, WI: Metropolitan Church Association, n.d.

Damon, A J. *A Brief History of the Wisconsin Conference of the Free Methodist Church.* [Place of publication not identified]: [publisher not identified], 1988.

Damon, C M. *Sketches and Incidents, or Reminiscences of Interest in the Life of the Author: With an Appendix Containing Treatises on "The Ministration of the Spirit," "National Religion," and "On Holiness," with Other Matter.* Chicago: Free Methodist Pub. House, 1900.

Daniels, W. *Illustrated History of Methodism in Great Britain and America, from the Days of the Wesleys to the Present Time,.* New York: Phillips & Hunt, 1880.

Daningburg, Todd Wayne. "An Equipping Model Applied to Valley Chapel Free Methodist Church," 2003.

Davenport, Mark Steven. "Six Ministry Strategies for Planting a Seeker Sensitive Church," 1996.

Davis, Joseph L, and Philip E rtMyette. *Official Bible Quiz Text: The Gospel of Mark.* Winona Lake, Ind.: Light and Life Press, 1960.

Davis, Joseph L, and Willard H Taylor. *Let's Learn Mark.* Winona Lake, IN: Light and Life Press, 1960.

Davis, LaVerne. *Daddy Is a Layman: A True Tale of Laughs, Loves and Ladders.* Los Angeles Calif.: Cowman Publications, 1953.

Davis, Rolland N. *Redeemed: A Remarkable Conversion in the Heart of India: The Story of Moses David, Superintendent of the Eastern District, and Evangelist, India Free Methodist Church ...* Winona Lake, Ind.: Woman's Missionary Society, Free Methodist Church, 1954.

———. *The Challenge in Central India.* Winona Lake, Ind.: Women's Missionary Society, Free Methodist Church, 1954.

Davison Free Methodist Church. "Directory of Davison Free Methodist Church." *Directory of Davison Free Methodist Church.* Davison, Mich.: The Church, n.d.

Dawson, Franklin. *Life Sketch and Sermons of Rev. B.C. Dewey,.* Chicago Ill.: Free Methodist Pub. House, 1929.

Dawson, Louise. *Vital Faith.* Seattle WA: Printed by L & H Print. Co., 1962.

Day, Bruce., Wesleyan Methodist Church of America., and Christian Youth Crusaders. *Cadet Trails*. Winona Lake, IN: Light and Life Press, 1979.

Day, Bruce., Wesleyan Methodist Church of America, Christian Youth Crusaders, Wesleyan Methodist Church of America., Christian Youth Crusaders., Wesleyan Church, Christian Youth Crusaders, and Wesleyan Church. Christian Youth Crusaders. *Cadet Trails*. [Winona Lake, Ind.]: Printed by Light and Life Press, 1970.

Dayton, Donald. *The American Holiness Movement a Bibliographic Introduction,.* Wilmore Ky.: B.L. Fisher Library Asbury Theological Seminary, 1971.

Dayton, Wilber T. *Romans: Leader's Guide*. Winona Lake, Ind.: Light and Life Press, 1960.

De Voist, M. *Foot-Prints in My Life, Or, the Story Told in Rhyme*. [Place of publication not identified]: [M. De Voist], 1920.

— — —. *History of the East Michigan Conference of the Free Methodist Church*. Owosso, Mich.: Times Print. Co., 1925.

Deaconess Hospital (Oklahoma City, Okla.), and Deaconess Hospital. *The Butterfields: 50 Years*. Oklahoma City, Okla.: Deaconess Hospital, 1975.

Deemer, Philip. *Ecumenical Directory of Retreat and Conference Centers*. Boston: Jarrow Press, 1974.

Degen, H. *The Guide to Holiness*. Wilmore, Ky. : Asbury Theological Seminary, 2013.

DeGroot, A T. *American Church Records. Series III, Series III,*. [United States]: Southwest Microfilm, n.d.

DeGroot, A T, Free Methodist Church of North America., Ind.) Church of God (Anderson, Fellowship of Grace Brethren Churches., Undenominational Fellowship of Christian Churches and Churches of Christ., Free Methodist Church of North America, Church of God, Fellowship of Grace Brethren Churches, and Undenominational Fellowship of Christian Churches and Churches of Christ. *Library of American Church Records Series III: An Introduction to the Evangelicals.* [Place of publication not identified]: [Ecumenism Research Agency], 1979.

Delamarter, George N. *Pastoral Support Team Manual.* Winona Lake, Ind.: Free Methodist Church of North America, 1985.

Demaray, Donald. *A Pulpit Manual.* Grand Rapids: Baker Book House, 1959.

———. *Bible Study Source-Book.* Grand Rapids MI: Zondervan, 1964.

———. *Loyalty to Christ: Sermons with Prayers for the Easter Season.* Grand Rapids: Baker Book House, 1958.

———. *Preacher Aflame.* Grand Rapids Mich.: Baker Book House, 1972.

———. *Pulpit Giants: What Made Them Great.* Chicago: Moody Press, 1973.

———. *The Minister's Ministries.* Winona Lake Ind.: Light and Life, 1974.

Demaray, Donald E. *Acts: Leader's Guide.* Winona Lake, Ind.: Light and Life Press, 1961.

———. *Alive to God through Praise.* Winona Lake, Ind.: Light and Life Press, 1976.

―――. *"Amazing Grace!"* Winona Lake, Ind.: Light and Life Press, 1958.

―――. *An Introduction to Homiletics*. Indianapolis, Ind.: Light and Life Press, 1990.

―――. *Basic Beliefs: An Introductory Guide to Christian Theology*. Grand Rapids: Baker Book House, 1958.

―――. *Laughter, Joy and Healing*. Indianapolis, Ind.: Light and Life Press, 1995.

―――. *Near Hurting People: The Pastoral Ministry of Robert Moffat Fine*. Winona Lake, Ind.: Light and Life Press, 1978.

―――. *Papers*, 1948.

―――. *The People Called Free Methodist: Snapshots*. Winona Lake, Ind.: Light and Life Press, 1985.

―――. *With His Joy: The Life and Leadership of David McKenna*. Indianapolis, IN: Light & Life Communications, 2000.

Demaray, Donald E, Free Methodist Church of North America, General Leadership and Service Training Council, Free Methodist Church of North America., and General Leadership and Service Training Council. *Alive to God through Prayer: A Manual on the Practices of Prayer*. Grand Rapids: Baker Book House, 1965.

Demaray, Donald E, and Yixun. Sun Liu. *Ji yao zhen li: Jidu jiao Weisili zong shen xue jian jie*. Gaoxiong Shi: Sheng guang shen xue yuan, 2009.

Demaray, Kathleen. *Train up a Child*. Winona Lake, IN: Light and Life Press, 1965.

DeMille, Lela. *Black Gold: A Story of Mozambique and Transvaal*. Winona Lake, Ind.: Light and Life Press, 1966.

———. *Prairie Rose*. Winona Lake, IN: Light and Life Press, 1987.

DeMille, Lela., Dave Hill. Grace. Abbott, Peggy. Payne, Free Methodist Church of North America., Free Methodist Church of North America, and Free Methodist Church of North America. *Stories from Southern Africa*. Winona lake, Ind.: Light and Life Press, 1984.

Denbo, Cleo T. *Wabash Centennial: Together We Serve, 1885-1985: The History of Wabash Conference, Free Methodist Church*. Camby, Ind.: The Church, 1985.

Denbo, Cleo T, Edna Erb. Schirack, and Larry. Schirack. *Wabash Centennial: Together We Serve, the History of Wabash Conference, Free Methodist Church*. [Greenville, Ohio]: [E.E. Schirack], 1989.

Denniss, Gary. *Free Methodist Hill, a Centennial History: Bracebridge Free Methodist Church, 1879-1979*. Bracebridge [Ont.]: Herald-Gazette, 1979.

Deratany, Edward. *When God Calls You*. Winona Lake, Ind.: Light and Life Press, 1988.

———. *Why Fear? Freedom from Fear in the Secret Place*. Winona Lake, IN: Light and Life Press, 2007.

Derr, Mary Krane. "Suggs, Eliza G." Oxford: Oxford University Press, 2006.

DeShazer, Jacob. "Jacob DeShazer's Personal Testimony." Wilmore, Ky.: DQB-LLC for the Marston Memorial Historical Center], 2012. http://place.asburyseminary.edu/ecommonsatsdigitalresources/38/.

Developing Christian Personality. Published for Aldersgate Associates by Beacon Hill Press of Kansas City, 1970.

Dictionary of American Biography. New York: C. Scribner's Sons, 1943.

Dieter, Melvin Easterday. *Revivalism and Holiness*, 1973.

"Directory of American Scholars," n.d. http://www.worldcat.org/title/directory-of-american-scholars/oclc/1246775&referer=brief_results.

"Directory of American Scholars. (Journal, Magazine, 1942) [WorldCat.org]," n.d. http://www.worldcat.org/title/directory-of-american-scholars/oclc/1246775&referer=brief_results.

"Directory of North American Protestant Foreign Missionary Agencies. (Journal, Magazine, 1958) [WorldCat.org]," n.d. http://www.worldcat.org/title/directory-of-north-american-protestant-foreign-missionary-agencies/oclc/2712345&referer=brief_results.

Discipline of the Missionary Bands of the World. Indianapolis IN: Grace Pub. House, 1926.

Discover Your Bible: A Course for Persons Who Believe They Should Be Getting More out of Their Bible Study. Published for Aldersgate Associates by Beacon Hill Press of Kansas City, 1970.

Dolan, T F. *A Bit of Experience: Showing the Dealings of Godmanandthedevil with T.F. Dolan, Convert from Romanism; to Which Is Added a Review of the Methodist Discipline and Selections from Wesley, Clarke, Bramwell, Carvosso, and Others*. Chicago: Baker & Arnold, Printers, 1880.

Dow, Lorenzo. *The Life, Travels, Labors, and Writings of Lorenzo Dow: Including His Singular and Erratic Wanderings in Europe and America: To Which Is Added His Chain Journey from Babylon to Jerusalem Dialogue*. New York: R. Worthington, 1881.

Drury, Keith W, and Sharon Drury. *Children as Learners*. Winona Lake, Ind.: Light and Life Press, 1979.

Duewel, Wesley L. *The Holy Spirit and Tongues*. Winona Lake, Ind.: Light and Life Press, 1974.

"Dunhard Church," n.d.

Dunn, Margaret. *God's Call: From Infilling to Outpouring*. Grantham, PA: Wesleyan/Holiness Women Clergy, Inc., 2000.

Dunning, Jane., S H Platt, and Benjamin Titus Roberts. *Brands from the Burning: An Account of a Work among the Sick and Destitute in Connection with Providence Mission, New York City*. [New York?]: [publisher not identified], 1877.

Dyer, Paul D, and Theological Research Exchange Network. "The Use of Oral Communication Methods (storytelling, Song/music, and Drama) in Health Education, Evangelism, and Christian Maturation." Bethel Theological Seminary 1994, 1994.

Dymale, Marjorie., Ken. Heer, Marie. Hubbard, Marjorie. Dymale, Ken. Heer, Marie. Hubbard, and Marjorie. Dymale. *Open Letters from a Roman Prison: Philippians/Colossians/Philemon: Study Guide*. Winona Lake, Ind.: Published for the Aldersgate Publications Association by Light and Life Press, 1980.

Earle, Ralph. *Ezekial, Haggai, Zechariah: Leader's Guide*. Winona Lake, Ind.: Light and Life Press, 1965.

―――. *Ezekiel, Haggai, Zechariah: Study Guide*. Winona Lake, Ind.: Light and Life Press, 1965.

―――. *Matthew: Leader's Guide*. Winona Lake, Ind.: Light and Life Press, 1961.

Easton, J B. *The Baptism and Indwelling of the Holy Ghost,*. Chicago: Light and life Press, n.d.

Eastside Free Methodist Church. *1986 Directory of Eastside Free Methodist Church*. Portland, Or.: Eastside Free Methodist Church : Oland Mills, 1986.

Education, U S Office of. *Education Directory*, n.d.

Elder, Russell M. *Healing Where the Hurt Is: A New Look at Some Old Problems*. Winona, Minn.: Justin Books, 1984.

— — —. *In Search of Sanity*. Place of publication not identified: publisher not identified, 1992.

Ellershaw, J Allan. *Apostolic Doctrine, Practice and Experience*. Fulwood Eng.: Free Methodist Church in the United Kingdom, 2005.

Ellis, Paul N. *To Keep Yourself Free*. Winona Lake, IN: Forward Movement, n.d.

Ellis, Paul N, Free Methodist Church of North America, General Council for the Church in Mission, Free Methodist Church of North America., and General Council for Church in Mission. *To Keep Yourself Free: A Question of Christian Loyalties*. Winona Lake, Ind.: Free Methodist Church of North America, General Council for Church in Mission, 1960.

Ellis, Raymond W. "A Christian Growth Manual for the Discipling of New Believers in the Local Church," 1980.

— — —. *How to Plant a Free Methodist Church: Effective Models for the 90's*. Indianapolis, Ind.: Free Methodist Church of N.A., 1993.

Embree, Esther. *Now Rings the Bell: The Story of Ralph Jacobs, Missionary Pioneer to Africa*. Winona Lake IN: Light and Life, 1978.

Embree, Esther. *Chikombedzi: A Missionary Wife Writes Home*. Winona Lake, Ind.: Light and Life Press, 1973.

Emerick, Samuel. *Spiritual Renewal for Methodism: A Discussion of the Early Methodist Class Meeting and the Values Inherent in Personal Groups Today*. Nashville: Methodist evangelistic materials, 1958.

Entering the Open Door in Formosa. [Winona Lake, Ind.]: [Light and Life], 1956.

Eugene First Free Methodist Church. *First Free Methodist Church, Eugene, Oregon: "Grow and Serve."* Eugene, Or.: First Free Methodist Church, 1978.

"Evangel." *Evangel*. Winona Lake, IN: Light and Life Press., n.d.

Evangelicals., National Association of, Evangelism-church Extension Commission., National Association of Evangelicals, and Evangelism-church Extension Commission. *New Churches for a New America*. Winona Lake, Ind.: Light and Life Press, 1957.

"Explore 1-6, No. 3." Winona Lake IN: Light and Life, 1969.

Fahs, Charles. *World Missionary Atlas*. New York: Institute of social and religious research, 1925.

Failing, George E. *I Corinthians: Leader's Guide*. Winona Lake, Ind.: Light and Life Press, 1963.

Fairbairn, Charles. ... *God's Plan for World Evangelism,*. Winona Lake Ind.: Light and Life Press, 1946.

———. *Purity and Power: Or the Baptism with the Holy Ghost*. Chicago: Christian Witness Co., 1930.

———. *The Secret of the True Revival (holiness Must Be Preached)*. Chicago Ill.: Pub. for the author by Free Methodist Pub.c House, 1929.

Fairbairn, Charles Victor. *A Primer in Evangelism: New "Secret of True Revival", Specially Revised, Rechaptered and Rewritten by the Author for Service Training Course 134A, "Evangelism in the Local Church."* Winona Lake, Ind.: Light and Life Press, 1947.

Fairbairn, Charles V. *A Primer on Evangelism*, n.d.

———. *A Symposium on Revivals and the Present Day Need.* Chicago: Free Methodist Pub. House, 1900.

———. *"Tarry Ye": With Other Sermons and Studies.* Winona Lake, Ind.: Light and Life Press, 1943.

———. *What We Believe: A Brief Manual of Christian Doctrine for Young Free Methodists and New Converts Based upon the Catechism and Articles of Religion of the Free Methodist Church of North America.* Winona Lake, IN: Light and Life Press, 1957.

Fairbarn, Charles Victor. *I Call to Remembrance.* Winona Lake, Ind.: Light and Life Press, 1960.

Fang, Lois Li-Huci., Theological Research Exchange Network, and Theological Research Exchange Network. "Formative Evaluation of a Leadership Development Course in Spiritual Formation for the China Free Methodist Church in Taiwan," 2000.

Faulkner, John. ... *The Methodists,.* New York: The Baker & Taylor Co., 1903.

Fear, Leona K. *New Ventures: Free Methodist Missions, 1960-1979.* Winona Lake, Ind.: Light and Life Press, 1979.

Fellowship., Christian Service, and Christian Service Fellowship. *Report of Evaluation Study of the Free Methodist Church of North America.* Fort Morgan, Colo.: Christian Service Fellowship, 1972.

Fellowship., Free Methodist World, Free Methodist World Fellowship, and Free Methodist World Fellowship. "News and Views." *News and Views.* Winona Lake, Ind.: Free Methodist Pub. House, 1962.

Fenwick, David L. *The Psalmist and His Critic.* [Place of publication not identified]: [publisher not identified], 1900.

Ferguson, Charles. *Organizing to Beat the Devil: Methodists and the Making of America*. Garden City N.Y.: Doubleday, 1971.

Ferm, Vergilius. *Pictorial History of Protestantism a Panoramic View of Western Europe and the United States*. New York: Philosophical Library, 1957.

———. *The American Church of the Protestant Heritage*. New York: Philosophical library, 1953.

Ferndale Free Methodist Church. *Ferndale Free Methodist Church, a Place for You, Ferndale, Michigan: [2009 Membership Directory]*. [Chattanooga, TN]: Olan Mills, 2010.

Ferrell, J David. "A Study of Institutional Identity and Direction : Central College at a Crossroads," 1997.

Fidler, Gloria. *Adventures in India*. St. Catherines, ON: Cornerstone Research & Pub., 2006.

Fields, Weston W. "Unformed and Unfilled : A Critique of the Gap Theory of Genesis 1:1,2." Light and Life Press, 1973.

Fine, Robert M. *Great Todays, Better Tomorrows*. Winona Lake, Ind.: Light and Life Press, 1976.

Fink, Newton W, Joseph B Lutz, and W B Rose. "Inspirational Songs for the Sunday School, Social Worship, Missionary and Evangelistic Work." Chicago: Light and Life Press, 1924.

Finley, Harvey E. *I and II Samuel (and Related Chronicles Passages): Leader's Guide*. Winona Lake, Ind.: Light and Life Press, 1961.

———. *Zephaniah, Nahum, Habakkuk, Obadiah, Daniel: Leader's Guide*. Winona Lake, Ind.: Light and Life Press, 1964.

First Free Methodist Church (Seattle, Wash.)., Modern Maturity Fellowship., First Free Methodist Church Seattle, and Modern Maturity Fellowship. "Modern Maturity Fellowship Herald." *Modern Maturity Fellowship Herald*. Seattle, Wash.: First Free Methodist Church, n.d.

"First Free Methodist Episcopal Church," 1910.

Flatbush, Adda M. *How She Was Lost: Or, Methods and Results of Rescue Work, from an Experience of Ten Years*. Kansas City, Mo.: Franklin Hudson Pub., 1908.

Fletcher, Cliff. "Sacramental Discipleship as a Pathway to Ecclesial Reformation in the Free Methodist Church in Canada." Gordon-Conwell Theological Seminary, 2011.

Folkestad, Robert H. "A Historical Survey of Free Methodist World Missions," 1969.

Ford, George L. *All the Money You Need*. Winona Lake, Ind.: Light and Life Press, 1976.

———. *Like a Tree Planted: The Life Story of Leslie Ray Marston*. Winona Lake, Ind.: Light and Life Press, 1985.

———. *To God with Love*. Winona Lake, IN: Free Methodist Church, 1973.

"Free Methodist Book Bulletin. (Journal, Magazine, 1943) [WorldCat.org]," n.d. http://www.worldcat.org/title/free-methodist-book-bulletin/oclc/28474317&referer=brief_results.

Free Methodist Bradbury Chun Lei Primary School. *Li qing 30: Xun li jian zheng ji*, 2013.

———. *Xun li hui Baipuli ji jin xun li xiao xue kai mu gan en dian li: ji nian te kan = Grand opening and thanksgiving of Free Methodist Bradbury Chun Lei Primary School: memorial issue*. [Xianggang]: [Xun li hui Baipuli ji jin xun li xiao xue], 1984.

———. *Xun li hui Baipuli ji jin xun li xiao xue shi wu zhou nian xiao qing ji nian te kan*. Xianggang: Xun li hui Baipuli ji jin xun li xiao xue, 1998.

Free Methodist Church (McPherson, Kan). *Free Methodist Church, McPherson, Kansas, 1880-1980: 1883, 1917, 1955, 1980*. [McPherson, Kan.]: [Free Methodist Church], 1980.

Free Methodist Church (Newberg, Ore). *Faith and Life of a Free Methodist*. Newberg, Ore.: Free Methodist Church, 1983.

Free Methodist Church (Niagara Falls, Ont). *The Dedication of Free Methodist Church, 397 Dorchester Road South, Niagara Falls, Ontario, October 8th, 1967*, 1967.

Free Methodist Church (Petersburg, Ind). *History of the Free Methodist Church, Petersburg, Indiana, 1924-1976*. [Petersburg, Ind.]: [The Church], 1976.

Free Methodist Church (Three Oaks, Mich). "Directory of Free Methodist Church." *Directory of Free Methodist Church*. Three Oaks, Mich. The Church, n.d.

Free Methodist Church, and Free Methodist Church. "Instrumental Music in Public Worship : The Position Held by the Free Methodist Church." Chicago, Ill.: Free Methodist Pub. House, 1927.

Free Methodist Church, Free Methodist Church., Free Methodist Church, and Free Methodist Church. *Yearbook*. Winona Lake, Ind.: Free Methodist Publishing House., n.d.

Free Methodist Church In Canada, Canada West Conference, Free Methodist Church in Canada., and Canada West Conference. *Annual Reports*. Cymric, Sask: Canada West Conference, Free Methodist Church, 1970.

Free Methodist Church In Canada, and Free Methodist Church in Canada. "Directory." *Directory*. Mississauga, ON: Free Methodist Church in Canada, Canadian Ministry Centre., n.d.

Free Methodist Church In Canada, Free Methodist Church in Canada., and Free Methodist Church In Canada. "Mosaic." *Mosaic*. Mississauga, Ont.: Free Methodist Church in Canada, 2003.

Free Methodist Church In Canada, Canadian General Conference, Donald N Bastian, R Wayne Kleinsteuber, Alan A Retzman, Glenn H Teal, Brian T Hartley, et al. *Symposium on Worship and Preaching*. S.l.: s.n.], 1992.

Free Methodist Church In Canada, East Ontario Conference, Free Methodist Church in Canada., and East Ontario Conference. *75 Years of Progress in Canadian Free Methodism, East Ontario Conference: 1895-1970*. S.l: s.n., 1970.

Free Methodist Church In Canada, National Task Force on a Canadian General Conference, Free Methodist Church in Canada., and National Task Force on a Canadian General Conference. *A Proposal for a Canadian General Conference*. Mississauga, Ont.: Free Methodist Church in Canada, 1988.

Free Methodist Church of Alpena. "Directory of Free Methodist Church of Alpena." *Directory of Free Methodist Church of Alpena*. Alpena, Mich.: The Church, n.d.

Free Methodist Church of North America. "2007 Book of Discipline." Indianapolis, Ind.: Free Methodist Publishing House, 2008.

— — —. "Current : For Concerned Church Leaders." *Current: For Concerned Church Leaders*. Winona Lake, Ind.: General Strategy Council of the Free Methodist Church of North America, 1968.

— — —. "El Mensajero Metodist Libra." *El Mensajero Metodist Libra*. Los Angeles, CA: Publicaciones Luz y Vida, n.d.

— — —. "Interracial News." *Interracial News*, n.d.

———. *Strategy Handbook*. Winona Lake, Ind.: General Strategy Council of the Free Methodist Church, 1965.

———. "Youth in Action." *Youth In Action*, n.d.

Free Methodist Church of North America, and Free Methodist Church of North America. "[Annual Conference Packet Materials for the 1994-1995 Annual Conferences of the Free Methodist Church of North America.]." Winona Lake, Ind.: Free Methodist Church, 1995.

———. *An Act to Incorporate the Free Methodist Chiurch in Canada: Assented to 8th July, 1959*. Ottawa: Queen's printer and controller of stationery, 1959.

———. "Annual Report." *Annual Report*. Winona Lake, IN: The Church, 1985.

———. "Doutrinas e disciplina da Igreja Metodista Livre da América do Norte." *Doutrinas e disciplina da Igreja Metodista Livre da América do Norte*. S.l.: Free Methodist Church of North America], n.d.

———. "Free Methodist Ministries Today." *Free Methodist Ministries Today*. Indianapolis, IN: Light and Life Press, n.d.

———. "Free Methodist World Mission People." *Free Methodist World Mission People*. Indianapolis, Ind.: Free Methodist World Missions, n.d.

———. "General Conference Daily." In *General Conference Daily*. Greenville, Ill.: S.K.J. Chesbro, n.d.

———. *God Made a Colorful World*. Winona Lake, Ind.: Light and Life Press, 1960.

———. "Living Holiness: Free Methodist in the Year 2001." [S.l.]: New Link Media, 2001.

———. "Minutes of the Annual Conference and General Conference of the Free Methodist Church for the Year Ending October, 1874." Rochester, N.Y.: The Earnest Christian Office, 1874.

———. *Probationer's Guide: Instruction to Candidates for Admission to Membership in the Free Methodist Church.* Chicago, Ill.: Free Methodist Pub. House, 1896.

———. *The Annual Minutes (combined Number): Free Methodist Church of North America.* Winona Lake, Ind.: Free Methodist Pub. House., n.d.

———. *The Vision Glorious: New York Conference of the Free Methodist Church, [1974 Centennial]; Sept. 2-6, 1874, Brooklyn, N.Y., Sept. 26-28, 1974, Beach Lake, Pa.* Winona Lake, Ind.: Free Methodist Church of North America, 1974.

———. "Yearbook : Official Personnel, Organization, and Statistics of the Free Methodist Church around the World." *Yearbook: Official Personnel, Organization, and Statistics of the Free Methodist Church around the World.* Winona Lake, Ind.: Office of the General Administrator, Free Methodist Church of North America., n.d.

Free Methodist Church of North America, Free Methodist Church of North America., Free Methodist Church of North America., and Free Methodist Church of North America. *Free Methodist Church, 1861-1978.* Sun City, Ariz.: Ecumenism Research Agency, 1973.

Free Methodist Church of North America, Free Methodist Church of North America., Free Methodist Church of North America, and Free Methodist Church of North America. *The Hymn Book of the Free Methodist Church.* Rochester, N.Y.: B.T. Roberts, 1891.

Free Methodist Church of North America, Atlantic Southeast Extension Conference, Free Methodist Church of North America., and Atlantic Southeast Extension Conference. "The Good Word." *The Good Word*. Lake City, AL: The Conference, n.d.

Free Methodist Church of North America, Board of Bishops, Free Methodist Church of North America., and Board of Bishops. "Confidentially Yours." *Confidentially Yours*. Winona Lake, Ind.: Free Methodist Church of North America, 1957.

— — —. *Is God Calling You to the Ordained Ministry?* Indianapolis, Ind.: Free Methodist Church of North America, 1960.

Free Methodist Church of North America, California Conference, Free Methodist Church of North America., and California Conference. "The Echoes." *The Echoes*. Sacramento, CA: California Conference, n.d.

Free Methodist Church of North America, Central Illinois Conference, Free Methodist Church of North America., and Central Illinois Conference. *Centennial of the Central Illinois Conference of the Free Methodist Church*. [Greenville, Ill.]: [publisher not identified], 1978.

— — —. "The Conference Gleaner : A Weekly Report of the Ministry in the Central Illinois Conference of the Free Methodist Church." *The Conference Gleaner: A Weekly Report of the Ministry in the Central Illinois Conference of the Free Methodist Church*. Greenville, IL: The Conference, n.d.

Free Methodist Church of North America, Christian Education Commision, Department of Sunday Schools, Free Methodist Church of North America., Christian Education Commission., and Department of Sunday Schools. *Manual of the Christian Youth Crusaders of the Free Methodist Church of North America*. Winona Lake, Ind.: A.L. Brown, 1944.

Free Methodist Church of North America, Commission on Christian Education, Free Methodist Church of North America., and Commission on Christian Education. *Concepts in Christian Education.* Winona Lake, Ind.: Light and Life Press, n.d.

Free Methodist Church of North America, Commission on Christian Education, Department of Service Training, Free Methodist Church of North America., Commission on Christian Education., and Department of Service Training. *Correspondence Study Courses.* McPherson, Kan.: Free Methodist Church of North America, 1957.

— — —. *Service Training Comes of Age, 1937-1960: Nineteen Hundred and Sixty, Centennial Year.* Winona Lake, Ind.: Free Methodist Church of North America, 1960.

— — —. *The Story of Service Training.* McPherson, Kan.: Free Methodist Church of North America, 1952.

Free Methodist Church of North America, Commission on Christian Education, Department of Service Training, Free Methodist Church of North America., Commission on Christian Education., Department of Service Training., Free Methodist Church of North America, et al. *Service Training Is for You.* McPherson, Kan.: Free Methodist Church of North America, 1957.

Free Methodist Church of North America, Commission on Christian Education, Departmetn of Service Training, Free Methodist Church of North America., Commission on Christian Education., and Department of Service Training. *So You're a Teacher.* McPherson, Kan.: Free Methodist Church of North America, 1958.

— — —. *Visual Aids for Service Training Courses.* McPherson, Kan.: Free Methodist Church of North America, 1955.

Free Methodist Church of North America, Commission on Missions, General Missionary Board, Free Methodist World Missions, Free Methodist Church of North America., Commission on Missions., Free Methodist Church of North America., General Missionary Board., and Free Methodist World Missions. "Missions Annual Report." *Missions Annual Report*. Winona Lake, Ind.: Commission on Missions, 1970.

Free Methodist Church of North America, Commission on Missions, Woman's Missionary Society, Young People's Missionary Society of the Free Methodist Church, Junior Missionary Society of the Free Methodist Church, Free Methodist Church of North America., Commission on Missions., et al. "Annual Report." In *Annual Report*. Chicago, Ill.: Free Methodist Pub. House, n.d.

Free Methodist Church of North America, Department of Evangelism and Church Growth, Free Methodist Church of North America., and Department of Evangelism and Church Growth. *Reach out in Love: A Manual for the Growing Church*. Winona Lake, Ind.: Department of Evangelism and Church Growth, assisted by the Department of Christian Education, Free Methodist Church of North America, 1980.

Free Methodist Church of North America, Department of Higher Education, Free Methodist Church of North America., and Department of Higher Education. "The Aldersgate Nexus." *The Aldersgate Nexus*. Winona Lake, IN: Dept. of Higher Education of the Free Methodist Church, 1968.

Free Methodist Church of North America, Department of Service Training, Commission on Christian Education, Free Methodist Church of North America., Department of Service Training., and Commission on Christian Education. "Free Methodist Book Bulletin." *Free Methodist Book Bulletin*. McPherson, KS: Dept. of Service Training of the Free Methodist Church of North America, 1943.

Free Methodist Church of North America, Department of Sunday Schools, Free Methodist Church of North America., and Department of Sunday Schools. *Sunday School Constitution*. S.l.: Free Methodist Church of North America, 1950.

Free Methodist Church of North America, Department of World Missions, Free Methodist Church of North America., and Department of World Missions. "Across the Miles--." *Across the Miles--*. Winona Lake, IN: Dept. of World Missions, The Free Methodist Church, 1989.

Free Methodist Church of North America, General Conference, Free Methodist Church of North America., and General Conference. *Free Methodist Centenary, June 14-26, 1960, Winona Lake, Indiana: 25th Annual Conference Guide Book*. Winona Lake, Ind.: Free Methodist Church of North America, 1960.

— — —. "General Conference Today." *General Conference Today*. Winona Lake, IN: Light and Life Press, n.d.

— — —. "Quinquennial Report of the General Missionary Secretary to the General Conference of the Free Methodist Church." In *Quinquennial Report of the General Missionary Secretary to the General Conference of the Free Methodist Church*. S.l.: s.n., 1960.

— — —. "Winona ... Daily." *Winona ... Daily*. Winona Lake, IN: Free Methodist Church, n.d.

Free Methodist Church of North America, General Conference, Study Commission on Doctrine, Free Methodist Church of North America., Study Commission on Doctrine., Free Methodist Church of North America., and General Conference. *Report of the Study Commission on Doctrine: Free Methodist Church of North America, 31st General Conference, August 3-13, 1989, Seattle, Washington.*, 1989.

Free Methodist Church of North America, General
   Missionary Board, Free Methodist Church of North
   America., and General Missionary Board. "Missions
   Perspective." *Missions Perspective*. Winona Lake, IN:
   General Missionary Board, n.d.

— — —. "Missions Quinquennial Report." *Missions
   Quinquennial Report*. Winona Lake, Ind.: Light and
   Life Press, 1974.

— — —. *Perspective in Missions Giving*. Winona Lake, Ind.:
   Free Methodist Church of North America, General
   Missionary Board, 1950.

Free Methodist Church of North America, General
   Missionary Board, Woman's Foreign Missionary
   Society, Free Methodist Church of North America.,
   General Missionary Board., Free Methodist Church
   of North America., Woman's Missionary Foreign
   Missionary Society., et al. *Proceedings of the General
   Missionary Board of the Free Methodist Church of
   North America. Proceedings of the General Missionary
   Board of the Free Methodist Church of North America*.
   [Chicago, Ill.]: [Board?], 1923.

Free Methodist Church of North America, Home Ministries,
   Free Methodist Church of North America., and Home
   Ministries. "Free Methodist Ministries Update." *Free
   Methodist Ministries Update*. Indianapolis, IN: Light
   and Life Press, n.d.

Free Methodist Church of North America, Illinois-Wisconsin
   Conference, Free Methodist Church of North America.,
   and Illinois-Wisconsin Conference. "Illinois-Wisconsin
   Messenger." *Illinois-Wisconsin Messenger*. Woodstock,
   IL: Illinois-Wisconsin Conference, n.d.

Free Methodist Church of North America, Kentucky-Tennessee Conference, Free Methodist Church of North America., and Kentucky-Tennessee Conference. "Builder : Newsletter of the Kentucky-Tennessee Conference." *Builder: Newsletter of the Kentucky-Tennessee Conference*. Jackson, KY: The Conference, n.d.

———. "Report Book : The ... Session of the Kentucky-Tennessee Annual Conference." *Report Book: The ... Session of the Kentucky-Tennessee Annual Conference*. KY: The Conference, n.d.

Free Methodist Church of North America, Keystone Conference, Free Methodist Church of North America., and Keystone Conference. "Keystone Conference News." *Keystone Conference News*. Oil City, PA: The Conference, n.d.

Free Methodist Church of North America, Light and Life Men International, Free Methodist Church of North America., and Light and Life Men International. "Light and Life Line." *Light and Life Line*. Winona Lake, Ind.: Free Methodist Church of North America, Light and Life Men International, n.d.

Free Methodist Church of North America, Light and Life Men's Fellowship, Free Methodist Church of North America., and Light and Life Men's Fellowship. *"Break through": The President's Manual*. Winona Lake, Ind.: Free Methodist Church of North America, 1960.

Free Methodist Church of North America, Louisianna Conference, Free Methodist Church of North America., and Louisiana Conference. "Louisiana Messenger of the Free Methodist Church." *Louisiana Messenger of the Free Methodist Church*. Effie, LA: The Conference, n.d.

Free Methodist Church of North America, New York
Conference, Free Methodist Church of North America.,
and New York Conference. "New York Conference
News." *New York Conference News*. NY: The Conference,
n.d.

Free Methodist Church of North America, North Michigan
Conference, Free Methodist Church of North America., and
North Michigan Conference. "The North Michigan Herald."
The North Michigan Herald. Cadillac, MI: The Conference,
n.d.

Free Methodist Church of North America, Ohio Conference, Free
Methodist Church of North America., and Ohio Conference.
"The Ohio Connection." *The Ohio Connection*. Baltimore,
Ohio: Ohio Conference, Free Methodist Church of N.
America, 1995.

Free Methodist Church of North America, Ohio Conference,
Board of Evangelism, Free Methodist Church of North
America., Ohio Conference., and Board of Evangelism.
"The Net." *The Net*. Mansfield, OH: Board of Evangelism
of the Ohio Annual Conference, Free Methodist Church of
North America, n.d.

Free Methodist Church of North America, Oil City Conference,
Free Methodist Church of North America., and Oil City
Conference. "The Oil City Conference News." *The Oil City
Conference News*. Pleasentville, PA: The Conference, n.d.

Free Methodist Church of North America, Oklahoma Conference,
Free Methodist Church of North America., and Oklahoma
Conference. "In Touch with Oklahoma Free Methodists."
In Touch with Oklahoma Free Methodists. Oklahoma City:
The Conference, 1993.

– – –. "Oklahoma Free Methodist." *Oklahoma Free Methodist*.
Oklahoma City: The Conference, n.d.

Free Methodist Church of North America, and Oregon Conference. "Annual Reports of the Oregon Annual Conference." *Annual Reports [of The] Oregon Annual Conference*. Turner, Ore.: Oregon Conference Free Methodist Church of North America, n.d.

Free Methodist Church of North America, Oregon Conference, Free Methodist Church of North America., and Oregon Conference. "Connection." *Connection*. Turner, OR: Oregon Conference of the Free Methodist Church of North America, 1997.

———. *Connection, 1895-1995: Oregon Conference*. Turner, Or.: Oregon Conference of the Free Methodist Church, 1995.

———. *Oregon Conference of the Free Methodist Church: 75th Anniversary, 1895-1970*. S.l.: Free Methodist Church of North America, Oregon Conference, 1970.

Free Methodist Church of North America, Pacific Northwest Conference, Free Methodist Church of North America., and Pacific Northwest Conferenc. "The Northwest Passage." *The Northwest Passage*. Seattle, WA: Pacific Conference of the Free Methodist Church of North America, n.d.

Free Methodist Church of North America, Pacific Northwest Conference, Free Methodist Church of North America., and Pacific Northwest Conference. "Conference News." *Conference News*. Seattle, WA: The Conference, n.d.

Free Methodist Church of North America, Pacific Northwest Conference, and Board of Social Action. "Social Action Issues." *Social Action Issues*. Seattle, WA: The Board, n.d.

Free Methodist Church of North America, Southeastern Regional Fellowship, Kentucky-Tennessee Conference, Atlantic Southeast Conference, Free Methodist Church of North America., Southeastern Regional Fellowship., Free Methodist Church of North America., Kentucky-Tennessee Conference., Free Methodist Church of North America., and Atlantic Southeast Conference. "Southern Breeze." *Southern Breeze*. Bowling Green, KY: Southeastern Regional Fellowship, Free Methodist Church of North America, 1995.

Free Methodist Church of North America, Southern California-Arizona Conference, Free Methodist Church of North America., and Southern California-Arizona Conference. "Observer." *Observer*. [S.l.]: The Conference, n.d.

Free Methodist Church of North America, Southern Michigan Conference, Free Methodist Church of North America., and Southern Michigan Conference. "Vision." *Vision*. Spring Arbor, MI: The Conference, n.d.

Free Methodist Church of North America, Wabash Conference, Free Methodist Church of North America., and Wabash Conference. "The Christian Courier : The Voice of the Wabash Conference." *The Christian Courier: The Voice of the Wabash Conference*. Hooperston, IL: Wabash Conference of the Free Methodist Church, n.d.

— — —. "The Wabash Christian Courier." *The Wabash Christian Courier*. Hooperston, IL: Free Methodist Church of North America, Wabash Conference, n.d.

Free Methodist Church of North America, Wesleyan Church, Committee on Merger Exploration, Free Methodist Church of North America., Committee on Merger Exploration., Wesleyan Church., and Committee on Merger Exploration. *Free Methodist Church of North America and the Wesleyan Church: Proposed Articles of Agreement and Constitution.* [Winona Lake, Ind.]: [publisher not identified], 1974.

Free Methodist Church of North America, West Virginia Conference, Free Methodist Church of North America., and West Virginia Conference. "West Virginia Echoes." *West Virginia Echoes.* Teays, WV: The Conference, n.d.

Free Methodist Church of North America, Woman's Missionary Society, Free Methodist Church of North America., and Woman's Missionary Society. *Then Jesus Came: True Stories of African Children.* Winona Lake, Ind.: Free Methodist Church, 1959.

– – –. *Twentieth General Session: August 20-24, 1979, Indianapolis, Indiana.* Indianapolis, Ind.: Women's Missionary Society of the Free Methodist Church, 1979.

Free Methodist Church of North America, Woman's Missionary Society, Young People's Missionary Society of the Free Methodist Church, Free Methodist Church of North America., Woman's Missionary Society., and Young People's Missionary Society of the Free Methodist Church. *Directory: Oregon Conference, Free Methodist Church, 1949-1950.* S.l.: s.n., 1949.

Free Methodist Church Of Watervilet. "Directory of Watervliet Free Methodist Church." *Directory of Watervliet Free Methodist Church.* Watervliet, Mich.: The Church, n.d.

Free Methodist Church, Topeka, Kansas, 1882-1982. [Topeka, Kan.]: [The Church], 1982.

"Free Methodist Church, Ypsilanti, Michigan." Ypsilanti Historical Society Photo Archives, n.d. http://name.umdl.umich.edu/IC-YHSIC1-X-711%5DYHS00711.TIF.

Free Methodist Historical Society, Marston Memorial Historical Center, Free Methodist Historical Society., Marston Memorial Historical Center., Free Methodist Church of North America, Men's Ministries International, Free Methodist Historical Society., Marston Memorial Historical Center., Free Methodist Church of North America., and Men's Ministries International. "Newsletter." *Newsletter*. Indianapolis, IN: Marston Memorial Historical Center, 2000.

"Free Methodist Hymnal / Published by Authority of the General Conference of the Free Methodist Church of North America." Chicago : Free Methodist Pub. House, n.d. http://hdl.handle.net/2027/mdp.39015054361087.

Free Methodist Mission. *Buku ya milawu ya Vandla ra Methodista Livre*. Germiston: the Mission, 1961.

Free Methodist Publishing House. "The Christian Minister." *The Christian Minister.*, 1949.

Free Methodist Youth. *The Official Guidebook of Free Methodist Youth*. Winona Lake, IN: World Headquarters, Free Methodist Youth, 1955.

Free Methodists Ministers' Associaton. "The Free Methodist Ministers' Magazine." *The Free Methodist Ministers' Magazine*. London: Free Methodist Minister's Association], 1895.

Freeland, Mariet Hardy, and One who loved her. *Missionary Martyrs Mary Louisa Ranf, Missionary to India*. Chicago: T.B. Arnold, 1892. http://ncco.galegroup.com/gdc/ncco/MonographsDetailsPage/MonographsDetailsWindow?disableHighlighting=false&prodId=NCCO&action=1&activityType=BasicSearch&javax.portlet.action=viewPortletAction&documentId=GALE|ASPQWH539177403&dviSelectedPage=1&userGroupNa.

Gaddis, Vincent. *The Story of Winona Lake: A Memory and a Vision*. Winona Lake Ind.: Winona Lake Christian Assembly, 1960.

Gagne, Real. "The Free Methodist Understanding of Baptism in the Light of John Wesley's Teaching and the American Methodist Tradition," 1991.

Galbreath, Marvin. *20 Centuries of Christianity*. Winona Lake IN: Light and Life Press, 1970.

Galbreath, Marvin L. *James and Peter: Leader's Guide*. Winona Lake, Ind.: Light and Life Press, 1962.

Gallaher Family, and Gallaher family. *Gallaher Family Papers*, 1800.

Garber, Paul. *The Methodists Are One People*. Nashville: Cokesbury Press, 1939.

Gaylord, Mary Loew. *Tender Heart*. Winona Lake, In.: Light and Life Press, 1976.

Gear, F B. "Book Review: Peloubet's Select Notes on the International Bible Lessons for Christian Teaching, Uniform Series, 1955, by Wilbur M. Smith. W. A. Wilde Co., Boston. 473 Pp. $2.75.; The Douglass Sunday School Lessons, 1955, by Earl L. Douglass. The Macmillan." *Interpretation: A Journal of Bible and Theology Interpretation: A Journal of Bible and Theology* 9, no. 2 (1955): 235–36.

Geiger, Kenneth. *Further Insights into Holiness: Nineteen Leading Wesleyan Scholars Present Various Phases of Holiness Thinking*. Kansas City MO: Beacon Hill Press, 1963.

———. *Insights into Holiness: Discussions of Holiness by Fifteen Leading Scholars of the Wesleyan Persuasion*. Kansas City MO: Beacon Hill Press, 1962.

"General Conference Daily. (Journal, Magazine, 1900s) [WorldCat.org]," n.d. http://www.worldcat.org/title/general-conference-daily/oclc/7904114&referer=brief_results.

General Council of the Church in Mission of the Free Methodist Church of North America, Free Methodist Church of North America, General Council for the Church in Mission, Free Methodist Church of North America., General Council of the Church in Mission., Leslie Ray Marston, Free Methodist Church of North America., Leslie Ray Marston, Free Methodist Church of North America., and Free Methodist Church of North America. *The Free Methodist. The Free Methodist*. Rochester, N.Y.: Levi Wood, 1868.

General Mission Board of the Free Methodist Church of North America. "Inhambane Tidings," n.d.

General Young People's Missionary Society Council, and General Young People's Missionary Society Council. *It's Time You Knew ...: The Facts about the Ministry and Operation of the Young People's Missionary Society through the Free Methodist Church around the World*. Winona Lake, Ind.: Young People's Missionary Society, 1952.

Ghormley, Newton Baxter. *The Land of the Heart of Livingstone; Or, The Genius of the Bantu. A Study of the Bantu Tribes of Africa, 100,000,000 Souls, with Special Reference to the Agencies Which Contribute to Their Civilization,*. Chicago: Published by the author; for sale by the Woman's Foreign Missionary Society of the Free Methodist Church, 1920.

Gilmore, Alene. *Treasure in the Dominican*. Winona Lake, IN: Light and Life Press, 1964.

Goddard, Burton. *The Encyclopedia of Modern Christian Missions the Agencies*. Camden N.J.: T. Nelson, 1967.

Godfroy, Clarence, and Martha Una. McClurg. *Miami Indian Stories*. Winona Lake, Ind.: Light and Life Press, 1961.

Goldstein, Donald M, and Carol Aiko Deshazer Dixon. *Return of the Raider*. Lake Mary, Fla.: Creation House, 2010.

Goodhew, Edna. *Echoes from Half a Century*. Los Angeles: Los Angeles Pacific College Press, 1960.

Gramento, Jean Hall. "Those Astounding Free Methodist Women! A Biographical History of Free Methodist Women in Ministry with an Extended Bibliography of Free Methodist Women's Studies : A Final Document Submitted to the Doctoral Studies Committee of United Theological Seminary." United Theological Seminary, 1992.

Green, Evaline D. *The Stewardship of the Mother Talent*. Winona Lake, Ind.: Woman's Missionary Society of the Free Methodist Church of North America, 1942.

Greenville College (Greenville, Ill.). "Annual Register of Greenville College." *Annual Register of Greenville College*. Chicago, IL.: Free Methodist Publishing House., n.d.

Greenville College, and Ill.) Greenville College (Greenville. "Greenville College Record." Greenville, IL: Greenville College, n.d. http://catalog.hathitrust.org/api/volumes/oclc/27723572.html.

Gregory, Dwight T. *Free Methodists and Cities, 1950-1980*. Winona Lake, Ind.: Free Methodist Urban Fellowship, 1982.

———. "From the New Day to the New Century : Free Methodist Strategies for Metropolitan Church Planting in Light of 1985-2000 Efforts and Results," 2005.

Griffith, Claude E. "Patterns of Free Methodist Worship : Historic Freedoms," 1984.

Griffith, George. *Daily Glow*. Los Angeles Calif., 1941.

Griffith, George W. *Lest We Forget: Selected Messages*. Los Angeles, CA: Mrs. G.W. Griffith, 1939.

———. *The Divine Program; an Interpretation of the Divine Method of Redemption and of the Nature and Nurture of the Christian Life,*. Chicago, Ill.: W.B. Rose, 1923.

Griffith, Lillian Bushnell, and George William Griffith. *Living Embers: The Life and Writings of George William Griffith*. Winona Lake, IN: Light and Life Press, 1937.

"Group Buys Ottawa County Church to Save It." *Minor Methodist Sects, Clippings*. 1 (1994).

Grubb, Kenneth. *World Christian Handbook*. London: World Dominion press, 1949.

Guthrie, Michael D. "Discovering the Life of Christ: A Biographical Study Approach to the Life of Jesus Christ Utilizing the Four Gospels : A Final Document Submitted to the Doctor of Ministry Program Committee of United Theological Seminary in Partial Fulfillment of the Requ." United Theological Seminary, 1992.

Gyertson, David John. "The Church Related College Higher Education in the Free Methodist Church during the Decade of the Seventies ; Implications for the Eighties," 1981.

Haley, John Wesley. *But Thy Right Hand*. Winona Lake, Ind.: Woman's Missionary Society of the Free Methodist Church, 1949.

Haley, John Wesley., William B Olmstead, Free Methodist Church of North America., Free Methodist Church of North America, and Free Methodist Church of North America. *Life in Mozambique and South Africa*. Chicago: Free Methodist Pub. House, 1926.

Hall, Bert H. *Job: Leader's Guide*. Winona Lake, Ind.: Light and Life Press, 1962.

Hamilton, Mary Elizabeth. *James R. Bishop: God's Chosen Man: The Life Story of the Founder of South India Biblical Seminary Bangarapet, Karnataka, South India*. Karnataka, India: South India Biblical Seminary, 1988.

Harmon, Nolan. *The Encyclopedia of World Methodism*. Nashville: United Methodist Pub. House, 1974.

Hart, Edward Payson. *Reminiscences of Early Free Methodism*. Chicago, Ill.: Free Methodist Publ. House, 1903. http://catalog.hathitrust.org/api/volumes/oclc/13683697.html.

Hartsough, Mary Mae., Lucy E Upson, and Lloyd W Babb. *A History of the Hartough - Hartsough - Hartsock Family*. Winona Lake, Indiana: The Free Methodist Publishing House, 1964.

Harvey, David. *STMO (submission, Transformation, Multiplication, Order): Building a Culture of Kingdom Fruitfulness*. [Indianapolis, Ind.]: Free Methodist Church of North America, 2006.

Harvey, J. *Faith plus: Search for the Holy Life*. Winona Lake Ind.: Light and Life, 1976.

Harvey, J D. *The Wesleyan Way Today*. Winona Lake, Ind.: Light and Life Press, 1979.

Harvey, James Dowell. *Dimensions in Christian Living*. Winona Lake, Ind.: Light and Life Press, 1973.

Haskins, Andrew M. "New Life for Old Churches : A Multi-Case Study of Four Turnaround Small Churches," 1997.

Haslam, Robert B. *Peepholes on Life: 44 Fun Looks at the Serious Side of Life*. Winona Lake, Ind.: Light and Life Press, 1977.

Haviland, Emma. *Under the Southern Cross: Or, a Woman's Life Work for Africa*. Cincinnati: God's Bible School and Revivalist, 1928.

Hawke, Joanna. "Hogue, Wilson Thomas." *American National Biography*. 11 (1999).

Hawkins, Richard. *Redemption or the Living Way: A Treatise on the Redemption of the Body Including a Doctrinal Outline of Experimental Religion*. Olean N.Y.: Herald Publ. House, 1888.

Hawkins, Richard Watson. *Life Eternal*, 1880.

Hawley, Doreen., and Jessie. Hardy. *Living Water, Living Letter: Free Methodist Missions in Egypt and India*. Winona Lake, IN: Light and Life Press, 1980.

Haywood, A L. "My Life Story." Stanwood, Mich.: Sanders Print Shop, 1942. http://books.google.com/books?id=E2bhAAAAMAAJ.

Hazzard, Aaron Harold, Montmorency County Historical Society, Montmorency County Tribune, Montmorency County Historical Society., and Montmorency County Tribune. *Blue Sky Circuit Montmorency County, Michigan, 1922-1926*. [Atlanta, Mich.]: [Montmorency County Historical Society] : Printed by the Montmorency County Tribune, 1991. http://books.google.com/books?id=H2bhAAAAMAAJ.

Helms, Elmer Ellsworth. *God in History*. Chicago, IL: Light and Life Press, 1923.

Helsel, E Walter. "When Is Jesus Coming Back?" *Light and Life* November 9 (1976): 6–7,12.

Helsel, E Walter. *Timothy, Titus: Leader's Guide*. Winona Lake, Ind.: Light and Life Press, 1965.

Hendrickson, Ford. *The "Livingstone" of the Orinoco (interior of South America): The Life Story of Ford Hendrickson (an Autobiography)...* Wausen Ohio: [publisher not identified], 1942.

Herndon, Barton T. "Discipleship out of Transition : A Study of the New Membership Policies and Procedures of the Free Methodist Church and Its Impact on Discipleship," 2001.

Herzog, J. *The New Schaff-Herzog Encyclopedia of Religious Knowledge, Embracing Biblical, Historical, Doctrinal, and Practical Theology and Biblical, Theological, and Ecclesiastical Biography from the Earliest*. New York ;London: Funk and Wagnalls Company, 1908.

Hill, Cyril D, Seattle Pacific University., Archives., and Seattle Pacific University Archives. *Cyril Hill Papers,* 1909.

Hill, Darold L, John E Van Valin, Free Methodist Church of North America Board of Bishops, Free Methodist Church of North America., and Board of Bishops. *Membership Care Committee Handbook, Free Methodist Church of North America*. Winona Lake, IN: Free Methodist Pub. House, 1988.

Hill, Nettie. *A Brief History of Holiness Movement & Free Methodist Missions, Egypt 1899-1986*. S.l.: s.n., 2007.

Hillman Free Methodist Church. "Directory of Hillman Free Methodist Church." *Directory of Hillman Free Methodist Church*. Hillman, Mich.: The Church, n.d.

Hillsdale Free Methodist Church. "Directory of Hillsdale Free Methodist Church." *Directory of Hillsdale Free Methodist Church*. Hillsdale, Mich.: The Church, n.d.

Hilson, James Benjamin. *History of the South Carolina Conference of Wesleyan Methodist Church of America; Fifty-Five Years of Wesleyan Methodism in South Carolina*. Winona Lake, Indiana: Light and Life Press, 1950.

"Historical Sketches of the Free Methodist Churches of the East Michigan Conference, 1924-1962." Linden, Mich.: Scottie's Printing, 1963. http://books.google.com/books?id=znXiAAAAMAAJ.

"History of Greenville College with Special Reference to the Curriculum (Book, 1934) [WorldCat.org]," n.d. http://www.worldcat.org/title/history-of-greenville-college-with-special-reference-to-the-curriculum/oclc/30659503&referer=brief_results.

Hitt, Russell T, Roy A Beltz, and C Hoyt. Watson. *Story of the Light and Life Hour*. [Winona Lake, IN]: [Forward Movement], n.d.

Hockett, Betty., and Grace. Abbott. *Life Changing Learning for Children: Resources That Work*. Winona Lake, Ind.: Light and Life Press, 1977.

Hockley, Robert G. *Sectarianism within Free Methodism: Its Contribution to the Formation of the Free Methodist Church and Its Continuing Influence Today*. S.l.: s.n.], 1991.

Hodson, Olive., Free Methodist Church of North America., and Women's Ministries International. *Free to Choose: Lessons from the Gospel of John*. Winona Lake, Ind.: printed for Women's Ministries International by Light and Life Press, 1990.

Hoffer, Mary. *George Pocre (1723-1810) and Descendants*. [Winona Lake, Ind.]: [Light and Life Press], 1982.

Hogg, W T. *A Hand-Book of Homiletics and Pastoral Theology*. Chicago: Free Methodist Pub. House, 1895.

———. *History of the Free Methodist Church of North America*. Winona Lake, Ind.: Free Methodist Pub. House, 1938.

Hogue, Emma. *India: A Mission Study for Juniors*. Chicago: Women's Foreign Missionary Society of the Free Methodist Church, 1920.

Hogue, Emma L. *Adella Paulina Carpenter: In Memory of a Beautiful Life*. Winona Lake, Ind.: Woman's Missionary Society, 1939.

Hogue, Wilson. *Revivals and Revival Work,*. Buffalo N.Y.: Published for the author, 1890.

———. *The Believer's Personal Experience of Christ in the Processes of Salvation*. Chicago: W.B. Rose, 1915.

———. *The Class-Meeting as a Means of Grace,*. Chicago: S.K.J. Chesbro, 1907.

Hogue, Wilson T. *A Hand-Book of Homiletics and Pastoral Theology*. Winona Lake, Ind.: Herald and Banner Press, 1940.

———. *G. Harry Agnew, a Pioneer Missionary*. Chicago: Free Methodist Pub. House, 1905.

———. *History of the Free Methodist Church of North America,*. Chicago: Free Methodist Pub. House, 1915.

———. *Hymns That Are Immortal: With Some Account of Their Authorship, Origin, History and Influence*. Chicago, Ill.: Light and Life Press, 1932.

———. "Missionary Hymns and Responsive Scripture Readings : For Use in Missionary Meetings." Chicago: Woman's Foreign Missionary Society of the Free Methodist Church, 1928.

———. *Retrospect and Prospect: A Semi-Centennial Sermon Preached by Bishop Wilson T. Hogue before the General Conference of the Free Methodist Church, in Chicago, June 18, 1911*. Chicago, IL: Free Methodist Pub. House, 1911.

———. *The Holy Spirit: A Study*. Chicago, Ill.: William B. Rose, 1916.

Elmer, Hogue. *Through the Years*. Parker, CO: Books To Believe In, 2005.

Hogue, Wilson T, and Ann E Chesbrough. *A Sermon: Preached at the Fiftieth Anniversary of the Marriage of Rev. Samuel K.J. and Mrs. Ann E. Chesbrough, February 6, 1898, Together with the Experience of Mrs. Ann E. Chesbrough, a Member of the First Class Ever Formed in the Free Methodist Church*. Chicago: Free Methodist Pub. House, 1906.

Hogue, Wilson T, Benjamin Titus Roberts, and W T Hogg. *A Symposium on Scriptural Holiness*. Chicago: Free Methodist Pub. House, 1896.

Holdren, David W. *The Power to Become: I, II, III John, Jude; Study Guide*. Winona Lake, Ind.: [Published for Aldersgate Publications] by Light and Life Press, 1986.

Holiness Alive and Well: The Meaning of Holy Living in Twentieth-Century Life. Published for Aldersgate Associates by Beacon Hill Press of Kansas City, 1970.

Hook, Edna M. *Centennial of Armadale Church, 1880-1980: In the Cradle of Free Methodism in Canada*. Scarborough, Ont.: Armadale Church], 1980.

Horner, Ralph. *Bible Doctrines*. Ottawa Can.: Holiness Movement Pub. House, 1908.

———. *From the Altar to the Upper Room in Four Parts*. Toronto ;Montréal: W. Briggs ;;C.W. Coates, 1891.

Horton, Claude A. *Money Counts: A Handbook on Local Church Finance*. Winona Lake, Ind.: Light and Life Press, 1980.

Houck, Larry Edward. "A Descriptive Dissertation on Trust Development between Pastor and Parish," 1988.

Houser, Gwen. *Boadi and Tembi of Africa's Grasslands*. Winona Lake, Ind.: Light and Life Press, 1969.

Houser, Gwen., Jean. Johnson, and Henry. Church. *Adventures in Africa's Grasslands: Stories from Southern Africa*. Winona Lake, Ind.: Light and Life Press, 1978.

Houser, Tillman. *Free Methodist and Other Missions in Zimbabwe*. Kopje, Harare: Priority Projects Pub., 2000.

Houser, Tillman., and Gwen. Houser. *Let Me Tell You: A Memoir*. [Charleston, SC]: Booksurge, 2007.

Howell, Roy. *Saved to Serve: Accent on Stewardship*. Grand Rapids MI: Baker Book House, 1965.

Howell, Roy W. *Christian Family: A Symposium*. Winona Lake, Ind.: Light and Life Press, 1965.

Howell, Roy W, and Wesley F Jeffery. *Relections*. Winona Lake, Ind.: Roy W. Howell, 1970.

Howland, Carl. *Manual of Missions,*. New York ;Chicago: Fleming H. Revell Co., 1913.

Howland, Carl Leroy. *A Brief Story of Our Church: An Historical Outline of the Origin and Growth of the Free Methodist Church of North America*. Winona Lakes, Ind.: Free Methodist Pub. House, 1953.

— — —. *Proofs of Inspiration: The Cumulative Proofs of the Inspiration of the Scriptures*. Winona Lake, Ind.: Free Methodist Pub. House, 1950.

— — —. *The Story of Our Church: Free Methodism, Some Facts and Some Reasons*. Winona Lake, IN: Free Methodist Pub. House, 1951.

Howland, Jenne. *Not Mine Steward*. Winona Lake In.: Published by Woman's Missionary Society of the Free Methodist Church, 1947.

Hoyer, Jeff. *Life-Changing Learning for Adults: Resources That Work*. Winona Lake, Ind.: Light and Life Press, 1984.

Hudson, Winthrop. *Religion in America*. New York: Scribner, 1965.

Huffman, Jasper A. *Building the Home Christian*. Winona Lake, Ind.: Light and Life Press, 1951.

———. *Golden Treasures from the Greek New Testament for English Readers*. Winona Lake, IN: Light and Life Press, 1951.

———. *The Holy Spirit*. Butler, Ind.: Higley Press, 1944.

———. *The Messianic Hope in Both Testaments*. Winona Lake, IN: Light and Life Press, 1939.

———. *The Stones Cry out*. Winona Lake, Ind.: Light and Life Press, 1948.

Humphrey, J M. *Crumbs from Heaven*. Salem, Ohio: Allegheny, 2000.

———. *Railroad Sermons from Railroad Stories*. Salem, OH: Schmul Pub. Co., 2003.

———. *Select Fruits from the Highlands of Beulah*. Lima, OH: True Gospel Grain Pub. Co., 1913.

———. *Seven Old Time Gospel Sermons*. Chicago: The Author, n.d.

———. *Spiritual Lessons from Every-Day Life*. Lima, Ohio: True Gospel Grain Pub. Co., 1914.

———. *X-Ray Sermons.*. Omaha, Neb.: "Anywhere" evangelistic workers' Pub. House, 1924.

Humphrey, J M, and J M Humphrey. *The Lost Soul's First Day in Eternity*. Salem, Ohio: Allegheny Publications, 2000.

Hunt, Sandford. *Methodism in Buffalo, from Its Origin to the Close of 1892,*. Buffalo N.Y.: H.H. Otis & Sons, 1893.

Hurst, J. *The History of Methodism,*. New York: Eaton & Mains, 1902.

Hyde, A. *The Story of Methodism throughout the World, from the Beginning to the Present Time ... Giving an Account of Its Various Influences and Institutions of to-Day*. Springfield Mass. ;Chicago Ill.: Wiley & Co.;;Johns Pub. House, 1889.

Iesalnieks, Karlis., Karlis Lesalnieks, and Karlis. Iesalnieks. *Unsearchable Ways of God: Isaiah 55: 8-9*. Bicknell, Ind.: Fellowship Promoter Press, 1970.

"In Touch." Winona Lake IN: Wesley Press, 1971.

Inc., World Book, and World Book Inc. "Free Methodist Church," 2014.

"India Letter Links (Journal, Magazine, 1937) [WorldCat.org]," n.d. http://www.worldcat.org/title/india-letter-links/oclc/59109876&referer=brief_results.

"Infant Baptism in Biblical and Wesleyan Theology (Book, 1975) [WorldCat.org]," n.d. http://www.worldcat.org/title/infant-baptism-in-biblical-and-wesleyan-theology/oclc/13461002&referer=brief_results.

Ingersol, Robert Stanley. *Burden of Dissent: Mary Lee Cagle and the Southern Holiness Movement*, 1990.

"Inhambane Tidings. (Journal, Magazine, 1900s) [WorldCat.org]," n.d. http://www.worldcat.org/title/inhambane-tidings/oclc/14815942&referer=brief_results.

"Interior of the Dunhard Church," n.d.

"International Uniform Series." Winona Lake IN: Light and Life Press, 1885.

"Interracial News. (Journal, Magazine, 1950) [WorldCat.org]," n.d. http://www.worldcat.org/title/interracial-news/oclc/10917576&referer=brief_results.

Ionia County Clerk, Free Methodist Church of Orleans, First Baptist Church of Otisco, Society of First Baptist Church of Otisco, and Orleans and Belding Circuit Free Methodist Church. *Records of the Ionia County Clerk*. Orleans, MI, 1848.

Ivers, Karl. *Golden Memories: God's Leading in the Lives of His People*. McPherson, KS.: McPherson Free Methodist Church, 1991.

Iwig-O'Byrne, Liam. "A Progression of Methodist Radicalism : An Examination of the History and Ethos of the First Sixty Years of the Nazarites and Their Heirs (1855-1915) in Their Social and Religious Context," 1993.

Jacobson, Byron. *Jacobson, Byron: Papers*, 1900.

Jacquet, Constant. *Yearbook of American and Canadian Churches 1975*. Nashville TN: Abingdon Press, 1975.

James, Gilbert. "The Sanctified Way of Life." Wilmore, Ky.: DQB-LLC for Asbury Theological Seminary, 2012. http://place.asburyseminary.edu/ecommonsatschapelservices/.

James, Joseph F. *On the Front Lines: A Guide to Church Planting*. Winona Lake, Ind.: [Light and Life Press], 1987.

James, Joseph F, Free Methodist Church of North America, General Conference, Free Methodist Church of North America., General Conference, Free Methodist Church of North America, and General Conference. *Our Calling to the Poor*. Indianapolis, Ind.: Light and Life Press, 2008.

Jernigan, C. *Pioneer Days of the Holiness Movement in the Southwest*. Kansas City Mo.: Pentecostal Nazarene Pub. House, 1919.

Jessop, Harry E. *Foundations of Doctrine in Scripture and Experience: A Students' Handbook on Holiness*. Winona Lake, Ind.: Free Methodist Pub. House, 1938.

———. *I Met a Man with a Shining Face: An Autobiography in the Things of God*. Winona Lake, Ind.: Light and Life Press, 1956.

———. *That Burning Question of Final Perseverance*. Winona Lake, Ind.: Light and Life Press, 1942.

Johnson, Bruce C. "An Analysis of the Pastor's Relationship to the Sunday School in the Oregon Conference of the Free Methodist Church," 1964.

———. "The Training of College Persons as Lay Ministers in the Free Methodist Church," 1984.

Johnson, Carl E. *How in the World?* Winona Lake, Ind.: Light and Life Press, 1969.

Johnson, Harrison Frederick. *Handbook of Free Methodist Missions*. Winona Lake, Ind.: Free Methodist Pub. House, 1900.

Johnson, Harry F. *Heroes of Other Lands*. Winona Lake, IN: Light and Life Press, 1939.

Johnson, Hazel O. *Programs and Suggestions for Public Junior Missionary Meetings*. Winona Lake, Ind.: Free Methodist Church of North America, 1955.

Johnson, Jeffrey Paul. "A Strategy for Using Spiritual Formation to Promote Community Renewal," 2002.

Johnson, Pearl Vennard., Free Methodist church. Woman's missionary society., and Woman's Missionary Society of the Free Methodist Church. *Our Neighbors the Dominicans,*. Winnona Lake, Ind.: Woman's missionary Society, Free Methodist church, 1942.

Johnston, Tom. *Yesterday's Hate, Today's Love: The Amazing Story of Tom & Roberta Johnston*. Winona Lake IN: Light & Life Men International, 1974.

"Joint Commission of the Free Methodist and Wesleyan Methodist Churches on the Matter of Church Union Records," 1944.

Jones, Burton Rensselaer. *Incidents in the Life and Labors of Burton Rensselaer Jones, Minister of the Gospel, with Extracts from His Diary*. Chicago: Free Methodist Pub. House, 1909.

Jones, Charles. *A Guide to the Study of the Holiness Movement*. Metuchen N.J.: Scarecrow Press, 1974.

———. *Perfectionist Persuasion: The Holiness Movement and American Methodism, 1867-1936*. Metuchen N.J.: Scarecrow Press, 1974.

Jordahl, Donald C. "A History of the Kansas Conference of the Free Methodist Church," 1960.

Joy, Donald. *Bonding: Relationships in the Image of God*. Waco Tex.: Word Books, 1985.

———. *Moral Development Foundations: Judeo-Christian Alternatives to Piaget Kohlberg*. Nashville: Abingdon, 1983.

Joy, Donald M. *A Preliminary Report on the Aldersgate Graded Curriculum Project*. Winona Lake, Ind.: Free Methodist Pub. House, 1967.

———. "A Survey and Analysis of the Experiences, Attitudes and Problems of Senior High Youth of the Free Methodist Church." Southern Methodist University, 1960. http://www.worldcat.org/title/survey-and-analysis-of-the-experiences-attitudes-and-problems-of-senior-high-youth-of-the-free-methodist-church/oclc/7378773&referer=brief_results.

———. *Aldersgate Biblical Series*. Winona Lake, Ind.: Light and Life Press, 1960.

———. *Psalms: Leader's Guide*. Winona Lake, Ind.: Light and Life Press, 1962.

———. *The Holy Spirit and You: Leadership and Service Training/ series*. Winona Lake, Ind.: Light and Life Press, 1965.

Joy, Donald M, Aldersgate Publications Association., and Aldersgate Publications Association. *Meaningful Learning in the Church*. Winona Lake, Ind.: Light and Life Press, 1969.

"Junior Manual, 1-16, No.4." Winona Lake IN: Light and Life Press, 1953.

"Junior Manual. 1-3, No. 3." Winona Lake IN: Light and Life Press, 1951.

"Junior's Friend, 1-14, No. 39." Winona Lake IN: Light and Life Press, 1929.

Junker, James Arthur. *Free Methodist Missionary Work among the Mexicans*. S.l.: s.n.], n.d.

Kahl, Maude. *His Guiding Hand: An Autobiography*. Overland Park Kan.: Herald and Banner Press, 1970.

Kaiser, C Ray. "Axiomatic Church Growth," 1980.

Kalamazoo Free Methodist Church. "Directory of Kalamazoo Free Methodist Church." *Directory of Kalamazoo Free Methodist Church*. Kalamazoo, Mich.: The Church, n.d.

Kaub, Verne Paul. *Collectivism Challenges Christianity*. Winona Lake, Ind.: Light and Life Press, 1946.

Kaufmann, U Milo. *The Church and the Channels of Power*. Winona Lake, IN: Free Methodist Church, 1972.

Kaufmann, U Milo. *Heaven: A Future Finer than Dreams*. Winona Lake, Ind.: Light and Life Press, 1981.

———. *The God Who Shows Himself*. Winona Lake, Ind.: Free Methodist Church of North America, General Council for Church in Mission, 1970.

Keen, J Osborne. *In Memoriam: Frederick William Bourne*. London, 1905.

Kelley, Augusta Tullis, and Walter W Kelley. *Memoirs of Mrs. Augusta Tullis Kelley Her Experience, Labors as Evangelist and Missionary to Africa, with Extracts from Her Writings*. Chicago: T.B. Arnold, 1889. https://dds.crl.edu/crldelivery/1950.

Kelley, Dean. *Why Conservative Churches Are Growing: A Study in Sociology of Religion*. New York: Harper & Row, 1972.

Kendall, David W, Karen Strand Winslow, Free Methodist Church of North America, and Free Methodist Church of North America. *The Female Pastor: Is There Room for "She" in Shepherd?* Indianapolis, Ind.: Light and Life Communications, 2006.

Kendall, Walter S. *Evangel of the Cross: Highlights, Devotion Depths, and Bits of Humor*. Stanwood, Wash.: Le Sabre, 1985.

———. *That the World May Know*. Winona Lake, Ind.: Light and Life Press, 1964.

———. *The Challenge of This Century: A Doctrinal Emphasis*. [Salem, Or.?]: Free Methodist Church of North America, 1955.

———. *The Holy Spirit in Christian Experience*. Stanwood, Wash.: Warm Beach Printing Services, 1981.

Kennedy, Jessie Harper. *The Lord Shall Preserve and Treasures out of the Darkness*. Bern, Ind.: Light and Hope Publications, 1954.

Kerby, R A. *A Shuffling Theology*. Winona Lake, IN: Light and Life Press, 1949.

Kettinger, LeRoy., and Catherine. Stonehouse. *Youth as Learners*. Winona Lake, Ind.: Light and Life Press, 1983.

Keys, Charles E, and Pauline H Todd. *Christian Youth Looks at Evolution: ... Bible Exploration Guide of the Christian Youth Camper Curriculum*. Winona Lake, In.: Light and life Press, 1965.

Kidney, Elsie Mae. *Our Father's Care*. Spring Arbor, MI.: The Author, 1988.

Killingray, David. "Soga, Tiyo." Oxford: Oxford University Press, 2005.

Killion, Mead W. "A History of Spring Arbor Seminary and Junior College." University of Michigan, 1941. http://www.worldcat.org/title/history-of-spring-arbor-seminary-and-junior-college/oclc/11605017&referer=brief_results.

"Kindergaren Activities." Kansas City MO: Beacon Hill Press, 1969.

"Kindergarten Activities." Winona Lake IN: Light and Life Press, 1954.

"Kindergarten Bible Stories, 1-16, No. 4." Winona Lake IN: Light and Life Press, 1954.

"Kindergarten Stories. 1-16, No. 4." Winona Lake IN: Light and Life Press, 1954.

"Kindergarten Teacher." Kansas City MO: Beacon Hill Press, n.d.

Kindschi, Paul. *Entire Sanctification: Studies in Christian Holiness*. Marion Ind.: Wesley Press, 1964.

King, Carroll Wesley. "Infant Baptism in Biblical and Wesleyan Theology." Asbury Theological Seminary, 1975.

———. "Mobilizing the Laity : A Strategy for Obtaining Greater Numerical Growth in the Wilmore Free Methodist Church," 1990.

King, Wesley. *The Joy of Ministry: My Role in Christian Education*. Winona Lake, Ind.: Light and Life Press, 1977.

Kingsley, Charles. *Do: Manifesto for Concerned Christian Community, Manual for Meaning in Mobilization of Manpower*. Winona Lake Ind.: Light and Life Men International, 1976.

———. *Go!: Revolutionary New Testament Christianity*. Grand Rapids: Zondervan, 1965.

Kingsley, Charles W. *I Stand by the Door: The Autobiography of Charles W. Kingsley*. Indianapolis, Ind.: Light and Life Men International, 1990.

Kirchhofer, William. *Fire among the Stubble: Church Renewal in the Wesleyan Tradition*, 2009.

Kirkpatrick, Charles D, Free Methodist Church of North America., Woman's Missionary Society., Free Methodist Church of North America, Woman's Missionary Society of the Free Methodist Church, Free Methodist Church of North America., and Woman's Missionary Society. *Cow in the Clinic, and Other Missionary Stories from around the World*. Winona Lake, Ind.: Light and Life Press, 1977.

Kirkpatrick, Charles D, Free Methodist Church of North America, and Free Methodist Church of North America. *Profile of Missions*. Winona Lake, Ind.: Light and Life Press, 1971.

Kleibscheidel, Denny. *Someone to Watch Over Me: Living the Last Verse*. Camarillo, CA: Salem Communications, 2006.

Klein, Matthias. *By Nippon's Lotus Ponds Pen Pictures of Real Japan*. New York ;Chicago: Fleming H. Revell Company, 1914.

Kleinsteuber, R Wayne. *Coming of Age: The Making of a Canadian Free Methodist Church*. [Hamilton, Ont.]: Light and Life Press, Canada, 1980.

———. *More than a Memory: The Renewal of Methodism in Canada*. [Mississauga, Ont.]: Light and Life Press Canada, 1984.

Knox, Lloyd H. *A Faith to Grow by*. Winona Lake, Ind.: Light and Life Press, 1977.

———. *Everybody Wants Your Money: How to Be Generous, Not Gullible*. Winona Lake, Ind.: Light and Life Press, 1976.

———. *Key Biblical Perspectives on Tongues*. Winona Lake, Ind.: Light and Life Press, 1974.

———. *Key to Holiness Theology: A Relational Understanding*. Winona Lake, Ind.: Light and Life Press, 1972.

———. *Philippians and Thessalonians: Leader's Guide*. Winona Lake, Ind.: Light and Life Press, 1963.

———. *Security for Believers*. Winona Lake, Ind.: Light and Life Press, 1970.

———. *The Free Methodist Minister*. Winona Lake, Ind.: Light and Life Press, 1976.

Knox, Lloyd H, Chet. Martin, and Ruth. Sparrow. *Building Holy Relationships: Prayers, Sermons, and Other Writings*. Indianapolis, IN: Light and Life Communications, 1999.

Knox, Lloyd Henry, John Wesley, Charles Wesley, Free Methodist Church of North America., Free Methodist Church of North America, and Free Methodist Church of North America. *The Faith and Life of a Free Methodist*. Winona Lake, Ind. Free Methodist Pub. House, 1976.

Krober, Leslie L, Free Methodist Church of North America Board of Bishops, Free Methodist Church of North America., and Board of Bishops. *Pastors and Church Leaders Manual: Resources for Leading Local Churches*. Indianapolis, Ind.: Light and Life Communications, 2006.

Kuhn, Harold B. *Colossians, Philemon: Leader's Guide*. Winona Lake, Ind.: Light and Life Press, 1966.

Kulaga, Jon S. *Edward Payson Hart: The Second Man of Free Methodism*. Spring Arbor, Mich.: Spring Arbor University Press, 2007.

Kysor, Kenneth. *A History of The Free Methodist Church of Cattaraugus, New York*. Cattaraugus, N.Y.?; [Randolph, N.Y.?]: Church?] : [Printed by the Randolph Register], 1976.

Kysor, Kenneth. *Benjamin Titus Roberts and the Free Methodist Church*. Cattaraugus, N.Y.: s.n., 1976.

———. *The Wonderful Ways and Works of God*. [Cattaraugus, N.Y.]: [The author], 1976.

La Due, Gertrude., and Mildred La Due. Mead. *Gertrude Black La Due and Family Papers*, 1900.

La Due, John., and William K La Due. *The Life of Rev. Thomas Scott La Due: With Some Sketches and Other Writings*. Chicago: Free Methodist Pub. House, 1898.

Lake, Charles. *Our Goodly Heritage: A History of the Gerry Homes*. Gerry N.Y. ;Falconer N.Y.: Heritage Village ;;Printed by Falconer Print. and Design Inc., 1971.

Lamb, E Wendell., and Lawrence W Shultz. *Indian Lore*. Winona Lake, Ind.: Light and Life Press, 1964.

Lamson, Byron S. *The Holiness Teachings of New Testament Literature: Part I: The Teachings of Jesus*. Winona Lake, Ind.: Light and Life Press, 1950.

Lamson, Byron Samuel. *Greater Works than These*. Winona Lake, Ind.: Light and Life Press, 1987.

— — —. *Lights in the World; Free Methodist Missions at Work*. Winona Lake, Ind.: General missionary board, 1951.

— — —. *To Catch the Tide*. Winona Lake, Ind.: General Missionary Board, 1963.

— — —. *Venture!: The Frontiers of Free Methodism*. Winona Lake, Ind.: Light and Life Press, 1960.

Lancashire Family History and Heraldry Society. *Blackburn Nonconformist Chapels Monumental Inscriptions, Lancashire*. Ramsbottom: Lancashire Family History and Heraldry Society, n.d.

Larm, Terry A. "A Grammar of Conversion," 2004.

Las Cruces Free Methodist Church, and Las Cruces Free Methodist Church. *Las Cruces Free Methodist Church Records,* 1958.

Latourette, Kenneth. *A History of the Expansion of Christianity*. New York ;;London: Harper & Brothers, 1937.

Leach, Larry. "Pastor Establishes Seminary," 1963.

"Leaders in Education, a Biographical Dictionary. (Journal, Magazine, 1932) [WorldCat.org]," n.d. http://www.worldcat.org/title/leaders-in-education-a-biographical-dictionary/oclc/42314538&referer=brief_results.

"Learn and Do." Marion Ind.: Wesley Press, 1969.

Lee, James. *The Illustrated History of Methodism the Story of the Origin and Progress of the Methodist Church, from Its Foundation by John Wesley to the Present Day. Written in Popular Style and Illustrated by*. St Louis;New York: The Methodist magazine Pub. Co., 1900.

Lee, Joel Chi-hung. "A Gospel Team Training Program for the Kaohsiung Tsz Chiang Free Methodist Church," 1994.

Lee, Luther., and Benjamin Titus Roberts. *Holiness Tracts Defending the Ministry of Women*. New York [u.a.]: Garland Publ., 1985.

Leech, Ken. *Dark Providence, Bright Promise*. Indianapolis: Light and Life Press, 1995.

— — —. *True Witness: The Amazing Story of Detective Leech*. Winona Lake Ind.: Christian Witness Crusades Light and Life Men International, 1976.

Leete, Frederick. *Methodist Bishops--Personal Notes and Bibliography: With Quotations from Unpublished Writings and Reminiscences*. Nashville: Parthenon Press, 1948.

— — —. *Methodist Bishops: Personal Notes and Bibliography,*. Nashville: Printed by the Parthenon Press, 1948.

Lewis, L G. *Mitama no mi = The Fruite of the Spirit*. Tokyo-to: Jiyu Mesojisutosha Shuppanbu, dc 1931, Showa 6., 1931.

Lewis, M E. *The Invisible Railway*. Winona Lake, Ind.: Light and Life Press, 1900.

Lieby, Robert J. *Here's Your Answer!* Winona Lake, Ind.: Published by Light and Life Press for the Forward Movement of the Free Methodist Church, 1960.

Life Line Homes Incorporated. "Life Lines." *Life Lines*. Kansas City, KS: Life Line Homes, Inc., n.d.

"Light and Life Adult." Chicago, IL: Light and Life Press, 1885.

"Light and Life Beginner Teacher. 1-4, No. 2." Winona Lake IN: Light and Life Press, 1948.

"Light and Life Evangel." Chicago, IL; Winona Lake, IN: Light and Life Press, 1912.

"Light and Life Graded Series." Winona Lake IN: Light and Life Press, n.d.

"Light and Life Junior." *Light and Life Junior.* Winona, Lake, Ind.: Light and Life Press, n.d.

Light and Life Press, and Light and Life Press. "The Junior's Friend." *The Junior's Friend*. Chicago, Ill.: Light and Life Press, n.d.

"Light and Life Teacher's Quarterly." Chicago, IL; Winona Lake, IN: Light and Life Press, 1889.

"Light and Life Teacher's Quarterly for the Graded Primary Series. 1-9, No. 1." Winona Lake IN: Light and Life Press, 1941.

"Light and Life Youth. 1-76, No. 3." Chicago, IL; Winona Lake, IN: Light and Life Press, 1885.

"Lily of the Valley. 1-10, No. 12." Chicago, IL: W.B. Rose, 1897.

Lincicome, F. *A Lot in Sodom.* Winona Lake, Ind.: Light and Life Press, 1932.

———. *A Tribute to Mothers.* [Place of publication not identified]: [publisher not identified], 1935.

———. *Behold the Man!* Apollo, Pa.: West Pub. Co., 1932.

———. *Enemies of the Home.* Winona Lake, IN: Light and Life Press, 1934.

———. *Prayer*. Winona Lake, Ind.: Light and Life Press, 1936.

———. *The Doubles of the Bible*. Atlanta, GA: Repairer Pub. Co, n.d.

———. *The Soul*. Apollo, Pa.: West Pub. Co., 1940.

———. *The Three D's of the Sanctified*. Winona Lake, Ind.: Light and life Press, 1932.

———. *What Is Your Life?* Chicago, Ill.: Light and life Press, 1933.

Linton, John. *From Coalpit to Pulpit: An Informal Autobiography*. [N.l.]: Light and Life Press, 1947.

———. *Tears in Heaven: And Other Sermons*. [S.l.]: Light and Life Press, 1947.

Livermore, Harry E. *Psalms*. Winona Lake, Ind.: Light and Life Press, 1962.

Livermore, Paul. *Resources for Renewal: Romans Study Guide*. Winona Lake, IN: Light and Life Press, 1982.

———. *The God of Our Salvation: Christian Theology from the Wesleyan Perspective*. Indianapolis, IN: Light and Life Press, 1995.

Living Hymns of Charles Wesley. The Singing Saint. [Winona Lake, Ind.: Light and Life Press, 1957.

Livingston, G Herbert. *Genesis*. Winona Lake, Ind.: Light and Life Press, 1960.

———. *Genesis: Leader's Guide*. Winona Lake, Ind.: Light and Life Press, 1971.

———. *God's Spokesman*. Winona Lake, IN: Light and Life Press, 1960.

———. *Origins of Life and Faith: Genesis A: Study Guide*. Winona Lake, Ind.: Light and Life Press, 1981.

———. *Roots of the Church in the Old Testament*. Winona Lake, IN: Light and Life Press, 1960.

———. *Trial and Triumph: Genesis B, Study Guide*. Winona Lake, Ind.: Light and Life Press, 1981.

Livingstone, G Herbert. *Jeremiah-B and Lamentations*. Winona Lake, Ind.: Light and Life Press, 1964.

———. *Jeremiah, Lamentations: Leader's Guide*. Winona Lake, Ind.: Light and Life Press, 1963.

"Lois Evelyn Worbois," n.d.

Looman, John. *The Story of My Life*. Allegan, Mich.: John Looman, n.d.

Lorenz, Glenn Virgil. "Leading from the Margins : Recovering the Christian Tradition of Hospitality in Church Leadership," 2005.

Los Angeles Pacific College, and Los Angeles Free Methodist Seminary. *Articles of Incorporation and by-Laws, 1903-1965*. Los Angeles, Calif.: Los Angeles Pacific College, 1903.

Loss, Myron. *Culture Shock: Dealing with Stress in Cross-Cultural Living*. Winona Lake, Ind.: Light and Life Press, 1983.

Louth Free Methodist Church. *Rules of the Free Methodist Church, Louth: And of the Country Churches in the Louth Circuit: Also the Louth Free Methodist Circuit Regulations*. Louth [England]: Printed at the Times Works, 1882.

———. *The Regulations of the Louth Free Methodist Church: With Introductory Observations*. Louth: E. Squire, printer, 1854.

Love, Marriage - and Other Hazards. Published for Aldersgate Associates by Beacon Hill Press of Kansas City, 1970.

Lovejoy, Clarence. *College Guide a Complete Reference Book to 2,049 American Colleges and Universities for Use by Students, Parents, Teachers, and Guidance Counselors. 1953-54.* New York: Simon and Schuster, 1952.

Lovell, O D. *Ephesians: Leader's Guide.* Winona Lake, Ind.: Light and Life Press, 1962.

Lowell, LeRoy M. *Building the House Beautiful: A Study in Personal Religious Living.* Winona Lake, Ind.: Light and Life Press, 1939.

Lyon, Demester. *My Life Story.* [Place of publication not identified]: [D. Lyon], 1953.

M'Geary, John S. *The Free Methodist Church: A Brief Outline History of Its Origin and Development.* Chicago: W.B. Rose, 1908.

MacGeary, Ella L. *A Sketch of the Woman's Foreign Missionary Society.* Chicago, Ill.: Foreign Missionary Society, Free Methodist Church, 1924.

Macmillian. "The College Blue Book," n.d. http://www.worldcat.org/title/college-blue-book/oclc/1244494&referer=brief_results.

Macy, Victor W. "A History of the Free Methodist Mission in Portugese East Africa," 1946.

Macy, Victor W, and Lela. DeMille. *Discovery under the Southern Cross: Below the Equator--Missions Adventures in Mozambique and South Africa.* Winona Lake, Ind.: Light and Life Press, 1984.

Magida, Arthur J. *How to Be a Perfect Stranger, Vol. 2: A Guide to Etiquette in Other People's Religious Ceremonies.* Woodstock, Vt.: Jewish Lights Publishing, 1997.

Mahoney, Michael A, and Theological Research Exchange Network. "The Impact of Formational Prayer upon Spiritual Vitality." Ashland Theological Seminary, 2007.

Mann, W. *Sect, Cult, and Church in Alberta*. Toronto: University of Toronto Press, 1955.

Manning, S J. *Crusade Day*. [Place of publication not identified]: [publisher not identified], 1890.

Mannoia, Florence., and Lucy. Huston. *Amigos*. Winona Lake, Ind.: Light and Life Press, 1979.

Mannoia, Kevin W. "A Study of the Perception of Faculty Concerning Integration of Faith and Learning at Free Methodist Colleges," 1988.

— — —. *Church Planting: The next Generation: Century 21 Network, Leader's Manual*. Indianapolis, IN: Light and Life Press, 1996.

— — —. *Church Planting: The next Generation: Introducing the Century 21 Church Planting System*. Indianapolis, IN: Light and Life Press, 1994.

Manual for Leaders of Light and Life Men. Winona Lake, Ind.: Light and Life, International, Free Methodist Headquarters, n.d.

Markell, Dave. *Origins of Life and Faith: Genesis a Leader's Guide*. Winona Lake, Ind.: Light and Life Press, 1981.

Markell, Dave., Allen. Cleveland, Free Methodist Church of North America., Free Methodist Church of North America, and Free Methodist Church of North America. *Young Teen Organizational Manual*. Winona Lake, Ind.: Light and Life Press, 1978.

Markell, Dave., Allen. Cleveland, Free Methodist Church of North America, and Free Methodist Church of North America. *FMY Organizational Manual*. Winona Lake, Ind.: Light and Life Press, 1977.

Markell, David. *Expanded Ministry to Youth: Program Guidelines*. Winona Lake, IN: Light and Life Press, 1981.

Markley, Rena, Joan Vandenberg, and Glenn Yoder. *Ancestors and Descendants of Thomas Bays Nelson and Frances Miller*. Winona Lake, Ind.: Light and Life Press, 1986.

Marsh, C. *American Universities and Colleges*. Washington D.C.: American Council on Education, 1936.

Marston, Clarence Dean. *Life Is for That*. Winona Lake, In.: Printed for the author by Light and Life Press, 1940.

Marston, L R, Free Methodist Church of North America, and Free Methodist Church of North America. *Your Bishops Speak*. Winona Lake, IN: Light and Life Press, 1949.

Marston, Leslie Ray. *Bring the Books*. [Place of publication not identified]: [publisher not identified], 1950.

— — —. *From Age to Age a Living Witness; a Historical Interpretation of Free Methodism's First Century*. Winona Lake, Ind.: Light and Life Press, 1960.

— — —. *From Chaos to Character, a Study in the Stewardship of Personality*. Winona Lake, Ind.: Light and life Press, 1944.

— — —. *He Lived on Our Street: Enduring Words for Today*. Winona Lake, Ind.: Light and Life Press, 1979.

— — —. *I Need a Chart*. Winona Lake, Ind.: Published for The National Association of Evangelicals by courtesy of Light and Life Press, 1946.

— — —. "*I Need a Chart*." Winona Lake, Ind.: Published for The National Association of Evangelicals by courtesy of Light and Life Press, 1946.

— — —. *My Church: A Living Witness from Age to Age*. Winona Lake, Ind.: Distributed by the Forward Movement, Free Methodist World Headquarters, 1964.

———. *The River of Spiritual Life.* Winona Lake, Ind.: Light and Life Press, 1965.

———. *The Spirit and Emphasis of Free Methodism.* Winona Lake, Ind.: Free Methodist Church of North America, 1950.

———. *Thumb-Nail Sketches of Doctrinal Patterns: John Calvin, Jacobus Arminius, John Wesley.* Winona Lake, Ind.: Free Methodist Heaquarters, n.d.

———. *Youth Speaks!* Winona Lake, Ind.: Light and life Press, 1939.

Martin, Chet., and Jeff. Hoyer. *Guidelines for Service: I, II Timothy Titus Study Guide.* Winona Lake, Indiana: Light and Life Press, 1987.

Martin, Dawn., and Jeff. Hoyer. *Guidelines for Service: I, II Timothy Titus Leader's Guide.* Winona Lake, Indiana: Light and Life Press, 1987.

Martinez, David L. "The Wesleyan Way to Spiritual Formation Teaching an Adult Sunday School Class," 1989.

Mason, Harold. *Abiding Values in Christian Education.* [Westwood N.J.]: Fleming H. Revell Co., 1955.

Mason, Harold Carlton. *The Teaching Task of the Local Church.* Winona Lake, Ind.: Light and Life Press, 1960.

Mason, Harold Carlton, National Sunday School Association, National Sunday School Association., and National Sunday School Association. *Reclaiming the Sunday School. The Sunday School.* Winona Lake, Ind.: Light and Life Press, 1946.

Mavis, Marion. *A Brief Story of the Kentucky-Tennessee Conference.* [Wilmore, Ky.]: [Mavis], 1970.

Mavis, W. *Personal Renewal through Christian Conversion.* Kansas City Mo.: Beacon Hill Press of Kansas City, 1969.

———. *The Psychology of Christian Experience*. Grand Rapids: Zondervan Pub. House, 1963.

Mavis, Walter Curry. *Advancing the Smaller Local Church*. Winona Lake, Ind.: Light and Life Press, 1957.

———. *Beyond Conformity*. Winona Lake, Ind.: Light and life Press, 1958.

———. *The Holy Spirit in the Christian Life*. Winona Lake, Ind.: Light and Life Press, 1977.

Mayer, June. *Free Methodist Churches in Lawrence County*. S.l.: s.n., n.d.

Maynard, J Louise. *God's Lamp: History [of The] Central Illinois Conference, Free Methodist Church*. Greenville, Ill.: Tower Press, 1989.

Mays, Ira Dale, Judith Dunning, Bancroft Library, and Regional Oral History Office. *Ira Dale Mays: Stories of a Second-Generation Ironworker from Iowa*. Berkeley, Calif.: Regional Oral History Office, the Bancroft Library, University of California, 1992.

Mayse, P Thomas. "A Brief Study of Our Philosophy of Ministry : As It Pertains to Our Current Position of Associate Pastor in the Winona Lake Free Methodist Church (Indiana)," 1982.

Mayse, P Thomas. *Confronting in Love: I and II Corinthians; Study Guide*. Winona Lake, Ind.: [Published for Aldersgate Publications] by Light and Life Press, 1987.

McAllaster, Elva. *My Heart Hears Heaven's Reveille*. [Winona Lake, Ind.]: [Light and Life Press], 1954.

McChesney, Audine., and Bill McChesney. *Through Congo Shadows*. Salem, Ohio: Convention Book Store Publishers, 1968.

McClintock, John. *Cyclopedia of Biblical, Theological, and Ecclesiastical Literature*. Grand Rapids Mich.: Baker Book House, 1981.

McConnell, Lela G. *Faith Victorious in the Kentucky Mountains: The Story of Twenty-Two Years of Spirit-Filled Ministry*. Winona Lake, Ind.: Printed for the author by Light and Life Press, 1946.

McCutchen, Retha. *Be Strong and Courageous: Joshua Study Guide*. Winona Lake, Ind.: Light and Life Press, 1986.

McDowell, Adine. *The Passion of Our Lord: Six Service Outlines and Poster Suggestions*. Winona Lake, Ind.: Light and Life Press, 1940.

McElhinney, Robert Stewart., and Henry Lester Smith. *Personality and Character Building,*. Winona Lake, Ind.: Light and life Press, 1942.

McGhie, Anna E. *Loving Talks to Young Christians*. Winona Lake, Ind.: Printed by Light and Life Press for the author Anna E. McGhie, 1942.

— — —. *The Miracle Hand around the World*. Ft. Valley, Ga.: Printed for the author, 1947.

McGrew, R S. *True Accounts of Divine Healing*. Freeport, Pa.: Fountain Press, 1978.

McKenna, David. *Renewing Our Ministry*. Waco TX: Word Books, 1986.

McKenna, David L. *A Future with a History: The Wesleyan Witness of the Free Methodist Church, 1960-1995*. Indianapolis, IN: Light and Life Press, 1995.

— — —. *Awake, My Conscience*. Winona Lake, Ind.: Light and Life Press, 1977.

———. "Free Methodist Education-1992." *Free Methodist* October 10 (1967): 23.

———. *The Sunday School Dropout: The Great Loss of the Church*. Winona Lake, Ind.: Dept. of Sunday Schools, Free Methodist Headquarters, 1955.

———. *The Works of Dr. David L. McKenna*. [Wilmore, Ky.]: [Asbury Theological Seminary], 1993.

McKenna, David L, E C John, Free Methodist Church of North America, Commission on Christian Education, Church-School Relations Committee, Association of Free Methodist Colleges, Free Methodist Church of North America., et al. *The Study of Free Methodist Higher Education*. [Place of publication not identified]: [publisher not identified], 1962.

McKeown, Mona E. *This Is How to Teach*. Winona Lake, Ind.: Light and Life Press, 1962.

McLaren, Rob C. "A Wesleyan Theology of Worship and Its Development in Free Methodism," 2003.

McLeister, Ira. *History of the Wesleyan Methodist Church of America*. Syracuse N.Y.: Wesleyan Methodist Pub. Association, 1934.

McPeak, Rick Hughes. "Earnest Christianity : The Practical Theology of Benjamin Titus Roberts," 2001.

McReynolds, Mary, Deaconess Hospital, and Okla.) Deaconess Hospital (Oklahoma City. *Redeeming Love: The Legacy of the Deaconess Ladies*. [Place of publication not identified]: The Author, 2000.

Mead, Frank. *Handbook of Denominations in the United States*. Nashville: Abingdon Press, 1970.

Mercer, F Dean. *The History of First Free Methodist Church of Moose Jaw, Saskatchewan*. Moose Jaw, Sask.: Quick Printing, 1989.

Mercer, Francis Dean. "The Liturgical and Sacramental Development of the Free Methodist Church in Canada : With Special Attention to the Rituals of Baptism and the Lord's Supper," 1991.

Merrill, Arch. *Stagecoach Towns*. Rochester N.Y.: [Gannett Co.], 1947.

Methodist Episcopal Church. "Minutes of the Annual Conferences of the Methodist Episcopal Church." *Minutes of the Annual Conferences of the Methodist Episcopal Church*, n.d.

Miles, Mary Lillian. *Quiet Moments with God*. Winona Lake, IN: Light and Life Press, 1957.

Miller, Donald. "History of Greenville College with Special Reference to the Curriculum." New York University, 1934.

———. *The Way to Biblical Preaching*. New York: Abingdon Press, 1957.

Miller, Terry, and Sugarcreek Free Methodist Church. *Adult Bible Fellowship Manual*. Sugarcreek, Ohio: Sugarcreek Free Methodist Church, 1993.

Miller, William. *Holiness Works: A Bibliography*. Kansas City Mo.: Printed for Nazarene Theological Seminary by Nazarene Pub. House, 1986.

Milner, Vincent. *Religious Denominations of the World: Comprising a General View of the Origin, History and Condition of the Various Sects of Christians, the Jews and Mahometans, as Well as the Pagan Forms of Religion Existing in the Different Countries of the Earth: Wi*. Philadelphia: William Garretson & Co., 1871.

"Minutes of the Annual Conferences of the Methodist Episcopal Church (eJournal / eMagazine, 1773) [WorldCat.org]," n.d. https://www.worldcat.org/title/minutes-of-the-annual-conferences-of-the-methodist-episcopal-church/oclc/659330924&referer=brief_results.

"Minutes of the Annual Conferences. (Journal, Magazine, 1864) [WorldCat.org]." Accessed July 17, 2015. http://www.worldcat.org/title/minutes-of-the-annual-conferences/oclc/9064597?referer=di&ht=edition.

Mission Handbook: North American Protestant Ministries Overseas. Monrovia Calif.: MARC, 1973.

Mission Manual. Winona Lake Ind.: Commission on Missions, 1966.

Mission Valley Free Methodist Church. "Misshonbare Hatsu Nozomi." *Misshonbare Hatsu Nozomi*. San Gabriel, Ca: Mission Valley Free Methodist Church, n.d.

Mission., American Indian Bible, Free Methodist Church of North America., American Indian Bible Mission, Free Methodist Church of North America, American Indian Bible Mission., and Free Methodist Church of North America. "Hane' Niji'a = It Carries the News." *Hane' Niji'a = It Carries the News*. Farmington, NJ: American Indian Bible Mission, 1992.

Missionary Research Library. "Directory of North American Protestant Foreign Missionary Agencies." *Directory of North American Protestant Foreign Missionary Agencies*, n.d.

Moore, Carl. *Hidden Strands from the Fabric of Early Chili*. [Chili N.Y.]: Moore, 1976.

Moore, Carl C. *Variety and Spice of a Minister's Life*. Lakeland, FL: C.C. Moore, 1978.

Mortenson, Alice Hansche. *Knee-Deep in Snow and Other Poems*. Winona Lake, In.: Light and Life Press, 1954.

Mosher, Craig E. "Free Methodist Educational Institutions as Perceived by Selected Constituents," 1983.

Mott, Edward., Free Methodist Church of North America., Free Methodist Church of North America, and Free Methodist Church of North America. *The Security of the Believers*. Seattle, Wa.: Board of Aggressive Evangelism, Washington Conference, Free Methodist Church, 1944.

Mottweiler, Jack Hugo. *Adults as Learners*. Winona Lake, Ind.: Light and Life Press, 1984.

———. "The Development of Self-Report Instrument for Pastor Effectiveness," 1981.

Mountcastle, William Drew. "Back to the Future : Evolving the Wesleyan Model for Renewal and Leadership Development for the Free Methodist Church." Regent University, 2006.

Moyer, Elgin. *Who Was Who in Church History*. Chicago: Moody Press, 1962.

Mullikin, James C. *James Clayland Mullikin Papers,* 1915.

Mumby, Eileen H, and Michael D Burch. *Methodism in Caistor*. Caistor: The Church, 1961.

"Muncie, Indiana Sanborn Map, 1911, Sheet 51." Sanborn Map Company, n.d. http://libx.bsu.edu/cdm/ref/collection/SanbrnMps/id/225.

Munn, Nettie Perkins., and Nahum. Perkins. *Dear Folks: Letters from Nahum Perkins, Missionary to the Caribbean*. Winona Lake, Ind.: Light and Life Press, 1982.

Murekezi, Francois Ferdinand. "Poverty, Environment and Church : A Christian Contribution to the Earth Crisis as a Key to Poverty Eradication : A Zambian Perspective." University of KwaZulu-Natal, 2004.

Murphy, Minnie Ferris. *A Memorial to Pauline Fowler Kimball.* El Paso, Texas: Minnie Ferris Murphy], 1921.

Murphy, T. *Religious Bodies, 1936.* Washington: U.S. G.P.O. ;For sale by the Supt. of Docs., 1941.

Mylander, Ruth., and Helen Isabel Root. *Japan Investment.* Winona Lake, Ind.: Woman's Missionary Society of the Free Methodist Church of North America, 1944.

Nakajima, Mamoru George. "Growth of Japan Free Methodist Church, 1945-1982," 1983.

National Task Force on Canadian General Conference, and National Task Force on a Canadian General Conference. *Five Questions about a Canadian General Conference: An Interim Report.* [Mississauga, Ont.]: [Free Methodist Church in Canada]. 1988.

Nazarene Theological Seminary. *Master Bibliography of Holiness Works.* Kansas City MO: Beacon Hill Press, 1965.

Nazarite Documents: Comprising the Obligations, Practical Propositions, Lamentations, Recommendations, &c. of the Nazarite Union of the Genesee Conference of the M.E. Church. Brockport. N.Y.: Wm. Haswell, Printer, 1856.

Nazarite Review of the Pastoral Address of the Genesee Conference of the M.E. Church. [Place of publication not identified]: [publisher not identified], 1857.

Nelson, Marven O. "The Administration of Guidance in Colleges Related to the Wesleyan and Free Methodist Churches (Book, 1952) [WorldCat.org]." State University of New York at Buffalo, 1952. http://www.worldcat. org/title/administration-of-guidance-in-colleges-related-to-the-wesleyan-and-free-methodist-churches/ oclc/50266021&referer=brief_results.

Nelson, Royal S, Free Methodist Church of North America., Commission on Christian Education., Free Methodist Church of North America, Commission on Christian Education, Free Methodist Church of North America., and Commission on Christian Education. *Here's the Answer: A Handbook for Sunday-School Workers*. Winona Lake, IN: Light and Life Press, 1963.

Nelson, Thomas H, and Vivian A Dake. *Life and Labors of Rev. Vivian A. Dake: Organizer and Leader of Pentecost Bands: Embracing an Account of His Travels in America, Europe and Africa, with Selections from His Sketches, Poems and Songs*. Chicago: Published for the author by T.B. Arnold ..., 1894.

Nelson, Walter O. *History of the Oklahoma Annual Conference of the Free Methodist Church*. Siloam Springs, AR: Silent Minister Booklet Press, 1949.

Newberg Free Methodist Church Wedding Committee. *A Guide for Planning a Wedding at Newberg Free Methodist Church*. [Newberg, Or.]: Newberg Free Methodist Church, 1970.

Nicholson, David Lee. "A Strategy for Implementing 'Natural Church Development' Quality Characteristics at Open Door Free Methodist Church," 2002.

"No." *Shortwave* 1 - (n.d.).

"No Title." *Sunday School Journal*, no. 1–52 (n.d.).

"No Title." *The Layman. Voice of the Light and Life Men's Fellowship*, n.d.

"No Title." *Ecos Evangelicos*, no. 1- (n.d.).

"No Title." *Light and Life Hour Transmitter*, n.d.

"No Title." *The Layman. Voice of the Light and Life Men's Fellowship*, n.d.

"No Title." *Encounter*, n.d.

"No Title." *Sunday School Journal*, no. 1–52 (n.d.).

"No Title." *Ecos Evangelicos*, no. 1- (n.d.).

"No Title." *Nzira Iboneye* 1- (n.d.).

"No Title." *Nzira Iboneye* 1- (n.d.).

"No Title." *Light and Life Hour Transmitter*, n.d.

"No Title." *Missions Outlook Leadership Letter* ? (n.d.).

"No Title." *Missions Outlook Leadership Letter* ? (n.d.).

"No Title." *Encounter*, n.d.

"No Title." *News and Views* 1- (1962).

"No Title." *News and Views* 1- (1962).

Noda, Shigeru. *A Grain of Wheat: Memories of a Missionary, Eva Bryan Millikan*. [Tokyo]: Free Methodist Kaganei Church ;Printed by Sanshu Printing Co., 1967.

Norbeck, Mildred. *The Challenge of the Hills*. Apollo Pa.: West Pub. Co., 1947.

― ― ― . *The Haitian Challenge and You*. Intercession City Fla.: Great Commission Crusades, 1964.

― ― ― . *The Lure of the Hills a Tale of Life in the Mountains of Kentucky, by Mildred E. Norbeck* ... [Cincinnati]: Pub. for the author by the Revivalist Press, 1931.

North American Protestant Ministries Overseas, 1970. Monrovia Calif.: MARC, 1970.

Northeast Michigan Genealogical and Historical Society. *Pleasant Valley Free Methodist Church, Montmorency County*. Alpena, MI: Northeast Michigan Genealogical Society, 1998.

Northrup, L W. *Ancient Mirrors for Modern Churches: A Study of the Seven Churches of the Book of Revelation Relating Them to the Church in Modern Society.* Winona Lake, IN: Light and Life Press, 1973.

— — —. *It Took a Miracle: The Life Story of L.W. Northrup.* [Place of publication not identified]: [L.W. Northrup], 1999.

Northrup, Lyle W. *Ambassadors for Christ: The Story of Free Methodism in Northern Ireland.* [Place of publication not identified]: [publisher not identified], 1988.

Norwood, Frederick. *The Story of American Methodism a History of the United Methodists and Their Relations.* Nashville: Abingdon Press, 1974.

Ntakirutimana, Ezekiel. "A Christian Development Appraisal of the Ubunye Cooperative Housing Initiative in Pietermaritzburg." University of KwaZulu-Natal, 2004.

— — —. "A Christian Development Appraisal of the Ubunye Cooperative Housing Inititiative in Pietermaritzburg." University of KwaZulu-Natal, 2004.

"Nursery Activities." Winona Lake IN: Beacon Hill Press, 1969.

"Nursery Bible Story Cards, 1-12." Winona Lake IN: Light and Life Press, 1958.

"Nursery Teacher." Kansas City MO: Beacon Hill Press, n.d.

Nye, George A. *Readings Concerning the History of Warsaw.* Winona Lake, Indiana: Free Methodist Pub. House, 1943.

— — —. *Readings in Early Local History.* Winona Lake, IN.: Free Methodist Pub. House, 1943.

— — —. *Warsaw in the 1870's and 1880's.* Winona Lake, IN: Free Methodist Pub. House, 1947.

Nye, George A., and Nye. George A. *Warsaw in 1890's and Other Stories*. Winona Lake, IN: Free Methodist Pub. House, 1944.

Nystrom, Gertrude. *Mama Married Me*. [Place of publication not identified], 1960.

O'Brien, Thomas. *Corpus Dictionary of Western Churches*. Washington: Corpus Publications, 1970.

Oda, Kaneo. *Oda Kaneo sekkyoshu*. Osaka-fu: Seitosha, 1979.

Olmstead, B L. *Three Types of Eternal Security: A Simple and Clear Discussion of a Doctrine Which, in Various Forms, Is Being Widely Propagated at the Present Time*. Winona Lake, Ind.: Light and Life Press, 1942.

Olmstead, Benjamin L. *Serving God and the Church: A Brief Discussion of How to Live the Christian Life Successfully*. Winona Lake, Ind.: Free Methodist Pub. House, n.d.

Olmstead, Benjamin Luce. *A Brief Life of Paul, with a Chart and Six Maps*. Winona Lake, Ind.: Light and life Press, 1938.

———. *Arnold's Practical Commentary on the International Sunday School Lessons Uniform Series for 1952: A Practical Help for All Who Use the Unform Lesson in the Sunday School, or Who Desire to Do Individual Bible Study. There Are Ample Explanatory Notes ...* Winona Lake, Ind.: Light and Life Press, 1960.

———. *Arnold's Practical Commentary on the International Sunday School Lessons; Uniform Series for 1952... 58th Annual v*. Winona Lake, Ind.: Light and Life Press, 1951.

———. *Being a Christian: A Guide for Early Youth*. Winona Lake, Ind.: Free Methodist Pub. House, 1950.

———. *Our Church at Work: A Brief Manual for the Instruction of Preparatory Members of the Free Methodist Church.* Winona Lake, Ind.: Free Methodist Pub. House, 1955.

Olmstead, William. "Gospel Truths in Song." Chicago,: W.B. Rose, 1915.

———. *Handbook for Sunday-School Workers.* Chicago: W.B. Rose, 1907.

———. "Light and Life Songs : Adapted Especially to Sunday Schools, Prayer Meetings and Other Social Services." Chicago : S.K.J. Chesbro, 1904.

———. "Light and Life Songs, No. 3 : For Sunday-Schools, Social Worship, Camp Meetings and Revival Services." Chicago, IL : W.B. Rose, 1918.

———. "Light and Life Songs, Number Two : Adapted Especially to Sunday Schools, Social Worship, Camp Meetings and Revival Services." Chicago : W.B. Rose, 1914.

Olmstead, William Backus, and Thoro Harris. "Light and life songs : no. 4, for the Sunday school, social worship, missionary and evangelistic work." Chicago: Light and Life Press, 1928.

Olver, Howard L. *Biblical Basis for Urban Ministry: A Paper Presented at the 1977 Continental Urban Exchange (CUE), Minneapolis, Minnesota.* Winona Lake, Ind.: Light and Life Men International, 1977.

———. "Resurrection Strategies for Urban Neighborhood Churches in the Wesleyan Holiness Tradition," 1999.

Olver, Paul S. "A Strategy for Urban Church Planting for the Free Methodist Church of North America," 1986.

Omi, Masahiro. *Bakure Jiyu Mesojisuto Kyokai soritsu yonjunen enkakushi*. [Berkeley, Calif.]: [Bakure Jiyu Mesojisuto Kyokai], 1956.

"One Way to a Whole World Sing : The Free Methodist Church 1974 General Conference Official Songbook." Winona Lake, Ind.: [publisher not identified], 1974.

Ongley, Mark L, and Theological Research Exchange Network. "The Impact of Training in Inner Healing for Sexual Brokenness upon Attitudes toward Homosexuals." Ashland Theological Seminary, 2005.

Ontario Genealogical Society, Thunder Bay Branch, Ontario Genealogical Society., and Thunder Bay Branch. *Free Methodist Cemetery: Con. 1, Lot 9, O'Connor Township, District of Thunder Bay, Ontario*. [Thunder Bay, Ont.]: [Thunder Bay Branch, Ontario Genealogical Society], 1980.

Ontario Genealogical Society, and Thunder Bay Branch. *Armadale Free Methodist Cemetery, Scarborough, Ontario: East 1/2 of Lot 19, Concession 5, City of Scarborough, Ontario*. Toronto: Ontario Genealogical Society, Toronto Branch, 1992.

"Oral Hisotory Interview: David Black," 2011. http://digital.library.wisc.edu/1793/55519.

Orr, J. *The Light of the Nations Evangelical Renewal and Advance in the Nineteenth Century*. Grand Rapids: W.B. Eerdmans Pub. Co., 1966.

Osborne, Zenas. *Born of the Spirit, Or, Gems from the Book of Life* ... Sarotage Springs, NY: John Johnson & Co., 1888.

Otto, Kenneth., Azusa Pacific University., Marshburn Memorial Library., Azusa Pacific University, and Marshburn Memorial Library. *Free Methodist Denominational Collection of Azusa Pacific University's Marshburn Memorial Library, 1992*. Azusa, Calif.: Azusa Pacific University, 1992.

Our Heritage We Cherish: Free Methodist Church, Thornbury-Peniel, 1904-1984: Eighty Years of History! Thornbury, Ontario: Thornbury Free Methodist Church, 1985.

"Our Young Folks. 1-10, No. 12." Chicago, IL: W.B. Rose, 1897.

Our Youth and Our Colleges: 1942 Supplement to --Your Church and Education. Winona Lake, Indiana: Commission on Christian Education of the Free Methodist Church, 1942.

Owen, Epenetus. *Struck by Lightning a True and Thrilling Narrative of One Who Was Struck by Lightning: With Incidents, Experiences, and Anecdotes for Old and Young.* Otterville Ont.: A. Sims, 1891.

–––. *Things New and Old.* Boston: Henry V. Degen, 1856.

Page, Ruby, and Ed Burns. "Oral History Interview with Ruby Page," 1988.

Palmer, A C, and Benjamin Titus Roberts. *Lay aside Every Weight.* Yarmouth, Me.: I.C. Wellcome, 1875.

Parker, Joseph. *Interpretative Statistical Survey of the World Mission of the Christian Church: Summary and Detailed Statistics of Churches and Missionary Societies, Interpretative Articles, and Indices.* New York ;London: International missionary council, 1938.

Parsons, Elmer E. *Witness to the Resurrection.* Winona Lake, Ind.: Light and Life Press, 1967.

Parsons, Elmer E, and John N Oswalt. *Living the Holy Life Today.* Indianapolis, Ind.: Light and Life Press, 1990.

Parsons, Ida Dake. *Kindling Watch-Fires; Being a Brief Sketch of the Life of Rev. Vivian A. Dake, Together with a Compilation of Selections from His Writings, Sermons, and Poems, to Which Is Appended a Few of His Best Songs with the Music,.* Chicago, Ill.: Free Methodist Pub. House, 1915.

Patil, Subhash. *History of the Free Methodist Church in India, 1881-1989.* Yavatmal, India: Literature Committee, India Free Methodist Conference, 1989.

Pauley, Rich. *DeShazer Returns.* Winona Lake, Ind.: Free Methodist Church of North America, General Missionary Board, 1970.

Payne, Peggy. *Teaching for Life-Changing Learning.* Winona Lake, Ind.: Light and Life Press, 1984.

Pearce, Bishop William. *Our Incarnate Lord.* Chicago, Ill.: Light and Life Press, 1900.

Pearce, William. "Choice Hymns : A Collection of Hymns from the Free Methodist Hymnal, Especially Adapted for Revival Services." Winona Lake, Ind.: Free Methodist Pub. House, 1942.

Pearce, William. *The Preacher and His Reading.* Winona Lake, Ind.: Light and Life Press, 1945.

— — —. "Worship in Song : An All Purpose Song Book for Use in the Church but Especially Adapted for Use in the Sunday School, Missionary, Young People's & Evangelistic Services." Winona Lake, Ind.: Light and Life Press, 1935.

Pearson, B. *Off to Panama: A True Adventure Story of the Opening Doors for Christian Missions in Panama.* L.A. Calif.: Free Tract Society, 1935

— — —. *Wings to Aztec Land: "Things to Do" with Each Chapter: Twenty-Five Attractive Patterns for Handwork.* Los Angeles Calif.: Harry Harper, 1930.

Pearson, B H. *Free Methodist Mexican Missions.* Winona Lake, Ind.: Woman's Missionary Society, Free Methodist Church, 1939.

— — —. *Mexican Missions: Home Mission Study Book.* Chicago: Woman's Missionary Society of the Free Methodist Church, 1925.

———. *The Lost Generation Returns*. Winona Lake, Ind.: Light and Life Press, 1937.

———. *The Monk Who Lived Again; a Tale of South America,.* Winona Lake, Ind.: Light and life Press, 1940.

Pearson, B H, Jenne Harroun. Howland, Mildred Williams. Harper, and Helen Isabel Root. *Sunday Evenings with Jesus: Volume II*. Winona Lake, Ind.: Light and Life Press, 1938.

Pearson, Benjamin Harold. *Next! Our Sunday-School Quest in South America: A "Caleb-Joshua" Story of the Expedition of "The Spies" Sent Forth by the "Birthday Pennies for South America Fund" into the Lands "Beyond the Amazon."* Winona Lake, Ind.: Light and life Press, 1940.

Peisker, Armor. *End Times: A Doctrinal Study on the Shape of Things to Come*. [Place of publication not identified]: [publisher not identified], 1970.

———. *Peace with God: Studies in Conversion*. [Marion Ind.]: [Wesley Press], 1969.

Pelton, Hannah. *The Pilgrim's Progress of the Twentieth Century*. Chicago, Ill.: Free Methodist Pub., 1904.

Pfouts, Neil. *A History of Roberts Wesleyan College*. [Rochester N.Y.?]: [The College?], 2000.

Phillips, Philip. "Metrical Tune Book with Hymns." Chicago : T.B. Arnold, 1891.

Phillips, Philip, J G Terrill, T B Arnold, Free Methodist Church of North America, and Free Methodist Church of North America. "Metrical Tune Book : With Hymns and Supplement." Chicago: Free Methodist Pub. House, 1906.

Phillips, Rose Myra. *Bird against the Wind,*. Winona Lake, Ind.: Light and Life Press, 1940.

— — —. *Journey by Night. [Poems]*. Winona Lake, Ind.: Light and Life Press, 1950.

Phillips, Hal V. *From the Door of an Orphanage*. Sandusky, Mich.: New Creation Ministries, 1987.

Pierce, Mitchell C. "Developing Structures for Health and Growth for Northgate Free Methodist Church in Batavia, New York." Asbury Theological Seminary, 1998. http://place.asburyseminary.edu/ecommonsatsdissertations/139/.

Pirie, Margaret. *The Inseparables*. Wimona Lake, Ind.: Light and Life Press, 1955.

Pitts, Robert Duane. "A Comparative Environmental Study of Four Denominational Colleges." Indiana University, 1969.

Prayer That Really Works. Published for Aldersgate Associates by Beacon Hill Press of Kansas City, 1970.

Press, Light and Life. "No Title." *Just Between Us*, n.d.

Press., Light and Life. "Hymns of the Living Faith." Winona Lake, Ind.: Light and Life Press, 1954.

"Primary Activities." Winona Lake IN: Light and Life Press, 1959.

"Primary Bible Lesson Stories. 1-17." Chicago, IL: W.B. Rose, 1953.

"Primary Bible Stories." Marion Ind.: Wesley Press, 1969.

"Primary Days. 17-19, No. 4." Chicago, IL: Scripture Press, 1951.

"Primary Friend." Marion Ind.: Wesley Press, 1969.

"Primary Teacher." Marion Ind.: Wesley Press, 1969.

"Primary World. 1-15, No. 3." Chicago, IL: Scripture Press, 1955.

Priset, Duane W, and Thomas William. Herringshaw. "Roberts, Benjamin Titus." *Herringshaw's National Library of American Biography: Contains Thirty-Five Thousand Biographies of the Acknowledged Leaders of Life and Thought of the United States; Illustrated with Three Thousand Vignette Portraits*. 18 (1999).

"Probe Student 1-3, No. 4." Marion Ind.: Wesley Press, 1974.

"Probe Teacher. 1-3, No. 4." Marion Ind.: Wesley Press, 1974.

Progressive Men and Women of Kosciusko County, Indiana and 1903 Plat Maps: Illustrated, Portraits of Many Well-Known Residents of Kosciusko County, Indiana. Winona Lake, Ind.: Light and Life Press, 1989.

"ProTeen." Winona Lake Indiana: Light and Life Press, 1971.

Pugerude, Daniel Guy. "Preaching from the Old Testament : A Study in Exegesis and Hermeneutics of the Free Methodist Church of North America," 1987.

Purkiser, W T. *Joel, Jonah, Amos, Hosea, and Micah: Leader's Guide*. Winona Lake, Ind.: Light and Life Press, 1963.

———. *Leviticus, Deuteronomy: Leader's Guide*. Winona Lake, Ind.: Light and Life Press, 1961.

"Quest Student." Winona Lake Indiana: Light and Life Press, 1976.

"Quest Teacher." Winona Lake Indiana: Light and Life Press, 1976.

R. B. Spencer Papers., 1910.

Rader, Lyell. *The Book of Books*. Winona Lake, Ind.: Light and Life Press, 1965.

Ray, L P, and L P Ray. *Twice Sold, Twice Ransomed Autobiography of Mr. and Mrs. L.P. Ray.* Chicago, Ill: Free Methodist Pub. House, 1926.

Reber, Carson E. "The Doctrine of Holiness as Taught by B.T. Roberts," 1985.

Reber, L B. *A Sketch of the Life and Labors of Rev. L.B. Reber in the North Michigan, Louisiana, New York, and Missouri Conferences.* Clarence, Mo.: Farmers Favorite Print, 1901.

"Records of the Congo-Nile Mission," 1938.

Redmond Free Methodist Church. *Free Methodist Church: Anniversary of Fifty Years; 1933-1983; "to God Be the Glory."* Redmond, Or.: Redmond Free Methodist Church, 1983.

Reed, Nellie. *World Treasure Trails: Africa.* Winona Lake Ind.: Woman's Missionary Society Free Methodist church of North America, 1936.

———. *World Treasure Trails II: India.* Winona Lake Ind.: Woman's Missionary Society Free Methodist church of North America, 1938.

Reed, Nellie A. *Ntombinkulu (Big Girl): Or a Zulu Girl in Fair View Girls' School, Natal, South Africa.* New York: Free Methodist Pub. House, 1914.

Reformed Free Methodist Church of North America. "The Sound of the Trumpet." *The Sound of the Trumpet.* Perryopolis, PA: Reformed Free Methodist Church], 1990.

Reinhard, James Arnold. "Personal and Sociological Factors in the Formation of the Free Methodist Church, 1852-1860," 1971.

"Rev. Aura Claire Showers : A Sketch of His Life / by His Wife ; Together with Tributes by Ministerial Brethren ; to Which Is Added a Treatise on the Doctrine of Eternal Punishment and Other Unpublished Manuscripts." Oil City, PA :H.D.W. Showers,1896., 1896. http://www.biodiversitylibrary.org/bibliography/32004.

Revell, James Alan. "The Nazirites : Burned-over District Methodism and the Buffalo Middle Class," 1994.

"Revell's Guide to Christian Colleges. (Journal, Magazine, 1965) [WorldCat.org]," n.d. http://www.worldcat.org/title/revells-guide-to-christian-colleges/oclc/8044133&referer=brief_results.

Reynolds, Michael., and Grace. Abbott. *Life Changing Learning for Youth: Resources That Work*. Winona Lake, Ind.: Light and Life Press, 1978.

Reynolds, Walter C. *A Flaming Cross: A Story of First Century Christians*. Winona Lake, Ind.: Light and Life Press, 1941.

Rhoden, Maurice M. "The Recent Progress and Methods of Evangelism of Holiness Missions in Japan," 1956.

Rhodes, M L. *Clifford B. Barrett: The "Happy Alleghenian."* Chicago: W.B. Rose, 1919.

Rich, Marion. *Hidden Treasure: A Missionary Story from Haiti*. Winona Lake, Ind.: Light and Life Press, 1980.

Richardson, Arleta. *A Heart for God in India*. Winona Lake, Ind.: Light and Life Press, 1988.

———. *Maria*. Indianapolis, IN: Light and Life Communications, 1998.

Richardson, Arleta., and Dora. Leder. *In Grandma's Attic*. Colorado Springs, CO: David C. Cook, 2004.

Richardson, Arleta., and Emiline Secaur. *Andrew's Secret.* Winona Lake, Ind.: Light and Life Press, 1988.

Richardson, Arleta., and Karl. Tiedemann. "Maria." Van Wyck, SC: NorthStar Pub., 2000.

Richardson, Jack D, Colgate Rochester Divinity School, Crozer Theological Seminary, and Bexley Hall Colgate Rochester Divinity School Crozer Theological Seminary. "B.T. Roberts and the Role of Women in Ministry in Nineteenth-Century Free Methodism : By Jack D. Richardson." [Colgate Rochester Divinity School/Bexley Hall/Crozer Theological Seminary], 1984.

Riggs, Donald E. *Make It Happen.* Warsaw, Ind.: LP Products, 1981.

Robb, J A. *Memories of Rev. Charles H. Sage: The Free Methodist Church Canadian Centennial, 1876-1976.* Ontario: West Ontario Conference of the Free Methodist Church, 1976.

Robb, James A. *And He Said unto Me, Write.* Woodstock, Ont.: Nethercott Press, 1979.

— — —. *Life's Golden Memories.* Woodstock, Ont.: Nethercott Press, 1979.

Roberts, Benjamin. *Why Another Sect.* New York: Garland Pub., 1984.

— — —. *Why Another Sect: Containing a Review of Articles by Bishop Simpson and Others on the Free Methodist Church,.* Rochester N.Y.: "The Earnest Christian" Pub. House, 1879.

Roberts, Benjamin Titus. *First Lessons on Money.* Rochester, N.Y.: Christian Classics Ethereal Library, 1886. http://books.google.com/books?id=yuszAQAAMAAJ.

— — —. *Fishers of Men.* Indianapolis, IN: Light and Life Communications, 1997.

———. *Fishers of Men, Or, Practical Hints to Those Who Would Win Souls*. Winona Lake, Ind.: Light and Life Press, 1948.

———. *Living Truths*. Winona Lake, Ind.: Light and Life Press, 1960.

———. *Ordaining Women*. Indianapolis, IN: Light and Life Press, 1992.

———. *Spiritual Songs and Hymns for Pilgrims*. Rochester, N.Y.: B.T. Roberts, 1878.

———. "The Earnest Christian and Golden Rule." *The Earnest Christian and Golden Rule*. Buffalo, N.Y.: Benjamin T. Roberts, 1862.

———. "The Earnest Christian." *The Earnest Christian*. Buffalo, N.Y.: B.T. Roberts, 1860.

———. "The Holiness Teachings." Grand Rapids, Mich.: Christian Classics Ethereal Library, n.d. http://search.ebscohost.com/login.aspx?direct=true&scope=site&db=nlebk&db=nlabk&AN=2008304.

———. *The Right of Women to Preach the Gospel*. Rochester, N.Y.: [publisher not identified], n.d.

———. *Why Another Sect Containing a Review of Articles by Bishop Simpson*. [S.l.]: Book On Demand Ltd, 2013.

Roberts, Benjamin Titus, and Gerald Wesley. Coates. *Practical Piety: Daily Reflections on Christian Virtue*. Indianapolis, Ind.: Wesleyan Pub. House, 2007.

Roberts, Benjamin Titus, and Donald E Demaray. *The Daily Roberts: Readings for Every Day in the Year from the Writings of B.T. Roberts*. Indianapolis, IN: Light and Life Press, 1996.

Roberts, Benjamin Titus, and William Brester Rose. *Pungent Truths: Being Extracts from the Writings of the Rev. Benjamin Titus Roberts ...* Chicago: Free Methodist Pub. House, 1912.

Roberts, Benjamin Titus, Wallace Omor Thornton, Adam Clarke, A M Hills. and W B Godbey. *Chained by a Leaf: The Use and Abuse of Tobacco*. Salem, Ohio: Schmul Pub. Co., 2001.

Roberts, Benson Howard. *Benjamin Titus Roberts: A Biography*. North Chili, N.Y.: "The Earnest Christian" Office, 1900.

— — —. *Benjamin Titus Roberts. Late General Superintendent of the Free Methodist Church. A Biography*. North Chili, N.Y.: "The Earnest Christian," 1900.

Roberts, Benson Howard. Benjamin Titus, Anna A Rice Roberts, Benson Howard. Benjamin Titus Roberts, Emma Sellew. Ellen Lois Stowe. Emma Sellew Roberts, Emma Sellew. Ellen Lois Stowe. Emma Sellew Roberts, George Lane. Roberts, Library of Congress Manuscript Division, Library of Congress., and Manuscript Division. *Benjamin T. Roberts Family Papers*. Washington, D.C.: Library of Congress, Photoduplication Service, 1990.

Roberts, Benson Howard. Benjamin Titus, Benson Howard. Benjamin Titus Roberts, Anna A Rice Roberts, Benson Howard. Benjamin Titus Roberts, Emma Sellew. Ellen Lois Stowe. Emma Sellew Roberts, Emma Sellew. Ellen Lois Stowe. Emma Sellew Roberts, and George Lane. Roberts. *Family Papers.*, 1832.

Roberts, Esther M. *The Bishop and His Lady*. Winona Lake, Ind.: Light and Life Press, 1962.

Roller, David T, Jonathan. Parker, Free Methodist Church of North America., and Free Methodist Church of North America. *Journey to Mexico*. Winona lake, Ind.: Light and Life Press, 1985.

Ronayne, Edmond. *Ronayne's Reminiscences: A History of His Life and Renunciation of Romanism and Freemasonry.* Chicago: Free Methodist Pub. House, 1900.

Ronsvalle, John L. *A Comparison of the Growth in the United States per Capita Income and Population with the Free Methodist Church Budget and Membership for the Years 1967 and 1982.* Urbana, Ill.: Empty Tomb, 1987.

Root, Helen. *A Corn of Wheat: The Life Story of Clara Leffingwell.* Winona Lake Ind.: Woman's Missionary Society Free Methodist Church, 1943.

———. *An Alabaster Box: The Life Story of Grace E. Barnes.* Chicago Ill.: Woman's Missionary Society Free Methodist Church, 1929.

Root, Helen I. *Our Africa Work: A Brief History of the Free Methodist Mission in Africa.* Chicago, IL: Woman's Missionary Society, Free Methodist Church, 1928.

Root, Loretta P. *Patches: Missionary Life in India as Seen by [drawing of the Dog Patches].* Winona Lake, Ind.: Light and Life Press, 1938.

Root, Loretta P, and Mary C Benson. *Outflowing Love: Auntie-Bai, Effie Southworth's Life of Loving Service during Her More than 50 Years in Central India.* Winona Lake, Ind.: Light & Life Communications, 1988.

Root, Loretta P, and Ann. Zahniser. *Friends from the East.* Winona Lake, Ind.: Light and Life Press, 1971.

Roper, Samuel G. *The Story of My Life from the Cradle to Now (1859-1935).* Portland, Or.: Samuel G. Roper, 1935.

Rose, Delbert R. *Epistles of John and Jude: Leader's Guide.* Winona Lake, Ind.: Light and Life Press, 1964.

———. *Hebrews: Leader's Guide*. Winona Lake, Ind.: Light and Life Press, 1961.

———. *Hebrews: Study Guide*. Winona Lake, Ind.: Light and Life Press, 1967.

Rose Lake Free Methodist Church. *Rose Lake Free Methodist Church: Centennial Directory, 1887 to 1987*. LeRoy, Mich.: The Church, 1988.

"Rose of Sharon, 1-10, No. 12." Chicago, IL: W.B. Rose, 1897.

Ross, Irene M. *Golden Bells: Poems and Songs*. Winona Lake, Ind.: Light and Life Press, 1984.

Roth, Richard H. "The History of the Southern Michigan Conference of the Free Methodist Church," 1967.

Rowe, A T. *Ideals for Earnest Youth*. Chicago: Light and Life Press, 1927.

Rowe, Kenneth. *Methodist Union Catalog, Pre-1976 Imprints*. Metuchen N.J.: Scarecrow Press, 1975.

Runyon, Daniel V. *World Mission People: The Best of the Missionary Tidings, 1990-95*. Spring Arbor, Mich.: Saltbox Press, 1995.

Runyon, Daniel V, Scott. Auch, Free Methodist World Missions., and Free Methodist World Missions. *Ferguson: Her Tractor-Biography*. Spring Arbor, Mich.: Saltbox Press, 1995.

Rupert, David A, Free Methodist Church of North America., California Conference., Free Methodist Church of North America, and California Conference. *Celebrating One Hundred Years: A Centennial Focus on the California Conference Free Methodist Church*. [Place of publication not identified]: [Free Methodist Church, California Conference], 1983.

Russell, C. *Youth Wants to Know*. Winona Lake IN: Christian Youth Supplies, 1959.

Russell, C Mervin. *Giving Our Young People Evangelism Know How*. Winona Lake, Ind.: Light and Life Press, 1960.

Ryckman, Lucile Damon. *Paid in Full: The Story of Harold Ryckman, Missionary Pioneer to Paraguay and Brazil*. Winona Lake, Ind.: Light and Life Press, 1979.

Ryff, Frederic J. "An Examination of the Indigenous Church Principle with Special Reference to the Free Methodist Church in South Africa," 1954.

Sage, Charles H, and William B Olmstead. *Autobiography of Rev. Charles H. Sage: Embracing an Account of His Pioneer Work in Michigan, of the Formation of the Canada Conference and of His Labors in Various States*. Chicago, Ill.: Free Methodist Pub. House, 1908.

Sager, Ida May. *Lights along the Shore: Some Memories*. Falconer, N.Y.: Falconer Print. & design, Inc., 1974.

"Salt Lake City, 1898: Sheet 049." J. Willard Marriott Library, University of Utah, n.d. http://content.lib.utah.edu/u?/sanborn-jp2,758.

Sanders, Howard. "History of the Oregon Conference of the Free Methodist Church," 1965.

Sayre, Geneva., and Glen. Williamson. *On the Brink*. Winona Lake, Ind.: Light and Life Press, 1974.

Sayre, Mary Geneva. *Missionary Triumphs in Occupied China*. Winona Lake, Ind.: Woman's Missionary Society of the Free Methodist Church, 1945.

Scearce, Marty. *Bless This House*. Winona Lake, IN: Light and Life Press, 1988.

Scherer, Frances E. *Aunt Edith & Lora*. Oak Park, Ill.: James A. Scherer, 1997.

Scherer, Frances Schlosser. *George and Mary Schlosser: Ambassadors for Christ in China*. Winona Lake, Ind.: Light and Life Press, 1975.

Schlosser, Frances E. *A Challenge from China*. [Place of publication not identified]: [publisher not identified], 1940.

Schlosser, George. *George and Mary Schlosser papers*, 1906.

Schlosser, John. *Church Planting in Mindanao*. [Winona Lake Ind.]: [General Missionary Board Free Methodist Church of North America], n.d.

Schlosser, John H. *The Free Methodist Church in the Philippines: Our Heritage and History*, 1977.

Schlosser, Ruby., and Gertrude H Groesbeck. *Lighting the Philippine Frontier*. Winona Lake, Ind.: Light and Life Press, 1956.

Schoenhals, G Roger. *When Trouble Comes: How to Find God's Help in Difficult Times*. Winona Lake, Ind.: Light and Life Press, 1978.

Schoenhals, Lawrence R. "Light and Life Choral Arrangements." Winona Lake, IN: Light and Life Press, 1960.

Schoenhals, Lawrence R, Free Methodist Church of North America., and Wesleyan Church. *Companion to Hymns of Faith and Life*. Winona lake, Ind.: Light and Life Press, 1980.

Schoenhals, Lawrence R, LeRoy M Lowell, Lawrence R Schoenhals, LeRoy M Lowell, Lawrence R Schoenhals, and LeRoy M Lowell. "Choice Light and Life Songs : A Collection of the Best Loved Gospel Songs and Choruses, Both Old and New for the Sunday School, Young People's Meeting, Evangelistic Service and Children's Service." Winona Lake, Ind.: Light and Life Press, 1950.

Schoenhals, Lawrence Russell. "Higher Education in the Free Methodist Church in the United States, 1860-1954," 1955.

Schwanz, Keith Duane. "The 'Wooden Brother' : Instrumental Music Restricted in Free Methodist Worship, 1860-1955," 1991.

Second Free Methodist Church. *Minutes of the Sunday School Board of the Second Free Methodist Sunday School: 1939-*. Peoria, Ill.: The Church, 1939.

Sellew, Walter A. *Why Not?: A Plea for the Ordination of Those Women Whom God Has Called to Preach the Gospel*. Chicago, Ill.: Published for the author by the Free Methodist Pub. House, 1914.

Sellew, Walter Ashbel. *Clara Leffingwell, a Missionary*. Chicago: Free Methodist Pub. House, 1907.

———. *Obligations of Civilization to Christianity; Or, The Influence of Christianity upon Civilization*. Chicago, Ill.: Light and Life Press, 1928.

———. *Why Not? A Plea for the Ordination of Those Women Whom God Has Called to Preach the Gospel*. North Chili, N.Y.: "Earnest Christian" Pub. House, 1981.

Sellew, Walter Ashbel, Wilson T Hogue, Free Methodist Church of North America., Free Methodist Church of North America, and Free Methodist Church of North America. *Clara Leffingwell, a Missionary*. Chicago: Free Methodist Pub. House, 1913.

"Senior Teen Student." Marion Ind.: Wesley Press, 1969.

"Senior Teen Teacher." Marion Ind.: Wesley Press, 1969.

"Senior Teen. 1-14, No. _." Winona Lake IN: Light and Life Press, 1956.

Service Training Handbook, Improvement Plans for Workers in Every Local Church. St. Louis, Mo.: Free Methodist Church of North America, Commission on Christian Education, Dept. of Service Training, 1938.

Sharpley, J B, and Inter Documentation Company. *The Scriptural Character of Louth Free Methodism Vindicated and the Class Leaders Proved to Be the True Pastors in Methodism, according to the Principles of the New Testament, and the Minutes of the Wesleyan Conference: In Reply to the Two Letters of "Ph*. Louth; London: William Shepherd ; Whittaker and Co.. 1858.

Shaw, S. *Children's Edition of Touching Incidents and Remarkable Answers to Prayer*. Grand Rapids Mich.: S.B. Shaw, 1895.

— — —. *God's Financial Plan, or Temporal Prosperity the Result of Faithful Stewardship*. Grand Rapids: S.B. Shaw, 1897.

— — —. *The Great Revival in Wales, Also an Account of the Great Revival in Ireland in 1859,*. Chicago Ill.: S.B. Shaw, 1905.

— — —. *Touching Incidents and Remarkable Answers to Prayer*. Grand Rapids: S.B. Shaw, 1893.

Shay, Emma Abigail Freeland, Free Methodist Church of North America., and Woman's Foreign Missionary Society. *Mariet Hardy Freeland, a Faithful Witness: A Biography*. Chicago: Woman's Foreign Missionary Society of the Free Methodist Church, 1914.

Shay, Emma Freeland. *Mariet Hardy Freeland: A Faithful Witness: A Biography*. Chicago: Free Methodist Pub. House, 1913.

Shelhamer, E. *5 Reasons Why I Do Not Seek the Gift of Tongues.* Wilmore Ky.: Mrs. E.E. Shelhamer, 1919.

———. *Heart Searching Sermons and Sayings,.* Atlanta Ga.: Repairer Pub. Co., 1917.

———. *Heart Searching Talks to Ministers,.* Louisville Ky.: Pentecostal Pub. Co., 1914.

———. *Pointed Bible Readings on Various Subjects.* Atlanta Ga.: [publisher not identified], 1900.

Shelhamer, E E. *A Bit of Experience.* [Los Angeles?]: [publisher not identified], n.d.

———. "E.E. Shelhamer's Life Story." Knoxville, TN: Evangelist of Truth, n.d.

———. *Experiences in Travel and Soul Saving: Also Some of My Mistakes and What They Have Taught Me.* Atlanta, Ga.: [publisher not identified], 1907.

———. *Pointed Preaching for Practical People.* Cincinnati, Ohio: God's Bible School and Revivalist, 1932.

———. *Searching Sermons for Saints and Sinners.* Cincinnati, Ohio: God's Bible School, 1920.

———. *Seven Searching Sermons.* Cincinnati, Ohio: God's Revivalist, 1900.

———. *Sixty Years of Thorns and Roses.* Cincinnati, Ohio: God's Bible School and Revivalist, 1900.

———. *The Ups and Downs of a Pioneer Preacher: Also Some of My Mistakes and What They Taught Me.* Salem, Ohio: Allegheny Publications, 1991.

Shelhamer, E E, and Julia A Shelhamer. *A Spartan Evangel: Life Story of E.E. Shelhamer.* Winona Lake, Ind.: Light and Life Press, 1951.

———. *Ragged Elzie Gave Hope to the Discouraged*. Winona Lake, IN: Mrs. E.E. Shelhamer, n.d.

Shelhamer, Elmer. *False Doctrines and Fanaticism Exposed,*. Atlanta: "The Repairer," n.d.

———. *Popular and Radical Holiness Contrasted*. Atlanta: [publisher not identified], 1906.

Shelhamer, Elmer Ellsworth. *Bible Holiness: How Obtained and How Retained*. Chicago: Free Methodist Pub. House, 1900.

———. *Sermons That Search the Soul*. Kansas City, Mo.: Nazarene Pub. House, 1926.

Shelhamer, Elmer Elsworth. *Plain Preaching for Practical People*. Cincinnati, Ohio: God's Bible School and Revivalist, 1929.

Shelhamer, Julia. *A Message to Men*. Kansas City Mo.: Nazarene Pub. House, 1900.

———. *God, Ghosts, and Demons, Or, A Glimpse into the beyond*. Cincinnati: God's Bible School, n.d.

———. *Trials and Triumphs of a Minister's Wife*. Atlanta: Repairer Pub. Co., 1923.

Shepherd, Victor A. *So Great a Cloud of Witnesses*. Mississagua, Ont.: Light and Life Press Canada, 1993.

Shepherd, Victor A, United Church of Canada., Division of Mission in Canada., United Church of Canada, Division of Mission in Canada, United Church of Canada., and Division of Mission in Canada. *Ponder and Pray: Seven Weeks of Meditations and Prayers for Personal Enrichment during Any Season of the Year*. Mississauga: Light and Life Press, 1993.

"Shortwave." *Shortwave* 1 - (n.d.).

Showers, H D W. *Rev. Aura Claire Showers a Sketch of His Life*. Oil City, PA: H.D.W. Showers, 1896. http://catalog.hathitrust.org/api/volumes/oclc/19467847.html.

Shultz, Lawrence W. *Paul Family Record, 1763-1963*. Winona Lake, Ind.: Printed by the Light and Life Press, 1963.

―――. *Schwarzenau Yesterday and Today: Where the Brethren Began in Europe; Told in Picture and Story*. Winona Lake, Indiana: Light and Life Press, 1954.

―――. *Shultz Family Record, 1716-1966: From Hesse-Darmstadt to Huntingdon and Hagerstown*. North Manchester, Ind.: Lawrence W. Shultz, 1966.

Shultz, Lawrence W, and Herman E Taylor. *Paul Family Records 1763-1963 ... Including the 1917 Record*. Winona Lake, Ind.: Printed by the Light and Life Press, 1963.

Shumaker, J Timothy. "Church Growth in Paraguay." Fuller Theological Seminary, 1972.

Shumaker, J Timothy. "'Having the Mind of Christ' Presenting Christian Holiness in the Local Church : A Final Document Submitted to the Doctoral Studies Committee of United Theological Seminary in Partial Fulfillment of the Requirements for the Degree Doctor of Ministry." United Theological Seminary, 1992.

Sigsworth, John. *Careers for Christian Youth*. Chicago: Moody Press, 1956.

Sigsworth, John Wilkins. *The Battle Was the Lord's: A History of the Free Methodist Church in Canada*. Oshawa, Ont.: Sage Pubilications, 1960.

Silver, Jesse. *The Lord's Return: Seen in History and in Scripture as Pre-Millennial and Imminent*. New York: F.H. Revell, 1914.

Simpson, Matthew. *A Hundred Years of Methodism*. New York: Phillips & Hunt, 1870.

———. *Cyclopedia of Methodism: Embracing Sketches of Its Rise, Progress, and Present Condition*. Philadelphia: Everts & Stewart, 1878.

Sims, A. *Beams of Light on Scripture Texts, Or, Selected Passages of the Word of God Illuminated by Striking Illustrations and Choice Explanations from Eminent Writers: Also Helpful Bible Readings and Suggestive Hints*. Toronto: A. Sims, 1900.

———. *Behold the Bridegroom Cometh: Or, Some Remarkable and Incontrovertible Signs Which Herald the near Approach of the Son of Man*. Kingston Ont.: A. Sims, 1900.

———. *Deepening Shadows and Coming Glories*. Toronto: A. Sims, 1905.

———. *Helps to Bible Study with Practical Notes on the Books of Scripture Designed for Ministers, Local Preachers, S.s Teachers, and All Christian Workers*. Uxbridge Ont.: [publisher not identified], 1886.

———. *Honey from the Rock of Ages*. Ottervile, Ont.: The author, 1890.

———. *Remarkable Narratives: Or, Records of Powerful Revivals, Striking Providences, Wonderful Religious Experiences, Tragic Death-Bed Scenes, and Other Authentic Incidents, to Which Is Added Some Valuable*. Kingston Ont.: The author, 1896.

———. *Valuable Bank Notes, Or, God's Immutable Promises, Searched, Tested, and Found True*. Toronto: A. Sims, 1902.

———. *Yet Not I, Or, A Brief Sketch of the Early Life, Conversion, Call to the Ministry, and Some of the Subsequent Labors in the Master's Vineyard of A. Sims*. Toronto: The Author, n.d.

Sims, Albert. *Bible Salvation and Popular Religion Contrasted.* Kingston Ont.: The Author, 1886.

———. *Grace and Glory: Or Godly Counsel and Encouragement for Waiting, Watching Hearts.* Toronto: the author, 1900.

Sing His Praise, and Sing his praise. "Camp Meeting Special : A Selection of Songs Specially Designed for Use in Camp Meetings and Other Evangelistic Campaigns." Chicago: Light and Life Press, 1925.

Single in a Couples' World. Published for Aldersgate Associates by Beacon Hill Press of Kansas City, 1970.

Sizelove, Rachel A Harper, and James F Corum. *A Sketch of My Life.* S.l.: s.n., 2011.

Skyline Free Methodist Church. *Skyline Free Methodist Church.* Coos Bay, Or.: Skyline Free Methodist Church, 1978.

Sloan, Harold Paul. *He Is Risen.* Winona Lake, IN: Light and Life Press, 1942.

Small Collections, 1870.

Smashey, David. *The Redeeming Purpose of God, Including a Statement of the Scriptural Idea of the Doctrine of Holiness and Its Advancement in the Church,.* Chicago: Goodspeed Press, 1913.

Smith, Alfred B, and Homer A Rodeheaver. "Youth Rally Songs and Choruses," 1945.

Smith, Bertha B. "A Brief Sketch of a Remarkable Life, the Life of Mrs. Minnie B. Shelhamer." Atlanta: The Repairer, 1903. http://catalog.hathitrust.org/api/volumes/oclc/18842150.html.

Smith, Bertha B, and Julia A Shelhamer. *"A Remarkable Woman": The Life of Mrs. Minnie B. Shelhamer.* Atlanta: Repairer Pub. Co., 1904.

———. *The Life Story of Minnie B. Shelhamer*. Atlanta: Repairer Pub. Co., n.d.

Smith, Bertha B, Julia A Shelhamer, Nancy P Swauger, and Gracia L Fero. *Remarkable Women*. Salem, Ohio: Allegheny Publications, 1992.

Smith, David Paul. *The Growth and Development of the Interracial Movement within the Free Methodist Church of North America: A Research Paper in History of Free Methodism*, 1950.

Smith, Dwayne A. *Central College: The First 100 Years*. North Newton, Kan.: Mennonite Press, 1984.

Smith, Ella M. *A Child Shall Lead Them*. Greenville, Ill.: Tower Press, 1943.

Smith, James. *Religion in American Life*. Princeton N.J.: Princeton University Press, 1961.

Smith, Rosa. *Youth's Incense, Or, Life and Writings of Blanche Charlotte Smith*. Cincinnati: God's Bible School and Revivalist, 1935.

Smith, Timothy. *Revivalism and Social Reform in Mid-Nineteenth-Century America. Chapters I-XI and XIV Comprise the Frank S. and Elizabeth D. Brewer Prize Essay for 1955, the American Society of Church History*. New York: Abingdon Press, 1957.

Smith, Wilbur M. *The Incomparable Book: To Guide You as You Read It through*. Winona Lake, Ind.: Light and Life Press, 1961.

Snell, Verlyn R. "The Theology of Smallness," 1976.

Snider, K. *Whose Ministry?: A Group Study Book on the Ministry of Every Christian*. Osaka Japan: Japan Free Methodist Mission, 1975.

Snider, K Lavern. *Ten More Growing Churches in Japan Today*. Osaka, Japan: Japan Free Methodist Church, 1985.

Snider, K Lavern., and Shoji. Nakae. *Seicho Suru Ju Kyokai No Kiroku: Ima, Nihon Demo ...2*. Tokyo: Inochi no Kotobasha, 1986.

Snider, Lois. *Snow Pearl, a Girl of Japan*. Winona Lake, IN: Light and Life Press, 1968.

Snyder, C Albert. *Weeping May Endure for a Night: A Spiritual Journey*. [S. l.]: Xulon Press, 2006.

Snyder, Howard A. *Aspects of Early Free Methodist History*. Dayton, OH: United Theological Seminary, 1994.

— — —. *Concept and Commitment: A History of Spring Arbor University, 1873-2007*. Spring Arbor, MI: Spring Arbor University Press, 2008.

— — —. *One Hundred Years at Spring Arbor: A History of Spring Arbor College 1873-1973*. Spring Arbor, Mich.: Spring Arbor College, 1973.

— — —. *Populist Saints: B.T. and Ellen Roberts and the First Free Methodists*. Grand Rapids, Mich.: William B. Eerdmans Pub. Co., 2006.

— — —. *Radical Holiness Evangelism: Vivian Dake and the Pentecost Bands*. [Dayton (Ohio)]: [[Published privately by the author], 1990.

— — —. *Radical Holiness Evangelism: Vivian Dake and the Pentecostal Bands*, 1990.

— — —. *Under Construction: Ephesians Study Guide*. Indianapolis, IN: Light and Life Press, 1981.

Snyder, Howard A, Kenneth W Pickerill, Legacy of John Wesley for the Twenty-first Century, and Legacy of John Wesley for the Twenty-first Century. "B.T. Roberts, the Farmers' Alliance and the Rise of American Populism." Wilmore, KY: Asbury College Tape Ministry, 2003.

Snyder, Howard A, Daniel V Runyon, and Howard A Snyder. *B. T. and Ellen Roberts and the First Free Methodists*. Indianapolis, Ind.: Committee on Free Methodist History & Archives, 2011.

Snyder, Lefa E, and Bernice E Weidman. *Servant of God: Life Story and Selected Articles of Bishop Arthur D. Zahniser*. Winona Lake, Ind.: Light and Life Press, 1940.

Snyder, Richard D. *Being Disciples, Making Disciples*. [Indianapolis, Ind.]: Free Methodist Church of North America, 2004.

Somers, Delmar O. "Ministry Hazards within the Free Methodist Church," 1986.

Spears, Arthur K, and Leanne Hinton. "LANGUAGES AND SPEAKERS: AN INTRODUCTION TO AFRICAN AMERICAN ENGLISH AND NATIVE AMERICAN LANGUAGES." *TRAA Transforming Anthropology* 18, no. 1 (2010): 3–14.

Stayt, Edward Hoke. *Water Baptism*. Chicago, Ill.: Free Methodist Pub., 1912.

Stedwell, Anson. *Itinerant Footprints*. Shambaugh, Iowa: Stedwell, 1915.

Stevens, Abel. *History of the Methodist Episcopal Church in the United States of America*. New York: Carlton & Porter, 1864.

Stewart, E Eugene. *Joshua, Judges, Ruth: Leader's Guide*. Winona Lake, Ind.: Light and Life Press, 1961.

Stewart, J Wesley. "Historical Factors in the Naming of the Free Methodist Church," 1963.

Stonehouse, Catherine. *Adventures in Belonging: Membership Labs for Young Churchmen; Leader's Guide [and Resource Packet].* Winona Lake, Ind.: Light and Life Press, 1980.

Stonehouse, Catherine., and Donald M Joy. *Leader's Discussion Guide*. Winona Lake, IN: Light and Life Press, 1969.

Stonehouse, CATHY. "Moral Development: The Process and the Pattern." *CVJ Counseling and Values* 24, no. 1 (1979): 2–9.

"Story Hour." Chicago, IL: Light and Life Press, 1885.

"Story Papers." Winona Lake IN: Light and Life Press, n.d.

"Story Trails. 1-87, No. 8." Winona Lake In.: Light and Life Press, 1943.

Strategies for Vital Christian Living. Published for Aldersgate Associates by Beacon Hill Press of Kansas City, 1970.

Stratton-Porter, Gene, Rufus. Liechty, Dean. Cornwell, Gene Stratton-Porter, Ind.) Light and Life Press (Winona Lake, and Light and Life Press. *Euphorbia*. [Berne, Ind.]: [Liechty], 1986.

Street, Norman Averill. *In Memory of Zion Chapel, F.M. Church*. Elk City, Okla.: N.A. Street, 1983.

———. *Zion Chapel, F.M. Church, 1905-: Souvenir Edition*. U.S.: s.n., 1983.

Suderman, John P, General Conference Mennonite Church., Commission on Home Ministries., General Conference Mennonite Church, and Commission on Home Missions. *Hopi Gospel Songs; for Church and Street Services in Hopi-Land*. Winona Lake, IN: Light and Life Press, 1972.

Summers, Ancel., and Grace. Summers. *Sanctified Wholly*. Estevan, Sask.: J. Cowan, 1952.

Sung, Felix, and Donald N Bastian. *In the Church and in Christ Jesus: Essays in Honour of Donald N. Bastian.* Mississauga, Ont.: Light and Life Press Canada, 1993.

Sweet, William. *Methodism in American History.* New York; Nashville: Abingdon Press, 1961.

"Table Talk." Winona Lake IN: Light and Life Press, 1969.

Tabor, Mary., Free Methodist Church of North, Woman's Missionary Society, Free Methodist Church of North America., and Woman's Missionary Society. *Puss.* Winona Lake, Ind.: Woman's Missionary Society of the Free Methodist Church, 1946.

Taiwan Alphabet Tour. Kaohsiung, Taiwan: China Free Methodist Mission, 1967.

Takeya, Toshiro David., and Donald N Bastian. "Membership class guidance for pastors in the Japanese Free Methodist Church the study of Free Methodism: and, a Japanese translation of, Belonging!: adventures in church membership," 1981.

Tamblyn, Jeremiah. *Sweet Memories of a Trustful Life.* Morristown N.J.: E.A. Smith & Sons Printers, 1924.

Tankidaigaku., Osaka Kirisutokyo. "Osaka Kirisutokyo Tankidaigaku Kiyo." *Osaka Kirisutokyo Tankidaigaku Kiyo.* Osaka Shi: Osaka Kirisutokyo Tankidaigaku, n.d.

Tapper, Ruth. *Full Years: The Life Story of Helen I. Root.* Winona Lake IN: Young People's Missionary Society, 1948.

Tapper, Ruth M, Young People's Missionary Society of the Free Methodist Church., and Young People's Missionary Society of the Free Methodist Church. *Glimpses of Victory.* Chicago: Y.P.M.S. Council of the Free Methodist Church, 1931.

Tapper, Ruth M, Young People's Missionary Society of the Free Methodist Church, and Young People's Missionary Society of the Free Methodist Church. *Life Stories of Foreign Missionaries of the Free Methodist Church: Supported by the Young People's Missionary Society, 1931-1935*. Winona Lake, Ind.: Y.P.M.S. Council, 1935.

Taylor, Alice Hayes. *Rescued from the Dragon: True Accounts from China*. Winona Lake, Ind.: Light and Life Press, 1982.

Taylor, Ethel., Olive Branch Mission., and Olive Branch Mission. *The Olive Branch Mission, 1876-1970*. Chicago, IL: Olive Branch Mission, 1970.

Taylor, J Paul. *All Roads Lead to Bethlehem*. Winona Lake, Ind.: Light and Life Press, 1964.

— — —. *Soldiers of Christ*. [Winona Lake, Ind.]: [Light and Life Press], 1960.

Taylor, Jesse Paul. *Goodly Heritage*. Winona Lake, Ind.: Light and Life Press, 1960.

— — —. *Holiness, the Finished Foundation*. Winona Lake, Ind.: Light and Life Press, 1963.

— — —. *The Music of Pentecost*. Winona Lake, Ind.: Light and life Press, 1951.

Taylor, Willard H. *II Corinthians: Leader's Guide*. Winona Lake, Ind.: Light and Life Press, 1963.

"Teaching Beginners." *Teaching Beginners*. Winona, Lake, Ind.: Light and Life Press, 1953.

"Teaching Beginners. 1-3, No. 3." Winona Lake IN: Light and Life Press, 1951.

"Teaching Junior Hi." *Teaching Junior Hi*. Winona, Lake, Ind.: Light and Life Press, 1953.

"Teaching Junior High." *Teaching Junior Hi*. Winona, Lake, Ind.: Light and Life Press, 1953.

"Teaching Juniors, 1-3, No. 3." Winona Lake IN: Light and Life Press, 1951.

"Teaching Juniors." *Teaching Juniors*. Winona, Lake, Ind.: Light and Life Press, 1953.

"Teaching Juniors. 1-16, No.4." Winona Lake IN: Light and Life Press, 1953.

"Teaching Preschool. 1-16, No. 4." Winona Lake IN: Light and Life Press, 1951.

"Teaching Primaries." *Teaching Primaries*. Winona, Lake, Ind.: Light and Life Press, 1953.

"Teaching Primaries, 1-3, No. 3." Winona Lake Indiana: Light and Life Press, 1951.

"Teaching Primaries. 1-16, No.4." Winona Lake IN: Light and Life Press, 1953.

"Teaching Senior Teens, 1-14, No.1." Winona Lake IN: Light and Life Press, 1956.

"Teaching Young Teens. 1-16, No.4." Winona Lake IN: Light and Life Press, 1953.

Teed, Florence Ernestine Schleicher, Paul S Rees, Seth Cook Rees, Joseph Henry Smith, and Ralph W Sockman. *Florence Ernestine Schleicher Teed Papers,* 1919.

Telford, John. *The Life of John Wesley*. Chicago: Free Methodist Pub. House, 1886.

Tenney, Mary. *Still Abides the Memory*. Greenville Ill.: Tower Press of Greenville College, 1942.

———. *"Still Abides the Memory."* Greenville Ill.: Tower Press of Greenville College, 1942.

Tenney, Mary Alice. *Adventures in Christian Love*. Winona Lake, Ind.: Light and Life Press, 1964.

———. *Blueprint for a Christian World; an Analysis of the Wesleyan Way*. Winona Lake, Indiana: Light and Life Press, 1953.

———. *Living in Two Worlds; How a Christian Does It!* Winona Lake, Ind.: Light and Life Press, 1958.

Terhune, Carol Parker. "McCray, Mary F." Oxford: Oxford University Press, 2006.

Terrill, Joseph Goodwin. "Talks to Sunday School Teachers." Syracuse, NY: A.W. Hall, 1891. http://catalog.hathitrust.org/api/volumes/oclc/16733668.html.

———. *The Life of Rev. John Wesley Redfield*. Chicago: Free Methodist Pub. House, 1889.

———. *The St. Charles Camp-Meeting, Embodying Its History and Several Sermons by Leading Ministers, with Some Practical Suggestions Concerning Campmeeting Management*. Chicago: T.B. Arnold, 1883.

Terrill, Joseph Goodwin. *The Life of John Wesley Redfield, M.D.* Salem, Ohio: Allegheny, 2000.

The Christian & Social Problems. Published for Aldersgate Associates by Beacon Hill Press of Kansas City, 1970.

"The Christian Minister. (Journal, Magazine, 1949) [WorldCat.org]," n.d. http://www.worldcat.org/title/christian-minister/oclc/9316490&referer=brief_results.

"The College Blue Book. (Journal, Magazine, 1923) [WorldCat.org]," n.d. http://www.worldcat.org/title/college-blue-book/oclc/1244494&referer=brief_results.

The Doctrines and Discipline of the Methodist Episcopal Church, 1860. With an Appendix. New York: Carlton & Porter, 1860.

The Free Methodist Church in Postwar Japan., 1971.

"The Free Methodist Pastor. (Journal, Magazine, 1974) [WorldCat.org]," n.d. http://www.worldcat.org/title/free-methodist-pastor/oclc/11028288&referer=brief_results.

"The Life and Letters of Mrs. Phoebe Palmer (Book, 1984) [WorldCat.org]," n.d. http://www.worldcat.org/title/life-and-letters-of-mrs-phoebe-palmer/oclc/11159757&referer=brief_results.

The National Faculty Directory. Detroit Mich.: Gale Research, 1970.

The Now Look of Evangelism. Published for Aldersgate Associates by Beacon Hill Press of Kansas City, 1970.

"The Repairer." *The Repairer*, n.d.

"The Repairer. (Journal, Magazine, 1800s) [WorldCat.org]," n.d. http://www.worldcat.org/title/repairer/oclc/15349658&referer=brief_results.

The Shape of Things to Come: God's Plan for the Future. Published for Aldersgate Associates by Beacon Hill Press of Kansas City, 1970.

The State of the Churches in the U.S.A., 1973, as Shown in Their Own Official Yearbooks: A Study Resource. Sun City Ariz.: The Agency, 1973.

The What and the Why of Free Methodism. Chicago: Free Methodist Pub. House, 1927.

The World Book Encyclopedia. Chicago: Field Enterprises Educational Corp., 1976.

The Young Minister's Companion: Or, A Collection of Valuable and Scarce Treatises on the Pastoral Office. Boston: Printed and sold by Samuel T. Armstrong, 1813.

Thomas, Fred L, Free Methodist Church of North America, and Adult Ministries. *Adult Ministries*. Salem, Or.: Free Methodist Church of North America, 1991.

Thomas, Fred L, Free Methodist Church of North America, Adult Ministries, Free Methodist Church of North America., and Adult Ministries. *Building the Church through Adult Sunday School*, 1980.

Thompson, Brian. *If I Settle on the Far Side of the Sea*. Cuyahoga, OH: Invisible Inc, 2015.

Thompson, Frank H. *Proverbs, Ecclesiastes, Song of Solomon: Leader's Guide*. Winona Lake, Ind.: Light and Life Press, 1963.

Thompson, W Ralph. *John: Official Quiz Text*. Winona Lake, Ind.: Light and Life Press, 1967.

— — —. *The Gospel of John: Book of Proofs of the Deity of Christ; Official Bible Quiz Text*. Winona Lake, Ind.: Light and Life Press, 1961.

— — —. *The Road to Heaven: The Way of Holiness*. Indianapolis, IN: Light and Life Press, 1992.

Thompson, William Ralph. "Factors in the Establishing of a Free Methodist Mission Training School in Paraguay," 1950.

— — —. "Factors in the Establishment of a Free Methodist Mission Training School in Paraguay," 1950.

Thomson, Frances. *The New York Times Guide to Continuing Education in America,*. [New York]: Quadrangle Books, 1972.

Thomson, John F. *The Life and Labors of Rev. William Bramwell: A Chosen, Approved, Valiant and Successful Minister of Christ, 1783-1820*. Chicago, Ill.: Free Methodist Pub. House, 1905.

Thrall, O C. *From Darkness to Light and from the Power of Satan unto God*. Titusville, PA: O.C. Thrall, n.d.

Tiffany-Holtwick History Society, and Greenville College Department of History. "The Tiffany-Holtwick Journal." *The Tiffany-Holtwick Journal*. Greenville, Ill.: Dept. of History, Greenville College., n.d.

Tinsley, Samuel H. "Community: A New Testament Model of Ministry : A Final Document Submitted to the Doctoral Studies Committee of United Theological Seminary in Partial Fulfillment of the Requirements for the Degree of Doctor of Ministry.' United Theological Seminary, 1992.

Todd, Floyd. *Camping for Christian Youth a Guide to Methods and Principles for Evangelical Camps*. New York: Harper & Row, 1963.

Todd, Floyd, Free Methodist Church of North America, and Christian Youth Crusaders. *Herald Highways*. Winona Lake, Ind.: Dept. of Intermediate Youth, 1965.

Todd, Floyd, Pauline Todd, Free Methodist Church of North America, and Christian Youth Crusaders. *Cadet Trails*. Winona Lake, IN: Dept. of Intermediate Youth, a member Dept. of the Commission on Christian Education Free Methodist Church World Headquarters, 1965.

Todd, Pauline H. *Becoming a Christian: The Beginning of a Happy Life*. Winona Lake, Ind.: Light and Life Press, 1963.

― ― ―. *Truth in Action*. Winona Lake, Ind.: Light and Life Press, 1961.

Tongue-Speaking in Historical Perspective. Indianapolis, IN: Light and Life Press, 1990.

Toole, I N. *Living or Dead*. Winona Lake, IN: Light and Life Press, 1939.

Townsend, W. *A New History of Methodism*. London: Hodder and Stoughton, 1909.

Township of Uxbridge Public Library. *Church Records*. Uxbridge, Ont.: Uxbridge Public Library, 1999.

Tracy, Wesley, ed. *Dare to Discipline*. Kansas City MO: Beacon Hill Press, n.d.

Tremain, Lloyd Carlos. "An Evaluation of the Organization and Structure of the Family Camp Program of the Pacific Northwest Conference of the Free Methodist Church (Book, 1968) [WorldCat.org]." Seattle Pacific University, 1968. http://www.worldcat.org/title/evaluation-of-the-organization-and-structure-of-the-family-camp-program-of-the-pacific-northwest-conference-of-the-free-methodist-church/oclc/253713838&referer=brief_results.

Trever, Robert. *Life and Labors of Rev. Robert Trever Both in England and America Also, A Sketch of Frontier Work in Connection with the Free Methodist Church with an Appendix Containing Temperance and Other Matter*. St. Louis: J.H. Flowers, 1905. http://catalog.hathitrust.org/api/volumes/oclc/3803612.html.

Tsuchiyama, Tetsuji. *Victory of the Cross, Or, An Account of My Trip in China*. Winona Lake, IN: Light and Life Press, n.d.

Tsuchiyama, Tetsuji., and William B Olmstead. *From Darkness to Light*. Chicago, IL: Light and Life Press, 1927.

Tsuchiyama, Tetsuji., Arleta. Richardson, Tetsuji. Tsuchiyama, and Kazuo. Kaneda. *Love Shining through: Tsuchiyama*. Winona Lake, IN: Light and Life Press, 1986.

Turnbull, Ralph. *A History of Preaching Volume III, from the Close of the Nineteenth Century to the Middle of the Twentieth Century (continuing the Work of the Volumes I and II by Edwin C. Dargan) and American*. Grand Rapids Mich.: Baker Book House, 1974.

Turner, George Allen. *Ezra, Nehemiah, Esther, Malachi*. Winona Lake, Ind.: Light and Life Press, 1966.

———. *Isaiah -- A: First of Two Units*. Winona Lake, Ind.: Light and Life Press, 1965.

———. *Isaiah: Leader's Guide*. Winona Lake, Ind.: Light and Life Press, 1966.

———. *John: Study Guide*. Winona Lake, Ind.: Light and Life Press, 1962.

———. *Revelation: Leader's Guide*. Winona Lake, Ind.: Light and Life Press, 1964.

———. "The More Excellent Way : The Scriptural Basis of the Wesleyan Message." Light and Life Press, 1952.

———. "Uesure shingaku no chushin mondai," 1959.

United for Action: Official Workshop Outlines & Program of the Pre-Centennial Convocation for Sunday School & Youth Leaders [of the Free Methodist Church]. [Winona Lake, Ind.]: Lloyd H. Knox, 1957.

University., Seattle Pacific, Archives., Seattle Pacific University Archives, Seattle Pacific University., and Archives. *Free Methodist Church records and publications*, 1950.

Upham, Thomas C. *Inward Divine Guidance*. Chicago: Free Methodist Pub. House, 1907.

US Office of Education. *Education Directory*, n.d.

Van Valin, Clyde E. *Pastor's Handbook*. [Place of publication not identified]: Board of Bishops, Free Methodist Church (USA), 1991.

———. *Tithing: God's Plan for the Church*. Indianapolis, IN.: Light and Life Press, 1990.

———. *Transforming Grace: A Biblical Guide for Holy Living*. Indianapolis, Ind.: Light and Life Press, 1990.

Van Valin, Frank. *Mark: Leader's Guide*. Winona Lake, Ind.: Light and Life Press, 1963.

Van Valin, William B. *Little White Girl in Eskimo Land*. Winona Lake, Ind.: Light and Life Press, 1913.

Veldman, Russell J. *Classic Catechism*. Indianapolis, Ind.: Light and Life Communications, 2006.

Village Green Free Methodist Church. *The Village Green Free Methodist Church*. Fort Wayne, Ind.: [The Church], 1964.

———. *The Village Green Free Methodist Church: Celebrating One Hundred Years, 1873-1973*. Fort Wayne, Ind.: [The Church], 1973.

Vincent, Burton. *"As Ye Go, Preach": Outlines and Notes from the Papers of Bishop Burton Jones Vincent, 1877-1931*. [Place of publication not identified]: [publisher not identified], 1975.

"Voices of Praise : Prepared with Especial Reference to the Needs of the Sunday School, It Will Also Be Found Suitable for the Prayer Meeting and Other Religious Gatherings." Chicago : W.B. Rose, 1909.

Vore, Ellen. *Mud Pies*. Winona Lake, Ind.: Light and Life Press, 1972.

Wabash Christian Courier, Cleo T Denbo, Wabash Christian Courier., and Cleo T Denbo. *Centennial: "Wabash Conference -- Courier to Every Age"; Free Methodist Church, 1860-1960; Wabash Conference, 1885-1960; 100 Years of Continuous Service to the Nations*. Wabash, Ind.: Wabash Christian Courier, 1960.

Waller, Fred L. "A History of Wessington Springs College." University of South Dakota, 1935. http://www.worldcat.org/title/history-of-wessington-springs-college/oclc/9497259&referer=brief_results.

Walls, Alice E, Ruth L Cochrane, and Mary Loretta. Rose. *Eighty Years: Historical Sketch of Thr Woman's Missionary Society of the Free Methodist Church*. [Place of publication not identified]: by the Society, 1975.

Walls, Francine E. *The Church Library Workbook: How to Start and Maintain the Church Library*. Winona Lake, Ind.: Light and Life Press, 1980.

— — —. *The Free Methodist Church: A Bibliography*. Winona Lake, Ind.: Free Methodist Historical Center, Free Methodist Headquarters, 1977.

Walrath, Brian., Theological Research Exchange Network, and Theological Research Exchange Network. "Exploring the Correlation between Authentic Worship and Health in Selected Congregations of the Free Methodist Church." Institute of Worship Studies, 2002.

Walsh, Gary., Brethren in Christ Holiness Camp Meeting, and Brethren in Christ Holiness Camp Meeting. "Clearing Life's Burdens." Chambersburg, PA: AV Ministries, 1993.

Walter, John., Margaret. Walter, and Doris Juhlin. Fisher. *History of the Ohio Conference of the Free Methodist Church*. Galion, Ohio: United Church Directories, 1978.

Walters, Orville Selkirk. *Christian Education in the Local Church*. Winona Lake, IN: Light and Life Press, 1939.

— — —. *The Christian and the Movies*. Winona Lake, Ind.: The Forward Movement, Free Methodist Church of North America, 1948.

— — —. *You Can Win Others; How to Adventure in Sharing the Good News*. Winona Lake, Ind.: Light and Life Press, 1951.

Walters, Stanley D. *Exodus - Numbers: Study Guide*. Winona Lake, Ind.: Light and Life Press, 1961.

— — —. *Exodus, Numbers: Leader's Guide.* Winona Lake, Ind.: Light and Life Press, 1961.

Walton, K M. *Western Convention: "The Springboard of Free Methodism."* S.l.: s.n., 1960.

Ward, Daniel T. "Theological Education by Extension : A Proposal for India's Free Methodist Church," 1983.

Ward, Daniel Thomas., Theological Research Exchange Network, and Theological Research Exchange Network. "Identifying Critical Areas of Need for the Future Development of Teaching Lesson Plans for the India Free Methodist Church." Trinity Evangelical Divinity School, 2001.

Ward, E F. *Papers*, 1880.

Ward, Ernest F. *Memory Links of "Our Own Chickabiddie", Or, Reminiscences of Mary Louise Vore.* Chicago: Free Methodist Pub. House, 1923.

Ward, Ernest F, and Phebe E Ward. *Echoes from Bharatkhand.* Chicago, ill.: Free Methodist Pub. House, 1908.

Ward, Ernest Fremont, Darden Asbury. Pyron, and Phebe E Ward. *Papers of This First Free Methodist Church Missionary to India*, 1878.

Ward, Ethel E, Free Methodist Church of North America., and Free Methodist Church of North America. "Letter Links." *Letter Links.* Lucknow: Methodist Pub. House, 1924.

Ward, Ethel E, Free Methodist Church of North America., Free Methodist Church of North America, and Free Methodist Church of North America. *Ordered Steps, Or, The Wards of India: A Biography of the Lives of Ernest Fremont Ward and Phebe Elizabeth Cox Ward, Missionaries to India, 1880-1927.* Winona Lake, Ind.: Light and Life Press, 1951.

Ward, Ethel E, Free Methodist Church of North America., Free Methodist Church of North America, Ethel E Ward, and Free Methodist Church of North America. "India Letter Links." *India Letter Links*, 1937.

Warner, David. *Glimpses of Palestine and Egypt*. Chicago: W.B. Rose, 1914.

———. *The Book We Study: A Brief Tribute to the Holy Scriptures*. Chicago: W.B. Rose, 1921.

Warner, David Snethen. *The Anointing of the Holy Spirit*. Chicago, Ill.: Light and Life Press, 1925.

Warren, R. *You Can Gain Spiritual Strength*. New York: Nelson, 1960.

Warren, Ralph. *Spiritual Strength for Today*. Toronto ;New York: T. Nelson, 1955.

Warrington, Janette Moffatt. *The Humpty Dumpty Syndrome*. Winona Lake, Ind.: Light and Life Press, 1981.

Washington County (N.Y.) Historian. *Town and Village of Argyle Collection*, 1728.

Watson, C Hoyt. *De Shazer: The Doolittle Raider Who Turned Missionary*. Winona Lake, Ind.: Light and Life Press, 1950.

———. *DeShazer*. Coquitlam, B.C., Canada: Galaxy Communications, 1998.

———. *The Fragrance of My Church*. S.l.: s.n., 1950.

Watson, C Hoyt. *Light and Life Scripture Memory Plan for Christian Workers*. Winona Lake, IN: Light and Life Press, 1946.

———. *Light and Life Scripture Memory Plan for Christian Workers: A Series of Pocket-Kits of Selected Scripture Verses Chosen to Be Hidden in the Heart for Ready Use*. Winona Lake, Ind.: Light and Life Press, 1946.

———. *The Free Methodist Church*. Winona Lake, Ind.: Free Methodist Church of North America, 1950.

Watson, C Hoyt., and R W Howell. *Exploring Church Membership: Pastor's Instruction Series, Junior Division*. Winona Lake Indiana: Light and Life Press, 1964.

Watson, C Hoyt., and Roy W Howell. *Advancing in Church Membership: Pastor's Instruction Series, Youth Division*. Winona Lake, Ind.: Light and Life Press, 1964.

Watson, Charles. *The Employer, the Wage Earner, and the Law of Love,*. [Lawrence]: University of Kansas, 1917.

Watson, Charles Hoyt. *De Shazer, the Doolittle Raider Who Turned Missionary: A True and Thrilling Story of How the Practical Demonstration of the Law of Love Is Bringing International Understanding and the Spirit of Christ to Japan*. Winona Lake, Ind.: Light and Life Press, 1950.

———. *DeShazer*. [Place of publication not identified]: [publisher not identified], 2002.

Watson, Charles Hoyt, and Leona K Fear. *De Shazer*. Winona Lake, Ind.: Light and Life Press, 1972.

Watson, Charles Hoyt. *De Shazer: Doolittle Raider Turned Missionary*. The Light and Life Press, 1950.

Watson, Claude A. *God's Plan for Civil Government*. Winona Lake, Ind.: Light and Life Press, 1946.

———. *Repeal Has Succeeded,*. Winona Lake, Ind.: Pub. by Light and life Press, 1945.

We Believe!: Insights into the Beliefs of Free Methodists. Winona Lake, Ind.: Light and Life Press, 1976.

Welliver, Dotsey. *Smudgkin Elves: And Other Lame Excuses*. Winona Lake, Ind.: Light and Life, 1981.

Welliver, Dotsey. *Dotsey's Diary: Her Daze ["X"-Figure Marked through Word] Days and Yours*. Winona Lake, Ind.: Light and Life Press, 1979.

― ― ―. *I Need You Now, God, While the Grape Juice Is Running All over the Floor*. Winona Lake, Ind.: Light and Life Press, 1975.

― ― ―. *Some of God's Miracles Wear Cowlicks*. Winona Lake, In.: Warner Press [Light and Life Press], 1978.

― ― ―. *Thank You, God, for Ninety-Five Pounds of Peanut Butter*. Winona Lake, Ind.: Light and Life Press, 1976.

Wesley, John. *A Plain Account of Christian Perfection*. Winona Lake, Ind.: Light and Life Press, n.d.

― ― ―. *John and Charles Wesley: Selected Prayers, Hymns, Journal Notes, Sermons, Letters and Treatises*. New York: Paulist Press, 1981.

― ― ―. *On Dress*. Chicago, Ill.: Published by the Free Methodist Pub. House, 1900.

― ― ―. *True Holiness as Taught by John Wesley: Comprising His Sermons on Sin in Believers, Repentance of Believers, Christian Perfection*. Chicago: Free Methodist Pub. House, 1902.

Wesley, John, Benjamin Titus Roberts, E P Hart, Gayle D Beebe, Jon S Kulaga, and David L McKenna. *A Concept to Keep: A Concept for Christian Higher Education in the Wesleyan Tradition*. Spring Arbor, MI: Spring Arbor University Press, 2003.

Wesley, John, John Wesley, and John Wesley. *On Dress and Evil Speaking*. Winona Lake, Ind.: Free Methodist Publishing House, 1940.

Wesleyan Church, Christian Youth Crusaders, and Wesleyan Church. Christian Youth Crusaders. *Herald Highways*. [Winona Lake, Ind.]: Light and Life Press, 1970.

Wesleyan Church Department of Youth, and Wesleyan Church. General Department of Youth. *First Studies in Christian Teachings*. Winona Lake, Ind.: Light and Life Press, 1969.

Wesleyan Methodist Church of America, and Wesleyan Methodist Connection (or Church) of America. "Hymns of the living faith : official hymnal of the Wesleyan Methodist Church of America." Syracuse, N.Y.: Wesleyan Methodist Pub. Assoc., 1951.

Wesleyan Theological Society, and Wesleyan Theological Society. *Wesleyan Theological Society Records*, 1963.

West, Betty J. *Forty Years of History at Flatwoods Camp, 1958-1998*. Perryopolis, Pa.: Sound of the Trumpet Tract Ministries, 1998.

West Morris Street Free Methodist Church, and Free Methodist Church of North America. "West Morris Street Free Methodist Church Good News." *West Morris Street Free Methodist Church Good News*. Indianapolis, Ind.: West Morris Street Free Methodist Church, n.d.

Westwood, N J. "Revell's Guide to Christian Colleges." *Revell's Guide to Christian Colleges*, n.d. http://www.worldcat.org/title/revells-guide-to-christian-/oclc/8044133&referer=brief_results.

Wheatlake, S K. *Casting Away Our Confidence*. Chicago: Free Methodist Publishing House, 2006.

― ― ―. *The Touch of Fire: Sermons on Holiness*. Chicago: Free Methodist Pub. House, 1900.

Whitcomb, A L. *Emmanuel and Stepping Stones to Union with God*. Winona Lake, Ind.: Light and Life Press, 1900.

White, Charles. *The Beauty of Holiness: Phoebe Palmer as Theologian, Revivalist, Feminist, and Humanitarian*. Grand Rapids Mich.: F. Asbury Press, 1986.

White, Jane Melville. *Sixty Years on the Way: Kindersley Free Methodist Church, 1921-1981*. Kindersley, Sask.: Kindersley Free Methodist Church, 1981.

White, Ronald., Theological Research Exchange Network., and Theological Research Exchange Network. "A Sacrament of Joy the Discovery of the Lord's Table as a Weekly Celebration at the Stanwood Free Methodist Church in Stanwood, Michigan." Northern Baptist Theological Seminary, 2001.

Whiteman, John H. *Amen Hallelujah*. Winona Lake, Ind.: Light and Life Press, 1920.

Who Was Who in America: A Companion Volume to Who's Who in America. Chicago: Marquis, 1943.

Who's Who in America, 1988-1989. Wilmette Ill.: Marquis Who's Who, 1988.

Wholesome Interpersonal Relationships. Published for Aldersgate Associates by Beacon Hill Press of Kansas City, 1970.

Why Don't You Do Something, God? Published for Aldersgate Associates by Beacon Hill Press of Kansas City, 1970.

Wilder, Justin E. *The Descendants of Harvey Wilder and His Ancestors to 1485 in England: With a History of the Wilder Name and Related Families of Warner, Barnhard, Benedict, Hepworth, Poore, Crocker, and Newman*. Winona Lake, Ind.: Printed by Light and Life Press, 1974.

Willard, F Burleigh. *Idol of Clay*. Winona Lake, Ind.: Light and Life Press, 1985.

Willard, Francis Burleigh. "A Proposal for the Training of Lay Ministers for Hispanic Free Methodist Churches," 1983.

Williamson, Glen. *Brother Kawabe*. Winona Lake, Ind.: Light and Life Press, 1977.

———. *Geneva: The Fascinating Story of Geneva Sayre, Missionary to the Chinese*. Winona Lake, Ind.: Light and Life Press, 1974.

———. *Gonzalo of Mexican Missions*. Winona Lake, Ind.: Light and Life Press, 1976.

———. *Julia: Giantess in Generosity; the Story of Julia Arnold Shelhamer*. Winona Lake, Ind.: Light and Life Press, 1969.

Williamson, Glenn. *Frank and Hazel: The Adamsons of Kibogora*. Winona Lake, IN: Light and Life Press, 1972.

"Wilson Street Mission, Wilson Street," n.d. http://www.leodis.net/display.aspx?id=2011510_172195.

Winget, B. *Historical Sketch of Members of the Free Methodist Church of North America Who Have Gone out to the Foreign Field of Missionaries*. Chicago, Ill.: Free Methodist Pub. House, 1903.

———. *Missions and Missionaries of the Free Methodist Church*. Chicago: Free Methodist Pub. House, 1911.

Winslow, Carolyn. *Forward with Christ*. Winona Lake Ind.: Young Peoples Missionary Society, 1947.

———. *Tomorrow*. Winona Lake Ind.: Young people's missionary Society, 1945.

Winslow, Carolyn Van Valin. *By Love Compelled: Life Story*. Winona Lake, Ind.: Light and Life Press, 1981.

———. *China's Four Sons*. Winona Lake, Ind.: Light and Life Pr., 1965.

Winslow, Ruth. *The Mountains Sing: God's Love Revealed to Taiwan Tribes*. Winona Lake, Ind.: Light and Life Press, 1984.

Winters, Peg. *Lab Brevities*. Winona Lake, Ind.: Light and Life Press, 1954.

Wiseman, Peter. *Purity and Power, Or, Sanctification at Pentecost*. Chicago: Christian Witness, 1900.

———. *Scriptural Sanctification*. Kansas City MO: Beacon Hill, 1951.

Wolfe, Karl G. "A History of the Founding of the Free Methodist Day-Schools in Southern California," 1999.

Wolfe, Mary-Elsie. "A Strategy for Mobilizing Integrated Local and Global Ministry in Free Methodist Congregations,with an Emphasis on Gateway Cities (urban Hubs for Unreached People Groups)," 2005.

Wood, J. *Perfect Love, Or, Plain Things for Those Who Need Them: Concerning the Doctrine, Experience, Profession, and Practice of Christian Holiness*. Oceanside Calif.: Standard of Zion Publications, 1996.

———. *Purity and Maturity*. Kansas City Mo.: Beacon hill Press, 1944.

Wood, J A, and W Roberto. Adell. *El perfecto amor: una explicaciÃ3n de la doctrina, la experienca, la profesiÃ3n y la practica de la santidid Cristiana*. Chiquimula, Guatemala: Mision de Los Amigos, 1927.

Woodruff, D O, Charles Duncombe, Aaron P Hammond, William. Hurd, Hurd Family., Thomas O'Callahan, Clarissa Hurd. Charles Clarissa Hurd Woodruff, et al. *D.O. Woodruff Papers*, 1836.

Woods, Dale A. *East Michigan's Great Adventure: A History of the East Michigan Conference of the Free Methodist Church, 1884-1984*. [Place of publication not identified]: East Michigan Conference of the Free Methodist Church, 1984.

———. *Tall Timber, Deep Roots: Autobiography of Dale A. Woods*. [Flint, Mich.?]: [D.A. Woods], 1989.

Woods, Dale Arthur. "Narrative Pastoral Leadership Pastor and People Working Together." Asbury Theological Seminary, 1998. http://place.asburyseminary.edu/ecommonsatsdissertations/143/.

Woodworth, Ralph. *Light in a Dark Place: The Story of Chicago's Oldest Rescue Mission*. Winona Lake, Ind.: Light and Life Press, 1978.

Worbois, Lois E. *The Thorn*. Winona Lake, Ind.: Light and Life Press, 1977.

Yamada, Miyoko. "The Pacific Coast Japanese Conference of the Free Methodist Church. (Book, 1966) [WorldCat.org]." Fuller Theological Seminary, 1966. http://www.worldcat.org/title/pacific-coast-japanese-conference-of-the-free-methodist-church/oclc/28961550&referer=brief_results.

Yardy, Jessie. *AadarsÃ¡ Khristi Grihajivana = Rearing a distinctive Christian family*. [New Delhi, India?] (31 Gurunanaka Nagar, Pune-2): Jivani Vacana Sahityalaya, 1966.

Yoder, Tamra., Dean. Smidderks, Free Methodist Church of North America, Department of Christian Education, Department of World Missions, Women's Missionary Fellowship International, Free Methodist Church of North America., et al. *The Great Discovery*. Winona Lake, Ind.: Light and Life Press, 1987.

Young, Brenda Mason. *Grace and Truth: Finding Balance in the Christian Life*. Uhrichsville, OH: Barbour Publishing Inc, 2013.

Young, Charles. *Seeds for Life: A Guide for New Believers, Leaders Guide*. Winona Lake, IN: Light and Life Press, 1991.

"Young Teen Student." Winona Lake IN: Light and Life Press, 1969.

"Young Teen. 1-16, No. 4." Winona Lake IN: Light and Life Press, 1953.

Your Church and Education: Christian Education Handbook of the Free Methodist Church. Winona Lake, Indiana: Commission on Christian Education, 1941.

"Youth in Action. (Journal, Magazine, 1900s) [WorldCat.org]," n.d. http://www.worldcat.org/title/youth-in-action/oclc/3970324&referer=brief_results.

Z.T. Gerganoff, Ralph Stevens Gerganoff, Stoyan T Gerganoff, and Zdravko T Gerganoff. *Z.T. Gerganoff Architectural Drawings*, 1928.

Zahniser, Arthur De France, and John B Easton. *History of the Pittsburgh Conference of the Free Methodist Church*. [Place of publication not identified]: [publisher not identified] Free Methodist Pub. House), 1932.

Zahniser, Clarence Howard. *Earnest Christian; Life and Works of Benjamin Titus Roberts*. [Place of publication not identified], 1957.

Zeeland Free Methodist Church. *History of the Zeeland Free Methodist Church, 1906-1981*. Zeeland, Mich.: The Church, 1981.

Content by Subject

Based on Library of Congress Subject Headings

Free Methodist Bibliography

A Brief history of Holiness Movement missions, 1899-1959. (1948). BOOK, Athens, Ont.: Y.P.M.S.

Ablard, G. C. (1981). The history and growth of the Winstanley Free Methodist Church, Wigan, Lancashire, England (THES). Western Evangelical Seminary.

Ablard, M., Baker, J., & Club, C. L. (1988). Discovery time : recreation fun, creativity fair, social event ; trailblazer ; grades 3 and 4 ; year one. BOOK, Winona Lake, Ind.: Light and Life Press.

Action. (1981). JFULL, Winona Lake, IN: for Aldersgate Publication Association by Light and Life Press.

Activity Time. (1969). GEN, Marion Ind.: Wesley Press.

Adams, F. A. (1999). A case study of the Elim Farm Project of the Filipino Free Methodist Church (Thesis). Trinity Evangelical Divinity School.

Adams, P. L. (2014). The lessons I've learned in politics. ELEC. Retrieved from http://place.asburyseminary.edu/ecommonsatschapelservices/

Ahern, A. A. (1965). Luke : leader's guide. BOOK, Winona Lake, Ind.: Light and Life Press.

Ahlstrom, S. (1972). A religious history of the American people. BOOK, New Haven: Yale University Press.

Aldersgate Dialogue Series. (n.d.). GEN, Winona Lake IN: Light and Life Press.

Aldersgate Doctrinal Studies. (n.d.). GEN, Winona Lake, IN: Light and Life Press.

Aldersgate Graded Curriculum. (n.d.). GEN, Winona Lake, IN: Light and Life Press.

Aldersgate Publications Association. (1938). The Railroad evangelist. JFULL. Winona Lake, Ind.: Light and Life Press.

Aldersgate Publications Association, & Association., A. P. (n.d.). Young teen study guide. JFULL, Winona Lake, Ind.: Light and Life Press.

Alexander, J. (1947). Thoughts from the sea. BOOK, Winona Lake, Ind.: Young Peoples Missionary Society.

All-Bible Graded Series. (n.d.). GEN, Winona Lake, IN: Light and Life Press.

Allen, M. S. (1898). From west to east, or, The Old world as I saw it : being a description of a journey from California to the Holy Land and Egypt, by the way of England, France, Switzerland and Italy. BOOK, Chicago, IL: Free Methodist Pub. House.

Altopp, D. P. (1981). A study of sexual attitudes, sexual behaviors, and the religiosity of high school students in Free Methodist church youth groups (THES). Southern Illinois University at Carbondale.

America., F. M. C. of N., & Action., C. on S. (1982). Servanthood : a manual. JFULL, Urbana, IL: The Council.

America., F. M. C. of N., America., W. M. C. (or C. of, Free Methodist Church of North America, America., F. M. C. of N., America., W. M. C. (or C. of, Light and Life Press, … Wesleyan Methodist Connection of America. (1951). Hymns of the living faith. MUSIC, Winona Lake, Ind.: Light and Life Press.

America., F. M. C. of N., Association., A. P., Free Methodist Church of North America, Aldersgate Publications Association, America., F. M. C. of N., & Association., A. P. (1971). Discovery. Discovery. JFULL, Winona Lake, Ind.: Light and Life Press [etc.].

America., F. M. C. of N., Bishops., B. of, Free Methodist Church of North America, & Board of Bishops. (1998). Pastor's handbook. BOOK, Board of Bishops, Free Methodist Church of North America.

America., F. M. C. of N., Conference., G., Free Methodist Church of North America, & General Conference. (1910). Free Methodist hymnal. MUSIC, Chicago: Free Methodist Pub. House.

America., F. M. C. of N., Conference., O., Free Methodist Church of North America, & Oregon Conference. (n.d.). Oregon Conference connection. Oregon Conference Connection. JFULL, OR: Free Methodist Church of North America, Oregon Conference.

America, F. M. C. N., & Maryland-Virginia Conference. (n.d.). The news-herald. The News-Herald. JFULL, Reisterstown, MD: Free Methodist Church, Maryland-Virginia Conference.

America, F. M. C. of N. (n.d.-a). Minutes of the annual conferences of the Free Methodist Church. CONF, Rochester, N.Y.: "The Earnest Christian" Print.

America, F. M. C. of N. (n.d.-b). Sunday school journal. JFULL, Winona Lake, Ind.: Dept. of Sunday Schools, Free Methodist Headquarters.

America, F. M. C. of N. (1864). Minutes of the Annual Conferences. CONF, Rochester, N.Y.: Earnest Christian Office.

America, F. M. C. of N. (1879). The annual minutes. JFULL, Chicago: Free Methodist Pub. House.

America, F. M. C. of N. (1891). Light and life primary. JFULL, Winona, Lake, Ind.: Light and Life Press.

America, F. M. C. of N. (1901). A digest of Free Methodist law; or, Guide in the administration of the discipline of the Free Methodist church ... BOOK, Chicago, Ill.: Free Methodist Pub. House.

America, F. M. C. of N. (1915). Doctrines and discipline of the Free Methodist Church. BOOK, Chicago, Ill.: Free Methodist Pub. House.

America, F. M. C. of N. (1935). The Y.P.M.S. story of Winona Lake. BOOK, Winona Lake, Ind.: Light and Life Press.

America, F. M. C. of N. (1950). God is calling you to minister. BOOK, Winona Lake, Ind.: Free Methodist Church of North America.

America, F. M. C. of N. (1951a). Conference minutes of the Free Methodist Church of North America. CONF, Winona Lake, IN: Free Methodist Pub. House.

America, F. M. C. of N. (1951b). Y. P. M. S. and W. M. S. Conference Missionary Convention : March 15 thru 18, 1951. BOOK, Winona Lake, Ind.: Free Methodist Church of North America.

America, F. M. C. of N. (1956). Records of the Free Methodist Church of North America (JFULL). Winona Lake, Ind: Free Methodist Pub. House.

America, F. M. C. of N. (1960). Yearbook of the Free Methodist Church around the world. JFULL, Winona Lake, Ind: Free Methodist Pub. House.

America, F. M. C. of N. (1967). Free Methodist Church, 1860-1978. BOOK, Sun City, Ariz.: Ecumenism Research Agency.

America, F. M. C. of N. (1970). Doctrines and discipline of the Free Methodist Church of North America. BOOK, Winona Lake, Ind.: Free Methodist Pub. House.

America, F. M. C. of N. (1971a). Discovery for juniors. JFULL, Marion, Ind.: Wesley Press, for the Aldersgate Publications Association.

America, F. M. C. of N. (1971b). Yearbook. JFULL, Winona Lake, Ind: Free Methodist Pub. House.

America, F. M. C. of N. (1974). One in love and mission : Winona '74, one way to a whole world, General Conference of the Free Methodist Church, June 24-July 1, 1974, Winona Lake, Indiana. CONF.

America, F. M. C. of N. (1983). Shoes, snakes, and shelves : missionary stories from Asia. BOOK, Winona lake, Ind.: Light and Life Press.

America, F. M. C. of N. (1990). The book of discipline, 1989. The Book of discipline. BOOK, Winona Lake, Ind.: Free Methodist Pub. House.

America, F. M. C. of N. (1999). Working together in the 21st century : the misison of the Free Methodist Church is to make known to all people everywhere God's call to wholeness through forgiveness and holiness in Jesus Christ, and to invite into membership and to equip for ministry. BOOK, Indianapolis, In: Free Methodist Communications.

America, F. M. C. of N. (2004). 2003 book of discipline. BOOK, Indianapolis, Ind.: Free Methodist Publishing House.

America, F. M. C. of N., & Bishops, B. of. (1980). Lay delegate's handbook. BOOK, Free Methodist Church of North America.

America, F. M. C. of N., & Bishops, B. of. (1988). Five Bishops speak to the church : foundations, building for the new day. BOOK, Winona Lake, Ind.: Board of Bishops, Free Methodist Church of North America.

America, F. M. C. of N., & Board, G. M. (1979). Missions heartbeat, '79. BOOK, Winona Lake, Ind.: Free Methodist Church of North America.

America, F. M. C. of N., & Committee, P. (1945). The glow of fifty years : a brief history of the Oregon Conference of the Free Methodist Church. BOOK, Winona Lake, Ind.: Free Methodist Church of North America.

America, F. M. C. of N., & Communication, W. M. (1972). "Communicating our United World Mission for Christ" : minister's manual. BOOK, Winona Lake, Ind.: Free Methodist Church of North America.

America, F. M. C. of N., & Conference, C. I. (1935). New and views. JFULL, Mulberry Grove, IL: Y.P.M.S. of the Central Illinois Conference.

America, F. M. C. of N., Conference, C. I., & Education, C. C. on C. (1938). Central Illinois advance. JFULL, Hillsboro, IL: Conference Committee on Christian Education.

America, F. M. C. of N., & Conference, E. M. (n.d.-a). The voice of the East Michigan Conference, Free Methodist Church. JFULL, Flint, MI: The Conference.

America, F. M. C. of N., & Conference, F. (1981). The Floridian challenge. JFULL, St. Petersburg, FL: Florida Conference, Free Methodist Church.

America, F. M. C. of N., & Conference, G. (n.d.-b). Quadrennial report of the General Missionary Secretary. CONF, S.l.: s.n.

America, F. M. C. of N., & Conference, G. (n.d.-c). The Convocation daily. JFULL, Indianapolis, IN: The Conference.

America, F. M. C. of N., & Conference, G. (1950). A catechism of the Free Methodist Church. BOOK, Winona Lake, Ind.: Free Methodist Pub. House.

America, F. M. C. of N., & Conference, G. P. (n.d.-d). Great Plains Conference reaper. JFULL, McPherson, KS: The Conference.

America, F. M. C. of N., & Conference, I. (1974). Commemoratin one hundred years of progress of the Iowa Conference, Free Methodist Church, 1874-1974. BOOK, Des Moines, Iowa: Free Methodist Church, Iowa Conference.

America, F. M. C. of N., Conference, I., & Committee, D. J. (1949). Commemorating seventy-five years of progress of the Iowa Conference, Free Methodist Church : 1874-1949 seventy-sixth conference and camp meeting, August 3-14, 1949. BOOK, Iowa: [Iowa Conference?].

America, F. M. C. of N., & Conference, M.-I.-K. (n.d.-e). Sharing. JFULL, Minneapolis, MN: The Conference.

America, F. M. C. of N., & Conference, M.-I.-K. (n.d.-f). Super-vision. JFULL, Wessington Springs, SD: Minn-I-Kota Conference of the Free Methodist Church.

America, F. M. C. of N., & Conference, N. M. (n.d.-g). Annual session. JFULL, Mich.: The Conference.

America, F. M. C. of N., & Conference, O. (n.d.-h). Ohio Conference newsletter. Ohio Conference Newsletter. JFULL, Mansfield, OH: Ohio Annual Conference, Free Methodist Church of North America.

America, F. M. C. of N., & Conference, O. (1945). Jubilee service honoring Golden Anniversary of the Oregon Conference of the Free Methodist Church : Wednesday evening, 7:30 o'clock, July 11, 1945 ; Oregon Conference Camp Ground, Portland, Oregon. BOOK, Portland, Or.: Free Methodist Church of North America, Oregon Conference.

America, F. M. C. of N., & Conference, O. (1987a). Leadership orientation : Septiember 26, 1987, Salem, Oregon ; "planning for 'a new day' in Oregon". BOOK, Turner, Ore.: Oregon Conference, Free Methodist Church of North America.

America, F. M. C. of N., & Conference, O. (1995a). Connection, Oregon Conference : keeping Oregon's Free Methodists informed ; March-April 1995. BOOK, Turner, Or.: Oregon Conference of the Free Methodist Church.

America, F. M. C. of N., & Conference, O. (1995b). Leadership link. JFULL, Mansfield, OH: Ohio Conference, Free Methodist Church.

America, F. M. C. of N., Conference, O., Free Methodist Church of North America, & Oregon Conference. (n.d.). Annual reports of the Oregon Annual Conference. JFULL, Turner, Ore.: Oregon Conference Free Methodist Church of North America.

America, F. M. C. of N., & Conference, P. (n.d.-i). The Pittsburgh Conference herald. JFULL, Apollo, PA: The Conference.

America, F. M. C. of N., Conference, P. N., & Board, C. M. (n.d.). On waves of faith. JFULL, Seattle, WA: Conference Mission Board, Pacific Conference of the Free Methodist Church of North America].

America, F. M. C. of N., & Conference, S. (n.d.-j). The Susquehanna advance. JFULL, Syracuse, NY: The Conference.

America, F. M. C. of N., & Conference, T. (1960). The Texas Conference of the Free Methodist Church its origin and present churches. BOOK, TX: The Conference.

America, F. M. C. of N., & Conference, W. V. (1987b). West Virginia Conference echoes. JFULL, St. Morgantown, WV: The Conference.

America, F. M. C. of N., & Cryderman, W. L. (1983). Songs for renewal. MUSIC, Winona Lake, Ind.: Light and Life Press.

America, F. M. C. of N., Department, B., & Ligth and Life Press. (n.d.). Just Between Us. JFULL.

America, F. M. C. of N., & Education, C. on C. (1961). Let's teach. BOOK, Winona Lake, Ind.: Light and Life Press.

America, F. M. C. of N., & Education, C. on C. (1986). Lay leadership training handbook. BOOK, Winona Lake, Ind.: Free Methodist Church of North America.

America, F. M. C. of N., Education, C. on C., & Training, D. of S. (1953). Better workers for your church. BOOK, McPherson, Kan.: Free Methodist Church of North America.

America, F. M. C. of N., Education, C. on C., & Training, D. of S. (1955). Service training in your church. BOOK, McPherson, Kan.: Free Methodist Church of North America.

America, F. M. C. of N., Education, C. on C., & Training, D. of S. (1958). Do-it-yourself plans for service training. BOOK, McPherson, Kan.: Free Methodist Church of North America.

America, F. M. C. of N., & Education, D. of C. (1989). What is a Free Methodist? BOOK, Winona Lake, Ind.: Department of Christian Education, Free Methodist Church of North America.

America, F. M. C. of N., Education, D. of C., Board, G. M., & International, W. M. F. (1981). All god's children : stories from Central Africa. BOOK, Winona Lake, Ind.: Light and Life Press.

America, F. M. C. of N., Education, D. of C., Board, G. M., & International, W. M. F. (1982). Island adventures : treasures in Dominican and Pierre, a boy from Haiti. BOOK, Winona Lake, Ind.: Light and Life Press.

America, F. M. C. of N., & Fettke, T. (1989). The hymnal for worship & celebration : containing Scriptures from the New American Standard Bible, Revised Standard Version, the Holy Bible, New International Version, the New King James Version. MUSIC, Irving, Tex.: Word Music.

America, F. M. C. of N., & Growth, D. of E. and C. (1980). Reach out in love. Winona Lake, Ind.: Light and Life Press.

America, F. M. C. of N., & Hart, E. P. (1908). A digest of Free Methodist law : or, Guide in the administration of the discipline of the Free Methodist church. BOOK, Chicago: Free Methodist Pub. House.

America, F. M. C. of N., & Houser, T. (1970). Foreign mission statistical reports of the Free Methodist Church, 1864-1969. BOOK, Winona Lake, IN.: General Missionary Board.

America, F. M. C. of N., & Institutions, A. of F. M. E. (n.d.). Heart & mind. Heart & Mind. JFULL, Indianapolis, IN: Association of Free Methodist Educational Institutions.

America, F. M. C. of N., & International, W. M. (1997). Trend analysis : number of women serving on Conference Boards and Committees, Free Methodist Church of North America, 1991-1996. BOOK, Indianapolis, IN: Women's Ministries International.

America, F. M. C. of N., & Kendall, W. S. (1955). From age to age, my church, a living witness. BOOK, Winona Lake, Ind.: Free Methodist Church of North America.

America, F. M. C. of N., & Livermore, P. (1996). Foundations of a living faith : the catechism of the Free Methodist Church. BOOK, Indianapolis, IN: Light and Life Communications.

America, F. M. C. of N., & Mission, G. C. for C. in. (1970). What is a Free Methodist? BOOK, Winona Lake, Ind.: General Council for Church in Mission, Free Methodist Church.

America, F. M. C. of N., & Missions, C. on. (n.d.). Report of the General Missionary Secretary. Report of the General Missionary Secretary. JFULL, Winona Lake, Ind.: General Missionary Secretary.

America, F. M. C. of N., & Missions, D. of W. (1987). World net. JFULL, Winona Lake, IN: Free Methodist Church, Dept. of World Missions.

America, F. M. C. of N., & Outreach, D. of E. (n.d.). Distinguished disciples : a new world of opportunity. BOOK, Winona Lake, IN: Free Methodist Church Headquarters.

America, F. M. C. of N., & Outreach, D. of E. (1969). North Michigan Conference survey : requested by the North Michigan Conference and conducted during the conference year 1967-68. BOOK, Winona Lake, Ind.: Dept. of Evangelistic Outreach, Free Methodist Church.

America, F. M. C. of N., Society, G. W. M., & International, G. W. M. F. (1897). The Missionary tidings. JFULL, Winona Lake, Ind.: General Woman's Missionary Fellowship International of the Free Methodist Church.

America, F. M. C. of N., & Society, W. F. M. (1899). Missionary tidings. JFULL, Chicago, Ill.: Woman's Foreign Missionary Society of the Free Methodist Church.

America, F. M. C. of N., & Society, W. M. (n.d.). Historical record of fifty years, 1899-1949 : Women's Missionary Society of Southern California Conference, Free Methodist Church. BOOK.

America, F. M. C. of N., & Society, W. M. (1931). Woman's Missionary Society of the Free Methodist Church, ninth quadrennial meeting : Greenville, Illinois, June 11-22, 1931. BOOK, Chicago, Ill.: Woman's Missionary Society.

America, F. M. C. of N., & Society, W. M. (1955). The Woman's Missionary Society of the Free Methodist Church, fifteenth quadrennial meeting : June 8-18, 1955, Winona Lake, Indiana. BOOK, Winona Lake, Ind.: Woman's Missionary Society.

America, F. M. C. of N., & Society, W. M. (1957). The living faith in Japan. BOOK, Winona Lake, Ind.

America, F. M. C. of N., & Training, C. B. of M. (1958). Recent books : a quarterly review for ministers. JFULL, Winona Lake, IN: Free Methodist Church of North America, Central Board of Ministerial Training.

America, F. M. C. of N., & Van Valin, C. E. (1986). Pastor's handbook of the Free Methodist Church. BOOK, Winona Lake, IN: Light and Life Press.

America, G. C. of the F. M. C. of N., Missions, C. on, & Missions, F. M. W. (1963). Quinquennial report of Free Methodist World Missions. CONF, Winona Lake, Ind.: Light and Life Press.

America, R. F. M. C. of N. (1960). Discipline of the Reformed Free Methodist Church. BOOK, Perryopolis, Pa.: Sound of the Trumpet Ministries.

American Free Methodist Mission. (n.d.). Praise and prayer : giving information of the work of the American Free Methodist Mission in China. JFULL, Kaifeng, Honan, China: American Free Methodist Mission.

Anderson, A. (1920). African jungle. BOOK, Anderson Ind.: Gospel Trumpet Co.

Anderson, A. (1931). Ukanya : life story of an African girl. BOOK, Anderson, Ind.: Warner Press.

Anderson, A. (1938). Nkosi : story of an African chief's son. BOOK, Anderson, In.: Warner Press.

Anderson, D. (1966). Man of compassion, Carl Eric Anderson. Essex Junction, Vt.: Roscoe Printing House.

Anderson, D. (1989). I have you in my heart : the delights of overseas ministry. BOOK, Indianapolis, Ind.: Wesley Press.

Anderson, M. (1985). The school in the vale : a history of Oakdale Christian High School. BOOK.

Anderson, M. (1988). Just over the hill : my four-score-plus years under God. BOOK, Gerry, NY: M. Anderson.

Andrews, E. A. (n.d.). A Symposium on instrumental music in public worship. BOOK, Chicago, Ill.: Free Methodist Pub. House.

Andrews, E. A. (1926). Reminiscent musings. BOOK, Spring Arbor MI: E.A. Andrews.

Andrews, E. A. (2005). Musings on self-deception. BOOK, Chicago, Ill.: Charles Edwin Jones.

Andrews, R. F. (n.d.). The web of emptiness. BOOK, Winona Lake, IN: Light & Life Hour.

Andrews, R. F. (1979). When you need a friend. BOOK, Winona Lake, Ind.: Light and Life Media, Dept. of Communications, Free Methodist Church of North America.

Angel, E., & Buswell, R. C. (1982). At ease under pressure : James, I, II Peter leader's guide. BOOK, Winona Lake, IN: Light and Life Press.

Antista, V. J. (1988). So it goes in America. BOOK, Winona Lake, IN: Light and Life Press.

Archer, A. C. (1930). The man with a thorn in his flesh. BOOK, Medford, Ore.: Schmul Pub. Co.

Archives, S. P. U. (1950). Free Methodist Church records and publications (UNPB).

Arksey, L. (2011). A mission boyhood in Mozambique. BOOK, S.l.: Tornado Creek.

Arnold's commentary : international Sunday school lessons. (1895). JFULL, Winona Lake, Ind: Light and Life Press.

Arnold's practical commentary on the International Sunday School lessons uniform series for 1949 : a practical help for all who use the uniform lessons in the Sunday School, or who desire to do individual Bible study ... (1947). BOOK, Winona Lake, Ind.: Light and Life Press.

Arnold's practical Sabbath school commentary on the international lessons. (1895). JFULL, Winona Lake, Ind.: Light and Life Press.

Arnold, H. (1924). Under southern skies : reminiscences in the life of Mrs. Adelia Arnold. BOOK, Atlanta Ga.: Repairer Pub.

Arthur, W. (1900). The tongue of fire, or, The true power of Christianity. BOOK, Winona Lake, Ind.: Light and Life Press.

Asher, M. G. (1955). Saints alive! BOOK, New York: Vantage Press.

Association, A. P. (n.d.-a). Junior teacher. JFULL, Winona Lake, Ind.: Light and Life Press.

Association, A. P. (n.d.-b). Young teen teacher. JFULL, Winona Lake, Ind.: Light and Life Press.

Association, A. P. (1975a). Explorer 1. JFULL, Winona Lake, Ind.: Light and Life Press.

Association, A. P. (1975b). Explorer 2. JFULL, Winona Lake, Ind.: Light and Life Press.

Atkinson, D. (1970). A study of methods used in the establishment and growth of selected churches in the Pacific Northwest Conference of the Free Methodist Church. BOOK.

Augustus L and Jennie D Hoffman Foundation, Frey, J. D., Clark, H. S., Dean, B. L., Partch, L. M., Garrett, H. P., ... Lincoln First Bank of Rochester. (1979). Hoffman Foundation Wayne County history scholarship essays : submitted for 1979 scholarship awards. BOOK.

Augustus L and Jennie D Hoffman Foundation, Miller, V., Olson, E., Baynes, S. A., Sturges, M. C., Oakley, C., ... Chase Manhattan Bank. (1999). Hoffman Foundation Wayne County history scholarship essays : submitted for 1999 scholarship awards. BOOK.

Azusa Pacific University Graduate School of Theology, Free Methodist Center for Transformational Leadership, & Winslow, K. S. (2013). The Free Methodist newsletter. JFULL, Azusa, Calif.: Azusa Pacific University Graduate School of Theology.

Babcock, C. A. (1938). Life and labours of Chas. A. Babcock : with a brief sketch of early days in the district in which he was born. BOOK, Brockville, Ont.: Standard Publishing House.

Back Lane, United Free Methodist Church. (n.d.). ELEC.

Backenstoe, M. (1944). Triumphant living. Kutztown Pa.: Kutztown Pub. Co.

Bai, Z. (2005). Ran dian yi sheng : zhang zhe shi feng shi kuang yu xin dong xiang, Xianggang Xun li hui zhang zhe shi gong yan jiu. BOOK, Xianggang: Jidu jiao zhuo yue shi tuan.

Bailey, A., Christian Life Club, Boyd, J., Christian Life Club, Club., C. L., Bailey, A., ... Club., C. L. (1988). Trailblazer squadron activities ; year one, grades 3 and 4. BOOK, Winona Lake, Ind.: Light and Life Press.

Baker, F. (1957). Methodism and the love-feast. BOOK, London: Epworth Press.

Baker, H. (1945). Sackcloth and purple. Indianapolis, Ind.: Pilgrim Pub. House.

Baker, H. E. (n.d.). Springs of water. BOOK, Freeport, NY: Transylvania Bible School Press.

Baker, H. E. (1944a). Sparks from the anvil of truth. BOOK, East Liverpool, Ohio: The author.

Baker, H. E. (1944b). Travailing for souls. BOOK, Freeport, PA: Transylvania Bible School Press.

Baker, H. E. (1972a). The wardrobe of Christ. BOOK, Olean, N.Y.: H.E. Baker.

Baker, H. E. (1972b). Unlighted glory. BOOK, Freeport, Pa.: Fountain Press.

Baker, H. E. (1978). Degrees of the Spirit. BOOK, Freeport, Pa.: Fountain Press.

Baker, H. E. (1980). Where the corn grows tall. BOOK, Freeport, Pa.: Fountain Press.

Baker, M. C., & Theological Research Exchange Network. (1982). Concerns of pastoral ministry with a biblical perspective from the Gospel of Mark. ELEC.

Baldwin, H. (1907). Lessons for seekers of holiness : containing numerous quotations from Wesley, Fletcher, and other standard authors, and designed to aid such as are groaning after purity of heart in entering upon the. BOOK, Chicago: W.B. Rose.

Baldwin, H. (1911). Objections to entire sanctification considered. BOOK, Pittsburgh: Published for the author.

Baldwin, H. (1923). The fisherman of Galilee: a devotional study of the Apostle Peter. BOOK, New York; Chicago: Fleming H. Revell Co.

Baldwin, H. (1926). The carnal mind; a doctrinal and experimental view of the subject. BOOK, Chicago, Ill.: Free Methodist Pub. House.

Baldwin, H. A. (1912). The indwelling Christ. BOOK, Chicago: Free Methodist Pub. House.

Baldwin, H. A. (1919). Holiness and the human element. BOOK, Chicago: Free Methodist Pub. House.

Baldwin, H. A. (1927). The coming judgment, general and at the end of time. BOOK, Chicago, Ill.: Free Methodist Pub. House.

Baldwin, H. A. (1987). The coming judgment : general and at the end of time. BOOK, Salem, Ohio: Allegheny Publications.

Ballard Free Methodist Church. (1986). Ballard Free Methodist Church : 1986-87 directory. BOOK, Ballard (Seattle), Wash.: Ballard Free Methodist Church.

Ballard Free Methodist Church. (1989). Celebrating God's family : August 6, 1989. BOOK, Seattle, Wash.: Ballard Free Methodisct Church.

Ballew, J., Sutton, M., & Christian Life Club. (1988). Guide squadron activities ; year two, grades 5 and 6. BOOK, Winona Lake, Ind.: Light and Life Press.

Banks, S. (1975). Saints in work clothes. BOOK, Winona Lake, Ind.: Light and Life Press.

Barber, G. A. (1990). Records of the Free Methodist Church, Ferndale, Sullivan County, N.Y. BOOK.

Barker, J. H. J. (1975). This is the will of God : a study in the doctrine of entire sanctification as a definite experience. BOOK, Salem, Ohio: Schmul.

Barnett, L. P. (1965). Yorokobi no otozure. BOOK, Rosanjerusu: Rosanjerusu Furi Mesojisuto Kyokai.

Barron's profiles of American colleges : an in-depth study. (1971). BOOK, Woodbur, NY: Barrons' Educational Series Inc.

Bartlette, W. (1971). Ethics, real or relative? : an inquiry into the place of Christianity in world ethical philosophies. BOOK, New York: Vantage Press.

Bastian, D. N. (n.d.). Leading the local church : for members of the official board. BOOK, Winona Lake, Ind.: Light and Life Press.

Bastian, D. N. (1963). The mature church member. BOOK, Winona Lake, Ind.: Light and Life Press.

Bastian, D. N. (1964). Galatians : leader's guide. BOOK, Winona Lake, Ind.: Light and Life Press.

Bastian, D. N. (1973). Temptations and what to do about them. BOOK, Winona Lake, IN: Free Methodist Church.

Bastian, D. N. (1977). Along the way. BOOK, Winona Lake, Ind.: Light and Life Press.

Bastian, D. N. (1978a). Belonging! : adventures in church membership. BOOK Winona Lake, Ind.: Light and Life Press.

Bastian, D. N. (1978b). Cultivating church members : for Free Methodist pastors on y. BOOK, Winona Lake, IN: Light and Life Press.

Bastian, D. N. (1980). The joy of Christian fathering : five first-person accounts. BOOK, Winona Lake, Ind.: Light and Life Press.

Bastian, D. N. (1988). Counterfeit : the lie of living together unmarried. BOOK, Toronto: Light and Life Press Canada.

Bastian, D. N. (1995). Sketches of Free Methodism. BOOK, Indianapolis, Ind.: Light & Life Press.

Bastian, D. N., & Free Methodist Church of North America. (2008). Give it a rest. BOOK, Indianapolis, Ind.: Light and Life Communications.

Bastion, D. N., & Marston, L. R. (1978). Thumb-nail sketches of doctrinal patterns. BOOK, Winona Lake, Ind.: Light and Life Press.

Bates, G. (1981). Soul afire : life of J.W. Haley. BOOK, Winona Lake, Ind.: Light and Life Press.

Bates, G. E. (1975). A study of the processes of conflict resolution between a protestant mission and selected national churches overseas (THES).

Bates, G., Snyder, H. A., & Marston Memorial Historic Center. (2007). Soul searching the church : Free Methodism at 150 years. BOOK, Indianapolis, Ind.: Light & Life Communications.

Bauer, D. R. (1986). Gospel of the king : Matthew study guide. BOOK, Winona Lake, IN: Light and Life Press.

Baym, N. (2011). A History of American Women's Western Books, 1833-1928, 63–80. JOUR.

Be ye holy : a study of the teaching of Scripture relative to entire sanctification : with a sketch of the history and the literature of the Holiness Movement. (n.d.). [ICOMM].

Beazley, S. W. (1929). Revival gems : number three, a great collection in a modest book. MUSIC, Chicago: Samuel W. Beazley & Son.

Beegle, B. L. (n.d.). Panama and the Canal Zone. BOOK, Chicago: Woman's Missionary Society.

Beers, A. (1922). The romance of a consecrated life : a biography of Alexander Beers. Chicago: Free Methodist Pub. House.

Benson, M. C. (1967). Church library manual,. BOOK, Winona Lake, Ind.: Light and Life Press.

Betania, R., & America, F. M. C. of N. (1991). Rancho Betania news. JFULL, Nogales, AZ: Free Methodist Mexican Missions.

Bible Lesson Stories. 1-31, No.4. (1930). GEN, Providence, Rhode Island: Religious Press.

Bible Stories for Threes. (1961). GEN, Kansas City MO: Beacon Hill Press.

Bible Stories for Twos. (1964). GEN, Kansas City MO: Beacon Hill Press.

Bidwell, D. (1995). Leading lay ministers : a study of the relationship between leadership and factors associated with lay minister job satisfaction in the Fort Worth Free Methodist Church (THES).

Bilezikian, V. S. (1951). Apraham Hoja of Aintap. BOOK, Winona Lake, IN: Light and Life Press.

Binney, A. (1902). Binneys' Theological compend improved : containing a synopsis of the evidences, doctrines, morals and institutions of Christianity. BOOK, New York ; Cincinnati: Methodist Book Concern.

Black, H. (n.d.-a). Is the end of the age at hand. BOOK, Los Angeles, CA: H. Black.

Black, H. (n.d.-b). Prophecy sermons by a newsboy preacher. BOOK, Redlands, Calif.: Black.

Black, H. (n.d.-c). Revival sermons on Bible prophecy. BOOK, Los Angeles, CA: Harry Black.

Black, H. (n.d.-d). The Holy Ghost baptism : and seven other sermons on sin, salvation, and holiness. BOOK, Los Angeles, CA.

Black, H. (n.d.-e). The price of a revival and other sermons. BOOK, Los Angeles, CA: Harry Black.

Black, H. (n.d.-f). The rich man and Lazarus and other sermons. BOOK, Los Angeles, Calif.

Black, H. (1900a). Signs of his coming and other sermons. BOOK, Los Angeles, Calif.: Mrs. H. Black.

Black, H. (1900b). Sunday morning (soul food) sermons. BOOK, Los Angeles, Calif.: Black.

Black, H. (1932). From newsboy to preacher : the story of my life.

Black, H. (1936). Soul food messages. BOOK, Los Angeles, CA: Harry Black.

Black, H. (1952). Tribulation plagues are coming : evangelistic messages on Revelation. BOOK, Los Angeles: Harry Black.

Black, H. (1953a). Satan's masterpiece, the Antichrist : evangelistic messages on Revelation. BOOK, Los Angeles: Harry Black.

Black, H. (1953b). The four horses of the Apocalypse : evangelistic messages on Revelation. BOOK, Los Angeles, CA: Harry Black.

Black, H., & Office, P. N. (1940). The four horses of the Apocalypse : evangelistic messages on Revelation : (an expository and evangelistic message for each chapter in the book of Revelation). Book 1. Messages on Revelation Book 1. Messages on Revelation. BOOK, Los Angeles, Calif.: Prophetic News Office.

Black, J. (1950). "The Word of the Lord came unto me also." BOOK, Winona Lake, Ind.: Light and Life Press.

Blackie Buffalo and other stories of North American missions. (1967). BOOK, Winona Lake, Ind.: Light and Life Press.

Blews, R. (1939). Master workmen biographies of the deceased bishops of the Free Methodist Church. Winona Lake, Ind.: Light and Life Press.

Blews, R. (1960). Master workmen biographies of the late bishops of the Free Methodist Church during her first century, 1860-1960. Winona Lake, Ind.: Light and Life Press.

Bliss, E. (1910). The encyclopedia of missions : descriptive, historical, biographical, statistical. BOOK, New York ; London: Funk & Wagnalls Co.

Boileau, E. L. (1950). It occurred to me. . . BOOK, Winona Lake, Ind.: Department of Information and Stewardship, Free Methodist Church.

Bonney, R. B. (1981). A program of ministry training opportunities for the Kentucky-Tennessee Conference of the Free Methodist Church (THES).

Book Review Doctors, I Salute . Emilie Conklin. 92 pp. Winona Lake, Indiana. (1939). N Engl J Med New England Journal of Medicine, 221(2), 84. JOUR.

Bosco, N. (1968). Rye field to pulpit: The life story of Rev. N.A. Bosko. Picton , Ontario.

Boulder Daily Camera, Wendt, C., Wilkes, P., & Ruby, P. C. (1965). Focus Magazine. BOOK.

Bounds, E. M. (1946). Preacher and prayer. BOOK, Winona Lake, Ind.: Light and Life Press.

Bowell, G. (2014). Reflections and thoughts on a hymnal : The 1910 Free Methodist hymnal. BOOK, Gary E. Bowell.

Bowen, B. F. L. (1989) Progressive men and women of Kosciusko County, Indiana and 1903 plat maps. BOOK, Winona Lake, Ind. Light and Life Press.

Bowen, E. (1859). Slavery in the Methodist Episcopal Church. GEN, Auburn, NY: William J. Moses, printer,.

Bowen, E. (1871). History of the origin of the Free Methodist Church. BOOK, Rochester, N.Y.: B.T. Roberts.

Bownes, L. K. (1962). A study of the Christian day school movement in the Arizona-Southern California conference of the Free Methodist Church (Book, 1962) (ICOMM). Seatlle Pacific University.

Boyd, M. (1958). Flame of a century, what made it burn? : Radio messages on John Wesley and early Methodism. BOOK, Winona Lake, Ind.: World-Wide Gospel Broadcast.

Boyd, M. F. (n.d.). A more excellent way : radio messasges on the deeper spiritual life. BOOK, Winona Lake, IN: Light and Life Hour.

Boyd, M. F. (1940). Finding, enjoying and retaining God! BOOK, Winona Lake, Ind.: Light and Life Hour.

Boyd, M. F. (1946). Light and life hour, sixteen radio messages : world-wide gospel broadcast. BOOK, Winona Lake, Ind.: Light and Life Press.

Boyd, M. F. (1953). Honoring the Spirit : 18 radio messages on love and the Holy Spirit. BOOK, Winona Lake, Ind.: Light and Life Hour.

Boyd, M. F. (1964). To tell the world : thirty radio messages. BOOK, Winona Lake, Ind.: Light and Life Hour.

Boyd, M. F., Andrews, R. F., Choir, S. A. L. and L. S. L. and L., Marston Memorial Historical Center (Winona Lake, I. ., Choir, S. A. L. and L., & Center, M. M. H. (1968). Moments of memory. SOUND, Winona Lake, Ind.: The Center.

Boyd, M. F., & Hour, L. and L. (1949). Light and life hour, eighteen radio messages : world-wide gospel broadcast. BOOK, Apollo, Pa.: West Pub. Co.

Brandt, M. E. (1980). Henry and Emma Brandt : memorabelia. BOOK, McPherson, KS: Brandt Family.

Branson, W. T. (1892). Hymns and songs of worship. BOOK, Chicago: Free Methodist Pub. House.

Brauer, J. (1971). The Westminster dictionary of church history. BOOK, Philadelphia: Westminster Press.

Brause, D. (1979). Expanded ministry to adults : program guidelines. BOOK, Winona Lake, Ind.: Light and Life Press.

Bready, J. W. (1952). Faith and freedom : the roots of democracy. BOOK, Winona Lake, Ind.: Light and Life Press.

Bready, J. W., & American Tract Society. (1950). This freedom - whence? BOOK, Winona Lake, Ind.: Light and Life Press.

Brito B., I. (1975). Historia de la Iglesia Metodista Libre Dominicana. BOOK, Santo Domingo, D.N.: Editora Educativa Dominicana.

Brock, L. W. (1987). The life story of Rev. Lyle and Doris Brock : pioneer pastors of the Free Methodist Church in the West Kansas Conference and the California Conference. BOOK, Stanwood, WA.

Brodhead, C. A. S. (1908). Our Free Methodist missions in Africa, to April, 1907. BOOK, Pittsburgh: Aldine.

Brooks, P. F. (1969). The history of Pacific Northwest conference of the Free Methodist Church (THES).

Brooks Hill Free Methodist Church. (1974). Brooks Hill Free Methodist Church history : 80th year anniversary, 1894-1974. BOOK, Portland, Or.: Brooks Hill Free Methodist Church.

Brown, A. L., Secord, A. W., & White, E. C. (1946). A handbook for Sunday school workers. BOOK, Winona Lake, Ind.: Department of Sunday Schools, Christian Education Commission : Light and Life Press.

Brown, A. S. (1981). The local church in a Christian academic community a process for discovering and developing its identity, mission and ministry (Thesis). Asbury Theological Seminary.

Brown, Z. (1977). Aldersgate : the college of the warm heart. BOOK, Moose Jaw, Sask.

Brown, Z. M. (1981). Trail-blazers in Livingstone country : the story of Ronald and Margaret Collett. BOOK, Winona Lake, Ind.: Light and Life Press.

Buchanan, J. (1990). The development of ecclesiastical autonomy for the Free Methodist Chuch in Canada. BOOK, S.l.: s.n.

Bucke, E. (1964). The History of American Methodism. BOOK, New York: Abingdon Press.

Bundy, D. (1975). Keswick : a bibliographic introduction to the Higher Life Movements. Wilmore, Ky.: B.L. Fisher Library Asbury Theological Seminary.

Burgess, R. J. (1900). Winning others : studies in evangelism for everyone. BOOK, Winona Lake, Ind.: Light and Life Press.

Burgess, S. (1988). Dictionary of Pentecostal and charismatic movements. Grand Rapids, Mich.: Regency Reference Library.

Burritt, C. T., America, F. M. C. of N., & Society, W. M. (1952). A guide for missionary workers. BOOK, Winona Lake, Ind.: Womans' Missionary Society, Free Methodist Church.

Burritt, C. T., & Hogue, E. L. (1935). The story of fifty years. BOOK, Winona Lake, Ind.: Light and Life Press.

Burritt, E. G. (1927). The pupil and how to teach him. BOOK, Chicago: Light and Life Press.

Buswell, R. C. (1982). At ease under pressure : James, I, II Peter study guide. BOOK, Winona Lake, IN: Light and Life Press.

Calkins, P. J. (1968). A comparative investigation of levels of attainment in the development of the indigenous church principle on Latin American Free Methodist mission fields (THES).

Cameron, R. (1961). Methodism and society in historical perspective. BOOK, New York: Abingdon.

Campbell Free Methodist Seminary. (1913). Fourth catalogue, 1913-1914. BOOK, Greenville, Tex.: Greenville Print. Co.

Canada. (1927). The Free Methodist Church Act, 1927. BOOK, Ottawa: Acland, Law Printer to the King.

Canada, F. M. C. I., & Free Methodist Church. (1990). The Book of discipline. JFULL, Mississauga, Ont.: Light and Life Press Canada.

Canon, C. H., Cowsert, E. W., & Page L, R. (1983). History of the Pittsburgh Conference of the Free Methodist Church : Centennial Edition, 1883-1983. BOOK, Pittsburgh: Pittsburgh Conference.

Carpenter, A. (1926). Ellen Lois Roberts, Life and writings. A sketch. Chicago: Woman's Missionary Society.

Casberg, J. (1919). Dhatu and his friends. BOOK, Winona Lake, Indiana.

Cathey, N. (1980). The First Free Methodist Church of Seattle, Washington : centennial year, 1880-1980. BOOK.

Cathey, N. (2002). Sharing God's vision : 1982-2002. BOOK, Seattle, WA: Vision Press.

Cathey, N. G., Free Methodist Church of North America, & Pacific Northwest Conference. (1995). Free Methodist Church centennial : Pacific Northwest Conference, 1895-1995. BOOK, Seattle, Wa.: Free Methodist Church of North America, Pacific Northwest Conference.

Cattell, J. (1906). American men of science : a biographical directory. BOOK, Lancaster, Pa. ; New York: Science Pr. ; Bowker.

Cattell, J. (1948). Leaders in education : a biographical dictionary. Lancaster, Pa.: Science Press.

Centz, H. B. (1951). Prelude to Armageddon : shadows on the sundial. BOOK, Winona Lake, Ind.: Light and Life Press.

Chalker, G. I. (1904). Papers (UNPB).

Chapman, M. (1896). Mother Cobb, or, Sixty years' walk with God. Chicago: Arnold.

Chauke, H. W. M., & Houser, T. (2009). H.M. Chauke research of African Hlengwe people. BOOK.

Cheeseman, S. (1981). Eight Gates Beyond. BOOK, Winona Lake, Ind.: Light and Life Press.

Cheeseman, S. (1984). Wee brown lambs. BOOK, Winona Lake, Ind.; Dept. of Evangelism and Church Growth: Free Methodist Church of North America.

Chesbro, S. K. J. (1900). Reopening the wells, a sermon. BOOK, Chicago, IL: Free Methodist Pub. House.

Chesbrough, S. K. J. (1983). Defence of Rev. B.T. Roberts, A.M., before the Genesee Conference of the Methodist Episcopal Church at Perry, N.Y., Oct. 13-21, 1858. BOOK, Buffalo: Clapp, Matthews & Co's Steam Printing House.

Christian-Life Graded Bible Lessons. (1948). GEN, Winona Lake, IN: Light and Life Press.

Christianity, F. for S. (1999). Discovery : basic belief studies for Free Methodists. BOOK, Indianapolis, Ind.: Light and LIfe Communications in cooperation with Bristol House.

Church, A. F. M. (1982). A century for Christ in the community, 1882-1982, Alma Free Methodist Church, September 4-5, 1982. BOOK, Alma, Neb.: Journal Print.

Church, F. M. (n.d.). Directory of Free Methodist Church. Directory of Free Methodist Church. JFULL, Three Oaks, Mich.: The Church.

Church, F. M. (1967). The dedication of Free Methodist Church, 397 Dorchester Road South, Niagara Falls, Ontario, October 8th, 1967. BOOK.

Church, F. M. (1976). History of the Free Methodist Church, Petersburg, Indiana, 1924-1976. BOOK, [Petersburg, Ind.]: [The Church].

Church, F. M. (1980). Free Methodist Church, McPherson, Kansas, 1880-1980 : 1883, 1917, 1955, 1980. BOOK, McPherson, Kan.: Free Methodist Church.

Church, F. M. (1983). Faith and life of a Free Methodist. BOOK, Newberg, Ore.: Free Methodist Church.

Church, H. (1987). Light is shining in the Africa I know. BOOK, Winona Lake, Ind.: Light and Life Press.

Church, H. G. (2002). Theological education that makes a difference : church growth in the Free Methodist Church in Malawi and Zimbabwe. BOOK, Blantyre, Malawi: Christian Literature Association in Malawi.

Church, W., & Crusaders, C. Y. (1969). Crusaders guide for young teens. BOOK, Winona Lake, Ind.: Light and Life Press.

Church, W., & Crusaders, C. Y. (1970). God and church -- doctrine : for young teens in all local churches. BOOK, Winona Lake, Ind.: Light and Life Press.

City Planning Department of Boulder Colorado. (1986). 2150 Pearl Street. BOOK, Boulder, Colorado: Boulder City Planning Department.

Clark, E. (1949). The small sects in America. BOOK, New York: Abingdon-Cokesbury Press.

Clark, E. (1952a). An album of Methodist history. BOOK, New York: Abingdon-Cokesbury Press.

Clark, E. (1952b). Who's who in methodism. BOOK, Chicago: A.N. Marquis.

Clark, J. P. (1990). A five year strategy of church growth for Wesley Free Methodist Church (THES).

Clarke, E. (1915). Mary E. Chynoweth : missionary to India. BOOK, Chicago: Woman's Foreign Missionary Society of the Free Methodist Church.

Clem, M., & Bailey, R. Q. (1980). The servant story : the Gospel of Mark : leader's guide. BOOK, Winona Lake, Ind.: Published for the Aldersgate Publications Association by Light and Life Press.

Clemente, D. W. (2002). Filipino group life : a contextual study of small groups in Free Methodist congregations (THES).

Cleveland Ohio Free Methodist Church. (1913). Year book reference manual and directory of the Free Methodist Church, Bridge Avenue and West 45th Street, 1913-1914. BOOK, Cleveland, OH.

Climenhaga, G. G. (1975). The call was clear. BOOK, Victoria, B.C.: Climenhaga.

Climenhaga, G. G., & Mercer, J. (2010). The call was clear : superintendents of the Free Methodist Church in the Canadian prairie provinces, 1901-1995. BOOK, Canada.

Clyde, A. A. (1954). A study of minimum requirements in religious education for Free Methodist missionaries (THES).

Clyde, A. A., America, F. M. C. of N., & Society, W. M. (1979). International cookbook. BOOK, Winona Lake, Ind.: Light and Life Press.

Coates, G., America, F. M. C. of N., & Conference, G. (2003). Passion of the founders : General Conference 2003. BOOK, Indianapolis, Ind.: Free Methodist Light and Life Communications.

Coates, G. R. (2015). Politics strangely warmed : political theology in the Wesleyan spirit. BOOK, Eugene, Ore.: Wipf & Stock Publishers.

Cochrane, R. L. (1960). Years of beginnings : Washinton Conference, 1880-1896 ; outline. BOOK.

Cockroft, B., Club, C. L., Staneart, F., & Christian Life Club. (1988). Guide chapel plans ; year one. BOOK, Winona Lake, Ind.: Light and Life Press.

Cockroft, M., & Cottrill, K. (1984). Expanded ministry to children : program guidelines. BOOK, Winona Lake, Ind.: Light and Life Press.

College, M. C. of G., & Kline, G. E. (1940). The Wesleyan message, its Scriptures and historical bases : addresses delivered at the 12th Annual Ministers' Conference, Greenville College, April 10-14, 1939. CONF, Winona Lake, IN: Light and Life Press.

Colorado Free Methodism. (1895). JFULL, Howard, Colo.: A.J. McKinney.

Compton, H. (1988). Through eyes of love : ventures of faith in India. BOOK, Winona Lake, Ind.

Conable, F. (1876). History of the Genesee Annual Conference of the Methodist Episcopal Church : from its organization by Bishops Asbury and M'Kendree in 1810, to the year 1872. BOOK, New York: Nelson & Phillips.

Conference, F. M. W., & Kline, F. J. (1960). Asia Fellowship Conference, April 19-28, Osaka, Japan : a compilation of reports, documents, interpretation. CONF, Winona Lake, Ind.: Continuing Committee of the Free Methodist World Fellowship. North American Division.

Conference, G. M. (1940). The Wesleyan message : addresses delivered at the 12th-14th sessions of the Ministers' Conference, Greenville College, 1939-1941. CONF, Winona Lake, Ind.: Light and Life P.

Conference, W. B. F. B., & America, F. M. C. of N. (n.d.). Notes. Notes. JFULL, [S.l.]: Warm Beach Family Bible Conference.

Conklin, E. (1938a). Doctors, I salute. BOOK, Winona Lake, Ind.: Light and Life Press.

Conklin, E. (1938b). Songs in the night. BOOK, Winona Lake, Ind.: Light and Life Press.

Conklin, E. C. (1939). Religion marches. BOOK, Winona Lake, Ind.: Printed for the author by Light and Life Press.

Cook, A. W. (1970). An analysis of the responsibilities and training of selected ministers in church business administration (ICOMM). East Tennessee State University.

Cook, E. D. (2005). Salt of the sea : a Navy chaplain's experience ashore and at sea. BOOK, Longwood, Fla.: Xulon Press.

Cook, E. D. (2010). Chaplaincy : being God's presence in closed communities : a Free Methodist history 1935-2010. BOOK, Bloomington, IN: AuthorHouse.

Cook, T. (1952). New Testament holiness. BOOK, London: Epworth Press.

Cooke, S. (1981). The handmaiden of the Lord, or, Wayside sketches. Chicago: Arnold.

Cooke, S. A. B. (1896). The handmaiden of the Lord, or, Wayside sketches. BOOK, Chicago: Shaw Pub. Co.

Cooke, S. A. B. (1983). Wayside sketches (abridged), or, The handmaiden of the Lord. BOOK, Salem, Ohio: Schmul Pub. Co.

Coolen, J., & Thunder Bay Branch of Ontario Genealogical Society. (2009). O'Connor Free Methodist Cemetery : grave marker transcriptions, OGS #5737, O'Connor Township, Thunder Bay District, Ontario. BOOK, Thunder Bay, Ont.: Ontario Genealogical Society, Thunder Bay Branch.

Coon, A. (1905). Life and labors of Auntie Coon. BOOK, Atlanta: Repairer Office.

Coon, H. A. (n.d.). Early Free Methodists. BOOK, Pueblo, Colo.: Mary Orem.

Cooper, R. E. (1976). A projected growth strategy for the Madras Free Methodist Church (THES).

Copeland, J. B. (2000). A strategy for relational evangelism at Skyline Family Fellowship (THES).

Cordell, B. (1948). Precious Pearl. BOOK, Winona Lake, Ind.: Light and Life Press.

Cordell, B. B. (1949). Blossoms from the flowery kingdom. BOOK, Winona Lake, Ind.: Light and Life Press.

Cox, B. E. (1963). Mwene of the Congo. BOOK, Winona Lake, Ind.: Light and Life Press.

Cox, B. E. (1998). Simply following : in all my journeying God went before. BOOK, Spring Arbor, Mich.: Saltbox Press.

Crandall, R. A. (1981). Ministry to persons : organization and administration. BOOK, Winona Lake, IN: Light and Life Press.

Cranston, R., & Cranston, C. (1983). Stars for the baliti tree : the story of Free Methodist missions in the Philippines. BOOK, Winona lake, Ind.: Published for Women's Missionary Fellowship International by Light and Life Press.

Cranston, R. J. (1984). A workable program of church growth for the Free Methodist Church of the Philippines (THES).

Crawford, D. L. (1993). Finding small healthy Free Methodist Churches in the state of Illinois (THES). Asbury Theological Seminary. Retrieved from http://place.asburyseminary.edu/ecommonsatsdissertations/75/

Crider, D. W. (1980). Development and rationale of theological education by extension of the Free Methodist Church in South Africa with a programmed text on pastoral theology for Africa (THES).

Cross, W. J. (1939). The great apostle and the great epistles ... BOOK, Winona Lake, Indiana: Free Methodist Pub. House.

Cryderman, L. (1999). Glory land : a memoir of a lifetime in church. BOOK, Grand Rapids, Mich.: Zondervan.

Cryderman, L. (2001). No swimming on Sunday : stories of a lifetime in church. BOOK, Grand Rapids, Mich.: Zondervan.

Cullum, D. R. (1991). What does it mean to be a Methodist? : an examination of denominational self-identity in John Wesley, the Methodist Episcopal Church and the Free Methodist Church (THES).

Cullum, D. R. (2002). Gospel simplicity : rhythms of faith and life among Free Methodists in Victorian America (THES).

Culumber, T. J. (1981). Church growth theology, strategy, and goals for the Department of Evangelism and church growth of the Free Methodist Church of North America (THES).

Curtiss, G. (1893). Manual of Methodist Episcopal Church history : showing the evolution of Methodism in the United States of America for the use of students and general readers. BOOK, New York: Hunt & Eaton.

Dake, V. A. (n.d.). Kindling watch-fires : choice extracts. BOOK, Waukesha, WI: Metropolitan Church Association.

Damon, A. J. (1988). A brief history of the Wisconsin Conference of the Free Methodist Church. BOOK.

Damon, C. M. (1900). Sketches and incidents, or reminiscences of interest in the life of the author. BOOK, Chicago: Free Methodist Pub. House.

Daniels, W. (1880). Illustrated history of Methodism in Great Britain and America, from the days of the Wesleys to the present time. BOOK, New York: Phillips & Hunt.

Daningburg, T. W. (2003). An equipping model applied to Valley Chapel Free Methodist Church (THES).

Davenport, M. S. (1996). Six ministry strategies for planting a seeker sensitive church (THES).

Davis, J. L., & rtMyette, P. E. (1960). Official Bible quiz text : the Gospel of Mark BOOK, Winona Lake, Ind.: Light and Life Press.

Davis, J. L., & Taylor, W. H. (1960). Let's learn Mark. BOOK, Winona Lake, IN: Light and Life Press.

Davis, L. (1953). Daddy is a layman : a true tale of laughs, loves and ladders. Los Angeles Calif.: Cowman Publications.

Davis, R. N. (1954a). Redeemed : a remarkable conversion in the heart of India : the story of Moses David, superintendent of the Eastern District. and evangelist, India Free Methodist Church ... BOOK, Winona Lake, Ind.: Woman's Missionary Society, Free Methodist Church.

Davis, R. N. (1954b). The Challenge in central India. BOOK, Winona Lake, Ind.: Women's Missionary Society, Free Methodist Church.

Davison Free Methodist Church. (n.d.). Directory of Davison Free Methodist Church. JFULL, Davison, Mich.: The Church.

Dawson, F. (1929). Life sketch and sermons of Rev. B.C. Dewey. Chicago Ill.: Free Methodist Pub. House.

Dawson, L. (1962). Vital faith. Seattle, WA: Printed by L & H Print. Co.

Day, B., Wesleyan Methodist Church of America, Christian Youth Crusaders, Church, W., America, W. M. C. of, & Crusaders, C. Y. (1970). Cadet trails. BOOK, Winona Lake, Ind.: Printed by Light and Life Press.

Dayton, D. (1971). The American Holiness movement a bibliographic introduction,. Wilmore, Ky.: B.L. Fisher Library Asbury Theological Seminary.

Dayton, W. T. (1960). Romans : leader's guide. BOOK, Winona Lake, Ind.: Light and Life Press.

De Voist, M. (1920). Foot-prints in my life, or, the story told in rhyme. BOOK.

De Voist, M. (1925). History of the East Michigan Conference of the Free Methodist Church. BOOK, Owosso, Mich.: Times Print Co.

Deemer, P. (1974). Ecumenical directory of retreat and conference centers. BOOK, Boston: Jarrow Press.

Degen, H. (2013). The guide to holiness. GEN, Wilmore, Ky. : Asbury Theological Seminary,.

DeGroot, A. T. (n.d.). American church records. BOOK, United States: Southwest Microfilm.

DeGroot, A. T., America, F. M. C. of N., God, C. of, Churches, F. of G. B., & Christ, U. F. of C. C. and C. of. (1979). Library of American church records series III : an introduction to the evangelicals. BOOK, Ecumenism Research Agency.

Delamarter, G. N. (1985). Pastoral support team manual. BOOK, Winona Lake, Ind.: Free Methodist Church of North America.

Demaray, D. (1958). Loyalty to Christ : sermons with prayers for the Easter season. BOOK, Grand Rapids: Baker Book House.

Demaray, D. (1959). A pulpit manual. BOOK, Grand Rapids: Baker Book House.

Demaray, D. (1964). Bible study source-book. BOOK, Grand Rapids, MI: Zondervan.

Demaray, D. (1972). Preacher aflame. BOOK, Grand Rapids, Mich.: Baker Book House.

Demaray, D. (1973). Pulpit giants : what made them great. BOOK, Chicago: Moody Press.

Demaray, D. (1974). The minister's ministries. BOOK, Winona Lake, Ind.: Light and Life.

Demaray, D. E. (1948). Papers. BOOK.

Demaray, D. E. (1958a). ' Amazing grace!" BOOK, Winona Lake, Ind.: Light and Life Press.

Demaray, D. E. (1958b). Basic beliefs : an introductory guide to Christian theology. BOOK, Grand Rapids: Baker Book House.

Demaray, D. E. (1961). Acts : leader's guide. BOOK, Winona Lake, Ind.: Light and Life Press.

Demaray, D. E. (1976). Alive to God through praise. BOOK, Winona Lake, Ind.: Light and Life Press.

Demaray, D. E. (1978). Near hurting people : the pastoral ministry of Robert Moffat Fine. BOOK, Winona Lake, Ind.: Light and Life Press

Demaray, D. E. (1985). The people called Free Methodist : snapshots. BOOK, Winona Lake, Ind.: Light and Life Press.

Demaray, D. E. (1990). An introduction to homiletics. BOOK, Indianapolis, Ind.: Light and Life Press.

Demaray, D. E. (1995). Laughter, joy and healing. BOOK, Indianapolis, Ind.: Light and Life Press.

Demaray, D. E. (2000). With His joy : the life and leadership of David McKenna. BOOK, Indianapolis, IN: Light & Life Communications.

Demaray, D. E., Free Methodist Church of North America, & General Leadership and Service Training Council. (1965). Alive to God through prayer : a manual on the practices of prayer. BOOK, Grand Rapids: Baker Book House.

Demaray, D. E., & Sun Liu, Y. (2009). Ji yao zhen li : Jidu jiao Weisili zong shen xue jian jie. BOOK, Gaoxiong Shi: Sheng guang shen xue yuan.

Demaray, K. (1965). Train up a child. BOOK, Winona Lake, IN: Light and Life Press.

DeMille, L. (1966). Black Gold : a story of Mozambique and Transvaal. BOOK, Winona Lake, Ind.: Light and Life Press.

DeMille, L. (1987). Prairie rose. BOOK, Winona Lake, IN: Light and Life Press.

DeMille, L., Hill, D., Abbott, G., Payne, P., & America, F. M. C. of N. (1984). Stories from Southern Africa. BOOK, Winona lake, Ind.: Light and Life Press.

Denniss, G. (1979). Free Methodist Hill, a centennial history : Bracebridge Free Methodist Church, 1879-1979. BOOK, Bracebridge, Ont.: Herald-Gazette.

Deratany, E. (1988). When God calls you. BOOK, Winona Lake, Ind.: Light and Life Press.

Deratany, E. (2007). Why fear? freedom from fear in the secret place. SOUND, Winona Lake, IN: Light and Life Press.

Derr, M. K. (2006). Suggs, Eliza G. Oxford: Oxford University Press.

DeShazer, J. (2012). Jacob DeShazer's personal testimony. ELEC, Wilmore, Ky.: DQB-LLC for the Marston Memorial Historical Center.

Developing Christian personality. (1970). BOOK, Published for Aldersgate Associates by Beacon Hill Press of Kansas City.

Dictionary of American biography. (1943). BOOK, New York: C. Scribner's Sons.

Dieter, M. E. (1973). Revivalism and Holiness (UNPB).

Discipline of the Missionary Bands of the World. (1926). BOOK, Indianapolis, IN: Grace Pub. House.

Discover your Bible : a course for persons who believe they should be getting more out of their Bible study. (1970). BOOK, Published for Aldersgate Associates by Beacon Hill Press of Kansas City.

Dolan, T. F. (1880). A bit of experience : showing the dealings of Godmanandthedevil with T.F. Dolan, convert from Romanism ; to which is added a review of the Methodist discipline and selections from Wesley, Clarke, Bramwell, Carvosso, and others. BOOK, Chicago: Baker & Arnold, Printers.

Dow, L. (1881). The life, travels, labors, and writings of Lorenzo Dow : including his singular and erratic wanderings in Europe and America : to which is added his chain journey from Babylon to Jerusalem   dialogue. BOOK, New York: R. Worthington.

Drury, K. W., & Drury, S. (1979). Children as learners. BOOK, Winona Lake, Ind.: Light and Life Press.

Duewel, W. L. (1974). The Holy Spirit and tongues. BOOK, Winona Lake, Ind.: Light and Life Press.

Dunhard Church. (n.d.).

Dunn, M. (2000). God's call : from infilling to outpouring. BOOK, Grantham, PA: Wesleyan/Holiness Women Clergy, Inc.

Dunning, J., Platt, S. H., & Roberts, B. T. (1877). Brands from the burning : an account of a work among the sick and destitute in connection with Providence Mission, New York City. BOOK, New York.

Dyer, P. D., & Theological Research Exchange Network. (1994). The use of oral communication methods (storytelling, song/music, and drama) in health education, evangelism, and Christian maturation (THES). Bethel Theological Seminary 1994.

Earle, R. (1961). Matthew : leader's guide. BOOK, Winona Lake, Ind.: Light and Life Press.

Earle, R. (1965a). Ezekial, Haggai, Zechariah : leader's guide. BOOK, Winona Lake, Ind.: Light and Life Press.

Earle, R. (1965b). Ezekiel, Haggai, Zechariah : study guide. BOOK, Winona Lake, Ind.: Light and Life Press.

Easton, J. B. (n.d.). The baptism and indwelling of the Holy Ghost,. BOOK, Chicago: Light and life Press.

Eastside Free Methodist Church. (1986). 1986 directory of Eastside Free Methodist Church. BOOK, Portland, Or.: Eastside Free Methodist Church : Oland Mills.

Elder, R. M. (1984). Healing where the hurt is : a new look at some old problems. BOOK, Winona, Minn.: Justin Books.

Elder, R. M. (1992). In search of sanity. BOOK, Place of publication not identified: publisher not identified.

Ellershaw, J. A. (2005). Apostolic doctrine, practice and experience. BOOK, Fulwood Eng.: Free Methodist Church in the United Kingdom.

Ellis, P. N. (n.d.). To keep yourself free. BOOK, Winona Lake, IN: Forward Movement.

Ellis, P. N., Free Methodist Church of North America, & General Council for the Church in Mission. (1960). To keep yourself free : a question of Christian loyalties. BOOK, Winona Lake, Ind.: Free Methodist Church of North America, General Council for Church in Mission.

Ellis, R. W. (1980). A Christian growth manual for the discipling of new believers in the local church (THES).

Ellis, R. W. (1993). How to plant a Free Methodist Church : effective models for the 90's. BOOK, Indianapolis, Ind.: Free Methodist Church of N.A.

Embree, E. (1973). Chikombedzi : a missionary wife writes home. BOOK, Winona Lake, Ind.: Light and Life Press.

Embree, E. (1978). Now rings the bell : the story of Ralph Jacobs, missionary pioneer to Africa. BOOK, Winona Lake, IN: Light and Life.

Emerick, S. (1958). Spiritual renewal for Methodism : a discussion of the early Methodist class meeting and the values inherent in personal groups today. BOOK, Nashville: Methodist evangelistic materials.

Entering the open door in Formosa. (1956). BOOK, Winona Lake, Ind.: Light and Life.

Eugene First Free Methodist Church. (1978). First Free Methodist Church, Eugene, Oregon : "grow and serve." BOOK, Eugene, Or.: First Free Methodist Church.

Evangel. (n.d.). JFULL, Winona Lake, IN: Light and Life Press.

Evangelicals, N. A. of, & Commission, E. E. (1957). New churches for a new America. BOOK, Winona Lake, Ind.: Light and Life Press.

Explore 1-6, No. 3. (1969). GEN, Winona Lake IN: Light and Life.

Fahs, C. (1925). World missionary atlas. BOOK, New York: Institute of social and religious research.

Failing, G. E. (1963). I Corinthians : leader's guide. BOOK, Winona Lake, Ind.: Light and Life Press.

Fairbairn, C. (1929). The secret of the true revival (holiness must be preached). BOOK, Chicago Ill.: Pub. for the author by Free Methodist Pub.c House.

Fairbairn, C. (1930). Purity and power : or the baptism with the Holy Ghost. BOOK, Chicago: Christian Witness Co.

Fairbairn, C. (1946). ... God's plan for world evangelism,. BOOK, Winona Lake Ind.: Light and Life Press.

Fairbairn, C. V. (1947). A primer in evangelism : new "Secret of true revival", specially revised, rechaptered and rewritten by the author for service training course 134A, "Evangelism in the local church." BOOK, Winona Lake, Ind.: Light and Life Press.

Fairbairn, C. V. (n.d.). A Primer on Evangelism. BOOK.

Fairbairn, C. V. (1900). A Symposium on revivals and the present day need. BOOK, Chicago: Free Methodist Pub. House.

Fairbairn, C. V. (1943). "Tarry ye" : with other sermons and studies. BOOK, Winona Lake, Ind.: Light and Life Press.

Fairbairn, C. V. (1957). What we believe : a brief manual of Christian doctrine for young Free Methodists and new converts based upon the catechism and articles of religion of the Free Methodist Church of North America. BOOK, Winona Lake, IN: Light and Life Press.

Fairbarn, C. V. (1960). I call to remembrance. BOOK, Winona Lake, Ind.: Light and Life Press.

Fang, L. L.-H., Theological Research Exchange Network, & Network., T. R. E. (2000). Formative evaluation of a leadership development course in spiritual formation for the China Free Methodist Church in Taiwan. ELEC.

Faulkner, J. (1903). ... The Methodists,. BOOK, New York: The Baker & Taylor Co.

Fear, L. K. (1979). New ventures : Free Methodist missions, 1960-1979. BOOK, Winona Lake, Ind.: Light and Life Press.

Fellowship, C. S. (1972). Report of evaluation study of the Free Methodist Church of North America. BOOK, Fort Morgan, Colo.: Christian Service Fellowship.

Fellowship, F. M. W. (1962). News and views. News and Views. JFULL, Winona Lake, Ind.: Free Methodist Pub. House.

Fenwick, D. L. (1900). The Psalmist and his critic. BOOK.

Ferguson, C. (1971). Organizing to beat the Devil : Methodists and the making of America. BOOK, Garden City N.Y.: Doubleday.

Ferm, V. (1953). The American church of the Protestant heritage. BOOK, New York: Philosophical Library.

Ferm, V. (1957). Pictorial history of Protestantism a panoramic view of western Europe and the United States. BOOK, New York: Philosophical Library.

Ferndale Free Methodist Church. (2010). Ferndale Free Methodist Church, a place for you, Ferndale, Michigan. BOOK, Chattanooga, TN: Olan Mills.

Ferrell, J. D. (1997). A study of institutional identity and direction : Central College at a crossroads (THES).

Fidler, G. (2006). Adventures in India. BOOK, St. Catherines, ON: Cornerstone Research & Pub.

Fields, W. W. (1973). Unformed and unfilled : a critique of the gap theory of Genesis 1:1,2 (THES). Light and Life Press, Winona Lake, Ind.

Fine, R. M. (1976). Great todays, better tomorrows. BOOK, Winona Lake, Ind.: Light and Life Press.

Fink, N. W., Lutz, J. B., & Rose, W. B. (1924). Inspirational songs for the Sunday school, social worship, missionary and evangelistic work. MUSIC, Chicago: Light and Life Press.

Finley, H. E. (1961). I and II Samuel (and related Chronicles passages) : leader's guide. BOOK, Winona Lake, Ind.: Light and Life Press.

Finley, H. E. (1964). Zephaniah, Nahum, Habakkuk, Obadiah, Daniel : leader's guide. BOOK, Winona Lake, Ind.: Light and Life Press.

First Free Methodist Episcopal Church. (1910).

Flatbush, A. M. (1908). How she was lost : or, methods and results of rescue work, from an experience of ten years. BOOK, Kansas City, Mo.: Franklin Hudson Pub.

Fletcher, C. (2011). Sacramental discipleship as a pathway to ecclesial reformation in the Free Methodist Church in Canada (THES). Gordon-Conwell Theological Seminary.

Folkestad, R. H. (1969). A historical survey of Free Methodist world missions (THES).

Ford, G. L. (1973). To God with love. BOOK, Winona Lake, IN: Free Methodist Church.

Ford, G. L. (1976). All the money you need. BOOK, Winona Lake, Ind.: Light and Life Press.

Ford, G. L. (1985). Like a tree planted : the life story of Leslie Ray Marston. BOOK, Winona Lake, Ind.: Light and Life Press.

Free Methodist book bulletin. (Journal, magazine, 1943) [WorldCat.org]. (n.d.). [ICOMM]. Retrieved from http://www.worldcat.org/title/free-methodist-book-bulletin/oclc/28474317&referer=brief_results

Free Methodist Bradbury Chun Lei Primary School. (1984). Xun li hui Baipuli ji jin xun li xiao xue kai mu gan en dian li : ji nian te kan = Grand opening and thanksgiving of Free Methodist Bradbury Chun Lei Primary School. BOOK, Xianggang: Xun li hui Baipuli ji jin xun li xiao xue.

Free Methodist Bradbury Chun Lei Primary School. (1998). Xun li hui Baipuli ji jin xun li xiao xue shi wu zhou nian xiao qing ji nian te kan. BOOK. Xianggang: Xun li hui Baipuli ji jin xun li xiao xue.

Free Methodist Bradbury Chun Lei Primary School. (2013). Li qing 30 : Xun li jian zheng ji. BOOK.

Free Methodist Church, Topeka, Kansas, 1882-1982. (1982). BOOK, Topeka, Kan.

Free Methodist Church, Ypsilanti, Michigan. (n.d.). ELEC, Ypsilanti Historical Society Photo Archives.

Free Methodist Church, Church., F. M., Church, F. M., & Church., F. M. (n.d.). Yearbook. BOOK, Winona Lake, Ind.: Free Methodist Publishing House.

Free Methodist Church, & Church, F. M. (1927). Instrumental music in public worship : the position held by the Free Methodist Church. CONF, Chicago, Ill.: Free Methodist Pub. House.

Free Methodist Church In Canada. (n.d.). Directory. Directory. JFULL, Mississauga, ON: Free Methodist Church in Canada, Canadian Ministry Centre.

Free Methodist Church in Canada. (2003). Mosaic. Mosaic. JFULL, Mississauga, Ont.: Free Methodist Church in Canada.

Free Methodist Church In Canada, & Canada West Conference. (1970). Annual reports. BOOK, Cymric, Sask: Canada West Conference, Free Methodist Church.

Free Methodist Church In Canada, Canadian General Conference, Bastian, D. N., Kleinsteuber, R. W., Retzman, A. A., Teal, G. H., ... Symposium on Worship and Preaching. (1992). Symposium on worship and preaching. BOOK, S.l.: s.n.

Free Methodist Church In Canada, & East Ontario Conference. (1970). 75 years of progress in Canadian Free Methodism, East Ontario Conference : 1895-1970. BOOK, S.l: s.n.

Free Methodist Church In Canada, & National Task Force on a Canadian General Conference. (1988). A proposal for a Canadian General Conference. BOOK, Mississauga, Ont.: Free Methodist Church in Canada.

Free Methodist Church of Alpena. (n.d.). Directory of Free Methodist Church of Alpena. JFULL, Alpena, Mich.: The Church.

Free Methodist Church of North America. (n.d.-a). Doutrinas e disciplina da Igreja Metodista Livre da América do Norte. JFULL, S.l.: Free Methodist Church of North America].

Free Methodist Church of North America. (n.d.-b). El Mensajero Metodist Libra. JFULL, Los Angeles, CA: Publicaciones Luz y Vida.

Free Methodist Church of North America. (n.d.-c). Free Methodist ministries today. JFULL, Indianapolis, IN: Light and Life Press.

Free Methodist Church of North America. (n.d.-d). Free Methodist World Mission people. JFULL, Indianapolis, Ind.: Free Methodist World Missions.

Free Methodist Church of North America. (n.d.-e). General conference daily. ICOMM, Greenville, Ill.: S.K.J. Chesbro.

Free Methodist Church of North America. (n.d.-f). Interracial news. JFULL.

Free Methodist Church of North America. (n.d.-g). The annual minutes : Free Methodist Church of North America. BOOK, Winona Lake, Ind.: Free Methodist Pub. House.

Free Methodist Church of North America. (n.d.-h). Yearbook : official personnel, organization, and statistics of the Free Methodist Church around the world. JFULL, Winona Lake, Ind.: Office of the General Administrator, Free Methodist Church of North America.

Free Methodist Church of North America. (n.d.-i). Youth in action. JFULL.

Free Methodist Church of North America. (1874). Minutes of the Annual Conference and General Conference of the Free Methodist Church for the year ending October, 1874. CONF, Rochester, N.Y.: The Earnest Christian Office.

Free Methodist Church of North America. (1891). The hymn book of the Free Methodist Church. BOOK, Rochester, N.Y.: B.T. Roberts.

Free Methodist Church of North America. (1896). Probationer's guide : instruction to candidates for admission to membership in the Free Methodist Church. BOOK, Chicago, Ill.: Free Methodist Pub. House.

Free Methodist Church of North America. (1959). An Act to incorporate the Free Methodist Chiurch in Canada : assented to 8th July, 1959. BOOK, Ottawa: Queen's printer and controller of stationery.

Free Methodist Church of North America. (1960). God made a colorful world. BOOK, Winona Lake, Ind.: Light and Life Press.

Free Methodist Church of North America. (1965). Strategy handbook. BOOK, Winona Lake, Ind.: General Strategy Council of the Free Methodist Church.

Free Methodist Church of North America. (1968). Current : for concerned church leaders. JFULL, Winona Lake, Ind.: General Strategy Council of the Free Methodist Church of North America.

Free Methodist Church of North America. (1973). Free Methodist Church, 1861-1978. BOOK, Sun City, Ariz.: Ecumenism Research Agency.

Free Methodist Church of North America. (1974). The vision glorious : New York Conference of the Free Methodist Church, 1974 Centennial ; Sept. 2-6, 1874, Brooklyn, N.Y., Sept. 26-28, 1974, Beach Lake, Pa. BOOK, Winona Lake, Ind.: Free Methodist Church of North America.

Free Methodist Church of North America. (1985). Annual report. JFULL, Winona Lake, IN: The Church.

Free Methodist Church of North America. (1995). Annual conference packet materials for the 1994-1995 annual conferences of the Free Methodist Church of North America. CONF, Winona Lake, Ind.: Free Methodist Church.

Free Methodist Church of North America. (2001). Living Holiness: Free Methodist in the Year 2001. VIDEO, New Link Media.

Free Methodist Church of North America. (2008). 2007 Book of Discipline. Book, Indianapolis, Ind.: Free Methodist Publishing House.

Free Methodist Church of North America, & Atlantic Southeast Extension Conference. (n.d.). The good word. JFULL, Lake City, AL: The Conference.

Free Methodist Church of North America, & Board of Bishops. (1957). Confidentially yours. JFULL, Winona Lake, Ind.: Free Methodist Church of North America.

Free Methodist Church of North America, & Board of Bishops. (1960). Is God calling you to the ordained ministry? BOOK, Indianapolis, Ind.: Free Methodist Church of North America.

Free Methodist Church of North America, & California Conference. (n.d.). The Echoes. JFULL, Sacramento, CA: California Conference.

Free Methodist Church of North America, & Central Illinois Conference. (n.d.). The conference gleaner : a weekly report of the ministry in the Central Illinois Conference of the Free Methodist Church. JFULL, Greenville, IL: The Conference.

Free Methodist Church of North America, & Central Illinois Conference. (1978). Centennial of the Central Illinois Conference of the Free Methodist Church. BOOK, Greenville, IL.

Free Methodist Church of North America, Christian Education Commision, & Department of Sunday Schools. (1944). Manual of the Christian Youth Crusaders of the Free Methodist Church of North America. BOOK, Winona Lake, Ind.: A.L. Brown.

Free Methodist Church of North America, & Commission on Christian Education. (n.d.). Concepts in Christian education. BOOK, Winona Lake, Ind.: Light and Life Press.

Free Methodist Church of North America, Commission on Christian Education, & Department of Service Training. (1952). The story of service training. BOOK, McPherson, Kan.: Free Methodist Church of North America.

Free Methodist Church of North America, Commission on Christian Education, & Department of Service Training. (1957a). Correspondence study courses. BOOK, McPherson, Kan.: Free Methodist Church of North America.

Free Methodist Church of North America, Commission on Christian Education, & Department of Service Training. (1957b). Service training is for you. BOOK, McPherson, Kan.: Free Methodist Church of North America.

Free Methodist Church of North America, Commission on Christian Education, & Department of Service Training. (1960). Service training comes of age, 1937-1960 : nineteen hundred and sixty, centennial year. BOOK, Winona Lake, Ind.: Free Methodist Church of North America.

Free Methodist Church of North America, Commission on Christian Education, & Departmetn of Service Training. (1955). Visual aids for service training courses. BOOK, McPherson, Kan.: Free Methodist Church of North America.

Free Methodist Church of North America, Commission on Christian Education, & Departmetn of Service Training. (1958). So you're a teacher. BOOK, McPherson, Kan.: Free Methodist Church of North America.

Free Methodist Church of North America, Commission on Missions, General Missionary Board, & Free Methodist World Missions. (1970). Missions annual report. Missions Annual Report. JFULL, Winona Lake, Ind.: Commission on Missions.

Free Methodist Church of North America, Commission on Missions, Woman's Missionary Society, Young People's Missionary Society of the Free Methodist Church, & Junior Missionary Society of the Free Methodist Church. (n.d.). Annual report. In Annual report. CONF, Chicago, Ill.: Free Methodist Pub. House.

Free Methodist Church of North America, & Department of
  Evangelism and Church Growth. (1980). Reach out in love :
  a manual for the growing church. BOOK, Winona Lake, Ind.:
  Department of Evangelism and Church Growth, assisted by the
  Department of Christian Education, Free Methodist Church of
  North America.

Free Methodist Church of North America, & Department of Higher
  Education. (1968). The Aldersgate nexus. The Aldersgate
  Nexus. JFULL, Winona Lake, IN: Dept. of Higher Education
  of the Free Methodist Church.

Free Methodist Church of North America, Department of Service
  Training, & Commission on Christian Education. (1943).
  Free Methodist book bulletin. JFULL, McPherson, KS: Dept.
  of Service Training of the Free Methodist Church of North
  America.

Free Methodist Church of North America, & Department of Sunday
  Schools. (1950). Sunday school constitution. BOOK, S.l.: Free
  Methodist Church of North America.

Free Methodist Church of North America, & Department of
  World Missions. (1989). Across the miles. Across the Miles.
  JFULL, Winona Lake, IN: Dept. of World Missions, The Free
  Methodist Church.

Free Methodist Church of North America, & General Conference.
  (n.d.-a). General Conference today. JFULL, Winona Lake, IN:
  Light and Life Press.

Free Methodist Church of North America, & General Conference.
  (n.d.-b). Winona daily. Winona Daily. JFULL, Winona Lake,
  IN: Free Methodist Church.

Free Methodist Church of North America, & General Conference.
  (1960a). Free Methodist centenary, June 14-26, 1960, Winona
  Lake, Indiana : 25th Annual Conference guide book. BOOK,
  Winona Lake, Ind.: Free Methodist Church of North America.

Free Methodist Church of North America, & General Conference. (1960b). Quinquennial report of the General Missionary Secretary to the General Conference of the Free Methodist Church. CONF, S.l.: s.n.

Free Methodist Church of North America, General Conference, & Study Commission on Doctrine. (1989). Report of the Study Commission on Doctrine : Free Methodist Church of North America, 31st General Conference, August 3-13, 1989, Seattle, Washington. BOOK.

Free Methodist Church of North America, & General Missionary Board. (n.d.). Missions perspective. Missions Perspective. JFULL, Winona Lake, IN: General Missionary Board.

Free Methodist Church of North America, & General Missionary Board. (1950). Perspective in missions giving. BOOK, Winona Lake, Ind.: Free Methodist Church of North America, General Missionary Board.

Free Methodist Church of North America, & General Missionary Board. (1974). Missions quinquennial report. JFULL, Winona Lake, Ind.: Light and Life Press.

Free Methodist Church of North America, General Missionary Board, Woman's Foreign Missionary Society, America., F. M. C. of N., Board., G. M., America., F. M. C. of N., … Woman's Foreign Missionary Society. (1923). Proceedings of the General Missionary Board of the Free Methodist Church of North America. BOOK, Chicago, Ill.

Free Methodist Church of North America, & Home Ministries. (n.d.). Free Methodist ministries update. JFULL, Indianapolis, IN: Light and Life Press.

Free Methodist Church of North America, & Illinois-Wisconsin Conference. (n.d.). Illinois-Wisconsin Messenger. JFULL, Woodstock, IL: Illinois-Wisconsin Conference.

Free Methodist Church of North America, & Kentucky-Tennessee Conference. (n.d.-a). Builder : newsletter of the Kentucky-Tennessee Conference. JFULL, Jackson, KY: The Conference.

Free Methodist Church of North America, & Kentucky-Tennessee Conference. (n.d.-b). Report book : the ... session of the Kentucky-Tennessee Annual Conference. JFULL, KY: The Conference.

Free Methodist Church of North America, & Keystone Conference. (n.d.). Keystone Conference news. JFULL, Oil City, PA: The Conference.

Free Methodist Church of North America, & Light and Life Men's Fellowship. (1960). "Break through" : the president's manual. BOOK, Winona Lake, Ind.: Free Methodist Church of North America.

Free Methodist Church of North America, & Light and Life Men International. (n.d.) Light and life line. JFULL, Winona Lake, Ind.: Free Methodist Church of North America, Light and Life Men International.

Free Methodist Church of North America, & Louisianna Conference. (n.d.). Louisiana messenger of the Free Methodist Church. JFULL, Effie, LA: The Conference.

Free Methodist Church of North America, & New York Conference. (n.d.). New York Conference news. JFULL, NY: The Conference.

Free Methodist Church of North America, & North Michigan Conference. (n.d.). The North Michigan herald. JFULL, Cadillac, MI: The Conference.

Free Methodist Church of North America, & Ohio Conference. (1995). The Ohio connection. JFULL, Baltimore, Ohio: Ohio Conference, Free Methodist Church of N. America.

Free Methodist Church of North America, Ohio Conference, & Board of Evangelism. (n.d.). The Net. JFULL, Mansfield, OH: Board of Evangelism of the Ohio Annual Conference, Free Methodist Church of North America.

Free Methodist Church of North America, & Oil City Conference. (n.d.). The Oil City Conference news. JFULL, Pleasentville, PA: The Conference.

Free Methodist Church of North America, & Oklahoma Conference. (1993). In touch with Oklahoma Free Methodists. JFULL, Oklahoma City: The Conference.

Free Methodist Church of North America, Oklahoma Conference, America., F. M. C. of N., & Conference., O. (n.d.). Oklahoma Free Methodist. Oklahoma Free Methodist. JFULL, Oklahoma City: The Conference.

Free Methodist Church of North America, & Oregon Conference. (1997). Connection. JFULL, Turner, OR: Oregon Conference of the Free Methodist Church of North America.

Free Methodist Church of North America, Oregon Conference, America., F. M. C. of N., & Conference., O. (1970). Oregon Conference of the Free Methodist Church : 75th anniversary, 1895-1970. BOOK, S.l.: Free Methodist Church of North America, Oregon Conference.

Free Methodist Church of North America, Oregon Conference, America., F. M. C. of N., & Conference., O. (1995). Connection, 1895-1995 : Oregon Conference. BOOK, Turner, Or.: Oregon Conference of the Free Methodist Church.

Free Methodist Church of North America, & Pacific Northwest Conference. (n.d.-a). Conference news. JFULL, Seattle, WA: The Conference.

Free Methodist Church of North America, & Pacific Northwest Conference. (n.d.-b). The Northwest passage. JFULL, Seattle, WA: Pacific Conference of the Free Methodist Church of North America.

Free Methodist Church of North America, Pacific Northwest Conference, & Board of Social Action. (n.d.). Social action issues. JFULL, Seattle, WA: The Board.

Free Methodist Church of North America, Southeastern Regional Fellowship, Kentucky-Tennessee Conference, & Atlantic Southeast Conference. (1995). Southern breeze. JFULL, Bowling Green, KY: Southeastern Regional Fellowship, Free Methodist Church of North America.

Free Methodist Church of North America, & Southern California-Arizona Conference (n.d.). Observer. JFULL, The Conference.

Free Methodist Church of North America, & Southern Michigan Conference. (n.d.). Vision. JFULL, Spring Arbor, MI: The Conference.

Free Methodist Church of North America, & Wabash Conference. (n.d.-a). The Christian courier : the voice of the Wabash Conference. JFULL, Hooperston, IL: Wabash Conference of the Free Methodist Church.

Free Methodist Church of North America, & Wabash Conference. (n.d.-b). The Wabash christian courier. The Wabash Christian Courier. JFULL, Hooperston, IL: Free Methodist Church of North America, Wabash Conference.

Free Methodist Church of North America, Wesleyan Church, & Committee on Merger Exploration. (1974). Free Methodist Church of North America and the Wesleyan Church : proposed articles of agreement and constitution. BOOK, Winona Lake, IN.

Free Methodist Church of North America, & West Virginia Conference. (n.d.). West Virginia echoes. JFULL, Teays, WV: The Conference.

Free Methodist Church of North America, & Woman's Missionary Society. (1959). Then Jesus came : true stories of African children. BOOK, Winona Lake, Ind.: Free Methodist Church.

Free Methodist Church of North America, Woman's Missionary Society, America., F. M. C. of N., & Society., W. M. (1979). Twentieth General Session : August 20-24, 1979, Indianapolis, Indiana. BOOK, Indianapolis, Ind.: Women's Missionary Society of the Free Methodist Church.

Free Methodist Church of North America, Woman's Missionary Society, & Young People's Missionary Society of the Free Methodist Church. (1949). Directory : Oregon Conference, Free Methodist Church, 1949-1950. BOOK, S.l.: s.n.

Free Methodist Church Of Watervilet. (n.d.). Directory of Watervliet Free Methodist Church. JFULL, Watervliet, Mich.: The Church.

Free Methodist Historical Society, Marston Memorial Historical Center, America, F. M. C. of N., & International, M. M. (2000). Newsletter. JFULL, Indianapolis, IN: Marston Memorial Historical Center.

Free Methodist hymnal / Published by authority of the General Conference of the Free Methodist Church of North America. (n.d.). ELEC, Chicago : Free Methodist Pub. House.

Free Methodist Mission. (1961). Buku ya milawu ya Vandla ra Methodista Livre. BOOK, Germiston: the Mission.

Free Methodist Publishing House. (1949). The Christian minister. The Christian Minister. JFULL.

Free Methodist Youth. (1955). The official guidebook of Free Methodist Youth. BOOK, Winona Lake, IN: World Headquarters, Free Methodist Youth.

Free Methodists Ministers' Associaton. (1895). The Free Methodist ministers' magazine. The Free Methodist Ministers' Magazine. JFULL, London.

Freeland, M. H., & Her., O. who loved. (1892). Missionary martyrs Mary Louisa Ranf, missionary to India. ELEC, Chicago: T.B. Arnold.

Gaddis, V. (1960). The story of Winona Lake : a memory and a vision. BOOK, Winona Lake Ind.: Winona Lake Christian Assembly.

Gagne, R. (1991). The Free Methodist understanding of baptism in the light of John Wesley's teaching and the American Methodist tradition (THES).

Galbreath, M. (1970). 20 centuries of Christianity. Winona Lake IN: Light and Life Press.

Galbreath, M. L. (1962). James and Peter : leader's guide. BOOK, Winona Lake, Ind.: Light and Life Press.

Gallaher Family. (1800). Gallaher family papers (UNPB).

Garber, P. (1939). The Methodists are one people. BOOK, Nashville: Cokesbury Press.

Gaylord, M. L. (1976). Tender heart. BOOK, Winona Lake, In.: Light and Life Press.

Gear, F. B. (1955). Book Review: Peloubet's Select Notes on the International Bible Lessons for Christian Teaching, Uniform Series, 1955, by Wilbur M. Smith. W. A. Wilde Co., Boston. 473; The Douglass Sunday School Lessons, 1955, by Earl L. Douglass. The Macmillan. Interpretation: A Journal of Bible and Theology Interpretation: A Journal of Bible and Theology, 9(2), 235–236. JOUR.

Geiger, K. (1962). Insights into holiness : discussions of holiness by fifteen leading scholars of the Wesleyan persuasion. BOOK, Kansas City, MO: Beacon Hill Press.

Geiger, K. (1963). Further insights into holiness : nineteen leading Wesleyan scholars present various phases of holiness thinking. BOOK, Kansas City, MO: Beacon Hill Press.

General Council of the Church in Mission of the Free Methodist Church of North America, Free Methodist Church of North America, General Council for the Church in Mission, America., F. M. C. of N., Mission., G. C. of the C. in, Marston, L. R., ... Free Methodist Church of North America. (1868). The Free Methodist. The Free Methodist. JFULL, Rochester, N.Y.: Levi Wood.

General Mission Board of the Free Methodist Church of North America. (n.d.). Inhambane tidings. JFULL.

General Young People's Missionary Society Council, & Council., G. Y. P. M. S. (1952). It's time you knew ... : the facts about the ministry and operation of the Young People's Missionary Society through the Free Methodist Church around the world. BOOK, Winona Lake, Ind.: Young People's Missionary Society.

Ghormley, N. B. (1920). The land of the heart of Livingstone; or, The genius of the Bantu. A study of the Bantu tribes of Africa, 100,000,000 souls, with special reference to the agencies which contribute to their civilization. BOOK, Chicago: Published by the author; for sale by the Woman's Foreign Missionary Society of the Free Methodist Church.

Gilmore, A. (1964). Treasure in the Dominican. BOOK, Winona Lake, IN: Light and Life Press.

Goddard, B. (1967). The Encyclopedia of modern Christian missions the agencies. BOOK, Camden N.J.: T. Nelson.

Godfroy, C., & McClurg, M. U. (1961). Miami Indian stories. BOOK, Winona Lake, Ind.: Light and Life Press.

Goldstein, D. M., & Dixon, C. A. D. (2010). Return of the raider. BOOK, Lake Mary, Fla.: Creation House.

Goodhew, E. (1960). Echoes from half a century. BOOK, Los Angeles: Los Angeles Pacific College Press.

Gramento, J. H. (1992). Those astounding Free Methodist women! a biographical history of Free Methodist women in ministry with an extended bibliography of Free Methodist women's studies : a final document submitted to the Doctoral Studies Committee of United Theological Seminary (THES). United Theological Seminary, Dayton, OH.

Green, E. D. (1942). The stewardship of the mother talent. BOOK, Winona Lake, Ind.: Woman's Missionary Society of the Free Methodist Church of North America.

Greenville College. (n.d.-a). Annual Register of Greenville College. Annual Register of Greenville College. JFULL, Chicago, IL.: Free Methodist Publishing House.

Greenville College. (n.d.-b). Greenville College record. JFULL, Greenville, IL: Greenville College. Retrieved from http://catalog.hathitrust.org/api/volumes/oclc/27723572.html

Gregory, D. T. (1982). Free Methodists and cities, 1950-1980. BOOK, Winona Lake, Ind.: Free Methodist Urban Fellowship.

Gregory, D. T. (2005). From the new day to the new century : Free Methodist strategies for metropolitan church planting in light of 1985-2000 efforts and results (THES).

Griffith, C. E. (1984). Patterns of Free Methodist worship : historic freedoms (THES).

Griffith, G. (1941). Daily glow. BOOK, Los Angeles, CA.

Griffith, G. W. (1923). The divine program; an interpretation of the divine method of redemption and of the nature and nurture of the Christian life,. BOOK, Chicago, Ill.: W.B. Rose.

Griffith, G. W. (1939). Lest we forget : selected messages. BOOK, Los Angeles, CA: Mrs. G.W. Griffith.

Griffith, L. B., & Griffith, G. W. (1937). Living embers : the life and writings of George William Griffith. BOOK, Winona Lake, IN: Light and Life Press.

Group buys Ottawa County church to save it. (1994). Minor Methodist Sects, Clippings., 1. JOUR.

Grubb, K. (1949). World Christian handbook. BOOK, London: World Dominion Press.

Guthrie, M. D. (1992). Discovering the life of Christ: a biographical study approach to the life of Jesus Christ utilizing the four gospels : a final document submitted to the Doctor of Ministry Program Committee of United Theological Seminary (THES). United Theological Seminary.

Gyertson, D. J. (1981). The church related college higher education in the Free Methodist Church during the decade of the seventies ; implications for the eighties (THES).

Haley, J. W. (1949). But thy right hand. BOOK, Winona Lake, Ind.: Woman's Missionary Society of the Free Methodist Church.

Haley, J. W., Olmstead, W. B., & America, F. M. C. of N. (1926). Life in Mozambique and South Africa. BOOK, Chicago: Free Methodist Pub. House.

Hall, B. H. (1962). Job : leader's guide. BOOK, Winona Lake, Ind.: Light and Life Press.

Hamilton, M. E. (1988). James R. Bishop : God's chosen man : the life story of the founder of South India Biblical Seminary Bangarapet, Karnataka, South India. BOOK, Karnataka, India: South India Biblical Seminary.

Harmon, N. (1974). The Encyclopedia of world Methodism. BOOK, Nashville: United Methodist Pub. House.

Hart, E. P. (1903). Reminiscences of early Free Methodism. BOOK, Chicago, Ill.: Free Methodist Publ. House.

Hartsough, M. M., Upson, L. E., & Babb, L. W. (1964). A history of the Hartough - Hartsough - Hartsock family. BOOK, Winona Lake, Indiana: The Free Methodist Publishing House.

Harvey, D. (2006). STMO (submission, transformation, multiplication, order) : building a culture of kingdom fruitfulness. BOOK, Indianapolis, IN: Free Methodist Church of North America.

Harvey, J. (1976). Faith Plus : search for the holy life. BOOK, Winona Lake, IN: Light and Life.

Harvey, J. D. (1973). Dimensions in Christian living. BOOK, Winona Lake, Ind.: Light and Life Press.

Harvey, J. D. (1979). The Wesleyan way today. BOOK, Winona Lake, Ind.: Light and Life Press.

Haskins, A. M. (1997). New life for old churches : a multi-case study of four turnaround small churches (THES).

Haslam, R. B. (1977). Peepholes on life : 44 fun looks at the serious side of life. BOOK, Winona Lake, Ind.: Light and Life Press.

Haviland, E. (1928). Under the Southern Cross : or, a woman's life work for Africa. BOOK, Cincinnati: God's Bible School and Revivalist.

Hawke, J. (1999). Hogue, Wilson Thomas. American National Biography., 11. JOUR.

Hawkins, R. (1888). Redemption or the living way : a treatise on the redemption of the body including a doctrinal outline of experimental religion. BOOK, Olean, NY: Herald Publ. House.

Hawkins, R. W. (1880). Life Eternal. BOOK.

Hawley, D., & Hardy, J. (1980). Living water, living letter : Free Methodist missions in Egypt and India. BOOK, Winona Lake, IN: Light and Life Press.

Haywood, A. L. (1942). My life story. ELEC, Stanwood, Mich.: Sanders Print Shop.

Hazzard, A. H., Montmorency County Historical Society, & Tribune., M. C. (1991). Blue Sky Circuit Montmorency County, Michigan, 1922-1926. ELEC, Atlanta, MI: Montmorency County Historical Society: Printed by the Montmorency County Tribune.

Heer, K., Hubbard, M., & Dymale, M. (1980). Open letters from a Roman prison : Philippians/Colossians/Philemon : study guide. BOOK, Winona Lake, Ind.: Published for the Aldersgate Publications Association by Light and Life Press.

Helms, E. E. (1923). God in history. BOOK, Chicago, IL: Light and Life Press.

Helsel, E. W. (1965). Timothy, Titus : leader's guide. BOOK, Winona Lake, Ind.: Light and Life Press.

Helsel, E. W. (1976). When is Jesus Coming Back? Light and Life, November 9, 6–7,12. JOUR.

Hendrickson, F. (1942). The "Livingstone" of the Orinoco (interior of South America) : the life story of Ford Hendrickson (an autobiography)... BOOK, Wausen, OH.

Herndon, B. T. (2001). Discipleship out of transition : a study of the new membership policies and procedures of the Free Methodist Church and its impact on discipleship (THES).

Herzog, J. (1908). The new Schaff-Herzog encyclopedia of religious knowledge, embracing Biblical, historical, doctrinal, and practical theology and Biblical, theological, and ecclesiastical biography from the earliest. BOOK, New York; London: Funk and Wagnalls Company.

Hill, C. D., & Archives, S. P. U. (1909). Cyril Hill Papers, (UNPB).

Hill, D. L., Van Valin, J. E., & Free Methodist Church of North America Board of Bishops. (1988). Membership Care Committee handbook, Free Methodist Church of North America. BOOK, Winona Lake, IN: Free Methodist Pub. House.

Hill, N. (2007). A brief history of Holiness Movement & Free Methodist missions Egypt 1899-1986. BOOK, S.l.: s.n.

Hillman Free Methodist Church. (n.d.). Directory of Hillman Free Methodist Church. Directory of Hillman Free Methodist Church. JFULL, Hillman, Mich.: The Church.

Hillsdale Free Methodist Church. (n.d.). Directory of Hillsdale Free Methodist Church. Directory of Hillsdale Free Methodist Church. JFULL, Hillsdale, Mich.: The Church.

Hilson, J. B. (1950). History of the South Carolina Conference of Wesleyan Methodist Church of America; fifty-five years of Wesleyan Methodism in South Carolina. BOOK, Winona Lake, Indiana: Light and life Press.

Hitt, R. T., Beltz, R. A., & Watson, C. H. (n.d.). Story of the Light and Life Hour. BOOK, Winona Lake, IN: Forward Movement.

Hockett, B., & Abbott, G. (1977). Life changing learning for children : resources that work. BOOK, Winona Lake, Ind.: Light and Life Press.

Hockley, R. G. (1991). Sectarianism within Free Methodism : its contribution to the formation of the Free Methodist Church and its continuing influence today. BOOK, S.l.: s.n.

Hoffer, M. (1982). George Poore (1723-1810) and descendants. BOOK, Winona Lake, IN: Light and Life Press.

Hogg, W. T. (1895). A hand-book of homiletics and pastoral theology. BOOK, Chicago: Free Methodist Pub. House.

Hogg, W. T. (1938). History of the Free Methodist Church of North America. BOOK, Winona Lake, Ind.: Free Methodist Pub. House.

Hogue, E. (1920). India : a mission study for juniors. BOOK, Chicago: Women's Foreign Missionary Society of the Free Methodist Church.

Hogue, E. L. (1939). Adella Paulina Carpenter : in memory of a beautiful life. BOOK, Winona Lake, Ind.: Woman's Missionary Society.

Hogue, W. (1890). Revivals and revival work. BOOK, Buffalo N.Y.: Published for the author.

Hogue, W. (1907). The class-meeting as a means of grace. Chicago: S.K.J. Chesbro.

Hogue, W. (1915). The believer's personal experience of Christ in the processes of salvation. BOOK, Chicago: W.B. Rose.

Hogue, W. T. (1905). G. Harry Agnew, a pioneer missionary. BOOK, Chicago: Free Methodist Pub. House.

Hogue, W. T. (1911). Retrospect and prospect : a semi-centennial sermon preached by Bishop Wilson T. Hogue before the General Conference of the Free Methodist Church, in Chicago, June 18, 1911. BOOK, Chicago, IL: Free Methodist Pub. House.

Hogue, W. T. (1915). History of the Free Methodist church of North America. BOOK, Chicago: Free Methodist Pub. House.

Hogue, W. T. (1916). The Holy Spirit : a study. BOOK, Chicago, Ill.: William B. Rose.

Hogue, W. T. (1928). Missionary hymns and responsive scripture readings : for use in missionary meetings. MUSIC, Chicago: Woman's Foreign Missionary Society of the Free Methodist Church.

Hogue, W. T. (1932). Hymns that are immortal : with some account of their authorship, origin, history and influence. BOOK, Chicago, Ill.: Light and Life Press.

Hogue, W. T. (1940). A hand-book of homiletics and pastoral theology. BOOK, Winona Lake, Ind.: Herald and Banner Press.

Hogue, W. T., & Chesbrough, A. E. (1906). A Sermon : preached at the fiftieth anniversary of the marriage of rev. Samuel K.J. and Mrs. Ann E. Chesbrough, February 6, 1898, together with the experience of Mrs. Ann E. Chesbrough, a member of the first class ever formed in the Free Methodist Church. BOOK, Chicago: Free Methodist Pub. House.

Hogue, W. T., & Roberts, B. T. (1896). A Symposium on scriptural holiness. BOOK, Chicago: Free Methodist Pub. House.

Holdren, D. W. (1986). The power to become : I, II, III John, Jude ; study guide. BOOK, Winona Lake, Ind.: Published for Aldersgate Publications by Light and Life Press.

Holiness alive and well : the meaning of holy living in twentieth-century life. (1970). BOOK, Published for Aldersgate Associates by Beacon Hill Press of Kansas City.

Hook, E. M. (1980). Centennial of Armadale Church, 1880-1980 : in the cradle of Free Methodism in Canada. BOOK, Scarborough, Ont.: Armadale Church.

Horner, R. (1891). From the altar to the upper room in four parts. BOOK, Toronto, Montréal: W. Briggs ;;C.W. Coates.

Horner, R. (1908). Bible doctrines. BOOK, Ottawa, Canada: Holiness Movement Pub. House.

Horton, C. A. (1980). Money counts : a handbook on local church finance. BOOK, Winona Lake, IN: Light and Life Press.

Hospital, D. (1975). The Butterfields : 50 years. BOOK, Oklahoma City, Okla.: Deaconess Hospital.

Houck, L. E. (1988). A descriptive dissertation on trust development between pastor and parish (THES).

Houser, G. (1969). Boadi and Tembi of Africa's grasslands. BOOK, Winona Lake, Ind.: Light and Life Press.

Houser, G., Johnson, J., & Church, H. (1978). Adventures in Africa's grasslands : stories from Southern Africa. BOOK, Winona Lake, Ind.: Light and Life Press.

Houser, T. (2000). Free Methodist and other missions in Zimbabwe. BOOK, Kopje, Harare: Priority Projects Pub.

Houser, T., & Houser, G. (2007). Let me tell you : a memoir. BOOK, Charleston, SC: Booksurge.

Howell, R. (1965). Saved to serve : accent on stewardship. BOOK, Grand Rapids, MI: Baker Book House.

Howell, R. W. (1965). Christian family : a symposium. BOOK, Winona Lake, Ind.: Light and Life Press.

Howell, R. W., & Jeffery, W. F. (1970). Relections. BOOK, Winona Lake, Ind.: Roy W. Howell.

Howland, C. (1913). Manual of missions. BOOK, New York ;Chicago: Fleming H. Revell Co.

Howland, C. L. (1950). Proofs of inspiration : the cumulative proofs of the inspiration of the scriptures. BOOK, Winona Lake, Ind.: Free Methodist Pub. House.

Howland, C. L. (1951). The story of our church : Free Methodism, some facts and some reasons. BOOK, Winona Lake, IN: Free Methodist Pub. House.

Howland, C. L. (1953). A brief story of our church : an historical outline of the origin and growth of the Free Methodist Church of North America. BOOK, Winona Lakes, Ind.: Free Methodist Pub. House.

Howland, J. (1947). Not mine Steward. BOOK, Winona Lake, IN: Published by Woman's Missionary Society of the Free Methodist Church.

Hoyer, J. (1984). Life-changing learning for adults : resources that work. BOOK, Winona Lake, Ind.: Light and Life Press.

Hudson, W. (1965). Religion in America. BOOK, New York: Scribner.

Huffman, J. A. (1939). The Messianic hope in both Testaments. BOOK, Winona Lake, IN: Light and Life Press.

Huffman, J. A. (1944). The Holy Spirit. BOOK, Butler, Ind.: Higley Press.

Huffman, J. A. (1948). The stones cry out. BOOK, Winona Lake, Ind.: Light and Life Press.

Huffman, J. A. (1951a). Building the home Christian. BOOK, Winona Lake, Ind.: Light and Life Press.

Huffman, J. A. (1951b). Golden treasures from the Greek New Testament for English readers. BOOK, Winona Lake, IN: Light and Life Press.

Humphrey, J. M. (n.d.). Seven old time gospel sermons. BOOK, Chicago: The Author.

Humphrey, J. M. (1913). Select fruits from the highlands of Beulah. BOOK, Lima, OH: True Gospel Grain Pub. Co.

Humphrey, J. M. (1914). Spiritual lessons from every-day life. BOOK, Lima, Ohio: True Gospel Grain Pub. Co.

Humphrey, J. M. (1924). X-ray sermons. BOOK, Omaha, Neb.: "Anywhere" evangelistic workers' Pub. House.

Humphrey, J. M. (2000). Crumbs from Heaven. BOOK, Salem, Ohio: Allegheny.

Humphrey, J. M. (2003). Railroad sermons from railroad stories. BOOK, Salem, OH: Schmul Pub. Co.

Humphrey, J. M., & Humphrey, J. M. (2000). The lost soul's first day in eternity. BOOK, Salem, Ohio: Allegheny Publications.

Hunt, S. (1893). Methodism in Buffalo, from its origin to the close of 1892,. BOOK, Buffalo, NY: H.H. Otis & Sons.

Hurst, J. (1902). The history of Methodism. BOOK, New York: Eaton & Mains.

Hyde, A. (1889). The story of Methodism throughout the world, from the beginning to the present time ... giving an account of its various influences and institutions of to-day. BOOK, Chicago, IL: Johns Publishing House.

In Touch. (1971). GEN, Winona Lake, IN: Wesley Press.

Ingersol, R. S. (1990). Burden of dissent : Mary Lee Cagle and the Southern Holiness movement. BOOK.

Interior of the Dunhard Church. (n.d.).

International Uniform Series. (1885). GEN, Winona Lake, IN: Light and Life Press.

Ionia County Clerk, Free Methodist Church of Orleans, First Baptist Church of Otisco, & Church, O. and B. C. F. M. (1848). Records of the Ionia County Clerk (UNPB). Orleans, MI.

Ivers, K. (1991). Golden memories : God's leading in the lives of His people. BOOK, McPherson, KS.: McPherson Free Methodist Church.

Iwig-O'Byrne, L. (1993). A Progression of Methodist radicalism : an examination of the history and ethos of the first sixty years of the Nazarites and their heirs (1855-1915) in their social and religious context (THES).

Jacobson, B. (1900). Jacobson, Byron: Papers (UNPB).

Jacquet, C. (1975). Yearbook of American and Canadian churches 1975. BOOK, Nashville, TN: Abingdon Press.

James, G. (2012). The sanctified way of life. ELEC, Wilmore, Ky.: DQB-LLC for Asbury Theological Seminary.

James, J. F. (1987). On the front lines : a guide to Church planting. BOOK, Winona Lake, Ind.: Light and Life Press.

James, J. F., Free Methodist Church of North America, & General Conference. (2008). Our calling to the poor. BOOK, Indianapolis, Ind.: Light and Life Press.

Jernigan, C. (1919). Pioneer days of the Holiness movement in the Southwest. BOOK, Kansas City, MO: Pentecostal Nazarene Pub. House.

Jessop, H. E. (1938). Foundations of doctrine in scripture and experience : a students' handbook on holiness. BOOK, Winona Lake, Ind.: Free Methodist Pub. House.

Jessop, H. E. (1942). That burning question of final perseverance. BOOK, Winona Lake, Ind.: Light and Life Press.

Jessop, H. E. (1956). I met a man with a shining face : an autobiography in the things of God. BOOK, Winona Lake, Ind.: Light and Life Press.

Johnson, B. C. (1964). An analysis of the pastor's relationship to the Sunday school in the Oregon conference of the Free Methodist Church (THES).

Johnson, B. C. (1984). The training of college persons as lay ministers in the Free Methodist Church (THES).

Johnson, C. E. (1969). How in the world? BOOK, Winona Lake, Ind.: Light and Life Press.

Johnson, H. F. (1900). Handbook of Free Methodist missions. BOOK, Winona Lake, Ind.: Free Methodist Pub. House.

Johnson, H. F. (1939). Heroes of other lands. BOOK, Winona Lake, IN: Light and Life Press.

Johnson, H. O. (1955). Programs and suggestions for public Junior Missionary meetings. BOOK, Winona Lake, Ind.: Free Methodist Church of North America.

Johnson, J. P. (2002). A strategy for using spiritual formation to promote community renewal (THES).

Johnson, P. V., & Church, W. M. S. of the F. M. (1942). Our neighbors the Dominicans. BOOK, Winnona Lake, Ind.: Woman's missionary Society, Free Methodist church.

Johnston, T. (1974). Yesterday's hate, today's love : the amazing story of Tom & Roberta Johnston. BOOK, Winona Lake, IN: Light & Life Men International.

Joint Commission of the Free Methodist and Wesleyan Methodist Churches on the Matter of Church Union records,. (1944). GEN.

Jones, B. R. (1909). Incidents in the life and labors of Burton Rensselaer Jones, Minister of the Gospel, with extracts from his diary. BOOK, Chicago: Free Methodist Pub. House.

Jones, C. (1974a). A guide to the study of the Holiness movement. Metuchen, NJ: Scarecrow Press.

Jones, C. (1974b). Perfectionist persuasion: the Holiness movement and American Methodism, 1867-1936. BOOK, Metuchen, NJ: Scarecrow Press.

Jordahl, D. C. (1960). A history of the Kansas Conference of the Free Methodist Church (THES).

Joy, D. (1983). Moral development foundations : Judeo-Christian alternatives to Piaget Kohlberg. BOOK, Nashville, TN: Abingdon.

Joy, D. (1985). Bonding : relationships in the image of God. BOOK, Waco, TX: Word Books.

Joy, D. M. (1960a). A survey and analysis of the experiences, attitudes and problems of senior high youth of the Free Methodist Church (COMM). Southern Methodist University.

Joy, D. M. (1960b). Aldersgate Biblical series. BOOK, Winona Lake, Ind.: Light and Life Press.

Joy, D. M. (1962). Psalms : leader's guide. BOOK, Winona Lake, Ind.: Light and Life Press.

Joy, D. M. (1965). The Holy Spirit and you : leadership and service training/series. BOOK, Winona Lake, Ind.: Light and Life Press.

Joy, D. M. (1967). A preliminary report on the Aldersgate Graded Curriculum Project. BOOK, Winona Lake, Ind.: Free Methodist Pub. House.

Joy, D. M., & Association, A. P. (1969). Meaningful learning in the church. BOOK, Winona Lake, Ind.: Light and Life Press.

Junior's Friend, 1-14, No. 39. (1929). GEN, Winona Lake, IN: Light and Life Press.

Junior Manual, 1-16, No.4. (1953). GEN, Winona Lake, IN: Light and Life Press.

Junior Manual. 1-3, No. 3. (1951). GEN, Winona Lake, IN: Light and Life Press.

Junker, J. A. (n.d.). Free Methodist missionary work among the Mexicans. BOOK, S.l.: s.n.

Kahl, M. (1970). His guiding hand : an autobiography. BOOK, Overland Park, KS: Herald and Banner Press.

Kaiser, C. R. (1980). Axiomatic church growth (THES).

Kalamazoo Free Methodist Church. (n.d.). Directory of Kalamazoo Free Methodist Church. JFULL, Kalamazoo, MI: The Church.

Kaub, V. P. (1946). Collectivism challenges Christianity. BOOK, Winona Lake, Ind.: Light and Life Press.

Kaufmann, U. M. (1970). The God who shows himself. BOOK, Winona Lake, Ind.: Free Methodist Church of North America, General Council for Church in Mission.

Kaufmann, U. M. (1972). The church and the channels of power. BOOK, Winona Lake, IN: Free Methodist Church.

Kaufmann, U. M. (1981). Heaven : a future finer than dreams. BOOK, Winona Lake, Ind.: Light and Life Press.

Keen, J. O. (1905). In memoriam : Frederick William Bourne. BOOK, London.

Kelley, A. T., & Kelley, W. W. (1889). Memoirs of Mrs. Augusta Tullis Kelley her experience, labors as evangelist and missionary to Africa, with extracts from her writings. ELEC, Chicago: T.E. Arnold.

Kelley, D. (1972). Why conservative churches are growing : a study in sociology of religion. BOOK, New York: Harper & Row.

Kendall, D. W., Winslow, K. S., & Free Methodist Church of North America. (2006). The female pastor : is there room for "she" in shepherd? BOOK, Indianapolis, Ind.: Light and Life Communications.

Kendall, W. S. (1955). The challenge of this century : a doctrinal emphasis. BOOK, Salem: Free Methodist Church of North America.

Kendall, W. S. (1964). That the world may know. BOOK, Winona Lake, Ind.: Light and Life Press.

Kendall, W. S. (1981). The Holy Spirit in Christian experience. BOOK, Stanwood, Wash.: Warm Beach Printing Services.

Kendall, W. S. (1985). Evangel of the cross : highlights, devotion depths, and bits of humor. BOOK, Stanwood, Wash.: Le Sabre.

Kennedy, J. H. (1954). The Lord shall preserve and Treasures out of the darkness. BOOK, Bern, Ind.: Light and Hope Publications.

Kerby, R. A. (1949). A shuffling theology. BOOK, Winona Lake, IN: Light and Life Press.

Kettinger, L., & Stonehouse, C. (1983). Youth as learners. BOOK, Winona Lake, Ind.: Light and Life Press.

Kidney, E. M. (1988). Our Father's care. BOOK, Spring Arbor, MI.: The Author.

Killingray, D. (2005). Soga, Tiyo. Oxford: Oxford University Press.

Killion, M. W. (1941). A history of Spring Arbor Seminary and Junior College (ICOMM). University of Michigan. Retrieved from http://www.worldcat.org/title/history-of-spring-arbor-seminary-and-junior-college/oclc/11605017&referer=brief_results

Kindergaren Activities. (1969). GEN, Kansas City, MO: Beacon Hill Press.

Kindergarten Activities. (1954). GEN, Winona Lake, IN: Light and Life Press.

Kindergarten Bible Stories, 1-16, No. 4. (1954). GEN, Winona Lake, IN: Light and Life Press.

Kindergarten Stories. 1-16, No. 4. (1954). GEN, Winona Lake, IN.: Light and Life Press.

Kindergarten Teacher. (n.d.). GEN, Kansas City, MO: Beacon Hill Press.

Kindschi, P. (1964). Entire sanctification : studies in Christian holiness. BOOK, Marion, IN: Wesley Press.

King, C. W. (1975). Infant baptism in Biblical and Wesleyan theology (THES). Asbury Theological Seminary.

King, C. W. (1990). Mobilizing the laity : a strategy for obtaining greater numerical growth in the Wilmore Free Methodist Church (THES).

King, W. (1977). The joy of ministry : my role in Christian education. BOOK, Winona Lake, Ind.: Light and Life Press.

Kingsley, C. (1965). Go! : Revolutionary New Testament Christianity. BOOK, Grand Rapids: Zondervan.

Kingsley, C. (1976). Do : manifesto for concerned Christian community, manual for meaning in mobilization of manpower. BOOK, Winona Lake Ind.: Light and Life Men International.

Kingsley, C. W. (1990). I stand by the door : the autobiography of Charles W. Kingsley. BOOK, Indianapolis, Ind.: Light and Life Men International.

Kirchhofer, W. (2009). Fire among the stubble : church renewal in the Wesleyan tradition. BOOK.

Kirkpatrick, C. D., & Church, W. M. S. of the F. M. (1977). Cow in the clinic, and other missionary stories from around the world. BOOK, Winona Lake, Ind.: Light and Life Press.

Kirkpatrick, C. D., & Free Methodist Church of North America. (1971). Profile of missions. BOOK, Winona Lake, Ind.: Light and Life Press.

Klein, M. (1914). By Nippon's lotus ponds pen pictures of real Japan. BOOK, New York ;Chicago: Fleming H. Revell Company.

Kleinsteuber, R. W. (1980). Coming of age : the making of a Canadian Free Methodist Church. BOOK, Hamilton, Ont.: Light and Life Press, Canada.

Kleinsteuber, R. W. (1984). More than a memory : the renewal of Methodism in Canada. BOOK, Mississauga, Ont.: Light and Life Press Canada.

Kline, G. E., College, M. C. of G., & Greenville, I. (1942). The Wesleyan message bearing fruit. BOOK, Winona Lake, Ind.: Light and Life Press.

Knox, L. H. (1963). Philippians and Thessalonians : leader's guide. BOOK, Winona Lake, Ind.: Light and Life Press.

Knox, L. H. (1970). Security for believers. BOOK, Winona Lake, Ind.: Light and Life Press.

Knox, L. H. (1972). Key to holiness theology : a relational understanding. BOOK, Winona Lake, Ind.: Light and Life Press.

Knox, L. H. (1974). Key Biblical perspectives on tongues. BOOK, Winona Lake, Ind.: Light and Life Press.

Knox, L. H. (1976a). Everybody wants your money : how to be generous, not gullible. BOOK, Winona Lake, Ind.: Light and Life Press.

Knox, L. H. (1976b). The Free Methodist minister. BOOK, Winona Lake, Ind.: Light and Life Press.

Knox, L. H. (1977). A faith to grow. BOOK, Winona Lake, IN: Light and Life Press.

Knox, L. H., Martin, C., & Sparrow, R. (1999). Building holy relationships : prayers, sermons, and other writings. BOOK, Indianapolis, IN: Light and Life Communications.

Knox, L. H., Wesley, J., Wesley, C., & Free Methodist Church of North America. (1976). The Faith and life of a Free Methodist. BOOK, Winona Lake, Ind.: Free Methodist Pub. House.

Krober, L. L., & Free Methodist Church of North America Board of Bishops. (2006). Pastors and church leaders manual : resources for leading local churches. BOOK, Indianapolis, Ind.: Light and Life Communications.

Kuhn, H. B. (1966). Colossians, Philemon : leader's guide. BOOK, Winona Lake, Ind.: Light and Life Press.

Kulaga, J. S. (2007). Edward Payson Hart : the second man of Free Methodism. BOOK, Spring Arbor, Mich.: Spring Arbor University Press.

Kysor, K. (1976a). A history of The Free Methodist Church of Cattaraugus, New York. BOOK, Cattaraugus, NY: Printed by the Randolph Register.

Kysor, K. (1976b). Benjamin Titus Roberts and the Free Methodist Church. BOOK, Cattaraugus, N.Y.: s.n.

Kysor, K. (1976c). The wonderful ways and works of God. BOOK, Cattaraugus, NY.

La Due, G., & Mead, M. L. D. (1900). Gertrude Black La Due and family papers (UNPB).

La Due, J., & La Due, W. K. (1898). The life of Rev. Thomas Scott La Due : with some sketches and other writings. BOOK, Chicago: Free Methodist Pub. House.

Lake, C. (1971). Our goodly heritage : a history of the Gerry homes. BOOK, Gerry, NY: Heritage Village; Printed by Falconer Print. and Design Inc.

Lamb, E. W., & Shultz, L. W. (1964). Indian lore. BOOK, Winona Lake, Ind.: Light and Life Press.

Lamson, B. S. (1950). The holiness teachings of New Testament literature : part I: the teachings of Jesus. BOOK, Winona Lake, Ind.: Light and Life Press.

Lamson, B. S. (1951). Lights in the world; Free Methodist missions at work. BOOK, Winona Lake, Ind.: General missionary board.

Lamson, B. S. (1960). Venture! : the frontiers of Free Methodism. BOOK, Winona Lake, Ind.: Light and Life Press.

Lamson, B. S. (1963). To catch the tide. BOOK, Winona Lake, Ind.: General Missionary Board.

Lamson, B. S. (1987). Greater works than these. BOOK, Winona Lake, Ind.: Light and Life Press.

Lancashire Family History and Heraldry Society. (n.d.). Blackburn nonconformist chapels monumental inscriptions, Lancashire. BOOK. Ramsbottom: Lancashire Family History and Heraldry Society.

Larm, T. A. (2004). A grammar of conversion (THES).

Las Cruces Free Methodist Church. (1958). Las Cruces Free Methodist Church records, (UNPB).

Latourette, K. (1937). A history of the expansion of Christianity. BOOK, New York; London: Harper & Brothers.

Leach, L. (1963). Pastor establishes seminary.

Learn and Do. (1969). GEN, Marion, Ind.: Wesley Press.

Lee, J. (1900). The illustrated history of Methodism the story of the origin and progress of the Methodist church, from its foundation by John Wesley to the present day. Written in popular style and illustrated by. BOOK, St Louis, MI: The Methodist Magazine Pub. Co.

Lee, J. C. (1994). A gospel team training program for the Kaohsiung Tsz Chiang Free Methodist Church (THES).

Lee, L., & Roberts, B. T. (1985). Holiness tracts defending the ministry of women. BOOK, New York: Garland Publ.

Leech, K. (1976). True witness : the amazing story of Detective Leech. BOOK, Winona Lake, IN: Christian Witness Crusades Light and Life Men International.

Leech, K. (1995). Dark providence, bright promise. BOOK, Indianapolis: Light and Life Press.

Leete, F. (1948a). Methodist bishops--personal notes and bibliography : with quotations from unpublished writings and reminiscences. BOOK, Nashville: Parthenon Press.

Leete, F. (1948b). Methodist bishops: personal notes and bibliography. BOOK, Nashville: Printed by the Parthenon Press.

Lesalnieks, K. (1970). Unsearchable ways of God : Isaiah 55: 8-9. BOOK, Bicknell, Ind.: Fellowship Promoter Press.

Lewis, L. G. (1931). Mitama no mi = The Fruite of the Spirit. BOOK, Tokyo-to: Jiyu Mesojisutosha Shuppanbu, dc 1931, Showa 6.

Lewis, M. E. (1900). The invisible railway. BOOK, Winona Lake, Ind.: Light and Life Press.

Lieby, R. J. (1960). Here's your answer! BOOK, Winona Lake, Ind.: Published by Light and Life Press for the Forward Movement of the Free Methodist Church.

Life Line Homes Incorporated. (n.d.). Life lines. JFULL, Kansas City, KS: Life Line Homes, Inc.

Light and Life Adult. (1885). GEN, Chicago, IL: Light and Life Press.

Light and Life Beginner Teacher. 1-4, No. 2. (1948). GEN, Winona Lake, IN: Light and Life Press.

Light and Life Evangel. (1912). GEN, Chicago, IL; Winona Lake, IN: Light and Life Press.

Light and Life Graded Series. (n.d.). GEN, Winona Lake, IN: Light and Life Press.

Light and Life Press. (n.d.). The Junior's friend. The Junior's Friend. JFULL, Chicago, IL: Light and Life Press.

Light and Life Teacher's Quarterly. (1889). GEN, Chicago, IL; Winona Lake, IN: Light and Life Press.

Light and Life Teacher's Quarterly for the Graded Primary Series. 1-9, No. 1. (1941). GEN, Winona Lake, IN: Light and Life Press.

Light and Life Youth. 1-76, No. 3. (1885). GEN, Chicago, IL; Winona Lake, IN: Light and Life Press.

Lily of the Valley. 1-10, No. 12. (1897). GEN, Chicago, IL: W.B. Rose.

Lincicome, F. (n.d.). The doubles of the Bible. BOOK, Atlanta, GA: Repairer Pub. Co.

Lincicome, F. (1932a). A lot in Sodom. BOOK, Winona Lake, Ind.: Light and Life Press.

Lincicome, F. (1932b). Behold the man! BOOK, Apollo, Pa.: West Pub. Co.

Lincicome, F. (1932c). The three D's of the sanctified. BOOK, Winona Lake, Ind.: Light and life Press.

Lincicome, F. (1933). What is your life? BOOK, Chicago, Ill.: Light and life Press.

Lincicome, F. (1934). Enemies of the home. BOOK, Winona Lake, IN: Light and Life Press.

Lincicome, F. (1935). A tribute to mothers. BOOK.

Lincicome, F. (1940). The soul. BOOK, Apollo, Pa.: West Pub. Co.

Linton, J. (1947a). From coalpit to pulpit : an informal autobiography. BOOK, NI: Light and Life Press.

Linton, J. (1947b). Tears in heaven : and other sermons. BOOK, SI: Light and Life Press.

Livermore, H. E. (1962). Psalms. BOOK, Winona Lake, Ind.: Light and Life Press.

Livermore, P. (1982). Resources for renewal : Romans study guide. BOOK, Winona Lake, IN: Light and Life Press.

Livermore, P. (1995). The God of our salvation : Christian theology from the Wesleyan perspective. BOOK, Indianapolis, IN: Light and Life Press.

Living hymns of Charles Wesley. The singing saint. (1957). BOOK, Winona Lake, Ind.: Light and Life Press.

Livingston, G. H. (1960a). Genesis. BOOK, Winona Lake, Ind.: Light and Life Press.

Livingston, G. H. (1960b). God's spokesman. BOOK, Winona Lake, IN: Light and Life Press.

Livingston, G. H. (1960c). Roots of the Church in the Old Testament. BOOK, Winona Lake, IN: Light and Life Press.

Livingston, G. H. (1971). Genesis : leader's guide. BOOK, Winona Lake, Ind.: Light and Life Press.

Livingston, G. H. (1981a). Origins of life and faith : Genesis A : study guide. BOOK, Winona Lake, Ind.: Light and Life Press.

Livingston, G. H. (1981b). Trial and triumph : Genesis B, study guide. BOOK, Winona Lake, Ind.: Light and Life Press.

Livingstone, G. H. (1963). Jeremiah, Lamentations : leader's guide. BOOK, Winona Lake, Ind.: Light and Life Press.

Livingstone, G. H. (1964). Jeremiah-B and Lamentations. BOOK, Winona Lake, Ind.: Light and Life Press.

Lois Evelyn Worbois. (n.d.).

Looman, J. (n.d.). The story of my life. BOOK, Allegan, Mich.: John Looman.

Lorenz, G. V. (2005). Leading from the margins : recovering the Christian tradition of hospitality in church leadership (THES).

Los Angeles Pacific College, & Los Angeles Free Methodist Seminary. (1903). Articles of incorporation and by-laws, 1903-1965. BOOK, Los Angeles, Calif.: Los Angeles Pacific College.

Loss, M. (1983). Culture shock : dealing with stress in cross-cultural living. BOOK, Winona Lake, Ind.: Light and Life Press.

Louth Free Methodist Church. (1854). The Regulations of the Louth Free Methodist Church : with introductory observations. BOOK, Louth: E. Squire.

Louth Free Methodist Church. (1882). Rules of the Free Methodist Church, Louth : and of the country churches in the Louth circuit : also the Louth Free Methodist circuit regulations. BOOK, Louth, England: Printed at the Times Works.

Love, marriage - and other hazards. (1970). BOOK, Published for Aldersgate Associates by Beacon Hill Press of Kansas City.

Lovejoy, C. (1952). College guide a complete reference book to 2,049 American colleges and universities for use by students, parents, teachers, and guidance counselors. 1953-54. BOOK, New York: Simon and Schuster.

Lovell, O. D. (1962). Ephesians : leader's guide. BOOK, Winona Lake, Ind.: Light and Life Press.

Lowell, L. M. (1939). Building the house beautiful : a study in personal religious living. BOOK, Winona Lake, Ind.: Light and Life Press.

Lyon, D. (1953). My life story. BOOK, D. Lyon.

M'Geary, J. S. (1908). The Free Methodist Church : a brief outline history of its origin and development. BOOK, Chicago: W.B. Rose.

MacGeary, E. L. (1924). A sketch of the Woman's Foreign Missionary Society. BOOK, Chicago, Ill.: Foreign Missionary Society, Free Methodist Church.

Macmillian. (n.d.). The College blue book. JFULL.

Macy, V. W. (1946). A history of the Free Methodist mission in Portugese East Africa (THES).

Macy, V. W., & DeMille, L. (1984). Discovery under the Southern Cross : below the equator--missions adventures in Mozambique and South Africa. BOOK, Winona Lake, Ind.: Light and Life Press.

Magida, A. J. (1997). How to be a perfect stranger, vol. 2 : a guide to etiquette in other people's religious ceremonies. BOOK, Woodstock, Vt.: Jewish Lights Publishing.

Mahoney, M. A., & Theological Research Exchange Network. (2007). The impact of formational prayer upon spiritual vitality (THES). Ashland Theological Seminary.

Mann, W. (1955). Sect, cult, and church in Alberta. BOOK, Toronto: University of Toronto Press.

Manning, S. J. (1890). Crusade day. BOOK.

Mannoia, F., & Huston, L. (1979). Amigos. BOOK, Winona Lake, Ind.: Light and Life Press.

Mannoia, K. W. (1988). A study of the perception of faculty concerning integration of faith and learning at Free Methodist colleges (THES).

Mannoia, K. W. (1996). Church planting : the next generation : Century 21 Network, leader's manual. BOOK, Indianapolis, IN: Light and Life Press.

Manual for leaders of Light and Life men. (n.d.). BOOK, Winona Lake, Ind.: Light and Life, International, Free Methodist Headquarters.

Markell, D. (1981). Expanded ministry to youth : program guidelines. BOOK, Winona Lake, IN: Light and Life Press.

Markell, D. (1981). Origins of life and faith : Genesis a leader's guide. BOOK, Winona Lake, Ind.: Light and Life Press.

Markell, D., Cleveland, A., & America, F. M. C. of N. (1978). Young teen organizational manual. BOOK, Winona Lake, Ind.: Light and Life Press.

Markell, D., Cleveland, A., Free Methodist Church of North America, & America., F. M. C. of N. (1977). FMY organizational manual. BOOK, Winona Lake, Ind.: Light and Life Press.

Markley, R., Vandenberg, J., & Yoder, G. (1986). Ancestors and descendants of Thomas Bays Nelson and Frances Miller. BOOK, Winona Lake, Ind.: Light and Life Press.

Marsh, C. (1936). American universities and colleges. BOOK, Washington, D.C.: American Council on Education.

Marston, C. D. (1940). Life is for that. BOOK, Winona Lake, In.: Printed for the author by Light and Life Press.

Marston, L. R. (n.d.). Thumb-nail sketches of doctrinal patterns : John Calvin, Jacobus Arminius, John Wesley. BOOK, Winona Lake, Ind.: Free Methodist Heaquarters.

Marston, L. R. (1939). Youth speaks! BOOK, Winona Lake, Ind.: Light and life Press.

Marston, L. R. (1944). From chaos to character, a study in the stewardship of personality. BOOK, Winona Lake, Ind.: Light and life Press.

Marston, L. R. (1946). I need a chart. BOOK, Winona Lake, Ind.: Published for The National Association of Evangelicals by courtesy of Light and Life Press.

Marston, L. R. (1950a). Bring the books. BOOK.

Marston, L. R. (1950b). The spirit and emphasis of Free Methodism. BOOK, Winona Lake, Ind.: Free Methodist Church of North America.

Marston, L. R. (1960). From age to age a living witness; a historical interpretation of Free Methodism's first century. BOOK, Winona Lake, Ind.: Light and Life Press.

Marston, L. R. (1964). My church : a living witness from age to age. BOOK, Winona Lake, Ind.: Distributed by the Forward Movement, Free Methodist World Headquarters.

Marston, L. R. (1965). The river of spiritual life. BOOK, Winona Lake, Ind.: Light and Life Press.

Marston, L. R. (1979). He lived on our street : enduring words for today. BOOK, Winona Lake, Ind.: Light and Life Press.

Marston, L. R., & Free Methodist Church of North America. (1949). Your bishops speak. BOOK, Winona Lake, IN: Light and Life Press.

Martin, C., & Hoyer, J. (1987). Guidelines for service : I, II Timothy Titus study guide. BOOK, Winona Lake, Indiana: Light and Life Press.

Martinez, D. L. (1989). The Wesleyan way to spiritual formation teaching an adult Sunday school class (THES).

Mason, H. (1955). Abiding values in Christian education. BOOK, Westwood, NJ: Fleming H. Revell Co.

Mason, H. C. (1960). The teaching task of the local church. BOOK, Winona Lake, Ind.: Light and Life Press.

Mason, H. C., & National Sunday School Association. (1946). Reclaiming the Sunday school. The Sunday school. JFULL, Winona Lake, Ind.: Light and Life Press.

Mavis, M. (1970). A brief story of the Kentucky-Tennessee Conference. BOOK, Wilmore, KY: Mavis.

Mavis, W. (1963). The psychology of Christian experience. BOOK, Grand Rapids: Zondervan Pub. House.

Mavis, W. (1969). Personal renewal through Christian conversion. BOOK, Kansas City, MO: Beacon Hill Press of Kansas City.

Mavis, W. C. (1957). Advancing the smaller local church. BOOK, Winona Lake, Ind.: Light and Life Press.

Mavis, W. C. (1958). Beyond conformity. BOOK, Winona Lake, Ind.: Light and life Press.

Mavis, W. C. (1977). The Holy Spirit in the Christian life. BOOK, Winona Lake, Ind.: Light and Life Press.

Mayer, J. (n.d.). Free methodist churches in Lawrence County. BOOK.

Maynard, J. L. (1989). God's lamp : history of the Central Illinois Conference, Free Methodist Church. BOOK, Greenville, Ill.: Tower Press.

Mays, I. D., Dunning, J., Bancroft Library, & Regional Oral History Office. (1992). Ira Dale Mays : stories of a second-generation ironworker from Iowa. BOOK, Berkeley, Calif.: Regional Oral History Office, the Bancroft Library, University of California.

Mayse, P. T. (1982). A brief study of our philosophy of ministry : as it pertains to our current position of associate pastor in the Winona Lake Free Methodist Church (THES).

Mayse, P. T. (1987). Confronting in love : I and II Corinthians ; study guide. BOOK, Winona Lake, Ind.: Published for Aldersgate Publications by Light and Life Press.

McAllaster, E. (1954). My heart hears heaven's reveille. BOOK, Winona Lake, Ind.: Light and Life Press.

McChesney, A., & McChesney, B. (1968). Through Congo shadows. BOOK, Salem, Ohio: Convention Book Store Publishers.

McClintock, J. (1981). Cyclopedia of Biblical, theological, and ecclesiastical literature. BOOK, Grand Rapids, MI: Baker Book House.

McConnell, L. G. (1946). Faith victorious in the Kentucky mountains : the story of twenty-two years of spirit-filled ministry. BOOK, Winona Lake, Ind.: Printed for the author by Light and Life Press.

McCutchen, R. (1986). Be strong and courageous : Joshua study guide. BOOK, Winona Lake, Ind.: Light and Life Press.

McDowell, A. (1940). The passion of our Lord : six service outlines and poster suggestions. BOOK, Winona Lake, Ind.: Light and Life Press.

McElhinney, R. S., & Smith, H. L. (1942). Personality and character building,. BOOK, Winona Lake, Ind.: Light and life Press.

McGhie, A. E. (1942). Loving talks to young Christians. BOOK, Winona Lake, Ind.: Printed by Light and Life Press for the author Anna E. McGhie.

McGhie, A. E. (1947). The miracle hand around the world. BOOK, Ft. Valley, Ga.: Printed for the author.

McGrew, R. S. (1978). True accounts of divine healing. BOOK, Freeport, Pa.: Fountain Press.

McKenna, D. (1986). Renewing our ministry. BOOK, Waco TX: Word Books.

McKenna, D. L. (1955). The Sunday school dropout : the great loss of the church. BOOK, Winona Lake, Ind.: Dept. of Sunday Schools, Free Methodist Headquarters.

McKenna, D. L. (1967). Free Methodist Education-1992. Free Methodist, October 10, 23. JOUR.

McKenna, D. L. (1977). Awake, my conscience. BOOK, Winona Lake, Ind.: Light and Life Press.

McKenna, D. L. (1993). The works of Dr. David L. McKenna. BOOK, Wilmore, KY: Asbury Theological Seminary.

McKenna, D. L. (1995). A future with a history : the Wesleyan witness of the Free Methodist Church, 1960-1995. BOOK, Indianapolis, IN: Light and Life Press.

McKenna, D. L., John, E. C., Free Methodist Church of North America, Commission on Christian Education, Church-School Relations Committee, Association of Free Methodist Colleges, ... Colleges., A. of F. M. (1962). The study of Free Methodist Higher Education. BOOK.

McKeown, M. E. (1962). This is how to teach. BOOK, Winona Lake, Ind.: Light and Life Press.

McLaren, R. C. (2003). A Wesleyan theology of worship and its development in Free Methodism (THES).

McLeister, I. (1934). History of the Wesleyan Methodist church of America. BOOK, Syracuse, NY: Wesleyan Methodist Pub. Association.

McPeak, R. H. (2001). Earnest Christianity : the practical theology of Benjamin Titus Roberts (THES).

McReynolds, M., & Deaconess Hospital. (2000). Redeeming love : the legacy of the Deaconess Ladies. BOOK, The Author.

Mead, F. (1970). Handbook of denominations in the United States. BOOK, Nashville: Abingdon Press.

Mercer, F. D. (1989). The history of First Free Methodist Church of Moose Jaw, Saskatchewan. BOOK, Moose Jaw, Sask.: Quick Printing.

Mercer, F. D. (1991). The liturgical and sacramental development of the Free Methodist Church in Canada : with special attention to the rituals of baptism and the Lord's Supper (THES).

Merrill, A. (1947). Stagecoach towns. BOOK, Rochester, NY: Gannett Co.

Methodist Episcopal Church. (n.d.). Minutes of the annual conferences of the Methodist Episcopal Church. Minutes of the Annual Conferences of the Methodist Episcopal Church. ICOMM.

Miles, M. L. (1957). Quiet moments with God. BOOK, Winona Lake, IN: Light and Life Press.

Miller, D. (1934). History of Greenville College with special reference to the curriculum (ICOMM). New York University.

Miller, D. (1957). The way to Biblical preaching. BOOK, New York: Abingdon Press.

Miller, T., & Sugarcreek Free Methodist Church. (1993). Adult Bible Fellowship manual. BOOK, Sugarcreek, Ohio: Sugarcreek Free Methodist Church.

Miller, W. (1986). Holiness works : a bibliography. Kansas City, MO: Printed for Nazarene Theological Seminary by Nazarene Pub. House.

Milner, V. (1871). Religious denominations of the world : comprising a general view of the origin, history and condition of the various sects of Christians, the Jews and Mahometans, as well as the pagan forms of religion existing in the different countries of the earth. BOOK, Philadelphia: William Garretson & Co.

Mission, A. I. B., & America, F. M. C. of N. (1992). Hane' niji'a = It carries the news. Hane' Niji'a = It Carries the News. JFULL, Farmington, NJ: American Indian Bible Mission.

Mission handbook: North American Protestant ministries overseas. (1973). BOOK, Monrovia, Calif.: MARC.

Mission manual. (1966). BOOK, Winona Lake, Ind.: Commission on Missions.

Missionary Research Library. (n.d.). Directory of North American Protestant foreign missionary agencies. JFULL.

Mission Valley Free Methodist Church. (n.d.). Misshonbare hatsu nozomi. JFULL, San Gabriel, Ca: Mission Valley Free Methodist Church.

Moore, C. (1976). Hidden strands from the fabric of early Chili. BOOK, Chili, NY: Moore.

Moore, C. C. (1978). Variety and spice of a minister's life. BOOK, Lakeland, FL: C.C. Moore.

Mortenson, A. H. (1954). Knee-deep in snow and other poems. BOOK, Winona Lake, In.: Light and Life Press.

Mosher, C. E. (1983). Free Methodist educational institutions as perceived by selected constituents (THES).

Mott, E., & America, F. M. C. of N. (1944). The security of the believers. BOOK, Seattle, Wa.: Board of Aggressive Evangelism, Washington Conference, Free Methodist Church.

Mottweiler, J. H. (1981). The development of self-report instrument for pastor effectiveness (THES).

Mottweiler, J. H. (1984). Adults as learners. BOOK, Winona Lake, Ind.: Light and Life Press.

Mountcastle, W. D. (2006). Back to the future : evolving the Wesleyan model for renewal and leadership development for the Free Methodist Church (THES). Regent University, Virginia Beach, Va.

Moyer, E. (1962). Who was who in church history. BOOK, Chicago: Moody Press.

Mullikin, J. C. (1915). James Clayland Mullikin papers, (UNPB).

Mumby, E. H., & Burch, M. D. (1961). Methodism in Caistor. BOOK, Caistor: The Church.

Muncie, Indiana Sanborn Map, 1911, Sheet 51. (n.d.). ELEC, Sanborn Map Company.

Munn, N. P., & Perkins, N. (1982). Dear folks : letters from Nahum Perkins, missionary to the Caribbean. BOOK, Winona Lake, Ind.: Light and Life Press.

Murekezi, F. F. (2004). Poverty, environment and church : a Christian contribution to the earth crisis as a key to poverty eradication : a Zambian perspective (THES). University of KwaZulu-Natal, Pietermaritzburg.

Murphy, M. F. (1921). A memorial to Pauline Fowler Kimball. BOOK, El Paso, Texas: Minnie Ferris Murphy.

Murphy, T. (1941). Religious bodies, 1936. BOOK, Washington: U.S. G.P.O.

Mylander, R., & Root, H. I. (1944). Japan investment. BOOK, Winona Lake, Ind.: Woman's Missionary Society of the Free Methodist Church of North America.

Nakajima, M. G. (1983). Growth of Japan Free Methodist Church, 1945-1982 (THES).

National Task Force on Canadian General Conference. (1988). Five questions about a Canadian general conference : an interim report. BOOK, Mississauga, Ont.: Free Methodist Church in Canada.

Nazarene Theological Seminary. (1965). Master bibliography of holiness works. Kansas City, MO: Beacon Hill Press.

Nazarite documents : comprising the obligations, practical propositions, lamentations, recommendations, &c. of the Nazarite Union of the Genesee Conference of the M.E. Church. (1856). BOOK, Brockport, N.Y.: Wm. Haswell, Printer.

Nazarite review of the pastoral address of the Genesee Conference of the M.E. Church. (1857). BOOK.

Nelson, M. O. (1952). The administration of guidance in colleges related to the Wesleyan and Free Methodist churches (ICOMM). State University of New York at Buffalo.

Nelson, R. S., America, F. M. C. of N., & Education, C. on C. (1963). Here's the answer : a handbook for Sunday-school workers. BOOK, Winona Lake, IN: Light and Life Press.

Nelson, T. H., & Dake, V. A. (1894). Life and labors of Rev. Vivian A. Dake : organizer and leader of Pentecost Bands : embracing an account of his travels in America, Europe and Africa, with selections from his sketches, poems and songs. BOOK, Chicago: Published for the author by T.B. Arnold ...

Nelson, W. O. (1949). History of the Oklahoma Annual Conference of the Free Methodist Church. BOOK, Siloam Springs, AR: Silent Minister Booklet Press.

Newberg Free Methodist Church Wedding Committee. (1970). A guide for planning a wedding at Newberg Free Methodist Church. BOOK, Newberg, OR: Newberg Free Methodist Church.

Nicholson, D. L. (2002). A strategy for implementing "natural church development" quality characteristics at Open Door Free Methodist Church (THES).

No Title. (n.d.-a). Light and Life Hour Transmitter. JOUR.

No Title. (n.d.-b). Sunday School Journal, (1–52). JOUR.

No Title. (n.d.-c). Missions Outlook Leadership Letter, ? JOUR.

No Title. (n.d.-d). Ecos Evangelicos, (1-). JOUR.

No Title. (n.d.-e). Encounter. JOUR.

No Title. (n.d.-f). The Layman. Voice of the Light and Life Men's Fellowship. JOUR.

No Title. (1962). News and Views, 1-. JOUR.

Noda, S. (1967). A Grain of wheat : memories of a missionary, Eva Bryan Millikan. BOOK, Tokyo, Jap.: Free Methodist Kaganei Church ;Printed by Sanshu Printing Co.

Norbeck, M. (1931). The Lure of the hills a tale of life in the mountains of Kentucky, by Mildred E. Norbeck ... BOOK, Cincinnati, OH: Pub. for the author by the Revivalist Press.

Norbeck, M. (1947). The challenge of the hills. BOOK, Apollo, PA: West Pub. Co.

Norbeck, M. (1964). The Haitian challenge and you. BOOK, Intercession City, Fla.: Great Commission Crusades.

North American Protestant ministries overseas, 1970. (1970). BOOK, Monrovia, Calif.: MARC.

Northeast Michigan Genealogical and Historical Society. (1998). Pleasant Valley Free Methodist Church, Montmorency County. BOOK, Alpena, MI: Northeast Michigan Genealogical Society.

Northrup, L. W. (1973). Ancient mirrors for modern churches : a study of the seven churches of the book of Revelation relating them to the church in modern society. BOOK, Winona Lake, IN: Light and Life Press.

Northrup, L. W. (1988). Ambassadors for Christ : the story of Free Methodism in Northern Ireland. BOOK.

Northrup, L. W. (1999). It took a miracle : the life story of L.W. Northrup. BOOK, L.W. Northrup.

Norwood, F. (1974). The story of American Methodism a history of the United Methodists and their relations. BOOK, Nashville: Abingdon Press.

Ntakirutimana, E. (2004). A Christian development appraisal of the Ubunye Cooperative Housing Inititiative in Pietermaritzburg (THES). University of KwaZulu-Natal, Pietermaritzburg.

Nursery Activities. (1969). GEN, Winona Lake, IN: Beacon Hill Press.

Nursery Bible Story Cards, 1-12. (1958). GEN, Winona Lake, IN: Light and Life Press.

Nursery Teacher. (n.d.). GEN, Kansas City, MO: Beacon Hill Press.

Nye, G. A. (1943a). Readings concerning the history of Warsaw. BOOK, Winona Lake, Indiana: Free Methodist Pub. House.

Nye, G. A. (1943b). Readings in early local history. BOOK, Winona Lake, IN.: Free Methodist Pub. House.

Nye, G. A. (1947). Warsaw in the 1870's and 1880's. BOOK, Winona Lake, IN: Free Methodist Pub. House.

Nystrom, G. (1960). Mama married me. BOOK.

O'Brien, T. (1970). Corpus dictionary of Western churches. BOOK, Washington: Corpus Publications.

Oda, K. (1979). Oda Kaneo sekkyoshu. BOOK, Osaka-fu: Seitosha.

Olmstead, B. L. (n.d.). Serving God and the church : a brief discussion of how to live the Christian life successfully. BOOK, Winona Lake, Ind.: Free Methodist Pub. House.

Olmstead, B. L. (1938). A brief life of Paul, with a chart and six maps. BOOK, Winona Lake, Ind.: Light and Life Press.

Olmstead, B. L. (1942). Three types of eternal security : a simple and clear discussion of a doctrine which, in various forms, is being widely propagated at the present time. BOOK, Winona Lake, Ind.: Light and Life Press.

Olmstead, B. L. (1950). Being a Christian : a guide for early youth. BOOK, Winona Lake, Ind.: Free Methodist Pub. House.

Olmstead, B. L. (1951). Arnold's practical commentary on the International Sunday school lessons, improved uniform series. JFULL, Winona Lake, Ind.: Light and Life Press.

Olmstead, B. L. (1955). Our church at work : a brief manual for the instruction of preparatory members of the Free Methodist Church. BOOK, Winona Lake, Ind.: Free Methodist Pub. House.

Olmstead, B. L. (1960). Arnold's practical commentary on the International Sunday School lessons uniform series for 1952 : a practical help for all who use the unform lesson in the Sunday School, or who desire to do individual Bible study. There are ample explanatory notes ... BOOK, Winona Lake, Ind : Light and Life Press.

Olmstead, W. (1904). Light and life songs : adapted especially to Sunday schools, prayer meetings and other social services. GEN, Chicago, IL: S.K.J. Chesbro,.

Olmstead, W. (1907). Handbook for Sunday-school workers. BOOK, Chicago: W.B. Rose.

Olmstead, W. (1914). Light and life songs, number two : adapted especially to Sunday schools, social worship, camp meetings and revival services. GEN, Chicago : W.B. Rose,.

Olmstead, W. (1915). Gospel truths in song. GEN, Chicago,: W.B. Rose.

Olmstead, W. (1918). Light and life songs, no. 3 : for Sunday-schools, social worship, camp meetings and revival services. GEN, Chicago, IL : W.B. Rose,.

Olmstead, W. B., & Harris, T. (1928). Light and life songs : no. 4, for the Sunday school, social worship, missionary and evangelistic work. MUSIC, Chicago: Light and Life Press.

Olver, H. L. (1977). Biblical basis for urban ministry : a paper presented at the 1977 Continental Urban Exchange (CUE), Minneapolis, Minnesota. BOOK, Winona Lake, Ind.: Light and Life Men International.

Olver, H. L. (1999). Resurrection strategies for urban neighborhood churches in the Wesleyan Holiness tradition (THES).

Olver, P. S. (1986). A strategy for urban church planting for the Free Methodist Church of North America (THES).

Omi, M. (1956). Bakure Jiyu Mesojisuto Kyokai soritsu yonjunen enkakushi. BOOK, Berkeley, CA: Bakure Jiyu Mesojisuto Kyokai.

One way to a whole world sing : the Free Methodist Church 1974 General Conference Official Songbook. (1974). MUSIC, Winona Lake, Ind.

Ongley, M. L., & Theological Research Exchange Network. (2005). The impact of training in inner healing for sexual brokenness upon attitudes toward homosexuals (THES). Ashland Theological Seminary.

Ontario Genealogical Society, & Branch, T. B. (1980). Free Methodist cemetery : con. 1, lot 9, O'Connor Township, District of Thunder Bay, Ontario. BOOK, Thunder Bay, Ont.: Thunder Bay Branch, Ontario Genealogical Society.

Ontario Genealogical Society, & Thunder Bay Branch. (1992). Armadale Free Methodist Cemetery, Scarborough, Ontario : East 1/2 of lot 19, concession 5, City of Scarborough, Ontario. BOOK, Toronto: Ontario Genealogical Society, Toronto Branch.

Oral Hisotory Interview: David Black. (2011). ELEC. Retrieved from http://digital.library.wisc.edu/1793/55519

Orr, J. (1966). The light of the nations evangelical renewal and advance in the nineteenth century. BOOK, Grand Rapids: W.B. Eerdmans Pub. Co.

Osborne, Z. (1888). Born of the Spirit, or, Gems from the book of life. BOOK, Sarotage Springs, NY: John Johnson & Co.

Otto, K., University., A. F., & Marshburn Memorial Library. (1992). Free Methodist Denominational collection of Azusa Pacific University's Marshburn Memorial Library, 1992. BOOK, Azusa, Calif.: Azusa Pacific University.

Our heritage we cherish : Free Methodist Church, Thornbury-Peniel, 1904-1984 : eighty years of history! (1985). BOOK, Thornbury, Ontario: Thornbury Free Methodist Church.

Our Young Folks. 1-10, No. 12. (1897). GEN, Chicago, IL: W.B. Rose.

Our youth and our colleges : 1942 supplement to --your church and education. (1942). BOOK, Winona Lake, Indiana: Commission on Christian Education of the Free Methodist Church.

Owen, E. (1856). Things new and old. BOOK, Boston: Henry V. Degen.

Owen, E. (1891). Struck by lightning a true and thrilling narrative of one who was struck by lightning : with incidents, experiences, and anecdotes for old and young. BOOK, Otterville, Ont.: A. Sims.

Page, R., & Burns, E. (1988). Oral history interview with Ruby Page. SOUND.

Palmer, A. C., & Roberts, B. T. (1875). Lay aside every weight. BOOK, Yarmouth, Me.: I.C. Wellcome.

Parker, J. (1938). Interpretative statistical survey of the world mission of the Christian church: summary and detailed statistics of churches and missionary societies, interpretative articles, and indices. BOOK, New York; London: International Missionary Council.

Parsons, E. E. (1967). Witness to the resurrection. BOOK, Winona Lake, Ind.: Light and Life Press.

Parsons, E. E., & Oswalt, J. N. (1990). Living the holy life today. BOOK, Indianapolis, Ind.: Light and Life Press.

Parsons, I. D. (1915). Kindling watch-fires; being a brief sketch of the life of Rev. Vivian A. Dake, together with a compilation of selections from his writings, sermons, and poems, to which is appended a few of his best songs with the music,. BOOK, Chicago, Ill.: Free Methodist Pub. House.

Patil, S. (1989). History of the Free Methodist Church in India, 1881-1989. BOOK, Yavatmal, India: Literature Committee, India Free Methodist Conference.

Pauley, R. (1970). DeShazer returns. BOOK, Winona Lake, Ind.: Free Methodist Church of North America, General Missionary Board.

Payne, P. (1984). Teaching for life-changing learning. BOOK, Winona Lake, Ind.: Light and Life Press.

Pearce, B. W. (1900). Our incarnate Lord. BOOK, Chicago, Ill.: Light and Life Press.

Pearce, W. (1935). Worship in song : an all purpose song book for use in the church but especially adapted for use in the Sunday school, missionary, young people's & evangelistic services. MUSIC, Winona Lake, Ind.: Light and Life Press.

Pearce, W. (1942). Choice hymns : a collection of hymns from the Free Methodist hymnal, especially adapted for revival services. MUSIC, Winona Lake, Ind.: Free Methodist Pub. House.

Pearce, W. (1945). The preacher and his reading. BOOK, Winona Lake, Ind.: Light and Life Press.

Pearson, B. (1930). Wings to Aztec Land : "things to do" with each chapter : twenty-five attractive patterns for handwork. BOOK, Los Angeles, CA: Harry Harper.

Pearson, B. (1935). Off to Panama : a true adventure story of the opening doors for Christian missions in Panama. BOOK, L.A. Calif.: Free Tract Society.

Pearson, B. H. (1925). Mexican missions : home mission study book. BOOK, Chicago: Woman's Missionary Society of the Free Methodist Church.

Pearson, B. H. (1937). The lost generation returns. BOOK, Winona Lake, Ind.: Light and Life Press.

Pearson, B. H. (1939). Free Methodist Mexican missions. BOOK, Winona Lake, Ind.: Woman's Missionary Society, Free Methodist Church.

Pearson, B. H. (1940). Next! Our Sunday-School quest in South America : a "Caleb-Joshua" story of the expedition of "The spies" sent forth by the "Birthday pennies for South America fund" into the lands "Beyond the Amazon." BOOK, Winona Lake, Ind.: Light and life Press.

Pearson, B. H. (1940). The monk who lived again; a tale of South America. BOOK, Winona Lake, Ind.: Light and Life Press.

Pearson, B. H., Howland, J. H., Harper, M. W., & Root, H. I. (1938). Sunday evenings with Jesus : volume II. BOOK, Winona Lake, Ind.: Light and Life Press.

Peisker, A. (1969). Peace with God : studies in conversion. BOOK, Marion, IN Wesley Press.

Peisker, A. (1970). End times : a doctrinal study on the shape of things to come. BOOK.

Pelton, H. (1904). The Pilgrim's progress of the twentieth century. BOOK, Chicago, Ill.: Free Methodist Pub.

Pfouts, N. (2000). A history of Roberts Wesleyan College. BOOK, Rochester, NY.

Phillips, P. (1891). Metrical tune book with hymns. GEN, Chicago: T.B. Arnold.

Phillips, P., Terrill, J. G., Arnold, T. B., & Free Methodist Church of North America. (1906). Metrical tune book : with hymns and supplement. MUSIC, Chicago: Free Methodist Pub. House.

Phillips, R. M. (1940). Bird against the wind. BOOK, Winona Lake, Ind.: Light and Life Press.

Phillips, R. M. (1950). Journey by night. [Poems]. BOOK, Winona Lake, Ind.: Light and Life Press.

Phillips, H. V. (1987). From the door of an orphanage. BOOK, Sandusky, Mich.: New Creation Ministries.

Pierce, M. C. (1998). Developing structures for health and growth for Northgate Free Methodist Church in Batavia, New York (ELEC). Asbury Theological Seminary.

Pirie, M. (1955). The inseparables. BOOK, Wimona Lake, Ind.: Light and Life Press.

Pitts, R. D. (1969). A comparative environmental study of four denominational colleges (THES). Indiana University.

Prayer that really works. (1970). BOOK, Published for Aldersgate Associates by Beacon Hill Press of Kansas City.

Primary Activities. (1959). GEN, Winona Lake IN: Light and Life Press.

Primary Bible Lesson Stories. 1-17. (1953). GEN, Chicago, IL: W.B. Rose.

Primary Bible Stories. (1969). GEN, Marion, Ind.: Wesley Press.

Primary Days. 17-19, No. 4. (1951). GEN, Chicago, IL: Scripture Press.

Primary Friend. (1969). GEN, Marion, Ind.: Wesley Press.

Primary Teacher. (1969). GEN, Marion, Ind.: Wesley Press.

Primary World. 1-15, No. 3. (1955). GEN, Chicago, IL: Scripture Press.

Priset, D. W., & Herringshaw, T. W. (1999). Roberts, Benjamin Titus. Herringshaw's National Library of American Biography : Contains Thirty-Five Thousand Biographies of the Acknowledged Leaders of Life and Thought of the United States; Illustrated with Three Thousand Vignette Portraits., 18. JOUR.

Probe Student 1-3, No. 4. (1974). GEN, Marion, Ind.: Wesley Press.

Probe Teacher. 1-3, No. 4. (1974). GEN, Marion, Ind.: Wesley Press.

Progressive men and women of Kosciusko County, Indiana and 1903 plat maps : illustrated, portraits of many well-known residents of Kosciusko County, Indiana. (1989). BOOK, Winona Lake, Ind.: Light and Life Press.

ProTeen. (1971). GEN, Winona Lake, Ind.: Light and Life Press.

Pugerude, D. G. (1987). Preaching from the Old Testament : a study in exegesis and hermeneutics of the Free Methodist Church of North America (THES).

Purkiser, W. T. (1961). Leviticus, Deuteronomy : leader's guide. BOOK, Winona Lake, Ind.: Light and Life Press.

Purkiser, W. T. (1963). Joel, Jonah, Amos, Hosea, and Micah : leader's guide. BOOK, Winona Lake, Ind.: Light and Life Press.

Quest Student. (1976). GEN, Winona Lake, Indiana: Light and Life Press.

Quest Teacher. (1976). GEN, Winona Lake, Indiana: Light and Life Press.

R. B. Spencer papers. (1910). BOOK.

Rader, L. (1965). The Book of Books. BOOK, Winona Lake, Ind.: Light and Life Press.

Ray, L. P. (1926). Twice sold, twice ransomed autobiography of Mr. and Mrs. L.P. Ray. BOOK, Chicago, Ill: Free Methodist Pub. House.

Reber, C. E. (1985). The doctrine of holiness as taught by B.T. Roberts (THES).

Reber, L. B. (1901). A sketch of the life and labors of Rev. L.B. Reber in the North Michigan, Louisiana, New York, and Missouri conferences. BOOK, Clarence, Mo.: Farmers Favorite Print.

Records of the Congo-Nile Mission. (1938). GEN.

Redmond Free Methodist Church. (1983). Free Methodist Church : anniversary of fifty years ; 1933-1983 ; "to God be the glory." BOOK, Redmond, OR: Redmond Free Methodist Church.

Reed, N. (1936). World treasure trails : Africa. BOOK, Winona Lake, IN: Woman's Missionary Society Free Methodist church of North America.

Reed, N. (1938). World treasure trails II : India. BOOK, Winona Lake, IN: Woman's Missionary Society Free Methodist church of North America.

Reed, N. A. (1914). Ntombinkulu (Big Girl) : or a Zulu girl in fair View Girls' School, Natal, South Africa. BOOK, New York: Free Methodist Pub. House.

Reformed Free Methodist Church of North America. (1990). The sound of the trumpet. JFULL, Perryopolis, PA: Reformed Free Methodist Church.

Reinhard, J. A. (1971). Personal and sociological factors in the formation of the Free Methodist Church, 1852-1860 (THES).

Revell, J. A. (1994). The Nazirites : burned-over district Methodism and the Buffalo middle class (THES).

Reynolds, M., & Abbott, G (1978). Life changing learning for youth : resources that work. BOOK, Winona Lake, Ind.: Light and Life Press.

Reynolds, W. C. (1941). A flaming cross : a story of first century Christians BOOK, Winona Lake, Ind.: Light and Life Press.

Rhoden, M. M. (1956). The recent progress and methods of evangelism of holiness missions in Japan (THES).

Rhodes, M. L. (1919). Clifford B. Barrett : the "Happy Alleghenian." BOOK, Chicago: W.B. Rose.

Rich, M. (1980). Hidden treasure : a missionary story from Haiti. BOOK, Winona Lake, Ind.: Light and Life Press.

Richardson, A. (1988). A heart for God in India. BOOK, Winona Lake, Ind.: Light and Life Press.

Richardson, A. (1998). Maria. BOOK, Indianapolis, IN: Light and Life Communications.

Richardson, A., & Leder, D. (2004). In grandma's attic. BOOK, Colorado Springs, CO: David C. Cook.

Richardson, A., & Secaur, E. (1988). Andrew's secret. BOOK, Winona Lake, Ind.: Light and Life Press.

Richardson, A., & Tiedemann, K. (2000). Maria. SOUND, Van Wyck, SC: NorthStar Pub.

Richardson, J. D., Colgate Rochester Divinity School, & Crozer Theological Seminary. (1984). B.T. Roberts and the role of women in ministry in nineteenth-century Free Methodism : by Jack D. Richardson (THES). Colgate Rochester Divinity School/Bexley Hall/Crozer Theological Seminary, Rochester, NY.

Riggs, D. E. (1981). Make it happen. BOOK, Warsaw, Ind.: LP Products.

Robb, J. A. (1976). Memories of Rev. Charles H. Sage : the Free Methodist Church Canadian centennial, 1876-1976. BOOK, Ontario: West Ontario Conference of the Free Methodist Church.

Robb, J. A. (1979a). And He said unto me, write. BOOK, Woodstock, Ont.: Nethercott Press.

Robb, J. A. (1979b). Life's golden memories. BOOK, Woodstock, Ont.: Nethercott Press.

Roberts, B. (1879). Why another sect: containing a review of articles by Bishop Simpson and others on the Free Methodist church,. Rochester, NY: "The Earnest Christian" Pub. House.

Roberts, B. (1984). Why another sect. New York: Garland Pub.

Roberts, B. H. (1900a). Benjamin Titus Roberts : a biography. BOOK, North Chili, N.Y.: "The Earnest Christian" Office.

Roberts, B. H. (1900b). Benjamin Titus Roberts. Late general superintendent of the Free Methodist Church. A Biography. BOOK, North Chili, N.Y.: "The Earnest Christian."

Roberts, B. H. B. T., Roberts, A. A. R., Roberts, E. S. E. L. S. E. S., & Roberts, G. L. (1832). Family papers. (UNPB).

Roberts, B. H. B. T., Roberts, A. A. R., Roberts, E. S. E. L. S. E. S., Roberts, G. L., & Division, L. of C. M. (1990). Benjamin T. Roberts family papers. BOOK, Washington, D.C.: Library of Congress, Photoduplication Service.

Roberts, B. T. (n.d.). The right of women to preach the gospel. BOOK, Rochester, N.Y.

Roberts, B. T. (1860). The Earnest Christian. JFULL, Buffalo, N.Y.: B.T. Roberts.

Roberts, B. T. (1862). The Earnest Christian and golden rule. JFULL, Buffalo, N.Y.: Benjamin T. Roberts.

Roberts, B. T. (1878). Spiritual songs and hymns for pilgrims. BOOK, Rochester, N.Y.: B.T. Roberts.

Roberts, B. T. (1886). First lessons on money. ELEC, Rochester, N.Y.: Christian Classics Ethereal Library.

Roberts, B. T. (1948). Fishers of men, or, Practical hints to those who would win souls. BOOK, Winona Lake, Ind.: Light and Life Press.

Roberts, B. T. (1960). Living truths. BOOK, Winona Lake, Ind.: Light and Life Press.

Roberts, B. T. (1992). Ordaining women. BOOK, Indianapolis, IN: Light and Life Press.

Roberts, B. T. (1997). Fishers of men. BOOK, Indianapolis, IN: Light and Life Communications.

Roberts, B. T. (2013). Why another sect containing a review of articles by bishop simpson. BOOK, SI: Book On Demand Ltd.

Roberts, B. T., & Coates, G. W. (2007). Practical piety : daily reflections on Christian virtue. BOOK, Indianapolis, Ind.: Wesleyan Pub. House.

Roberts, B. T., & Demaray, D. E. (1996). The daily Roberts : readings for every day in the year from the writings of B.T. Roberts. BOOK, Indianapolis, IN: Light and Life Press.

Roberts, B. T., & Rose, W. B. (1912). Pungent truths : being extracts from the writings of the Rev. Benjamin Titus Roberts ... BOOK, Chicago: Free Methodist Pub. House.

Roberts, B. T., Thornton, W. O., Clarke, A., Hills, A. M., & Godbey, W. B. (2001). Chained by a leaf : the use and abuse of tobacco. BOOK, Salem, Ohio: Schmul Pub. Co.

Roberts, E. M. (1962). The bishop and his lady. BOOK, Winona Lake, Ind.: Light and Life Press.

Roller, D. T., Parker, J., & America, F. M. C. of N. (1985). Journey to Mexico. BOOK, Winona lake, Ind.: Light and Life Press.

Ronayne, E. (1900). Ronayne's reminiscences: a history of his life and renunciation of Romanism and freemasonry. BOOK, Chicago: Free Methodist Pub. House.

Ronsvalle, J. L. (1987). A comparison of the growth in the United States per capita income and population with the Free Methodist Church budget and membership for the years 1967 and 1982. BOOK, Urbana, Ill.: Empty Tomb.

Root, H. (1929). An alabaster box : the life story of Grace E. Barnes. BOOK, Chicago, IL: Woman's Missionary Society Free Methodist Church.

Root, H. (1943). A corn of wheat : the life story of Clara Leffingwell. BOOK, Winona Lake, IN: Woman's Missionary Society Free Methodist Church.

Root, H. I. (1928). Our Africa work : a brief history of the Free Methodist Mission in Africa. BOOK, Chicago, IL: Woman's Missionary Society, Free Methodist Church.

Root, L. P. (1938). Patches : missionary life in India as seen by drawing of the dog Patches. BOOK, Winona Lake, Ind.: Light and Life Press.

Root, L. P., & Benson, M. C. (1988). Outflowing love : Auntie-bai, Effie Southworth's life of loving service during her more than 50 years in central India. BOOK, Winona Lake, Ind.: Light & Life Communications.

Root, L. P., & Zahniser, A. (1971). Friends from the East. BOOK, Winona Lake, Ind.: Light and Life Press.

Roper, S. G. (1935). The story of my life from the cradle to now (1859-1935). BOOK, Portland, Or.: Samuel G. Roper.

Rose, D. R. (1961). Hebrews : leader's guide. BOOK, Winona Lake, Ind.: Light and Life Press.

Rose, D. R. (1964). Epistles of John and Jude : leader's guide. BOOK, Winona Lake, Ind.: Light and Life Press.

Rose, D. R. (1967). Hebrews : study guide. BOOK, Winona Lake, Ind.: Light and Life Press.

Rose Lake Free Methodist Church. (1988). Rose Lake Free Methodist Church : centennial directory, 1887 to 1987. BOOK, LeRoy, Mich.: The Church.

Rose of Sharon, 1-10, No 12. (1897). GEN, Chicago, IL: W.B. Rose.

Ross, I. M. (1984). Golden bells : poems and songs. BOOK, Winona Lake, Ind.: Light and Life Press.

Roth, R. H. (1967). The history of the Southern Michigan Conference of the Free Methodist Church (THES).

Rowe, A. T. (1927). Ideals for earnest youth. BOOK, Chicago: Light and Life Press.

Rowe, K. (1975). Methodist union catalog, pre-1976 imprints. Metuchen, NJ: Scarecrow Press.

Runyon, D. V. (1995). World mission people : the best of the missionary tidings, 1990-95. BOOK, Spring Arbor, Mich.: Saltbox Press.

Runyon, D. V, Auch, S., & Missions, F. M. W. (1995). Ferguson: her tractor-biography. BOOK, Spring Arbor, Mich.: Saltbox Press.

Rupert, D. A., America, F. M. C. of N., & Conference, C. (1983). Celebrating one hundred years : a centennial focus on the California Conference Free Methodist Church. BOOK, Free Methodist Church, California Conference.

Russell, C. (1959). Youth wants to know. BOOK, Winona Lake, IN: Christian Youth Supplies.

Russell, C. M. (1960). Giving our young people evangelism know how. BOOK, Winona Lake, Ind.: Light and Life Press.

Ryckman, L. D. (1979). Paid in full : the story of Harold Ryckman, missionary pioneer to Paraguay and Brazil. BOOK, Winona Lake, Ind.: Light and Life Press.

Ryff, F. J. (1954). An examination of the indigenous church principle with special reference to the Free Methodist church in South Africa (THES).

Sage, C. H., & Olmstead, W. B. (1908). Autobiography of Rev. Charles H. Sage : embracing an account of his pioneer work in Michigan, of the formation of the Canada Conference and of his labors in various states. BOOK, Chicago, Ill.: Free Methodist Pub. House.

Sager, I. M. (1974). Lights along the shore : some memories. BOOK, Falconer, N.Y.: Falconer Print. & design, Inc.

Salt Lake City, 1898: Sheet 049. (n.d.). ELEC, J. Willard Marriott Library, University of Utah.

Sanders, H. (1965). History of the Oregon Conference of the Free Methodist Church (THES).

Sayre, G., & Williamson, G. (1974). On the brink. BOOK, Winona Lake, Ind.: Light and Life Press.

Sayre, M. G. (1945). Missionary triumphs in occupied China. BOOK, Winona Lake, Ind.: Woman's Missionary Society of the Free Methodist Church.

Scearce, M. (1988). Bless this house. BOOK, Winona Lake, IN: Light and Life Press.

Scherer, F. E. (1997). Aunt Edith & Lora. BOOK, Oak Park, Ill.: James A. Scherer.

Scherer, F. S. (1976). George and Mary Schlosser : ambassadors for Christ in China. BOOK, Winona Lake, Ind.: Light and Life Press.

Schlosser, F. E. (1940). A Challenge from China. BOOK.

Schlosser, G. (1906). George and Mary Schlosser papers, (UNPB).

Schlosser, J. (n.d.). Church planting in Mindanao. BOOK, Winona Lake, IN: General Missionary Board Free Methodist Church of North America.

Schlosser, J. H. (1977). The Free Methodist Church in the Philippines : our heritage and history. BOOK.

Schlosser, R., & Groesbeck, G. H. (1956). Lighting the Philippine Frontier. BOOK, Winona Lake, Ind.: Light and Life Press.

Schoenhals, G. R. (1978). When trouble comes : How to find God's help in difficult times. BOOK, Winona Lake, Ind.: Light and Life Press.

Schoenhals, L. R. (1955). Higher education in the Free Methodist Church in the United States, 1860-1954 (THES).

Schoenhals, L. R. (1960). Light and Life choral arrangements. MUSIC, Winona Lake, IN: Light and Life Press.

Schoenhals, L. R., Church, W., & America, F. M. C. of N. (1976). Hymns of faith and life. BOOK, Winona Lake, Ind.; Marion, Ind.: Light and Life Press ; Wesley Press.

Schoenhals, L. R., Lowell, L. M., Schoenhals, L. R., Lowell, L. M., Schoenhals, L. R., & Lowell, L. M. (1950). Choice light and life songs : a collection of the best loved gospel songs and choruses, both old and new for the Sunday School, Young People's meeting, evangelistic service and children's service. MUSIC, Winona Lake, Ind.: Light and Life Press.

Schwanz, K. D. (1991). The "wooden brother" : instrumental music restricted in Free Methodist worship, 1860-1955 (THES).

Seattle, F. F. M. C., & Fellowship, M. M. (n.d.). Modern maturity fellowship herald. Modern Maturity Fellowship Herald. JFULL, Seattle, Wash.: First Free Methodist Church.

Second Free Methodist Church. (1939). Minutes of the Sunday School Board of the Second Free Methodist Sunday School : 1939-. BOOK, Peoria, Ill.: The Church.

Sellew, W. A. (1907). Clara Leffingwell, a missionary. BOOK, Chicago: Free Methodist Pub. House.

Sellew, W. A. (1914). Why not? : a plea for the ordination of those women whom God has called to preach the Gospel. BOOK, Chicago, Ill.: Published for the author by the Free Methodist Pub. House.

Sellew, W. A. (1928). Obligations of civilization to Christianity; or, The influence of Christianity upon civilization. BOOK, Chicago, Ill.: Light and Life Press.

Sellew, W. A. (1981). Why not? a plea for the ordination of those women whom God has called to preach the Gospel. BOOK, North Chili, N.Y.: "Earnest Christian" Pub. House.

Sellew, W. A., Hogue, W. T., & America, F. M. C. of N. (1913). Clara Leffingwell, a missionary. BOOK, Chicago: Free Methodist Pub. House.

Senior Teen. 1-14, No.1. (1956). GEN, Winona Lake, IN: Light and Life Press.

Senior Teen Student. (1969). GEN, Marion, Ind.: Wesley Press.

Senior Teen Teacher. (1969). GEN, Marion, Ind.: Wesley Press.

Service training handbook, improvement plans for workers in every local church. (1938). BOOK, St. Louis, Mo.: Free Methodist Church of North America, Commission on Christian Education, Dept. of Service Training.

Sharpley, J. B., & Inter Documentation Company. (1858). The scriptural character of Louth Free Methodism vindicated and the class leaders proved to be the true pastors in Methodism, according to the principles of the New Testament, and the minutes of the Wesleyan Conference. BOOK, Louth; London: William Shepherd ; Whittaker and Co.

Shaw, S. (1893). Touching incidents and remarkable answers to prayer. BOOK, Grand Rapids: S.B. Shaw.

Shaw, S. (1895). Children's edition of touching incidents and remarkable answers to prayer. BOOK, Grand Rapids, MI: S.B. Shaw.

Shaw, S. (1897). God's financial plan, or temporal prosperity the result of faithful stewardship. BOOK, Grand Rapids: S.B. Shaw.

Shaw, S. (1905). The great revival in Wales, also an account of the great revival in Ireland in 1859,. BOOK, Chicago, IL: S.B. Shaw.

Shay, E. F. (1913). Mariet Hardy Freeland : a faithful witness : a biography. BOOK, Chicago: Free Methodist Pub. House.

Shelhamer, E. (n.d.). False doctrines and fanaticism exposed. BOOK, Atlanta, GA: "The Repairer."

Shelhamer, E. (1900). Pointed Bible readings on various subjects. BOOK, Atlanta, GA.

Shelhamer, E. (1906). Popular and radical holiness contrasted. BOOK, Atlanta.

Shelhamer, E. (1914). Heart searching talks to ministers. BOOK, Louisville, KY: Pentecostal Pub. Co.

Shelhamer, E. (1917). Heart searching sermons and sayings. BOOK, Atlanta, GA: Repairer Pub. Co.

Shelhamer, E. (1919). 5 reasons why I do not seek the gift of tongues. BOOK, Wilmore, KY: Mrs. E.E. Shelhamer.

Shelhamer, E. E. (n.d.). A bit of experience. BOOK, Los Angeles, CA.

Shelhamer, E. E. (n.d.). E.E. Shelhamer's life story. SOUND, Knoxville, TN: Evangelist of Truth.

Shelhamer, E. E. (1900). Bible holiness : how obtained and how retained. BOOK, Chicago: Free Methodist Pub. House.

Shelhamer, E. E. (1900a). Seven searching sermons. BOOK, Cincinnati, Ohio: God's Revivalist.

Shelhamer, E. E. (1900b). Sixty years of thorns and roses. BOOK, Cincinnati, Ohio: God's Bible School and Revivalist.

Shelhamer, E. E. (1907). Experiences in travel and soul saving : also some of my mistakes and what they have taught me. BOOK, Atlanta, Ga.

Shelhamer, E. E. (1920). Searching sermons for saints and sinners. BOOK, Cincinnati, Ohio: God's Bible School.

Shelhamer, E. E. (1926). Sermons that search the soul. BOOK, Kansas City, Mo.: Nazarene Pub. House.

Shelhamer, E. E. (1929). Plain preaching for practical people. BOOK, Cincinnati, Ohio: God's Bible School and Revivalist.

Shelhamer, E. E. (1932). Pointed preaching for practical people. BOOK, Cincinnati, Ohio: God's Bible School and Revivalist.

Shelhamer, E. E. (1991). The ups and downs of a pioneer preacher : also some of my mistakes and what they taught me. BOOK, Salem, Ohio: Allegheny Publications.

Shelhamer, E. E., & Shelhamer, J. A. (n.d.). Ragged Elzie gave hope to the discouraged. BOOK, Winona Lake, IN: Mrs. E.E. Shelhamer.

Shelhamer, E. E., & Shelhamer, J. A. (1951). A spartan evangel : life story of E.E. Shelhamer. BOOK, Winona Lake, Ind.: Light and Life Press.

Shelhamer, J. (n.d.). God, ghosts, and demons, or, A glimpse into the beyond. BOOK, Cincinnati: God's Bible School.

Shelhamer, J. (1900). A message to men. BOOK, Kansas City, MO: Nazarene Pub. House.

Shelhamer, J. (1923). Trials and triumphs of a minister's wife. BOOK, Atlanta: Repairer Pub. Co.

Shepherd, V. A. (1993). So great a cloud of witnesses. BOOK, Mississagua, Ont.: Light and Life Press Canada.

Shepherd, V. A., Canada, U. C. of, & Canada, D. of M. in. (1993). Ponder and pray : seven weeks of meditations and prayers for personal enrichment during any season of the year. BOOK, Mississauga: Light and Life Press.

Shortwave. (n.d.). Shortwave, 1. JOUR.

Showers, H. D. W. (1896). Rev. Aura Claire Showers a sketch of his life. ELEC, Oil City, PA: H.D.W. Showers.

Shultz, L. W. (1963). Paul family record, 1763-1963. BOOK, Winona Lake, Ind.: Printed by the Light and Life Press.

Shultz, L. W. (1966). Shultz family record, 1716-1966 : from Hesse-Darmstadt to Huntingdon and Hagerstown. BOOK, North Manchester, Ind.: Lawrence W. Shultz.

Shultz, L. W., & Taylor, H. E. (1963). Paul family records 1763-1963 ... including the 1917 record. BOOK, Winona Lake, Ind.: Printed by the Light and Life Press.

Shumaker, J. T. (1972). Church growth in Paraguay (ICOMM). Fuller Theological Seminary.

Shumaker, J. T. (1992). "Having the mind of Christ" presenting christian holiness in the local church : a final document submitted to the Doctoral Studies Committee of United Theological Seminary in partial fulfillment of the requirements for the degree Doctor of Ministry (THES). United Theological Seminary, Dayton, OH.

Sigsworth, J. (1956). Careers for Christian youth. BOOK, Chicago: Moody Press.

Sigsworth, J. W. (1960). The Battle was the Lord's : a history of the Free Methodist Church in Canada. BOOK, Oshawa, Ont.: Sage Pubilications.

Silver, J. (1914). The Lord's return : seen in history and in Scripture as pre-millennial and imminent. BOOK, New York: F.H. Revell.

Simpson, M. (1878). Cyclopedia of Methodism : embracing sketches of its rise, progress, and present condition. BOOK, Philadelphia: Everts & Stewart.

Simpson, M. (1970). A hundred years of Methodism. BOOK, New York: Phillips & Hunt.

Sims, A. (n.d.). Yet not I, or, A brief sketch of the early life, conversion, call to the ministry, and some of the subsequent labors in the Master's vineyard of A. Sims. BOOK, Toronto.

Sims, A. (1886). Bible salvation and popular religion contrasted. BOOK, Kingston Ont.: The Author.

Sims, A. (1886). Helps to Bible study with practical notes on the books of Scripture designed for ministers, local preachers, S.s teachers, and all Christian workers. BOOK, Uxbridge, Ont.

Sims, A. (1896). Remarkable narratives : or, records of powerful revivals, striking providences, wonderful religious experiences, tragic death-bed scenes, and other authentic incidents, to which is added some valuable. BOOK, Kingston, Ont.

Sims, A. (1900a). Beams of light on scripture texts, or, Selected passages of the Word of God illuminated by striking illustrations and choice explanations from eminent writers : also helpful Bible readings and suggestive hints. BOOK, Toronto: A. Sims.

Sims, A. (1900b). Behold the bridegroom cometh : or, Some remarkable and incontrovertible signs which herald the near approach of the Son of Man. BOOK, Kingston, Ont.: A. Sims.

Sims, A. (1900). Grace and glory : or Godly counsel and encouragement for waiting, watching hearts. BOOK, Toronto.

Sims, A. (1902). Valuable bank notes, or, God's immutable promises, searched, tested, and found true. BOOK, Toronto: A. Sims.

Sims, A. (1905). Deepening shadows and coming glories. BOOK, Toronto: A. Sims.

Sing His Praise. (1925). Camp meeting special : a selection of songs specially designed for use in camp meetings and other evangelistic campaigns. MUSIC, Chicago: Light and Life Press.

Single in a couples' world. (1970). BOOK, Published for Aldersgate Associates by Beacon Hill Press of Kansas City.

Sizelove, R. A. H., & Corum, J. F. (2011). A sketch of my life. BOOK, S.l.: s.n.

Skyline Free Methodist Church. (1978). Skyline Free Methodist Church. BOOK, Coos Bay, Or.: Skyline Free Methodist Church.

Sloan, H. P. (1942). He is risen. BOOK, Winona Lake, IN: Light and Life Press.

Small Collections. (1870). (UNPB).

Smashey, D. (1913). The redeeming purpose of God, including a statement of the Scriptural idea of the doctrine of holiness and its advancement in the church. BOOK, Chicago: Goodspeed Press.

Smith, A. B., & Rodeheaver, H. A. (1945). Youth rally songs and choruses. MUSIC.

Smith, B. B., & Shelhamer, J. A. (n.d.). The life story of Minnie B. Shelhamer. BOOK, Atlanta: Repairer Pub. Co.

Smith, B. B., & Shelhamer, J. A. (1904). "A remarkable woman" : the life of Mrs. Minnie B. Shelhamer. BOOK, Atlanta: Repairer Pub. Co.

Smith, B. B., Shelhamer, J. A., Swauger, N. P., & Fero, G. L. (1992). Remarkable women. BOOK, Salem, Ohio: Allegheny Publications.

Smith, D. A. (1984). Central College : the first 100 years. BOOK, North Newton, Kan.: Mennonite Press.

Smith, D. P. (1950). The growth and development of the interracial movement within the Free Methodist Church of North America : a research paper in history of Free Methodism. BOOK.

Smith, E. M. (1943). A child shall lead them. BOOK, Greenville, Ill.: Tower Press.

Smith, J. (1961). Religion in American life. BOOK, Princeton, NJ: Princeton University Press.

Smith, R. (1935). Youth's incense, or, Life and writings of Blanche Charlotte Smith. BOOK, Cincinnati: God's Bible School and Revivalist.

Smith, T. (1957). Revivalism and social reform in mid-nineteenth-century America. Chapters I-XI and XIV comprise the Frank S. and Elizabeth D. Brewer prize essay for 1955, the American Society of Church History. BOOK, New York: Abingdon Press.

Smith, W. M. (1961). The incomparable Book : to guide you as you read it through. BOOK, Winona Lake, Ind.: Light and Life Press.

Snell, V. R. (1976). The theology of smallness (THES).

Snider, K. (1975). Whose ministry? : a group study book on the ministry of every Christian. BOOK, Osaka Japan: Japan Free Methodist Mission.

Snider, K. L. (1985). Ten more growing churches in Japan today. BOOK, Osaka, Japan: Japan Free Methodist Church.

Snider, K. L., & Nakae, S. (1986). Seicho suru ju kyokai no kiroku : ima, nihon demo ...2. BOOK, Tokyo: Inochi no Kotobasha.

Snider, L. (1968). Snow Pearl, a girl of Japan. BOOK, Winona Lake, IN: Light and Life Press.

Snyder, C. A. (2006). Weeping may endure for a night : a spiritual journey. BOOK, Xulon Press.

Snyder, H. A. (1973). One hundred years at Spring Arbor : a history of Spring Arbor College 1873-1973. BOOK, Spring Arbor, Mich.: Spring Arbor College.

Snyder, H. A. (1981). Under construction : Ephesians study guide. BOOK, Indianapolis, IN: Light and Life Press.

Snyder, H. A. (1990a). Radical holiness evangelism : Vivian Dake and the Pentecost Bands. BOOK, Dayton, OH.

Snyder, H. A. (1990b). Radical holiness evangelism : Vivian Dake and the Pentecostal Bands. BOOK.

Snyder, H. A. (1994). Aspects of early Free Methodist history. BOOK, Dayton, OH: United Theological Seminary.

Snyder, H. A. (2006). Populist saints : B.T. and Ellen Roberts and the first Free Methodists. BOOK, Grand Rapids, Mich.: William B. Eerdmans Pub. Co.

Snyder, H. A. (2008). Concept and commitment : a history of Spring Arbor University, 1873-2007. BOOK, Spring Arbor, MI: Spring Arbor University Press.

Snyder, H. A., Pickerill, K. W., Century, L. of J. W. for the T., & Legacy of John Wesley for the Twenty-first Century. (2003). B.T. Roberts, the Farmers' Alliance and the rise of American populism. SOUND, Wilmore, KY: Asbury College Tape Ministry.

Snyder, H. A., Runyon, D. V, & Snyder, H. A. (2011). B. T. and Ellen Roberts and the first Free Methodists. BOOK, Indianapolis, Ind.: Committee on Free Methodist History & Archives.

Snyder, L. E., & Weidman, B. E. (1940). Servant of God : life story and selected articles of Bishop Arthur D. Zahniser. BOOK, Winona Lake, Ind.: Light and Life Press.

Snyder, R. D. (2004). Being disciples, making disciples. BOOK, Indianapolis, IN: Free Methodist Church of North America.

Somers, D. O. (1986). Ministry hazards within the Free Methodist Church (THES).

Spears, A. K., & Hinton, L. (2010). Languages and Speakers: An Introduction to African American English and Native American Languages. TRAA Transforming Anthropology, 18(1), 3–14. JOUR.

Stayt, E. H. (1912). Water baptism. BOOK, Chicago, Ill.: Free Methodist Pub.

Stedwell, A. (1915). Itinerant footprints. BOOK, Shambaugh, Iowa: Stedwell.

Stevens, A. (1864). History of the Methodist Episcopal Church in the United States of America. BOOK, New York: Carlton & Porter.

Stewart, E. E. (1961). Joshua, Judges, Ruth : leader's guide. BOOK, Winona Lake, Ind.: Light and Life Press.

Stewart, J. W. (1963). Historical factors in the naming of the Free Methodist Church (THES).

Stonehouse, C. (1979). Moral Development: The Process and the Pattern. CVJ Counseling and Values, 24(1), 2–9. JOUR.

Stonehouse, C. (1980). Adventures in Belonging : membership labs for young churchmen ; leader's guide. BOOK, Winona Lake, Ind.: Light and Life Press.

Stonehouse, C., & Joy, D. M. (1969). Leader's discussion guide. BOOK, Winona Lake, IN: Light and Life Press.

Story Hour. (1885). GEN, Chicago, IL: Light and Life Press.

Story Papers. (n.d.). GEN, Winona Lake, IN: Light and Life Press.

Story Trails. 1-87, No. 8. (1943). GEN, Winona Lake, IN.: Light and Life Press.

Strategies for vital Christian living. (1970). BOOK, Published for Aldersgate Associates by Beacon Hill Press of Kansas City.

Stratton-Porter, G., Liechty, R., Cornwell, D., & Press, L. and L. (1986). Euphorbia. BOOK, Berne, IN: Liechty.

Street, N. A. (1983a). In memory of Zion Chapel, F.M. Church. BOOK, Elk City, Okla.: N.A. Street.

Street, N. A. (1983b). Zion Chapel, F.M. Church, 1905- : souvenir edition. BOOK, U.S.: s.n.

Suderman, J. P., Church, G. C. M., & Missions, C. on H. (1972). Hopi gospel songs; for church and street services in Hopi-Land. BOOK, Winona Lake, IN: Light and Life Press.

Summers, A., & Summers, G. (1952). Sanctified wholly. BOOK, Estevan, Sask.: J. Cowan.

Sung, F., & Bastian, D. N. (1993). In the church and in Christ Jesus : essays in honour of Donald N. Bastian. BOOK, Mississauga, Ont.: Light and Life Press Canada.

Sweet, W. (1961). Methodism in American history. BOOK, New York; Nashville: Abingdon Press.

Table Talk. (1969). GEN, Winona Lake, IN: Light and Life Press.

Tabor, M., Free Methodist Church of North, & Woman's Missionary Society. (1946). Puss. BOOK, Winona Lake, Ind.: Woman's Missionary Society of the Free Methodist Church.

Taiwan alphabet tour. (1967). BOOK, Kaohsiung, Taiwan: China Free Methodist Mission.

Takeya, T. D., & Bastian, D. N. (1981). Membership class guidance for pastors in the Japanese Free Methodist Church the study of Free Methodism : and, a Japanese translation of, Belonging! : adventures in church membership (THES).

Tamblyn, J. (1924). Sweet memories of a trustful life. BOOK, Morristown N.J.: E.A. Smith & Sons Printers.

Tankidaigaku, O. K. (n.d.). Osaka Kirisutokyo Tankidaigaku Kiyo. JFULL, Osaka Shi: Osaka Kirisutokyo Tankidaigaku.

Tapper, R. (1948). Full years : the life story of Helen I. Root. BOOK, Winona Lake, In.: Young People's Missionary Society.

Tapper, R. M., & Church, Y. P. M. S. of the F. M. (1931). Glimpses of victory. BOOK, Chicago: Y.P.M.S. Council of the Free Methodist Church.

Tapper, R. M., & Young People's Missionary Society of the Free Methodist Church. (1935). Life stories of foreign missionaries of the Free Methodist Church : supported by the Young People's Missionary Society, 1931-1935. BOOK, Winona Lake, Ind.: Y.P.M.S. Council.

Taylor, A. H. (1982). Rescued from the dragon : true accounts from China. BOOK, Winona Lake, Ind.: Light and Life Press.

Taylor, E., & Mission, O. B. (1970). The Olive Branch Mission, 1876-1970. BOOK, Chicago, IL: Olive Branch Mission.

Taylor, J. P. (1951). The music of Pentecost. BOOK, Winona Lake, Ind.: Light and life Press.

Taylor, J. P. (1960). Goodly heritage. BOOK, Winona Lake, Ind.: Light and Life Press.

Taylor, J. P. (1960). Soldiers of Christ. BOOK, Winona Lake, Ind.: Light and Life Press.

Taylor, J. P. (1963). Holiness, the finished foundation. BOOK, Winona Lake, Ind.: Light and Life Press.

Taylor, J. P. (1964). All roads lead to Bethlehem. BOOK, Winona Lake, Ind.: Light and Life Press.

Taylor, W. H. (1963). II Corinthians : leader's guide. BOOK, Winona Lake, Ind.: Light and Life Press.

Teaching beginners. (1953). JFULL, Winona Lake, Ind.: Light and Life Press.

Teaching Beginners. 1-3, No. 3. (1951). GEN, Winona Lake, IN: Light and Life Press.

Teaching junior high. (1953). JFULL, Winona, Lake, Ind.: Light and Life Press.

Teaching Juniors, 1-3, No. 3. (1951). GEN, Winona Lake, IN: Light and Life Press.

Teaching juniors. (1953). JFULL, Winona, Lake, Ind.: Light and Life Press.

Teaching Juniors. 1-16, No.4. (1953). GEN, Winona Lake, IN: Light and Life Press.

Teaching Preschool. 1-16, No. 4. (1951). GEN, Winona Lake, IN: Light and Life Press.

Teaching primaries. (1953). Teaching Primaries. JFULL, Winona Lake, Ind.: Light and Life Press.

Teaching Primaries, 1-3, No. 3. (1951). GEN, Winona Lake, Indiana: Light and Life Press.

Teaching Primaries. 1-16, No.4. (1953). GEN, Winona Lake, IN: Light and Life Press.

Teaching Senior Teens, 1-14, No.1. (1956). GEN, Winona Lake, IN: Light and Life Press.

Teaching Young Teens. 1-16, No.4. (1953). GEN, Winona Lake, IN: Light and Life Press.

Teed, F. E. S., Rees, P. S., Rees, S. C., Smith, J. H., & Sockman, R. W. (1919). Florence Ernestine Schleicher Teed papers, (UNPB).

Telford, J. (1886). The life of John Wesley. BOOK, Chicago: Free Methodist Pub. House.

Tenney, M. (1942). Still abides the memory. BOOK, Greenville, IL: Tower Press of Greenville College.

Tenney, M. A. (1953). Blueprint for a Christian world; an analysis of the Wesleyan way. BOOK, Winona Lake, Indiana: Light and Life Press.

Tenney, M. A. (1958). Living in two worlds; how a Christian does it! BOOK, Winona Lake, Ind.: Light and Life Press.

Tenney, M. A. (1964). Adventures in Christian love. BOOK, Winona Lake, Ind.: Light and Life Press.

Terhune, C. P. (2006). McCray, Mary F. Oxford: Oxford University Press.

Terrill, J. G. (1883). The St. Charles camp-meeting, embodying its history and several sermons by leading ministers, with some practical suggestions concerning campmeeting management. BOOK, Chicago: T.B. Arnold.

Terrill, J. G. (1889). The life of Rev. John Wesley Redfield. BOOK, Chicago: Free Methodist Pub. House.

Terrill, J. G. (1891). Talks to Sunday school teachers. ELEC, Syracuse, NY: A.W Hall.

Terrill, J. G. (2000). The life of John Wesley Redfield, M.D. BOOK, Salem, Ohio: Allegheny.

The Christian & social problems. (1970). BOOK, Published for Aldersgate Associates by Beacon Hill Press of Kansas City.

The doctrines and discipline of the Methodist Episcopal Church, 1860. With an appendix. (1860). BOOK, New York: Carlton & Porter.

The Free Methodist Church in postwar Japan. (1971). BOOK.

The national faculty directory. (1970). BOOK, Detroit, Mich.: Gale Research.

The now look of evangelism. (1970). BOOK, Published for Aldersgate Associates by Beacon Hill Press of Kansas City.

The Repairer. (n.d.). JFULL.

The shape of things to come : God's plan for the future. (1970). BOOK, Published for Aldersgate Associates by Beacon Hill Press of Kansas City.

The state of the churches in the U.S.A., 1973, as shown in their own official yearbooks : a study resource. (1973). BOOK, Sun City, Ariz.: The Agency.

The what and the why of Free Methodism. (1927). BOOK, Chicago: Free Methodist Pub. House.

The World book encyclopedia. (1976). BOOK, Chicago: Field Enterprises Educational Corp.

The young minister's companion : or, A collection of valuable and scarce treatises on the pastoral office. (1813). BOOK, Boston: Printed and sold by Samuel T. Armstrong.

Thomas, F. L., Free Methodist Church of North America, & Adult Ministries. (1980). Building the church through adult Sunday school. BOOK.

Thomas, F. L., Free Methodist Church of North America, & Adult Ministries. (1991). Adult ministries. BOOK, Salem, Or.: Free Methodist Church of North America.

Thompson, F. H. (1963). Proverbs, Ecclesiastes, Song of Solomon : leader's guide. BOOK, Winona Lake, Ind.: Light and Life Press.

Thompson, W. R. (1950). Factors in the establishment of a Free Methodist mission training school in Paraguay (THES).

Thompson, W. R. (1961). The Gospel of John : book of proofs of the deity of Christ ; official Bible quiz text. BOOK, Winona Lake, Ind.: Light and Life Press.

Thompson, W. R. (1967). John : official quiz text. BOOK, Winona Lake, Ind.: Light and Life Press.

Thompson, W. R. (1992). The road to heaven : the way of holiness. BOOK, Indianapolis, IN: Light and Life Press.

Thomson, F. (1972). The New York Times guide to continuing education in America,. BOOK, New York: Quadrangle Books.

Thomson, J. F. (1905). The life and labors of Rev. William Bramwell : a chosen, approved, valiant and successful minister of Christ, 1783-1820. BOOK, Chicago, Ill.: Free Methodist Pub. House.

Thrall, O. C. (n.d.). From darkness to light and from the power of Satan unto God. BOOK, Titusville, PA: O.C. Thrall.

Tiffany-Holtwick History Society, & Greenville College Department of History. (n.d.). The Tiffany-Holtwick journal. JFULL, Greenville. Ill.: Dept. of History, Greenville College.

Tinsley, S. H. (1992). Community: a New Testament model of ministry : a final document submitted to the Doctoral Studies Committee of United Theological Seminary in partial fulfillment of the requirements for the degree of Doctor of Ministry (THES). United Theological Seminary, Dayton, OH.

Todd, F. (1963). Camping for Christian youth a guide to methods and principles for evangelical camps. BOOK, New York: Harper & Row.

Todd, F., Free Methodist Church of North America, & Christian Youth Crusaders. (1965). Herald highways. BOOK, Winona Lake, Ind.: Dept. of Intermediate Youth.

Todd, F., Todd, P., Free Methodist Church of North America, & Christian Youth Crusaders. (1965). Cadet trails. BOOK, Winona Lake, IN: Dept. of Intermediate Youth, a member Dept. of the Commission on Christian Education Free Methodist Church World Headquarters.

Todd, P. H. (1961). Truth in action. BOOK, Winona Lake, Ind.: Light and Life Press.

Todd, P. H. (1963). Becoming a Christian : the beginning of a happy life. BOOK, Winona Lake, Ind.: Light and Life Press.

Tongue-speaking in historical perspective. (1990). BOOK, Indianapolis, IN: Light and Life Press.

Toole, I. N. (1939). Living or dead. BOOK, Winona Lake, IN: Light and Life Press.

Townsend, W. (1909). A new history of Methodism. BOOK, London: Hodder and Stoughton.

Township of Uxbridge Public Library. (1999). Church records. BOOK, Uxbridge, Ont.: Uxbridge Public Library.

Tracy, W. (Ed.). (n.d.). Dare to Discipline. BOOK, Kansas City, MO: Beacon Hill Press.

Tremain, L. C. (1968). An evaluation of the organization and structure of the family camp program of the Pacific Northwest Conference of the Free Methodist Church (ICOMM). Seattle Pacific University.

Trever, R. (1905). Life and labors of Rev. Robert Trever both in England and America also, A sketch of frontier work in connection with the Free Methodist church with an appendix containing temperance and other matter. ELEC, St. Louis: J.H. Flowers.

Tsuchiyama, T. (n.d.). Victory of the cross, or, An account of my trip in China. BOOK, Winona Lake, IN: Light and Life Press.

Tsuchiyama, T., & Olmstead, W. B. (1927). From darkness to light. BOOK, Chicago, IL: Light and Life Press.

Tsuchiyama, T., Richardson, A., & Kaneda, K. (1986). Love shining through : Tsuchiyama. BOOK, Winona Lake, IN: Light and Life Press.

Turnbull, R. (1974). A history of preaching volume III, from the close of the nineteenth century to the middle of the twentieth century (continuing the work of the volumes I and II by Edwin C. Dargan) and American. BOOK, Grand Rapids Mich.: Baker Book House.

Turner, G. A. (1952). The more excellent way : the Scriptural basis of the Wesleyan message (THES). Light and Life Press, Winona Lake, Ind.

Turner, G. A. (1959). Uesure shingaku no chushin mondai (THES).

Turner, G. A. (1962). John : study guide. BOOK, Winona Lake, Ind.: Light and Life Press.

Turner, G. A. (1964). Revelation : leader's guide. BOOK, Winona Lake, Ind.: Light and Life Press.

Turner, G. A. (1966a). Ezra, Nehemiah, Esther, Malachi. BOOK, Winona Lake, Ind.: Light and Life Press.

Turner, G. A. (1966b). Isaiah : leader's guide. BOOK, Winona Lake, Ind.: Light and Life Press.

Turner, G. A. (1966c). Isaiah -- A : first of two units. BOOK, Winona Lake, Ind.: Light and Life Press.

United for action: official workshop outlines & program of the pre-centennial convocation for Sunday school & youth leaders of the Free Methodist Church. (1957). BOOK, Winona Lake, Ind.: Lloyd H. Knox.

Upham, T. C. (1907). Inward divine guidance. BOOK, Chicago: Free Methodist Pub. House.

US Office of Education. (n.d.). Education Directory (RPRT).

Van Valin, C. E. (1990a). Tithing : God's plan for the church. BOOK, Indianapolis, IN.: Light and Life Press.

Van Valin, C. E. (1990b). Transforming grace : a biblical guide for holy living. BOOK, Indianapolis, Ind.: Light and Life Press.

Van Valin, C. E. (1991). Pastor's handbook. BOOK, Board of Bishops, Free Methodist Church (USA).

Van Valin, F. (1963). Mark : leader's guide. BOOK, Winona Lake, Ind.: Light and Life Press.

Van Valin, W. B. (1913). Little white girl in Eskimo land. BOOK, Winona Lake, Ind.: Light and Life Press.

Veldman, R. J. (2006). Classic catechism. BOOK, Indianapolis, Ind.: Light and Life Communications.

Village Green Free Methodist Church. (1964). The Village Green Free Methodist Church. BOOK, Fort Wayne, Ind.

Village Green Free Methodist Church. (1973). The Village Green Free Methodist Church : celebrating one hundred years, 1873-1973. BOOK, Fort Wayne, Ind.

Vincent, B. (1975). "As ye go, preach" : outlines and notes from the papers of Bishop Burton Jones Vincent, 1877-1931. BOOK.

Voices of praise : prepared with especial reference to the needs of the Sunday school, it will also be found suitable for the prayer meeting and other religious gatherings. (1909). GEN, Chicago : W.B. Rose,.

Vore, E. (1972). Mud pies. BOOK, Winona Lake, Ind.: Light and Life Press.

Wabash Christian Courier, & Denbo, C. T. (1960). Centennial : "Wabash Conference -- courier to every age" ; Free Methodist Church, 1860-1960 ; Wabash Conference, 1885-1960 ; 100 years of continuous service to the nations. BOOK, Wabash, Ind.: Wabash Christian Courier.

Waller, F. L. (1935). A history of Wessington Springs College. (ICOMM). University of South Dakota.

Walls, A. E., Cochrane, R. L., & Rose, M. L. (1975). Eighty years : historical sketch of thr Woman's Missionary Society of the Free Methodist Church. BOOK, by the Society.

Walls, F. E. (1977). The Free Methodist Church : a bibliography. BOOK, Winona Lake, Ind.: Free Methodist Historical Center, Free Methodist Headquarters.

Walls, F. E. (1980). The church library workbook : how to start and maintain the church library. BOOK, Winona Lake, Ind.: Light and Life Press.

Walrath, B., & Theological Research Exchange Network. (2002). Exploring the correlation between authentic worship and health in selected congregations of the Free Methodist Church (THES). Institute of Worship Studies.

Walsh, G., Meeting, B. in C. H. C., & Brethren in Christ Holiness Camp Meeting. (1993). Clearing life's burdens. SOUND, Chambersburg, PA: AV Ministries.

Walter, J., Walter, M., & Fisher, D. J. (1978). History of the Ohio Conference of the Free Methodist Church. BOOK, Galion, Ohio: United Church Directories.

Walters, O. S. (1939). Christian education in the local church. BOOK, Winona Lake, IN: Light and Life Press.

Walters, O. S. (1948). The Christian and the movies. BOOK, Winona Lake, Ind.: The Forward Movement, Free Methodist Church of North America.

Walters, O. S. (1951). You can win others; how to adventure in sharing the good news. BOOK, Winona Lake, Ind.: Light and Life Press.

Walters, S. D. (1961). Exodus - Numbers : study guide. BOOK, Winona Lake, Ind.: Light and Life Press.

Walton, K. M. (1960). Western convention : "the springboard of Free Methodism." BOOK, S.l.: s.n.

Ward, D. T. (1983). Theological education by extension : a proposal for India's Free Methodist Church (THES).

Ward, D. T., & Theological Research Exchange Network. (2001). Identifying critical areas of need for the future development of teaching lesson plans for the India Free Methodist Church (THES). Trinity Evangelical Divinity School.

Ward, E. E., America., F. M. C. of N., & Free Methodist Church of North America. (1924). Letter links. Letter Links. JFULL, Lucknow: Methodist Pub. House.

Ward, E. E., America., F. M. C. of N., Free Methodist Church of North America, & America., F. M. C. of N. (1951). Ordered steps, or, The Wards of India : a biography of the lives of Ernest Fremont Ward and Phebe Elizabeth Cox Ward, missionaries to India, 1880-1927. BOOK, Winona Lake, Ind.: Light and Life Press.

Ward, E. E., & America, F. M. C. of N. (1937). India letter links. JFULL.

Ward, E. F. (1880). Papers. BOOK.

Ward, E. F. (1923). Memory links of "our own Chickabiddie", or, Reminiscences of Mary Louise Vore. BOOK, Chicago: Free Methodist Pub. House.

Ward, E. F., Pyron, D. A., & Ward, P. E. (1878). Papers of this first Free Methodist Church missionary to India. BOOK.

Ward, E. F., & Ward, P. E. (1908). Echoes from Bharatkhand. BOOK, Chicago, Ill.: Free Methodist Pub. House.

Warner, D. (1914). Glimpses of Palestine and Egypt. BOOK, Chicago: W.B. Rose.

Warner, D. (1921). The book we study : a brief tribute to the Holy Scriptures. BOOK, Chicago: W.B. Rose.

Warner, D. S. (1925). The anointing of the Holy Spirit. BOOK, Chicago, Ill.: Light and Life Press.

Warren, R. (1955). Spiritual strength for today. BOOK, Toronto ;New York: T. Nelson.

Warren, R. (1960). You can gain spiritual strength. BOOK, New York: Nelson.

Warrington, J. M. (1981). The Humpty Dumpty syndrome. BOOK, Winona Lake, Ind.: Light and Life Press.

Watson, C. (1917). The employer, the wage earner, and the law of love,. BOOK, Lawrence: University of Kansas.

Watson, C. A. (1945). Repeal has succeeded,. BOOK, Winona Lake, Ind.: Pub. by Light and life Press.

Watson, C. A. (1946). God's plan for civil government. BOOK, Winona Lake, Ind.: Light and Life Press.

Watson, C. H. (1946a). Light and Life Scripture memory plan for Christian workers. BOOK, Winona Lake, IN: Light and Life Press.

Watson, C. H. (1946b). Light and Life scripture memory plan for Christian workers : a series of pocket-kits of selected scripture verses chosen to be hidden in the heart for ready use. BOOK, Winona Lake, Ind.: Light and Life Press.

Watson, C. H. (1950). De Shazer : Doolittle Raider Turned Missionary. BOOK, The Light and Life Press.

Watson, C. H. (1950a). De Shazer : the Doolittle raider who turned missionary. BOOK, Winona Lake, Ind.: Light and Life Press.

Watson, C. H. (1950). De Shazer, the Doolittle raider who turned missionary : a true and thrilling story of how the practical demonstration of the law of love is bringing international understanding and the spirit of Christ to Japan. BOOK, Winona Lake, Ind.: Light and Life Press.

Watson, C. H. (1950b). The fragrance of my church. BOOK, S.l.: s.n.

Watson, C. H. (1950). The Free Methodist Church. BOOK, Winona Lake, Ind.: Free Methodist Church of North America.

Watson, C. H. (1998). DeShazer. BOOK, Coquitlam, B.C., Canada: Galaxy Communications.

Watson, C. H. (2002). DeShazer. BOOK.

Watson, C. H., & Howell, R. W. (1964a). Advancing in church membership : Pastor's instruction series, youth division. BOOK, Winona Lake, Ind.: Light and Life Press.

Watson, C. H., & Howell, R. W. (1964b). Exploring church membership : pastor's instruction series, junior division. BOOK, Winona Lake Indiana: Light and Life Press.

We believe! : insights into the beliefs of Free Methodists. (1976). BOOK, Winona Lake, Ind.: Light and Life Press.

Welliver, D. (1975). I need you now, God, while the grape juice is running all over the floor. BOOK, Winona Lake, Ind.: Light and Life Press.

Welliver, D. (1976). Thank you, God, for ninety-five pounds of peanut butter. BOOK, Winona Lake, Ind.: Light and Life Press.

Welliver, D. (1978). Some of God's miracles wear cowlicks. BOOK, Winona Lake, In.: Warner Press; Light and Life Press.

Welliver, D. (1979). Dotsey's diary : her daze ["X"-figure marked through word] days and yours. BOOK, Winona Lake, Ind.: Light and Life Press.

Welliver, D. (1981). Smudgkin elves : and other lame excuses. BOOK, Winona Lake, Ind.: Light and Life.

Wesley, J. (n.d.). A plain account of Christian perfection. BOOK, Winona Lake, Ind.: Light and Life Press.

Wesley, J. (1900). On dress. BOOK, Chicago, Ill.: Published by the Free Methodist Pub. House.

Wesley, J. (1902). True holiness as taught by John Wesley : comprising his sermons on Sin in believers, Repentance of believers, Christian perfection. BOOK, Chicago: Free Methodist Pub. House.

Wesley, J. (1940). On dress and evil speaking. BOOK, Winona Lake, Ind.: Free Methodist Publishing House.

Wesley, J. (1981). John and Charles Wesley : selected prayers, hymns, journal notes, sermons, letters and treatises. BOOK, New York: Paulist Press.

Wesleyan Church, & Crusaders, C. Y. (1970). Herald highways. BOOK, Winona Lake, Ind.: Light and Life Press.

Wesleyan Church Department of Youth, & Youth. (1969). First studies in Christian teachings. BOOK, Winona Lake, Ind.: Light and Life Press.

Wesleyan Methodist Church of America, & America. (1951). Hymns of the living faith : official hymnal of the Wesleyan Methodist Church of America. MUSIC, Syracuse, N.Y.: Wesleyan Methodist Pub. Assoc.

Wesleyan Theological Society. (1963). Wesleyan Theological Society Records (UNPB).

West, B. J. (1998). Forty years of history at Flatwoods Camp, 1958-1998. BOOK, Perryopolis, Pa.: Sound of the Trumpet Tract Ministries.

West Morris Street Free Methodist Church, & Free Methodist Church of North America. (n.d.). West Morris Street Free Methodist Church good news. JFULL, Indianapolis, Ind.

Westwood, N. J. (n.d.). Revell's guide to Christian colleges. Revell's Guide to Christian Colleges. JFULL.

Wheatlake, S. K. (1900). The touch of fire : sermons on holiness. BOOK, Chicago: Free Methodist Pub. House.

Wheatlake, S. K. (2006). Casting away our confidence. BOOK, Chicago: Free Methodist Publishing House.

Whitcomb, A. L. (1900). Emmanuel and stepping stones to union with God. BOOK, Winona Lake, Ind.: Light and Life Press.

White, C. (1986). The beauty of holiness : Phoebe Palmer as theologian, revivalist, feminist, and humanitarian. BOOK, Grand Rapids, Mich.: F. Asbury Press.

White, J. M. (1981). Sixty years on the way : Kindersley Free Methodist Church, 1921-1981. BOOK, Kindersley, Sask.: Kindersley Free Methodist Church.

White, R., & Network, T. R. E. (2001). A sacrament of joy the discovery of the Lord's Table as a weekly celebration at the Stanwood Free Methodist Church in Stanwood, Michigan (THES). Northern Baptist Theological Seminary.

Whiteman, J. H. (1920). Amen hallelujah. BOOK, Winona Lake, Ind.: Light and Life Press.

Free Methodist Biography | 299

Who's who in America. 1988-1989. (1988). BOOK, Wilmette Ill.: Marquis Who's Who.

Who was who in America : a companion volume to Who's who in America. (1943). BOOK, Chicago: Marquis.

Wholesome interpersonal relationships. (1970). BOOK, Published for Aldersgate Associates by Beacon Hill Press of Kansas City.

Why don't you do something, God? (1970). BOOK, Published for Aldersgate Associates by Beacon Hill Press of Kansas City.

Wilder, J. E. (1974). The descendants of Harvey Wilder and his ancestors to 1485 in England : with a history of the Wilder name and related families of Warner, Barnhard, Benedict, Hepworth, Poore, Crocker, and Newman. BOOK, Winona Lake, Ind.: Printed by Light and Life Press.

Willard, F. B. (1983). A proposal for the training of lay ministers for Hispanic Free Methodist Churches (THES).

Willard, F. B. (1985). Idol of clay. BOOK, Winona Lake, Ind.: Light and Life Press.

Williamson, G. (1969). Julia : giantess in generosity ; the story of Julia Arnold Shelhamer. BOOK, Winona Lake, Ind.: Light and Life Press.

Williamson, G. (1972). Frank and Hazel : the Adamsons of Kibogora. BOOK, Winona Lake, IN: Light and Life Press.

Williamson, G. (1974). Geneva : the fascinating story of Geneva Sayre, missionary to the Chinese. BOOK, Winona Lake, Ind.: Light and Life Press.

Williamson, G. (1976). Gonzalo of Mexican missions. BOOK, Winona Lake, Ind.: Light and Life Press.

Williamson, G. (1977). Brother Kawabe. BOOK, Winona Lake, Ind.: Light and Life Press.

Wilson Street Mission, Wilson Street. (n.d.). ELEC.

Winget, B. (1903). Historical sketch of members of the Free Methodist Church of North America who have gone out to the foreign field of missionaries. BOOK, Chicago, Ill.: Free Methodist Pub. House.

Winget, B. (1911). Missions and missionaries of the Free Methodist Church. BOOK, Chicago: Free Methodist Pub. House.

Winslow, C. (1945). Tomorrow. BOOK, Winona Lake, Ind.: Young people's missionary Society.

Winslow, C. (1947). Forward with Christ. BOOK, Winona Lake, Ind.: Young Peoples Missionary Society.

Winslow, C. V. V. (1965). China's four sons. BOOK, Winona Lake, Ind.: Light and Life Pr.

Winslow, C. V. V. (1981). By love compelled : life story. BOOK, Winona Lake, Ind.: Light and Life Press.

Winslow, R. (1984). The mountains sing : God's love revealed to Taiwan tribes. BOOK, Winona Lake, Ind.: Light and Life Press.

Winters, P. (1954). Lab brevities. BOOK, Winona Lake, Ind.: Light and Life Press.

Wiseman, P. (1900). Purity and power, or, Sanctification at Pentecost. BOOK, Chicago: Christian Witness.

Wiseman, P. (1951). Scriptural sanctification. BOOK, Kansas City, MO: Beacon Hill.

Wolfe, K. G. (1999). A history of the founding of the Free Methodist day-schools in Southern California (THES).

Wolfe, M.-E. (2005). A strategy for mobilizing integrated local and global ministry in Free Methodist congregations, with an emphasis on gateway cities (urban hubs for unreached people groups) (THES).

Wood, J. (1944). Purity and maturity. BOOK, Kansas City, Mo.: Beacon hill Press.

Wood, J. (1996). Perfect love, or, Plain things for those who need them : concerning the doctrine, experience, profession, and practice of Christian holiness. BOOK, Oceanside, Calif.: Standard of Zion Publications.

Wood, J. A., & Adell, W. R. (1927). El perfecto amor : una explicaciÃ3n de la doctrina, la experienca, la profesiÃ3n y la practica de la santidid Cristiana. BOOK, Chiquimula, Guatemala: Mision de Los Amigos.

Woodruff, D. O., Duncombe, C., Hammond, A. P., Hurd, W., Family., H., O'Callahan, T., … Family., W. (1836). D.O. Woodruff papers (UNPB).

Woods, D. A. (1984). East Michigan's great adventure : a history of the East Michigan Conference of the Free Methodist Church, 1884-1984. BOOK, [Place of publication not identified]: East Michigan Conference of the Free Methodist Church.

Woods, D. A. (1989). Tall timber, deep roots : autobiography of Dale A. Woods. BOOK, Flint, Mich.: D.A. Woods].

Woods, D. A. (1998). Narrative pastoral leadership pastor and people working together (THES). Asbury Theological Seminary.

Woodworth, R. (1978). Light in a dark place : the story of Chicago's oldest rescue mission. BOOK, Winona Lake, Ind.: Light and Life Press.

Worbois, L. E. (1977). The thorn. BOOK, Winona Lake, Ind.: Light and Life Press.

World Book Inc. (2014). Free Methodist Church.

Yamada, M. (1966). The Pacific Coast Japanese Conference of the Free Methodist Church. (ICOMM). Fuller Theological Seminary.

Yardy, J. (1966). AadarsÃ¡ Khristi Grihajivana = Rearing a distinctive Christian family. BOOK, New Delhi, India: Jivani Vacana Sahityalaya.

Yoder, T., Smidderks, D., Free Methodist Church of North America, Department of Christian Education, Department of World Missions, & Women's Missionary Fellowship International. (1987). The great discovery. BOOK, Winona Lake, Ind.: Light and Life Press.

Young, C. (1991). Seeds for life: a guide for new believers, leaders guide. BOOK, Winona Lake, IN: Light and Life Press.

Young Teen. 1-16, No. 4. (1953). GEN, Winona Lake IN: Light and Life Press.

Young Teen Student. (1969). GEN, Winona Lake, IN: Light and Life Press.

Your church and education : Christian education handbook of the Free Methodist Church. (1941). BOOK, Winona Lake, Indiana: Commission on Christian Education.

Z.T. Gerganoff, Gerganoff, R. S., Gerganoff, S. T., & Gerganoff, Z. T. (1928). Z.T. Gerganoff architectural drawings (UNPB).

Zahniser, A. D. F., & Easton, J. B. (1932). History of the Pittsburgh Conference of the Free Methodist Church. BOOK, Free Methodist Pub. House.

Zahniser, C. H. (1957). Earnest Christian; life and works of Benjamin Titus Roberts. BOOK.

Zeeland Free Methodist Church. (1981). History of the Zeeland Free Methodist Church, 1906-1981. BOOK, Zeeland, Mich.: The Church.

Free Methodist Church

Allen, F. G. (1920). Fair View Mission Station. BOOK, Chicago: Woman's Foreign Missionary Society, Free Methodist Church.

America., F. M. C. of N. (1860). Doctrines and discipline. CONF, Winona Lake, Ind.: Free Methodist Pub. House.

America., F. M. C. of N. (1962). Recent books for ministers. JFULL, Winona Lake, IN: Free Methodist Church of North America.

America., F. M. C. of N., & Action., C. on S. (1982). Servanthood : a manual. JFULL, Urbana, IL: The Council.

America., F. M. C. of N., America., W. M. C. (or C. of, Free Methodist Church of North America, America., F. M. C. of N., America., W. M. C. (or C. of, Light and Life Press, ... Wesleyan Methodist Connection of America. (1951). Hymns of the living faith. MUSIC, Winona Lake, Ind.: Light and Life Press.

America., F. M. C. of N., Bishops., B. of, Free Methodist Church of North America, & Board of Bishops. (1998). Pastor's handbook. BOOK, Board of Bishops, Free Methodist Church of North America.

America., F. M. C. of N., Conference., G., Free Methodist Church of North America, & General Conference. (1910). Free Methodist hymnal. MUSIC, Chicago: Free Methodist Pub. House.

America., F. M. C. of N., Conference., O., Free Methodist Church of North America, & Oregon Conference. (n.d.). Oregon Conference connection. Oregon Conference Connection. JFULL, OR: Free Methodist Church of North America, Oregon Conference.

America, F. M. C. N., & Maryland-Virginia Conference. (n.d.). The news-herald. The News-Herald. JFULL, Reisterstown, MD: Free Methodist Church, Maryland-Virginia Conference.

America, F. M. C. of N. (n.d.-a). Minutes of the annual conferences of the Free Methodist Church. CONF, Rochester, N.Y.: "The Earnest Christian" Print.

America, F. M. C. of N. (n.d.-b). Sunday school journal. JFULL, Winona Lake, Ind.: Dept. of Sunday Schools, Free Methodist Headquarters.

America, F. M. C. of N. (1864). Minutes of the Annual Conferences. CONF, Rochester, N.Y.: Earnest Christian Office.

America, F. M. C. of N. (1879). The annual minutes. JFULL, Chicago: Free Methodist Pub. House.

America, F. M. C. of N. (1891). Light and life primary. JFULL, Winona, Lake, Ind.: Light and Life Press.

America, F. M. C. of N. (1901). A digest of Free Methodist law; or, Guide in the administration of the discipline of the Free Methodist church . BOOK, Chicago, Ill.: Free Methodist Pub. House.

America, F. M. C. of N. (1915). Doctrines and discipline of the Free Methodist Church. BOOK, Chicago, Ill.: Free Methodist Pub. House.

America, F. M. C. of N. (1950). God is calling you to minister. BOOK, Winona Lake, Ind.: Free Methodist Church of North America.

America, F. M. C. of N. (1951a). Conference minutes of the Free Methodist Church of North America. CONF, Winona Lake, IN: Free Methodist Pub. House.

America, F. M. C. of N. (1951b). Y. P. M. S. and W. M. S. Conference Missionary Convention : March 15 thru 18, 1951. BOOK, Winona Lake, Ind.: Free Methodist Church of North America.

America, F. M. C. of N. (1956). Records of the Free Methodist Church of North America (JFULL). Winona Lake, Ind: Free Methodist Pub. House.

America, F. M. C. of N. (1960). Yearbook of the Free Methodist Church around the world. JFULL, Winona Lake, Ind: Free Methodist Pub. House.

America, F. M. C. of N. (1967). Free Methodist Church, 1860-1978. BOOK, Sun City, Ariz.: Ecumenism Research Agency.

America, F. M. C. of N. (1970). Doctrines and discipline of the Free Methodist Church of North America. BOOK, Winona Lake, Ind.: Free Methodist Pub. House.

America, F. M. C. of N. (1971a). Discovery for juniors. JFULL, Marion, Ind.: Wesley Press, for the Aldersgate Publications Association.

America, F. M. C. of N. (1971b). Yearbook. JFULL, Winona Lake, Ind: Free Methodist Pub. House.

America, F. M. C. of N. (1974). One in love and mission : Winona '74, one way to a whole world, General Conference of the Free Methodist Church, June 24-July 1, 1974, Winona Lake, Indiana. CONF.

America, F. M. C. of N. (1983). Shoes, snakes, and shelves : missionary stories from Asia. BOOK, Winona lake, Ind.: Light and Life Press.

America, F. M. C. of N. (1990). The book of discipline, 1989. The Book of discipline. BOOK, Winona Lake, Ind.: Free Methodist Pub. House.

America, F. M. C. of N. (1999). Working together in the 21st century : the misiscn of the Free Methodist Church is to make known to all people everywhere God's call to wholeness through forgiveness and holiness in Jesus Christ, and to invite into membership and to equip for ministry. BOOK, Indianapolis, In: Free Methodist Communications.

America, F. M. C. of N., & Bishops, B. of. (1980). Lay delegate's handbook. BOOK, Free Methodist Church of North America.

America, F. M. C. of N., & Bishops, B. of. (1988). Five Bishops speak to the church : foundations, building for the new day. BOOK, Winona Lake, Ind.: Board of Bishops, Free Methodist Church of North America.

America, F. M. C. of N., & Board, G. M. (1979). Missions heartbeat, '79. BOOK, Winona Lake, Ind.: Free Methodist Church of North America.

America, F. M. C. of N., & Committee, P. (1945). The glow of fifty years : a brief history of the Oregon Conference of the Free Methodist Church. BOOK, Winona Lake, Ind.: Free Methodist Church of North America.

America, F. M. C. of N., & Communication, W. M. (1972). "Communicating cur United World Mission for Christ" : minister's manual. BOOK, Winona Lake, Ind.: Free Methodist Church of North America.

America, F. M. C. of N., & Conference, C. I. (1935). New and views. JFULL, Mulberry Grove, IL: Y.P.M.S. of the Central Illinois Conference.

America, F. M. C. of N., Conference, C. I., & Education, C. C. on C. (1938). Central Illinois advance. JFULL, Hillsboro, IL: Conference Committee on Christian Education.

America, F. M. C. of N., & Conference, E. M. (n.d.-a). The voice of the East Michigan Conference, Free Methodist Church. JFULL, Flint, MI: The Conference.

America, F. M. C. of N., & Conference, F. (1981). The Floridian challenge. JFULL, St. Petersburg, FL: Florida Conference, Free Methodist Church.

America, F. M. C. of N., & Conference, G. (n.d.-b). Quadrennial report of the General Missionary Secretary. CONF, S.l.: s.n.

America, F. M. C. of N., & Conference, G. (n.d.-c). The Convocation daily. JFULL, Indianapolis, IN: The Conference.

America, F. M. C. of N., & Conference, G. (1950). A catechism of the Free Methodist Church. BOOK, Winona Lake, Ind.: Free Methodist Pub. House.

America, F. M. C. of N., & Conference, G. P. (n.d.-d). Great Plains Conference reaper. JFULL, McPherson, KS: The Conference.

America, F. M. C. of N., & Conference, I. (1974). Commemoratin one hundred years of progress of the Iowa Conference, Free Methodist Church, 1874-1974. BOOK, Des Moines, Iowa: Free Methodist Church, Iowa Conference.

America, F. M. C. of N., Conference, I., & Committee, D. J. (1949). Commemorating seventy-five years of progress of the Iowa Conference, Free Methodist Church : 1874-1949 seventy-sixth conference and camp meeting, August 3-14, 1949. BOOK, Iowa: [Iowa Conference?].

America, F. M. C. of N., & Conference, M.-I.-K. (n.d.-e). Sharing. JFULL, Minneapolis, MN: The Conference.

America, F. M. C. of N., & Conference, M.-I.-K. (n.d.-f). Supervision. JFULL, Wessington Springs, SD: Minn-I-Kota Conference of the Free Methodist Church.

America, F. M. C. of N., & Conference, N. M. (n.d.-g). Annual session. JFULL, Mich.: The Conference.

America, F. M. C. of N., & Conference, O. (n.d.-h). Ohio Conference newsletter. Ohio Conference Newsletter. JFULL, Mansfield, OH: Ohio Annual Conference, Free Methodist Church of North America.

America, F. M. C. of N., & Conference, O. (1945). Jubilee service honoring Golden Anniversary of the Oregon Conference of the Free Methodist Church : Wednesday evening, 7:30 o'clock, July 11, 1945 ; Oregon Conference Camp Ground, Portland, Oregon. BOOK, Portland, Or.: Free Methodist Church of North America, Oregon Conference.

America, F. M. C. of N., & Conference, O. (1987a). Leadership orientation : September 26, 1987, Salem, Oregon ; "planning for 'a new day' in Oregon". BOOK, Turner, Ore.: Oregon Conference, Free Methodist Church of North America.

America, F. M. C. of N., & Conference, O. (1995a). Connection, Oregon Conference keeping Oregon's Free Methodists informed ; March-April 1995. BOOK, Turner, Or.: Oregon Conference of the Free Methodist Church.

America, F. M. C. of N., & Conference, O. (1995b). Leadership link. JFULL, Mansfield, OH: Ohio Conference, Free Methodist Church.

America, F. M. C. of N., Conference, O., Free Methodist Church of North America, & Oregon Conference. (n.d.). Annual reports of the Oregon Annual Conference. JFULL, Turner, Ore.: Oregon Conference Free Methodist Church of North America.

America, F. M. C. of N., & Conference, P. (n.d.-i). The Pittsburgh Conference herald. JFULL, Apollo, PA: The Conference.

America, F. M. C. of N., Conference, P. N., & Board, C. M. (n.d.). On waves of faith. JFULL, Seattle, WA: Conference Mission Board, Pacific Conference of the Free Methodist Church of North America].

America, F. M. C. of N., & Conference, S. (n.d.-j). The Susquehanna advance. JFULL, Syracuse, NY: The Conference.

America, F. M. C. of N., & Conference, T. (1960). The Texas Conference of the Free Methodist Church its origin and present churches. BOOK, TX: The Conference.

America, F. M. C. of N., & Conference, W. V. (1987b). West Virginia Conference echoes. JFULL, St. Morgantown, WV: The Conference.

America, F. M. C. of N., & Cryderman, W. L. (1983). Songs for renewal. MUSIC, Winona Lake, Ind.: Light and Life Press.

America, F. M. C. of N., Department, B., & Ligth and Life Press. (n.d.). Just Between Us. JFULL.

America, F. M. C. of N., & Education, C. on C. (1986). Lay leadership training handbook. BOOK, Winona Lake, Ind.: Free Methodist Church of North America.

America, F. M. C. of N., Education, C. on C., & Training, D. of S. (1953). Better workers for your church. BOOK, McPherson, Kan.: Free Methodist Church of North America.

America, F. M. C. of N., Education, C. on C., & Training, D. of S. (1955). Service training in your church. BOOK, McPherson, Kan.: Free Methodist Church of North America.

America, F. M. C. of N., Education, C. on C., & Training, D. of S. (1958). Do-it-yourself plans for service training. BOOK, McPherson, Kan.: Free Methodist Church of North America.

America, F. M. C. of N., & Education, D. of C. (1989). What is a Free Methodist? BOOK, Winona Lake, Ind.: Department of Christian Education, Free Methodist Church of North America.

America, F. M. C. of N., Education, D. of C., Board, G. M., & International, W. M. F. (1981). All god's children : stories from Central Africa. BOOK, Winona Lake, Ind.: Light and Life Press.

America, F. M. C. of N., Education, D. of C., Board, G. M., & International, W. M. F. (1982). Island adventures : treasures in Dominican and Pierre, a boy from Haiti. BOOK, Winona Lake, Ind.: Light and Life Press.

America, F. M. C. of N., & Fettke, T. (1989). The hymnal for worship & celebration : containing Scriptures from the New American Standard Bible, Revised Standard Version, the Holy Bible, New International Version, the New King James Version. MUSIC, Irving, Tex.: Word Music.

America, F. M. C. of N., & Growth, D. of E. and C. (n.d.). Reaching out in love. JFULL, Indianapolis, IN: Free Methodist Church of North America, Dept. of Evangelism and Church Growth.

America, F. M. C. of N., & Growth, D. of E. and C. (1980). Reach out in love. Winona Lake, Ind.: Light and Life Press.

America, F. M. C. of N., & Hart, E. P. (1908). A digest of Free Methodist law : or, Guide in the administration of the discipline of the Free Methodist church. BOOK, Chicago: Free Methodist Pub. House.

America, F. M. C. of N., & Institutions, A. of F. M. E. (n.d.). Heart & mind. Heart & Mind. JFULL, Indianapolis, IN: Association of Free Methodist Educational Institutions.

America, F. M. C. of N., & International, W. M. (1997). Trend analysis : number of women serving on Conference Boards and Committees, Free Methodist Church of North America, 1991-1996. BOOK, Indianapolis, IN: Women's Ministries International.

America, F. M. C. of N., & Kendall, W. S. (1955). From age to age, my church, a living witness. BOOK, Winona Lake, Ind.: Free Methodist Church of North America.

America, F. M. C. of N., & Livermore, P. (1996). Foundations of a living faith : the catechism of the Free Methodist Church. BOOK, Indianapolis, IN: Light and Life Communications.

America, F. M. C. of N., & Mission, G. C. for C. in. (1970). What is a Free Methodist? BOOK, Winona Lake, Ind.: General Council for Church in Mission, Free Methodist Church.

America, F. M. C. of N., & Missions, C. on. (n.d.). Report of the General Missionary Secretary. Report of the General Missionary Secretary. JFULL, Winona Lake, Ind.: General Missionary Secretary.

America, F. M. C. of N., & Missions, D. of W. (1987). World net. JFULL, Winona Lake, IN: Free Methodist Church, Dept. of World Missions.

America, F. M. C. of N., & Outreach, D. of E. (n.d.). Distinguished disciples : a new world of opportunity. BOOK, Winona Lake, IN: Free Methodist Church Headquarters.

America, F. M. C. of N., & Outreach, D. of E. (1969). North Michigan Conference survey : requested by the North Michigan Conference and conducted during the conference year 1967-68. BOOK, Winona Lake, Ind.: Dept. of Evangelistic Outreach, Free Methodist Church.

America, F. M. C. of N., Society, G. W. M., & International, G. W. M. F. (1897). The Missionary tidings. JFULL, Winona Lake, Ind.: General Woman's Missionary Fellowship International of the Free Methodist Church.

America, F. M. C. of N., & Society, W. F. M. (1899). Missionary tidings. JFULL, Chicago, Ill.: Woman's Foreign Missionary Society of the Free Methodist Church.

America, F. M. C. of N., & Society, W. M. (n.d.). Historical record of fifty years, 1899-1949 : Women's Missionary Society of Southern California Conference, Free Methodist Church. BOOK.

America, F. M. C. of N., & Society, W. M. (1931). Woman's Missionary Society of the Free Methodist Church, ninth quadrennial meeting : Greenville, Illinois, June 11-22, 1931. BOOK, Chicago, Ill.: Woman's Missionary Society.

America, F. M. C. of N., & Society, W. M. (1955). The Woman's Missionary Society of the Free Methodist Church, fifteenth quadrennial meeting : June 8-18, 1955, Winona Lake, Indiana. BOOK, Winona Lake, Ind.: Woman's Missionary Society.

America, F. M. C. of N., & Society, W. M. (1957). The living faith in Japan. BOOK, Winona Lake, Ind.

America, F. M. C. of N., & Training, C. B. of M. (1958). Recent books : a quarterly review for ministers. JFULL, Winona Lake, IN: Free Methodist Church of North America, Central Board of Ministerial Training.

America, F. M. C. of N., & Van Valin, C. E. (1986). Pastor's handbook of the Free Methodist Church. BOOK, Winona Lake, IN: Light and Life Press.

America, G. C. of the F. M. C. of N., Missions, C. on, & Missions, F. M. W. (1963). Quinquennial report of Free Methodist World Missions. CONF, Winona Lake, Ind.: Light and Life Press.

American Free Methodist Mission. (n.d.). Praise and prayer : giving information of the work of the American Free Methodist Mission in China. JFULL, Kaifeng, Honan, China: American Free Methodist Mission.

Anderson, D. (1989). I have you in my heart : the delights of overseas ministry. BOOK, Indianapolis, Ind.: Wesley Press.

Anderson, M. (1988). Just over the hill : my four-score-plus years under God. BOOK, Gerry, NY: M. Anderson.

Andrews, E. A. (1926). Reminiscent musings. BOOK, Spring Arbor MI: E.A. Andrews.

Andrews, R. F. (1979). When you need a friend. BOOK, Winona Lake, Ind.: Light and Life Media, Dept. of Communications, Free Methodist Church of North America.

Archer, A. C. (1930). The man with a thorn in his flesh. BOOK, Medford, Ore.: Schmul Pub. Co.

Arksey, L. (2011). A mission boyhood in Mozambique. BOOK, S.l.: Tornado Creek.

Asher, M. G. (1955). Saints alive! BOOK, New York: Vantage Press.

Babcock, C. A. (1938). Life and labours of Chas. A. Babcock : with a brief sketch of early days in the district in which he was born. BOOK, Brockville, Ont.: Standard Publishing House.

Bai, Z. (2005). Ran dian yi sheng : zhang zhe shi feng shi kuang yu xin dong xiang, Xianggang Xun li hui zhang zhe shi gong yan jiu. BOOK, Xianggang: Jidu jiao zhuo yue shi tuan.

Baker, H. (1945). Sackcloth and purple. Indianapolis, Ind.: Pilgrim Pub. House.

Baker, H. E. (n.d.). Springs of water. BOOK, Freeport, NY: Transylvania Bible School Press.

Baker, H. E. (1944). Travailing for souls. BOOK, Freeport, PA: Transylvania Bible School Press.

Baker, H. E. (1972). Unlighted glory. BOOK, Freeport, Pa.: Fountain Press.

Baker, H. E. (1978). Degrees of the Spirit. BOOK, Freeport, Pa.: Fountain Press.

Baker, H. E. (1980). Where the corn grows tall. BOOK, Freeport, Pa.: Fountain Press.

Baldwin, H. A. (1987). The coming judgment : general and at the end of time. BOOK, Salem, Ohio: Allegheny Publications.

Bastian, D. N. (n.d.). Leading the local church : for members of the official board. BOOK Winona Lake, Ind.: Light and Life Press.

Bastian, D. N. (1963). The mature church member. BOOK, Winona Lake, Ind.: Light and Life Press.

Bastian, D. N. (1973). Temptations and what to do about them. BOOK, Winona Lake, IN: Free Methodist Church.

Bastian, D. N. (1978a). Belonging! : adventures in church membership. BOOK, Winona Lake, Ind.: Light and Life Press.

Bastian, D. N. (1978b). Cultivating church members : for Free Methodist pastors only. BOOK, Winona Lake, IN: Light and Life Press.

Bates, G. (1981). Soul afire : life of J.W. Haley. BOOK, Winona Lake, Ind.: Light and Life Press.

Bates, G. E. (1975). A study of the processes of conflict resolution between a protestant mission and selected national churches overseas (THES).

Bates, G., Snyder, H. A., & Marston Memorial Historic Center. (2007). Soul searching the church : Free Methodism at 150 years. BOOK, Indianapolis, Ind.: Light & Life Communications.

Beegle, B. L. (n.d.). Panama and the Canal Zone. BOOK, Chicago: Woman's Missionary Society.

Beers, A. (1922). The romance of a consecrated life : a biography of Alexander Beers. Chicago: Free Methodist Pub. House.

Betania, R., & America, F. M. C. of N. (1991). Rancho Betania news. JFULL, Nogales, AZ: Free Methodist Mexican Missions.

Black, H. (n.d.). Is the end of the age at hand. BOOK, Los Angeles, CA: H. Black.

Black, H. (n.d.). Revival sermons on Bible prophecy. BOOK, Los Angeles, CA: Harry Black.

Black, H. (n.d.). The Holy Ghost baptism : and seven other sermons on sin, salvation, and holiness. BOOK, Los Angeles, CA.

Black, H. (n.d.). The price of a revival and other sermons. BOOK, Los Angeles, CA: Harry Black.

Black, H. (n.d.). The rich man and Lazarus and other sermons. BOOK, Los Angeles, Calif.

Black, H. (1900a). Signs of his coming and other sermons. BOOK, Los Angeles, Calif.: Mrs. H. Black.

Black, H. (1900b). Sunday morning (soul food) sermons. BOOK, Los Angeles, Calif.: Black.

Black, H. (1932). From newsboy to preacher : the story of my life.

Black, H. (1936). Soul food messages. BOOK, Los Angeles, CA: Harry Black.

Black, H. (1952). Tribulation plagues are coming : evangelistic messages on Revelation. BOOK, Los Angeles: Harry Black.

Black, H. (1953a). Satan's masterpiece, the Antichrist : evangelistic messages on Revelation. BOOK, Los Angeles: Harry Black.

Black, H. (1953b). The four horses of the Apocalypse : evangelistic messages on Revelation. BOOK, Los Angeles, CA: Harry Black.

Black, H., & Office, P. N. (1940). The four horses of the Apocalypse : evangelistic messages on Revelation : (an expository and evangelistic message for each chapter in the book of Revelation). Book 1. Messages on Revelation Book 1. Messages on Revelation. BOOK, Los Angeles, Calif.: Prophetic News Office.

Blews, R. (1939). Master workmen biographies of the deceased bishops of the Free Methodist Church. Winona Lake, Ind.: Light and Life Press

Blews, R. (1960). Master workmen biographies of the late bishops of the Free Methodist Church during her first century, 1860-1960. Winona Lake, Ind.: Light and Life Press.

Bonney, R. B. (1981). A program of ministry training opportunities for the Kentucky-Tennessee Conference of the Free Methodist Church (THES).

Bowen, E. (1871). History of the origin of the Free Methodist Church. BOOK, Rochester, N.Y.: B.T. Roberts.

Boyd, M. F. (n.d.). A more excellent way : radio messasges on the deeper spiritual life. BOOK, Winona Lake, IN: Light and Life Hour.

Boyd, M. F. (1946). Light and life hour, sixteen radio messages : world-wide gospel broadcast. BOOK, Winona Lake, Ind.: Light and Life Press

Boyd, M. F. (1953). Honoring the Spirit : 18 radio messages on love and the Holy Spirit. BOOK, Winona Lake, Ind.: Light and Life Hour.

Boyd, M. F. (1964). To tell the world : thirty radio messages. BOOK, Winona Lake, Ind.: Light and Life Hour.

Boyd, M. F., & Hour, L. and L. (1949). Light and life hour, eighteen radio messages : world-wide gospel broadcast. BOOK, Apollo, Pa.: West Pub. Co.

Brock, L. W. (1987). The life story of Rev. Lyle and Doris Brock : pioneer pastors of the Free Methodist Church in the West Kansas Conference and the California Conference. BOOK, Stanwood, WA.

Brodhead, C. A. S. (1908). Our Free Methodist missions in Africa, to April, 1907. BOOK, Pittsburgh: Aldine.

Brooks, P. F. (1969). The history of Pacific Northwest conference of the Free Methodist Church (THES).

Brown, Z. M. (1981). Trailblazers in Livingston country / by Zella M. Brown. BOOK, Winona Lake, Ind.: Light and Life Press.

Buchanan, J. (1990). The development of ecclesiastical autonomy for the Free Methodist Chuch in Canada. BOOK, S.l.: s.n.

Buchanan, R. J., Canada, F. M. C. in, & Conference, N. T. F. on a C. G. (1990). The development of ecclesiastical autonomy for the Free Methodist Church in Canada (THES).

Burritt, C. T., & Hogue, E. L. (1935). The story of fifty years. BOOK, Winona Lake, Ind.: Light and Life Press.

Calkins, P. J. (1968). A comparative investigation of levels of attainment in the development of the indigenous church principle on Latin American Free Methodist mission fields (THES).

Canada. (1927). The Free Methodist Church Act, 1927. BOOK, Ottawa: Acland, Law Printer to the King.

Canada, F. M. C. I., & Free Methodist Church. (1990). The Book of discipline. JFULL, Mississauga, Ont.: Light and Life Press Canada.

Canon, C. H., Cowsert, E. W., & Page L, R. (1983). History of the Pittsburgh Conference of the Free Methodist Church : Centennial Edition, 1883-1983. BOOK, Pittsburgh: Pittsburgh Conference.

Carpenter, A. (1926). Ellen Lois Roberts, Life and writings. A sketch. Chicago: Woman's Missionary Society.

Cathey, N. G., Free Methodist Church of North America, & Pacific Northwest Conference. (1995). Free Methodist Church centennial : Pacific Northwest Conference, 1895-1995. BOOK, Seattle, Wa.: Free Methodist Church of North America, Pacific Northwest Conference.

Chalker, G. I. (1904). Papers (UNPB).

Chauke, H. W. M., & Houser, T. (2009). H.M. Chauke research of African Hlengwe people. BOOK.

Cheeseman, S. (1981). Eight Gates Beyond. BOOK, Winona Lake, Ind.: Light and Life Press.

Cheeseman, S. (1984). Wee brown lambs. BOOK, Winona Lake, Ind.; Dept. of Evangelism and Church Growth: Free Methodist Church of North America.

Church, H. G. (2002). Theological education that makes a difference : church growth in the Free Methodist Church in Malawi and Zimbabwe. BOOK, Blantyre, Malawi: Christian Literature Association in Malawi.

Church (General) : [vertical file]. (n.d.). BOOK.

Clemente, D. W. (2002). Filipino group life : a contextual study of small groups in Free Methodist congregations (THES).

Climenhaga, G. G. (1975). The call was clear. BOOK, Victoria, B.C.: Climenhaga.

Climenhaga, G. G., & Mercer, J. (2010). The call was clear : superintendents of the Free Methodist Church in the Canadian prairie provinces, 1901-1995. BOOK, Canada.

Coates, G., America, F. M. C. of N., & Conference, G. (2003). Passion of the founders : General Conference 2003. BOOK, Indianapolis, Ind.: Free Methodist Light and Life Communications.

College, M. C. of G., & Kline, G. E. (1940). The Wesleyan message, its Scriptures and historical bases : addresses delivered at the 12th Annual Ministers' Conference, Greenville College, April 10-14, 1939. CONF, Winona Lake, IN: Light and Life Press.

Conference, F. M. W., & Kline, F. J. (1960). Asia Fellowship Conference, April 19-28, Osaka, Japan : a compilation of reports, documents, interpretation. CONF, Winona Lake, Ind.: Continuing Committee of the Free Methodist World Fellowship, North American Division.

Conference, W. B. F. B., & America, F. M. C. of N. (n.d.). Notes. Notes. JFULL, [S.l.]: Warm Beach Family Bible Conference.

Cook, E. D. (2010). Chaplaincy : being God's presence in closed communities : a Free Methodist history 1935-2010. BOOK, Bloomington, IN: AuthorHouse.

Cooke, S. A. B. (1896). The handmaiden of the Lord, or, Wayside sketches. BOOK, Chicago: Shaw Pub. Co.

Cooke, S. A. B. (1983). Wayside sketches (abridged), or, The handmaiden of the Lord. BOOK, Salem, Ohio: Schmul Pub. Co.

Coon, H. A. (n.d.). Early Free Methodists. BOOK, Pueblo, Colo.: Mary Orem.

Cox, B. E. (1998). Simply following : in all my journeying God went before. BOOK. Spring Arbor, Mich.: Saltbox Press.

Cranston, R., & Cranston, C. (1983). Stars for the baliti tree : the story of Free Methodist missions in the Philippines. BOOK, Winona lake, Ind.: Published for Women's Missionary Fellowship International by Light and Life Press.

Cranston, R. J. (1984). A workable program of church growth for the Free Methodist Church of the Philippines (THES).

Crider, D. W. (1980). Development and rationale of theological education by extension of the Free Methodist Church in South Africa with a programmed text on pastoral theology for Africa (THES).

Cryderman, L. (1999). Glory land : a memoir of a lifetime in church. BOOK, Grand Rapids, Mich.: Zondervan.

Cryderman, L. (2001). No swimming on Sunday : stories of a lifetime in church. BOOK, Grand Rapids, Mich.: Zondervan.

Cullum, D. R. (1991). What does it mean to be a Methodist? : an examination of denominational self-identity in John Wesley, the Methodist Episcopal Church and the Free Methodist Church (THES).

Cullum, D. R. (2002). Gospel simplicity : rhythms of faith and life among Free Methodists in Victorian America (THES).

Culumber, T. J. (1981). Church growth theology, strategy, and goals for the Department of Evangelism and church growth of the Free Methodist Church of North America (THES).

Damon, C. M. (1900). Sketches and incidents, or reminiscences of interest in the life of the author. BOOK, Chicago: Free Methodist Pub. House.

Davis, R. N. (1954a). Redeemed : a remarkable conversion in the heart of India : the story of Moses David, superintendent of the Eastern District, and evangelist, India Free Methodist Church ... BOOK, Winona Lake, Ind.: Woman's Missionary Society, Free Methodist Church.

Davis, R. N. (1954b). The Challenge in central India. BOOK, Winona Lake, Ind.: Women's Missionary Society, Free Methodist Church.

Dawson, L. (1962). Vital faith. Seattle, WA: Printed by L & H Print. Co.

De Voist, M. (1920). Foot-prints in my life, or, the story told in rhyme. BOOK.

De Voist, M. (1925). History of the East Michigan Conference of the Free Methodist Church. BOOK, Owosso, Mich.: Times Print Co.

DeGroot, A. T. (n.d.). American church records. BOOK, United States: Southwest Microfilm.

DeGroot, A. T., America, F. M. C. of N., God, C. of, Churches, F. of G. B., & Christ, U. F. of C. C. and C. of. (1979). Library of American church records series III : an introduction to the evangelicals. BOOK, Ecumenism Research Agency.

Demaray, D. E. (1948). Papers. BOOK.

Demaray, D. E. (1958). Basic beliefs : an introductory guide to Christian theology. BOOK, Grand Rapids: Baker Book House.

Demaray, D. E. (1978). Near hurting people : the pastoral ministry of Robert Moffat Fine. BOOK, Winona Lake, Ind.: Light and Life Press.

Demaray, D. E. (1985). The people called Free Methodist : snapshots. BOOK, Winona Lake, Ind.: Light and Life Press.

Demaray, D. E. (1990). An introduction to homiletics. BOOK, Indianapolis, Ind.: Light and Life Press.

Demaray, D. E. (2000). With His joy : the life and leadership of David McKenna. BOOK, Indianapolis, IN: Light & Life Communications.

Demaray, D. E., Free Methodist Church of North America, & General Leadership and Service Training Council. (1965). Alive to God through prayer : a manual on the practices of prayer. BOOK, Grand Rapids: Baker Book House.

DeMille, L., Hill, D., Abbott, G., Payne, P., & America, F. M. C. of N. (1984). Stories from Southern Africa. BOOK, Winona lake, Ind.: Light and Life Press.

DeShazer, J. (2012). Jacob DeShazer's personal testimony. ELEC, Wilmore, Ky.: DQB-LLC for the Marston Memorial Historical Center.

Ellershaw, J. A. (2005). Apostolic doctrine, practice and experience. BOOK, Fulwood Eng.: Free Methodist Church in the United Kingdom.

Ellis, P. N. (n.d.). To keep yourself free. BOOK, Winona Lake, IN: Forward Movement.

Ellis, P. N., Free Methodist Church of North America, & General Council for the Church in Mission. (1960). To keep yourself free : a question of Christian loyalties. BOOK, Winona Lake, Ind.: Free Methodist Church of North America, General Council for Church in Mission.

Ellis, R. W. (1993). How to plant a Free Methodist Church : effective models for the 90's. BOOK, Indianapolis, Ind.: Free Methodist Church of N.A.

Entering the open door in Formosa. (1956). BOOK, Winona Lake, Ind.: Light and Life.

Fairbairn, C. V. (1943). "Tarry ye" : with other sermons and studies. BOOK, Winona Lake, Ind.: Light and Life Press.

Fairbairn, C. V. (1957). What we believe : a brief manual of Christian doctrine for young Free Methodists and new converts based upon the catechism and articles of religion of the Free Methodist Church of North America. BOOK, Winona Lake, IN: Light and Life Press.

Fairbarn, C. V. (1960). I call to remembrance. BOOK, Winona Lake, Ind.: Light and Life Press.

Fear, L. K. (1979). New ventures : Free Methodist missions, 1960-1979. BOOK, Winona Lake, Ind.: Light and Life Press.

Fellowship, C. S. (1972). Report of evaluation study of the Free Methodist Church of North America. BOOK, Fort Morgan, Colo.: Christian Service Fellowship.

Fenwick, D. L. (1900). The Psalmist and his critic. BOOK.

Ferrell, J. D. (1997). A study of institutional identity and direction : Central College at a crossroads (THES).

Fidler, G. (2006). Adventures in India. BOOK, St. Catherines, ON: Cornerstone Research & Pub.

Fletcher, C. (2011). Sacramental discipleship as a pathway to ecclesial reformation in the Free Methodist Church in Canada (THES). Gordon-Conwell Theological Seminary.

Folkestad, R. H. (1969). A historical survey of Free Methodist world missions (THES).

Ford, G. L. (1985). Like a tree planted : the life story of Leslie Ray Marston. BOOK, Winona Lake, Ind.: Light and Life Press.

Free Methodist Church In Canada. (n.d.). Directory. Directory. JFULL, Mississauga, ON: Free Methodist Church in Canada, Canadian Ministry Centre.

Free Methodist Church in Canada. (2003). Mosaic. Mosaic. JFULL, Mississauga, Ont.: Free Methodist Church in Canada.

Free Methodist Church In Canada, & Canada West Conference. (1970). Annual reports. BOOK, Cymric, Sask: Canada West Conference, Free Methodist Church.

Free Methodist Church In Canada, Canadian General Conference, Bastian, D. N., Kleinsteuber, R. W., Retzman, A. A., Teal, G. H., ... Symposium on Worship and Preaching. (1992). Symposium on worship and preaching. BOOK, S.l.: s.n.

Free Methodist Church In Canada, & East Ontario Conference. (1970). 75 years of progress in Canadian Free Methodism, East Ontario Conference : 1895-1970. BOOK, S.l: s.n.

Free Methodist Church In Canada, & National Task Force on a Canadian General Conference. (1988). A proposal for a Canadian General Conference. BOOK, Mississauga, Ont.: Free Methodist Church in Canada.

Free Methodist Church of North America. (n.d.). Doutrinas e disciplina da Igreja Metodista Livre da América do Norte. JFULL, S.l.: Free Methodist Church of North America].

Free Methodist Church of North America. (n.d.). Free Methodist ministries today. JFULL, Indianapolis, IN: Light and Life Press.

Free Methodist Church of North America. (n.d.). Free Methodist World Mission people. JFULL, Indianapolis, Ind.: Free Methodist World Missions.

Free Methodist Church of North America. (n.d.). General conference daily. ICOMM, Greenville, Ill.: S.K.J. Chesbro.

Free Methodist Church of North America. (n.d.). Yearbook : official personnel, organization, and statistics of the Free Methodist Church around the world. JFULL, Winona Lake, Ind.: Office of the General Administrator, Free Methodist Church of North America.

Free Methodist Church of North America. (1874). Minutes of the Annual Conference and General Conference of the Free Methodist Church for the year ending October, 1874. CONF, Rochester, N.Y.: The Earnest Christian Office.

Free Methodist Church of North America. (1891). The hymn book of the Free Methodist Church. BOOK, Rochester, N.Y.: B.T. Roberts.

Free Methodist Church of North America. (1896). Probationer's guide : instruction to candidates for admission to membership in the Free Methodist Church. BOOK, Chicago, Ill.: Free Methodist Pub. House.

Free Methodist Church of North America. (1959). An Act to incorporate the Free Methodist Chiurch in Canada : assented to 8th July, 1959. BOOK, Ottawa: Queen's printer and controller of stationery.

Free Methodist Church of North America. (1973). Free Methodist Church, 1861-1978. BOOK, Sun City, Ariz.: Ecumenism Research Agency.

Free Methodist Church of North America. (1974). The vision glorious : New York Conference of the Free Methodist Church, 1974 Centennial ; Sept. 2-6, 1874, Brooklyn, N.Y., Sept. 26-28, 1974, Beach Lake, Pa. BOOK, Winona Lake, Ind.: Free Methodist Church of North America.

Free Methodist Church of North America. (1985). Annual report. JFULL, Winona Lake, IN: The Church.

Free Methodist Church of North America. (1995). Annual conference packet materials for the 1994-1995 annual conferences of the Free Methodist Church of North America. CONF, Winona Lake, Ind.: Free Methodist Church.

Free Methodist Church of North America, & Atlantic Southeast Extension Conference. (n.d.). The good word. JFULL, Lake City, AL: The Conference.

Free Methodist Church of North America, & Board of Bishops. (1957). Confidentially yours. JFULL, Winona Lake, Ind.: Free Methodist Church of North America.

Free Methodist Church of North America, & Board of Bishops. (1960). Is God calling you to the ordained ministry? BOOK, Indianapolis, Ind.: Free Methodist Church of North America.

Free Methodist Church of North America, & California Conference. (n.d.). The Echoes. JFULL, Sacramento, CA: California Conference.

Free Methodist Church of North America, & Central Illinois Conference. (n.d.). The conference gleaner : a weekly report of the ministry in the Central Illinois Conference of the Free Methodist Church. JFULL, Greenville, IL: The Conference.

Free Methodist Church of North America, & Central Illinois Conference. (1978). Centennial of the Central Illinois Conference of the Free Methodist Church. BOOK, Greenville, IL.

Free Methodist Church of North America, Christian Education Commision, & Department of Sunday Schools. (1944). Manual of the Christian Youth Crusaders of the Free Methodist Church of North America. BOOK, Winona Lake, Ind.: A.L. Brown.

Free Methodist Church of North America, Commission on Christian Education, & Department of Service Training. (1952). The story of service training. BOOK, McPherson, Kan.: Free Methodist Church of North America.

Free Methodist Church of North America, Commission on Christian Education, & Department of Service Training. (1957a). Correspondence study courses. BOOK, McPherson, Kan.: Free Methodist Church of North America.

Free Methodist Church of North America, Commission on Christian Education, & Department of Service Training. (1957b). Service training is for you. BOOK, McPherson, Kan.: Free Methodist Church of North America.

Free Methodist Church of North America, Commission on Christian Education, & Department of Service Training. (1960). Service training comes of age, 1937-1960 : nineteen hundred and sixty, centennial year. BOOK, Winona Lake, Ind.: Free Methodist Church of North America.

Free Methodist Church of North America, Commission on Christian Education, & Departmetn of Service Training. (1955). Visual aids for service training courses. BOOK, McPherson, Kan.: Free Methodist Church of North America.

Free Methodist Church of North America, Commission on Christian Education, & Departmetn of Service Training. (1958). So you're a teacher. BOOK, McPherson, Kan.: Free Methodist Church of North America.

Free Methodist Church of North America, Commission on Missions, General Missionary Board, & Free Methodist World Missions. (1970). Missions annual report. Missions Annual Report. JFULL, Winona Lake, Ind.: Commission on Missions.

Free Methodist Church of North America, Commission on Missions, Woman's Missionary Society, Young People's Missionary Society of the Free Methodist Church, & Junior Missionary Society of the Free Methodist Church. (n.d.). Annual report. In Annual report. CONF, Chicago, Ill.: Free Methodist Pub. House.

Free Methodist Church of North America, & Department of Evangelism and Church Growth. (1980). Reach out in love : a manual for the growing church. BOOK, Winona Lake, Ind.: Department of Evangelism and Church Growth, assisted by the Department of Christian Education, Free Methodist Church of North America.

Free Methodist Church of North America, & Department of Higher Education. (1968). The Aldersgate nexus. The Aldersgate Nexus. JFULL, Winona Lake, IN: Dept. of Higher Education of the Free Methodist Church.

Free Methodist Church of North America, Department of Service Training, & Commission on Christian Education. (1943). Free Methodist book bulletin. JFULL, McPherson, KS: Dept. of Service Training of the Free Methodist Church of North America.

Free Methodist Church of North America, & Department of Sunday Schools. (1950). Sunday school constitution. BOOK, S.l.: Free Methodist Church of North America.

Free Methodist Church of North America, & Department of World Missions. (1989). Across the miles. Across the Miles. JFULL, Winona Lake, IN: Dept. of World Missions, The Free Methodist Church.

Free Methodist Church of North America, & General Conference. (n.d.-a). General Conference today. JFULL, Winona Lake, IN: Light and Life Press.

Free Methodist Church of North America, & General Conference. (n.d.-b). Winona daily. Winona Daily. JFULL, Winona Lake, IN: Free Methodist Church.

Free Methodist Church of North America, & General Conference. (1960a). Free Methodist centenary, June 14-26, 1960, Winona Lake, Indiana : 25th Annual Conference guide book. BOOK, Winona Lake, Ind.: Free Methodist Church of North America.

Free Methodist Church of North America, & General Conference. (1960b). Quinquennial report of the General Missionary Secretary to the General Conference of the Free Methodist Church. CONF, S.l.: s.n.

Free Methodist Church of North America, General Conference, & Study Commission on Doctrine. (1989). Report of the Study Commission on Doctrine : Free Methodist Church of North America, 31st General Conference, August 3-13, 1989, Seattle, Washington. BOOK.

Free Methodist Church of North America, & General Missionary Board. (n.d.). Missions perspective. Missions Perspective. JFULL, Winona Lake, IN: General Missionary Board.

Free Methodist Church of North America, & General Missionary Board. (1950). Perspective in missions giving. BOOK, Winona Lake, Ind.: Free Methodist Church of North America, General Missionary Board.

Free Methodist Church of North America, & General Missionary Board. (1974). Missions quinquennial report. JFULL, Winona Lake, Ind.: Light and Life Press.

Free Methodist Church of North America, General Missionary Board, Woman's Foreign Missionary Society, America., F. M. C. of N., Board., G. M., America., F. M. C. of N., … Woman's Foreign Missionary Society. (1923). Proceedings of the General Missionary Board of the Free Methodist Church of North America. BOOK, Chicago, Ill.

Free Methodist Church of North America, & Home Ministries. (n.d.). Free Methodist ministries update. JFULL, Indianapolis, IN: Light and Life Press.

Free Methodist Church of North America, & Illinois-Wisconsin Conference. (n.d.). Illinois-Wisconsin Messenger. JFULL, Woodstock, IL: Illinois-Wisconsin Conference.

Free Methodist Church of North America, & Kentucky-Tennessee Conference. (n.d.-a). Builder : newsletter of the Kentucky-Tennessee Conference. JFULL, Jackson, KY: The Conference.

Free Methodist Church of North America, & Kentucky-Tennessee Conference. (n.d.-b). Report book : the ... session of the Kentucky-Tennessee Annual Conference. JFULL, KY: The Conference.

Free Methodist Church of North America, & Keystone Conference. (n.d.). Keystone Conference news. JFULL, Oil City, PA: The Conference.

Free Methodist Church of North America, & Light and Life Men's Fellowship. (1960). "Break through" : the president's manual. BOOK, Winona Lake, Ind.: Free Methodist Church of North America.

Free Methodist Church of North America, & Light and Life Men International. (n.d.). Light and life line. JFULL, Winona Lake, Ind.: Free Methodist Church of North America, Light and Life Men International.

Free Methodist Church of North America, & Louisianna Conference. (n.d.). Louisiana messenger of the Free Methodist Church. JFULL, Effie, LA: The Conference.

Free Methodist Church of North America, & New York Conference. (n.d.). New York Conference news. JFULL, NY: The Conference.

Free Methodist Church of North America, & North Michigan Conference. (n.d.). The North Michigan herald. JFULL, Cadillac, MI: The Conference.

Free Methodist Church of North America, & Ohio Conference. (1995). The Ohio connection. JFULL, Baltimore, Ohio: Ohio Conference, Free Methodist Church of N. America.

Free Methodist Church of North America, Ohio Conference, & Board of Evangelism. (n.d.). The Net. JFULL, Mansfield, OH: Board of Evangelism of the Ohio Annual Conference, Free Methodist Church of North America.

Free Methodist Church of North America, & Oil City
    Conference. (n.d.). The Oil City Conference news. JFULL,
    Pleasentville, PA: The Conference.

Free Methodist Church of North America, & Oklahoma
    Conference. (1993). In touch with Oklahoma Free
    Methodists. JFULL, Oklahoma City: The Conference.

Free Methodist Church of North America, Oklahoma
    Conference, America., F. M. C. of N., & Conference.,
    O. (n.d.). Oklahoma Free Methodist. Oklahoma Free
    Methodist. JFULL, Oklahoma City: The Conference.

Free Methodist Church of North America, & Oregon
    Conference. (1997). Connection. JFULL, Turner, OR:
    Oregon Conference of the Free Methodist Church of North
    America.

Free Methodist Church of North America, Oregon Conference,
    America., F. M. C. of N., & Conference., O. (1970).
    Oregon Conference of the Free Methodist Church : 75th
    anniversary, 1895-1970. BOOK, S.l.: Free Methodist
    Church of North America, Oregon Conference.

Free Methodist Church of North America, Oregon Conference,
    America., F. M. C. of N., & Conference., O. (1995).
    Connection, 1895-1995 : Oregon Conference. BOOK,
    Turner, Or.: Oregon Conference of the Free Methodist
    Church.

Free Methodist Church of North America, & Pacific Northwest
    Conference. (n.d.-a). Conference news. JFULL, Seattle,
    WA: The Conference.

Free Methodist Church of North America, & Pacific Northwest
    Conference. (n.d.-b). The Northwest passage. JFULL,
    Seattle, WA: Pacific Conference of the Free Methodist
    Church of North America.

Free Methodist Church of North America, Southeastern Regional Fellowship, Kentucky-Tennessee Conference, & Atlantic Southeast Conference. (1995). Southern breeze. JFULL, Bowling Green, KY: Southeastern Regional Fellowship, Free Methodist Church of North America.

Free Methodist Church of North America, & Southern California-Arizona Conference. (n.d.). Observer. JFULL, The Conference.

Free Methodist Church of North America, & Southern Michigan Conference. (n.d.). Vision. JFULL, Spring Arbor, MI: The Conference.

Free Methodist Church of North America, & Wabash Conference. (n.d.-a). The Christian courier : the voice of the Wabash Conference. JFULL, Hooperston, IL: Wabash Conference of the Free Methodist Church.

Free Methodist Church of North America, & Wabash Conference. (n.d.-b). The Wabash christian courier. The Wabash Christian Courier. JFULL, Hooperston, IL: Free Methodist Church of North America, Wabash Conference.

Free Methodist Church of North America, Wesleyan Church, & Committee on Merger Exploration. (1974). Free Methodist Church of North America and the Wesleyan Church : proposed articles of agreement and constitution. BOOK, Winona Lake, IN.

Free Methodist Church of North America, & West Virginia Conference. (n.d.). West Virginia echoes. JFULL, Teays, WV: The Conference.

Free Methodist Church of North America, & Woman's Missionary Society. (1959). Then Jesus came : true stories of African children. BOOK, Winona Lake, Ind.: Free Methodist Church.

Free Methodist Church of North America, Woman's Missionary Society, America., F. M. C. of N., & Society., W. M. (1979). Twentieth General Session : August 20-24, 1979, Indianapolis, Indiana. BOOK, Indianapolis, Ind.: Women's Missionary Society of the Free Methodist Church.

Free Methodist Church of North America, Woman's Missionary Society, & Young People's Missionary Society of the Free Methodist Church. (1949). Directory : Oregon Conference, Free Methodist Church, 1949-1950. BOOK, S.l.: s.n.

Free Methodist Historical Society, Marston Memorial Historical Center, America, F. M. C. of N., & International, M. M. (2000). Newsletter. JFULL, Indianapolis, IN: Marston Memorial Historical Center.

Free Methodist Publishing House. (1949). The Christian minister. The Christian Minister. JFULL.

Freeland, M. H., & Her., O. who loved. (1892). Missionary martyrs Mary Louisa Ranf, missionary to India. ELEC, Chicago: T.B. Arnold.

Gagne, R. (1991). The Free Methodist understanding of baptism in the light of John Wesley's teaching and the American Methodist tradition (THES).

Gallaher Family. (1800). Gallaher family papers (UNPB).

General Council of the Church in Mission of the Free Methodist Church of North America, Free Methodist Church of North America, General Council for the Church in Mission, America., F. M. C. of N., Mission., G. C. of the C. in, Marston, L. R., ... Free Methodist Church of North America. (1868). The Free Methodist. The Free Methodist. JFULL, Rochester, N.Y.: Levi Wood.

Ghormley, N. B. (1920). The land of the heart of Livingstone; or, The genius of the Bantu. A study of the Bantu tribes of Africa, 100,000,000 souls, with special reference to the agencies which contribute to their civilization. BOOK, Chicago: Published by the author; for sale by the Woman's Foreign Missionary Society of the Free Methodist Church.

Goldstein, D. M., & Dixon, C. A. D. (2010). Return of the raider. BOOK, Lake Mary, Fla.: Creation House.

Gramento, J. H. (1992). Those astounding Free Methodist women! a biographical history of Free Methodist women in ministry with an extended bibliography of Free Methodist women's studies : a final document submitted to the Doctoral Studies Committee of United Theological Seminary (THES). United Theological Seminary, Dayton, OH.

Greenville College. (n.d.). Greenville College record. JFULL, Greenville, IL: Greenville College. Retrieved from http://catalog.hathitrust.org/api/volumes/oclc/27723572.html

Gregory, D. T. (2005). From the new day to the new century : Free Methodist strategies for metropolitan church planting in light of 1985-2000 efforts and results (THES).

Griffith, C. E. (1984). Patterns of Free Methodist worship : historic freedoms (THES).

Griffith, G. W. (1923). The divine program; an interpretation of the divine method of redemption and of the nature and nurture of the Christian life,. BOOK, Chicago, Ill.: W.B. Rose.

Griffith, G. W. (1939). Lest we forget : selected messages. BOOK, Los Angeles, CA: Mrs. G.W. Griffith.

Griffith, L. B., & Griffith, G. W. (1937). Living embers : the life and writings of George William Griffith. BOOK, Winona Lake, IN: Light and Life Press.

Gyertson, D. J. (1981). The church related college higher education in the Free Methodist Church during the decade of the seventies ; implications for the eighties (THES).

Haley, J. W. (1949). But thy right hand. BOOK, Winona Lake, Ind.: Woman's Missionary Society of the Free Methodist Church.

Haley, J. W., Olmstead, W. B., & America, F. M. C. of N. (1926). Life in Mozambique and South Africa. BOOK, Chicago: Free Methodist Pub. House.

Hamilton, M. E. (1988). James R. Bishop : God's chosen man : the life story of the founder of South India Biblical Seminary Bangarapet, Karnataka, South India. BOOK, Karnataka, India: South India Biblical Seminary.

Hart, E. P. (1903). Reminiscences of early Free Methodism. BOOK, Chicago, Ill.: Free Methodist Publ. House.

Hawley, D., & Hardy, J. (1980). Living water, living letter : Free Methodist missions in Egypt and India. BOOK, Winona Lake, IN: Light and Life Press.

Haywood, A. L. (1942). My life story. ELEC, Stanwood, Mich.: Sanders Print Shop.

Hazzard, A. H., Montmorency County Historical Society, & Tribune., M. C. (1991). Blue Sky Circuit Montmorency County, Michigan, 1922-1926. ELEC, Atlanta, MI: Montmorency County Historical Society: Printed by the Montmorency County Tribune.

Herndon, B. T. (2001). Discipleship out of transition : a study of the new membership policies and procedures of the Free Methodist Church and its impact on discipleship (THES).

Hill, C. D., & Archives, S. P. U. (1909). Cyril Hill Papers, (UNPB).

Historical sketches of the Free Methodist Churches of the East Michigan Conference, 1924-1962. (1963). ELEC, Linden, Mich.: Scottie's Printing.

Hitt, R. T., Beltz, R. A., & Watson, C. H. (n.d.). Story of the Light and Life Hour BOOK, Winona Lake, IN: Forward Movement.

Hockley, R. G. (1991). Sectarianism within Free Methodism : its contribution to the formation of the Free Methodist Church and its continuing influence today. BOOK, S.l.: s.n.

Hogg, W. T. (1938). History of the Free Methodist Church of North America. BOOK, Winona Lake, Ind.: Free Methodist Pub. House.

Hogue, E. L. (1939). Adella Paulina Carpenter : in memory of a beautiful life. BOOK, Winona Lake, Ind.: Woman's Missionary Society.

Hogue, W. T. (1911). Retrospect and prospect : a semi-centennial sermon preached by Bishop Wilson T. Hogue before the General Conference of the Free Methodist Church, in Chicago, June 18, 1911. BOOK, Chicago, IL: Free Methodist Pub. House.

Hogue, W. T. (1915). History of the Free Methodist church of North America. BOOK, Chicago: Free Methodist Pub. House.

Hogue, W. T. (1916). The Holy Spirit : a study. BOOK, Chicago, Ill.: William B. Rose.

Hogue, W. T. (1928). Missionary hymns and responsive scripture readings : for use in missionary meetings. MUSIC, Chicago: Woman's Foreign Missionary Society of the Free Methodist Church.

Hook, E. M. (1980). Centennial of Armadale Church, 1880-1980 : in the cradle of Free Methodism in Canada. BOOK, Scarborough, Ont.: Armadale Church.

Horton, C. A. (1980). Money counts : a handbook on local church finance. BOOK, Winona Lake, IN: Light and Life Press.

Houser, G., Johnson, J., & Church, H. (1978). Adventures in Africa's grasslands : stories from Southern Africa. BOOK, Winona Lake, Ind.: Light and Life Press.

Houser, T. (2000). Free Methodist and other missions in Zimbabwe. BOOK, Kopje, Harare: Priority Projects Pub.

Houser, T., & Houser, G. (2007). Let me tell you : a memoir. BOOK, Charleston, SC: Booksurge.

Howland, C. L. (1951). The story of our church : Free Methodism, some facts and some reasons. BOOK, Winona Lake, IN: Free Methodist Pub. House.

Howland, C. L. (1953). A brief story of our church : an historical outline of the origin and growth of the Free Methodist Church of North America. BOOK, Winona Lakes, Ind.: Free Methodist Pub. House.

Humphrey, J. M. (1913). Select fruits from the highlands of Beulah. BOOK, Lima, OH: True Gospel Grain Pub. Co.

Humphrey, J. M. (1924). X-ray sermons. BOOK, Omaha, Neb.: "Anywhere" evangelistic workers' Pub. House.

Humphrey, J. M. (2003). Railroad sermons from railroad stories. BOOK, Salem, OH: Schmul Pub. Co.

Humphrey, J. M., & Humphrey, J. M. (2000). The lost soul's first day in eternity. BOOK, Salem, Ohio: Allegheny Publications.

Ingersol, R. S. (1990). Burden of dissent : Mary Lee Cagle and the Southern Holiness movement. BOOK.

James, J. F. (1987). On the front lines : a guide to Church planting. BOOK, Winona Lake, Ind.: Light and Life Press.

James, J. F., Free Methodist Church of North America, & General Conference. (2008). Our calling to the poor. BOOK, Indianapolis, Ind.: Light and Life Press.

Johnson, B. C. (1964). An analysis of the pastor's relationship to the Sunday school in the Oregon conference of the Free Methodist Church (THES).

Johnson, B. C. (1984). The training of college persons as lay ministers in the Free Methodist Church (THES).

Johnson, H. F. (1900). Handbook of Free Methodist missions. BOOK, Winona Lake, Ind.: Free Methodist Pub. House.

Johnson, P. V., & Church, W. M. S. of the F. M. (1942). Our neighbors the Dominicans. BOOK, Winnona Lake, Ind.: Woman's missionary Society, Free Methodist church.

Jordahl, D. C. (1960). A history of the Kansas Conference of the Free Methodist Church (THES).

Junker, J. A. (n.d.). Free Methodist missionary work among the Mexicans. BOOK, S.l.: s.n.

Kelley, A. T., & Kelley, W. W. (1889). Memoirs of Mrs. Augusta Tullis Kelley her experience, labors as evangelist and missionary to Africa, with extracts from her writings. ELEC, Chicago: T.B. Arnold.

Kingsley, C. W. (1990). I stand by the door : the autobiography of Charles W. Kingsley. BOOK, Indianapolis, Ind.: Light and Life Men International.

Kirchhofer, W. (2009). Fire among the stubble : church renewal in the Wesleyan tradition. BOOK.

Kirkpatrick, C. D., & Church, W. M. S. of the F. M. (1977). Cow in the clinic, and other missionary stories from around the world. BOOK, Winona Lake, Ind.: Light and Life Press.

Kleinsteuber, R. W. (1980). Coming of age : the making of a Canadian Free Methodist Church. BOOK, Hamilton, Ont.: Light and Life Press, Canada.

Kleinsteuber, R. W. (1984). More than a memory : the renewal of Methodism in Canada. BOOK, Mississauga, Ont.: Light and Life Press Canada.

Kline, G. E., College, M. C. of G., & Greenville, I. (1942). The Wesleyan message bearing fruit. BOOK, Winona Lake, Ind.: Light and Life Press.

Knox, L. H. (1976). The Free Methodist minister. BOOK, Winona Lake, Ind.: Light and Life Press.

Knox, L. H., Martin, C., & Sparrow, R. (1999). Building holy relationships : prayers, sermons, and other writings. BOOK, Indianapolis, IN: Light and Life Communications.

Knox, L. H., Wesley, J., Wesley, C., & Free Methodist Church of North America. (1976). The Faith and life of a Free Methodist. BOOK, Winona Lake, Ind.: Free Methodist Pub. House.

Krober, L. L., & Free Methodist Church of North America Board of Bishops. (2006). Pastors and church leaders manual : resources for leading local churches. BOOK, Indianapolis, Ind.: Light and Life Communications.

Kulaga, J. S. (2007). Edward Payson Hart : the second man of Free Methodism. BOOK, Spring Arbor, Mich.: Spring Arbor University Press.

Kysor, K. (1976). Benjamin Titus Roberts and the Free Methodist Church. BOOK, Cattaraugus, N.Y.: s.n.

La Due, G., & Mead, M. L. D. (1900). Gertrude Black La Due and family papers (UNPB).

La Due, J., & La Due, W. K. (1898). The life of Rev. Thomas Scott La Due : with some sketches and other writings. BOOK, Chicago: Free Methodist Pub. House.

Lamson, B. S. (1951). Lights in the world; Free Methodist missions at work. BOOK, Winona Lake, Ind.: General missionary board.

Lamson, B. S. (1960). Venture! : the frontiers of Free Methodism. BOOK, Winona Lake, Ind.: Light and Life Press.

Lamson, B. S. (1963). To catch the tide. BOOK, Winona Lake, Ind.: General Missionary Board.

Lamson, B. S. (1987). Greater works than these. BOOK, Winona Lake, Ind.: Light and Life Press.

Las Cruces Free Methodist Church. (1958). Las Cruces Free Methodist Church records, (UNPB).

Lesalnieks, K. (1970). Unsearchable ways of God : Isaiah 55: 8-9. BOOK, Bicknell, Ind.: Fellowship Promoter Press.

Lewis, L. G. (1931). Mitama no mi = The Fruite of the Spirit. BOOK, Tokyo-to: Jiyu Mesojisutosha Shuppanbu, dc 1931, Showa 6.

Lincicome, F. (n.d.). The doubles of the Bible. BOOK, Atlanta, GA: Repairer Pub. Co.

Lincicome, F. (1932). A lot in Sodom. BOOK, Winona Lake, Ind.: Light and Life Press.

Lincicome, F. (1932). Behold the man! BOOK, Apollo, Pa.: West Pub. Co.

Lincicome, F. (1935). A tribute to mothers. BOOK.

Lincicome, F. (1940). The soul. BOOK, Apollo, Pa.: West Pub. Co.

Livingston, G. H. (1981). Origins of life and faith : Genesis A : study guide. BOOK, Winona Lake, Ind.: Light and Life Press.

Looman, J. (n.d.). The story of my life. BOOK, Allegan, Mich.: John Looman.

Lorenz, G. V. (2005). Leading from the margins : recovering the Christian tradition of hospitality in church leadership (THES).

Lyon, D. (1953). My life story. BOOK, D. Lyon.

M'Geary, J. S. (1908). The Free Methodist Church : a brief outline history of its origin and development. BOOK, Chicago: W.B. Rose.

MacGeary, E. L. (1924). A sketch of the Woman's Foreign Missionary Society. BOOK, Chicago, Ill.: Foreign Missionary Society, Free Methodist Church.

Macy, V. W. (1946). A history of the Free Methodist mission in Portugese East Africa (THES).

Macy, V. W., & DeMille, L. (1984). Discovery under the Southern Cross : below the equator--missions adventures in Mozambique and South Africa. BOOK, Winona Lake, Ind.: Light and Life Press.

Magida, A. J. (1997). How to be a perfect stranger, vol. 2 : a guide to etiquette in other people's religious ceremonies. BOOK, Woodstock, Vt.: Jewish Lights Publishing.

Mannoia, F., & Huston, L. (1979). Amigos. BOOK, Winona Lake, Ind.: Light and Life Press.

Mannoia, K. W. (1988). A study of the perception of faculty concerning integration of faith and learning at Free Methodist colleges (THES).

Manual for leaders of Light and Life men. (n.d.). BOOK, Winona Lake, Ind.: Light and Life, International, Free Methodist Headquarters.

Marston, L. R. (1950). Bring the books. BOOK.

Marston, L. R. (1960). From age to age a living witness; a historical interpretation of Free Methodism's first century. BOOK, Winona Lake, Ind.: Light and Life Press.

Marston, L. R. (1964). My church : a living witness from age to age. BOOK, Winona Lake, Ind.: Distributed by the Forward Movement, Free Methodist World Headquarters.

Marston, L. R. (1979). He lived on our street : enduring words for today. BOOK, Winona Lake, Ind.: Light and Life Press.

Mavis, M. (1970). A brief story of the Kentucky-Tennessee Conference. BOOK, Wilmore, KY: Mavis.

Maynard, J. L. (1989). God's lamp : history of the Central Illinois Conference, Free Methodist Church. BOOK, Greenville, Ill.: Tower Press.

McChesney, A., & McChesney, B. (1968). Through Congo shadows. BOOK, Salem, Ohio: Convention Book Store Publishers.

McKenna, D. L. (1993). The works of Dr. David L. McKenna. BOOK, Wilmore, KY: Asbury Theological Seminary.

McKenna, D. L. (1995) A future with a history : the Wesleyan witness of the Free Methodist Church, 1960-1995. BOOK, Indianapolis, IN: Light and Life Press.

McKenna, D. L., John, E. C., Free Methodist Church of North America, Commission on Christian Education, Church-School Relations Committee, Association of Free Methodist Colleges, … Colleges., A. of F. M. (1962). The study of Free Methodist Higher Education. BOOK.

McLaren, R. C. (2003). A Wesleyan theology of worship and its development in Free Methodism (THES).

McPeak, R. H. (2001). Earnest Christianity : the practical theology of Benjamin Titus Roberts (THES).

McReynolds, M., & Deaconess Hospital. (2000). Redeeming love : the legacy of the Deaconess Ladies. BOOK, The Author.

Mercer, F. D. (1989). The history of First Free Methodist Church of Moose Jaw, Saskatchewan. BOOK, Moose Jaw, Sask.: Quick Printing.

Mercer, F. D. (1991). The liturgical and sacramental development of the Free Methodist Church in Canada : with special attention to the rituals of baptism and the Lord's Supper (THES).

Mission, A. I. B., & America, F. M. C. of N. (1992). Hane' niji'a = It carries the news. Hane' Niji'a = It Carries the News. JFULL, Farmington, NJ: American Indian Bible Mission.

Moore, C. C. (1978). Variety and spice of a minister's life. BOOK, Lakeland, FL: C.C. Moore.

Mosher, C. E. (1983). Free Methodist educational institutions as perceived by selected constituents (THES).

Mott, E., & America, F. M. C. of N. (1944). The security of the believers. BOOK, Seattle, Wa.: Board of Aggressive Evangelism, Washington Conference, Free Methodist Church.

Mullikin, J. C. (1915). James Clayland Mullikin papers, (UNPB).

Mumby, E. H., & Burch, M. D. (1961). Methodism in Caistor. BOOK, Caistor: The Church.

Mylander, R., & Root, H. I. (1944). Japan investment. BOOK, Winona Lake, Ind.: Woman's Missionary Society of the Free Methodist Church of North America.

Nakajima, M. G. (1983). Growth of Japan Free Methodist Church, 1945-1982 (THES).

National Task Force on Canadian General Conference. (1988). Five questions about a Canadian general conference : an interim report. BOOK, Mississauga, Ont.: Free Methodist Church in Canada.

Nazarite documents : comprising the obligations, practical propositions, lamentations, recommendations, &c. of the Nazarite Union of the Genesee Conference of the M.E. Church. (1856). BOOK, Brockport, N.Y.: Wm. Haswell, Printer.

Nelson, T. H., & Dake, V. A. (1894). Life and labors of Rev. Vivian A. Dake : organizer and leader of Pentecost Bands : embracing an account of his travels in America, Europe and Africa, with selections from his sketches, poems and songs. BOOK, Chicago: Published for the author by T.B. Arnold ...

Nelson, W. O. (1949). History of the Oklahoma Annual Conference of the Free Methodist Church. BOOK, Siloam Springs, AR: Silent Minister Booklet Press.

Northrup, L. W. (1988). Ambassadors for Christ : the story of Free Methodism in Northern Ireland. BOOK.

Northrup, L. W. (1999). It took a miracle : the life story of L.W. Northrup. BOOK, L.W. Northrup.

Ntakirutimana, E. (2004). A Christian development appraisal of the Ubunye Cooperative Housing Inititiative in Pietermaritzburg (THES). University of KwaZulu-Natal, Pietermaritzburg.

Olmstead, B. L. (1955). Our church at work : a brief manual for the instruction of preparatory members of the Free Methodist Church. BOOK, Winona Lake, Ind.: Free Methodist Pub. House.

Olver, P. S. (1986). A strategy for urban church planting for the Free Methodist Church of North America (THES).

One way to a whole world sing : the Free Methodist Church 1974 General Conference Official Songbook. (1974). MUSIC, Winona Lake, Ind.

Ontario Genealogical Society, & Branch, T. B. (1980). Free Methodist cemetery : con. 1, lot 9, O'Connor Township, District of Thunder Bay, Ontario. BOOK, Thunder Bay, Ont.: Thunder Bay Branch, Ontario Genealogical Society.

Osborne, Z. (1888). Born of the Spirit, or, Gems from the book of life. BOOK, Sarotage Springs, NY: John Johnson & Co.

Otto, K., University., A. P., & Marshburn Memorial Library. (1992). Free Methodist Denominational collection of Azusa Pacific University's Marshburn Memorial Library, 1992. BOOK, Azusa, Calif.: Azusa Pacific University.

Our heritage we cherish : Free Methodist Church, Thornbury-Peniel, 1904-1984 : eighty years of history! (1985). BOOK, Thornbury, Ontario: Thornbury Free Methodist Church.

Page, R., & Burns, E. (1988). Oral history interview with Ruby Page. SOUND.

Patil, S. (1989). History of the Free Methodist Church in India, 1881-1989. BOOK, Yavatmal, India: Literature Committee, India Free Methodist Conference.

Pauley, R. (1970). DeShazer returns. BOOK, Winona Lake, Ind.: Free Methodist Church of North America, General Missionary Board.

Pearce, W. (1942). Choice hymns : a collection of hymns from the Free Methodist hymnal, especially adapted for revival services. MUSIC, Winona Lake, Ind.: Free Methodist Pub. House.

Pearson, B. H. (1925). Mexican missions : home mission study book. BOOK, Chicago: Woman's Missionary Society of the Free Methodist Church.

Pearson, B. H. (1940). Next! Our Sunday-School quest in South America : a "Caleb-Joshua" story of the expedition of "The spies" sent forth by the "Birthday pennies for South America fund" into the lands "Beyond the Amazon." BOOK, Winona Lake, Ind.: Light and life Press.

Phillips, H. V. (1987). From the door of an orphanage. BOOK, Sandusky, Mich.: New Creation Ministries.

Pugerude, D. G. (1987). Preaching from the Old Testament : a study in exegesis and hermeneutics of the Free Methodist Church of North America (THES).

Reber, L. B. (1901). A sketch of the life and labors of Rev. L.B. Reber in the North Michigan, Louisiana, New York, and Missouri conferences. BOOK, Clarence, Mo.: Farmers Favorite Print.

Reinhard, J. A. (1971). Personal and sociological factors in the formation of the Free Methodist Church, 1852-1860 (THES).

Rev. Aura Claire Showers : a sketch of his life / by his wife ; together with tributes by ministerial brethren ; to which is added a treatise on the doctrine of eternal punishment and other unpublished manuscripts. (1896). ELEC, Oil City, PA :H.D.W. Showers,1896.

Revell, J. A. (1994). The Nazirites : burned-over district Methodism and the Buffalo middle class (THES).

Rhoden, M. M. (1956). The recent progress and methods of evangelism of holiness missions in Japan (THES).

Rhodes, M. L. (1919). Clifford B. Barrett : the "Happy Alleghenian." BOCK, Chicago: W.B. Rose.

Richardson, A. (1988). A heart for God in India. BOOK, Winona Lake, Ind.: Light and Life Press.

Richardson, A. (1998). Maria. BOOK, Indianapolis, IN: Light and Life Communications.

Richardson, A., & Secaur, E. (1988). Andrew's secret. BOOK, Winona Lake, Ind.: Light and Life Press.

Riggs, D. E. (1981). Make it happen. BOOK, Warsaw, Ind.: LP Products.

Robb, J. A. (1976). Memories of Rev. Charles H. Sage : the Free Methodist Church Canadian centennial, 1876-1976. BOOK, Ontario: West Ontario Conference of the Free Methodist Church.

Robb, J. A. (1979a). And He said unto me, write. BOOK, Woodstock, Ont.: Nethercott Press.

Robb, J. A. (1979b). Life's golden memories. BOOK, Woodstock, Ont.: Nethercott Press.

Roberts, B. (1984). Why another sect. New York: Garland Pub.

Roberts, B. H. (1900). Benjamin Titus Roberts. Late general superintendent of the Free Methodist Church. A Biography. BOOK, North Chili, N.Y.: "The Earnest Christian."

Roberts, B. H. B. T., Roberts, A. A. R., Roberts, E. S. E. L. S. E. S., & Roberts, G. L. (1832). Family papers. (UNPB).

Roberts, B. H. B. T., Roberts, A. A. R., Roberts, E. S. E. L. S. E. S., Roberts, G. L., & Division, L. of C. M. (1990). Benjamin T. Roberts family papers. BOOK, Washington, D.C.: Library of Congress, Photoduplication Service.

Roberts, B. T., & Demaray, D. E. (1996). The daily Roberts : readings for every day in the year from the writings of B.T. Roberts. BOOK, Indianapolis, IN: Light and Life Press.

Roberts, E. M. (1962). The bishop and his lady. BOOK, Winona Lake, Ind.: Light and Life Press.

Roller, D. T., Parker, J., & America, F. M. C. of N. (1985). Journey to Mexico. BOOK, Winona lake, Ind.: Light and Life Press.

Ronsvalle, J. L. (1987). A comparison of the growth in the United States per capita income and population with the Free Methodist Church budget and membership for the years 1967 and 1982. BOOK. Urbana, Ill.: Empty Tomb.

Root, H. I. (1928). Our Africa work : a brief history of the Free Methodist Mission in Africa. BOOK, Chicago, IL: Woman's Missionary Society, Free Methodist Church.

Root, L. P., & Benson, M. C. (1988). Outflowing love : Auntie-bai, Effie Southworth's life of loving service during her more than 50 years in central India. BOOK, Winona Lake, Ind.: Light & Life Communications.

Roth, R. H. (1967). The history of the Southern Michigan Conference of the Free Methodist Church (THES).

Runyon, D. V. (1995). World mission people : the best of the missionary tidings, 1990-95. BOOK, Spring Arbor, Mich.: Saltbox Press.

Runyon, D. V, Auch, S., & Missions, F. M. W. (1995). Ferguson: her tractor-biography. BOOK, Spring Arbor, Mich.: Saltbox Press.

Rupert, D. A., America, F. M. C. of N., & Conference, C. (1983). Celebrating one hundred years : a centennial focus on the California Conference Free Methodist Church. BOOK, Free Methodist Church, California Conference.

Ryff, F. J. (1954). An examination of the indigenous church principle with special reference to the Free Methodist church in South Africa (THES).

Sage, C. H., & Olmstead, W. B. (1908). Autobiography of Rev. Charles H. Sage : embracing an account of his pioneer work in Michigan, of the formation of the Canada Conference and of his labors in various states. BOOK, Chicago, Ill.: Free Methodist Pub. House.

Sager, I. M. (1974). Lights along the shore : some memories. BOOK, Falconer, N.Y.: Falconer Print. & design, Inc.

Sanders, H. (1965). History of the Oregon Conference of the Free Methodist Church (THES).

Sayre, M. G. (1945). Missionary triumphs in occupied China. BOOK, Winona Lake, Ind.: Woman's Missionary Society of the Free Methodist Church.

Scherer, F. E. (1997). Aunt Edith & Lora. BOOK, Oak Park, Ill.: James A. Scherer.

Schlosser, G. (1906). George and Mary Schlosser papers, (UNPB).

Schlosser, J. H. (1977). The Free Methodist Church in the Philippines : our heritage and history. BOOK.

Schlosser, R., & Groesbeck, G. H. (1956). Lighting the Philippine Frontier. BOOK, Winona Lake, Ind.: Light and Life Press.

Schoenhals, L. R. (1955). Higher education in the Free Methodist Church in the United States, 1860-1954 (THES).

Schwanz, K. D. (1991). The "wooden brother" : instrumental music restricted in Free Methodist worship, 1860-1955 (THES).

Sellew, W. A. (1981). Why not? a plea for the ordination of those women whom God has called to preach the Gospel. BOOK, North Chili, N.Y.: "Earnest Christian" Pub. House.

Sellew, W. A., Hogue, W. T., & America, F. M. C. of N. (1913). Clara Leffingwell, a missionary. BOOK, Chicago: Free Methodist Pub. House.

Shay, E. A. F., America, F. M. C. of N., & Society, W. F. M. (1914). Mariet Hardy Freeland, a faithful witness : a biography. BOOK, Chicago: Woman's Foreign Missionary Society of the Free Methodist Church.

Shelhamer, E. E. (n.d.). A bit of experience. BOOK, Los Angeles, CA.

Shelhamer, E. E. (n.d.). E.E. Shelhamer's life story. SOUND, Knoxville, TN: Evangelist of Truth.

Shelhamer, E. E. (1900a). Seven searching sermons. BOOK, Cincinnati, Ohio: God's Revivalist.

Shelhamer, E. E. (1900). Sixty years of thorns and roses. BOOK, Cincinnati, Ohio: God's Bible School and Revivalist.

Shelhamer, E. E. (1907). Experiences in travel and soul saving : also some of my mistakes and what they have taught me. BOOK, Atlanta, Ga.

Shelhamer, E. E. (1920). Searching sermons for saints and sinners. BOOK, Cincinnati, Ohio: God's Bible School.

Shelhamer, E. E. (1926). Sermons that search the soul. BOOK, Kansas City, Mo.: Nazarene Pub. House.

Shelhamer, E. E. (1929). Plain preaching for practical people. BOOK, Cincinnati, Ohio: God's Bible School and Revivalist.

Shelhamer, E. E. (1932). Pointed preaching for practical people. BOOK, Cincinnati, Ohio: God's Bible School and Revivalist.

Shelhamer, E. E. (1991). The ups and downs of a pioneer preacher : also some of my mistakes and what they taught me. BOOK, Salem, Ohio: Allegheny Publications.

Shelhamer, E. E., & Shelhamer, J. A. (n.d.). Ragged Elzie gave hope to the discouraged. BOOK, Winona Lake, IN: Mrs. E.E. Shelhamer.

Showers, H. D. W. (1896). Rev. Aura Claire Showers a sketch of his life. ELEC, Oil City, PA: H.D.W. Showers.

Sigsworth, J. W. (1960). The Battle was the Lord's : a history of the Free Methodist Church in Canada. BOOK, Oshawa, Ont.: Sage Pubilications.

Sims, A. (n.d.). Yet not I, or, A brief sketch of the early life, conversion, call to the ministry, and some of the subsequent labors in the Master's vineyard of A. Sims. BOOK, Toronto.

Smith, B. B. (1903). A brief sketch of a remarkable life, the life of Mrs. Minnie B. Shelhamer. ELEC, Atlanta: The Repairer.

Smith, B. B., & Shelhamer, J. A. (n.d.). The life story of Minnie B. Shelhamer. BOOK, Atlanta: Repairer Pub. Co.

Smith, B. B., Shelhamer, J. A., Swauger, N. P., & Fero, G. L. (1992). Remarkable women. BOOK, Salem, Ohio: Allegheny Publications.

Smith, D. A. (1984). Central College : the first 100 years. BOOK, North Newton, Kan.: Mennonite Press.

Smith, D. P. (1950). The growth and development of the interracial movement within the Free Methodist Church of North America : a research paper in history of Free Methodism. BOOK.

Smith, E. M. (1943). A child shall lead them. BOOK, Greenville, Ill.: Tower Press.

Snell, V. R. (1976). The theology of smallness (THES).

Snider, K. L. (1985). Ten more growing churches in Japan today. BOOK, Osaka, Japan: Japan Free Methodist Church.

Snider, K. L., & Nakae, S. (1986). Seicho suru ju kyokai no kiroku : ima, nihon demo ...2. BOOK, Tokyo: Inochi no Kotobasha.

Snyder, C. A. (2006). Weeping may endure for a night : a spiritual journey. BOOK, Xulon Press.

Snyder, H. A. (1994). Aspects of early Free Methodist history. BOOK, Dayton, OH: United Theological Seminary.

Snyder, H. A. (2006). Populist saints : B.T. and Ellen Roberts and the first Free Methodists. BOOK, Grand Rapids, Mich.: William B. Eerdmans Pub. Co.

Snyder, H. A., Runyon, D. V, & Snyder, H. A. (2011). B. T. and Ellen Roberts and the first Free Methodists. BOOK, Indianapolis, Ind.: Committee on Free Methodist History & Archives.

Snyder, L. E., & Weidman, B. E. (1940). Servant of God : life story and selected articles of Bishop Arthur D. Zahniser. BOOK, Winona Lake, Ind.: Light and Life Press.

Somers, D. O. (1986). Ministry hazards within the Free Methodist Church (THES).

Stedwell, A. (1915). Itinerant footprints. BOOK, Shambaugh, Iowa: Stedwell.

Stewart, J. W. (1963). Historical factors in the naming of the Free Methodist Church (THES).

Summers, A., & Summers, G. (1952). Sanctified wholly. BOOK, Estevan, Sask.: J. Cowan.

Takeya, T. D., & Bastian, D. N. (1981). Membership class guidance for pastors in the Japanese Free Methodist Church the study of Free Methodism : and, a Japanese translation of, Belonging! : adventures in church membership (THES).

Tankidaigaku, O. K. (n.d.). Osaka Kirisutokyo Tankidaigaku Kiyo. JFULL, Osaka Shi: Osaka Kirisutokyo Tankidaigaku.

Tapper, R. M., & Church, Y. P. M. S. of the F. M. (1931). Glimpses of victory. BOOK, Chicago: Y.P.M.S. Council of the Free Methodist Church.

Tapper, R. M., & Young People's Missionary Society of the Free Methodist Church. (1935). Life stories of foreign missionaries of the Free Methodist Church : supported by the Young People's Missionary Society, 1931-1935. BOOK, Winona Lake, Ind.: Y.P.M.S. Council.

Taylor, J. P. (1960). Goodly heritage. BOOK, Winona Lake, Ind.: Light and Life Press.

Taylor, J. P. (1960). Soldiers of Christ. BOOK, Winona Lake, Ind.: Light and Life Press.

Taylor, J. P. (1964). All roads lead to Bethlehem. BOOK, Winona Lake, Ind.: Light and Life Press.

Terrill, J. G. (1883). The St. Charles camp-meeting, embodying its history and several sermons by leading ministers, with some practical suggestions concerning campmeeting management. BOOK, Chicago: T.B. Arnold.

Terrill, J. G. (1891). Talks to Sunday school teachers. ELEC, Syracuse, NY: A.W. Hall.

Terrill, J. G. (2000). The life of John Wesley Redfield, M.D. BOOK, Salem, Ohio: Allegheny.

The Free Methodist Church in postwar Japan. (1971). BOOK.

Thomas, F. L., Free Methodist Church of North America, & Adult Ministries. (1980). Building the church through adult Sunday school. BOOK.

Thompson, W. R. (1950a). Factors in the establishing of a Free Methodist mission training school in Paraguay (THES).

Thompson, W. R. (1950ɔ). Factors in the establishment of a Free Methodist mission training school in Paraguay (THES).

Thrall, O. C. (n.d.). From darkness to light and from the power of Satan unto God. BOOK, Titusville, PA: O.C. Thrall.

Trever, R. (1905). Life and labors of Rev. Robert Trever both in England and America also, A sketch of frontier work in connection with the Free Methodist church with an appendix containing temperance and other matter. ELEC, St. Louis: J.H. Flowers.

Tsuchiyama, T., & Olmstead, W. B. (1927). From darkness to light. BOOK, Chicago, IL: Light and Life Press.

Tsuchiyama, T., Richardson, A., & Kaneda, K. (1986). Love shining through : Tsuchiyama. BOOK, Winona Lake, IN: Light and Life Press.

United for action: official workshop outlines & program of the pre-centennial convocation for Sunday school & youth leaders of the Free Methodist Church. (1957). BOOK, Winona Lake, Ind.: Lloyd H. Knox.

Van Valin, C. E. (1990). Transforming grace : a biblical guide for holy living. BOOK, Indianapolis, Ind.: Light and Life Press.

Van Valin, C. E. (1991). Pastor's handbook. BOOK, Board of Bishops, Free Methodist Church (USA).

Veldman, R. J. (2006). Classic catechism. BOOK, Indianapolis, Ind.: Light and Life Communications.

Walls, A. E., Cochrane, R. L., & Rose, M. L. (1975). Eighty years : historical sketch of thr Woman's Missionary Society of the Free Methodist Church. BOOK, by the Society.

Walls, F. E. (1977). The Free Methodist Church : a bibliography. BOOK, Winona Lake, Ind.: Free Methodist Historical Center, Free Methodist Headquarters.

Walrath, B., & Theological Research Exchange Network. (2002). Exploring the correlation between authentic worship and health in selected congregations of the Free Methodist Church (THES). Institute of Worship Studies.

Walter, J., Walter, M., & Fisher, D. J. (1978). History of the Ohio Conference of the Free Methodist Church. BOOK, Galion, Ohio: United Church Directories.

Ward, E. E., America., F. M. C. of N., & Free Methodist Church of North America. (1924). Letter links. Letter Links. JFULL, Lucknow: Methodist Pub. House.

Ward, E. E., America., F. M. C. of N., Free Methodist Church of North America, & America., F. M. C. of N. (1951). Ordered steps, or, The Wards of India : a biography of the lives of Ernest Fremont Ward and Phebe Elizabeth Cox Ward, missionaries to India, 1880-1927. BOOK, Winona Lake, Ind.: Light and Life Press.

Ward, E. E., & America, F. M. C. of N. (1937). India letter links. JFULL.

Ward, E. F. (1880). Papers. BOOK.

Ward, E. F. (1923). Memory links of "our own Chickabiddie", or, Reminiscences of Mary Louise Vore. BOOK, Chicago: Free Methodist Pub. House.

Ward, E. F., Pyron, D. A., & Ward, P. E. (1878). Papers of this first Free Methodist Church missionary to India. BOOK.

Washington County Historian. (1728). Town and Village of Argyle collection (UNPB).

Watson, C. H. (2002). DeShazer. BOOK.

Watson, C. H., & Fear, L. K. (1972). De Shazer. BOOK, Winona Lake, Ind.: Light and Life Press.

Watson, C. H., & Howell, R. W. (1964a). Advancing in church membership : Pastor's instruction series, youth division. BOOK, Winona Lake, Ind.: Light and Life Press.

Watson, C. H., & Howell, R. W. (1964b). Exploring church membership : pastor's instruction series, junior division. BOOK, Winona Lake Indiana: Light and Life Press.

We believe! : insights into the beliefs of Free Methodists. (1976). BOOK, Winona Lake, Ind.: Light and Life Press.

Wesleyan Methodist Church of America, & America. (1951). Hymns of the living faith : official hymnal of the Wesleyan Methodist Church of America. MUSIC, Syracuse, N.Y.: Wesleyan Methodist Pub. Assoc.

West, B. J. (1998). Forty years of history at Flatwoods Camp, 1958-1998. BOOK, Perryopolis, Pa.: Sound of the Trumpet Tract Ministries.

White, J. M. (1981). Sixty years on the way : Kindersley Free Methodist Church, 1921-1981. BOOK, Kindersley, Sask.: Kindersley Free Methodist Church.

White, R., & Network, T. R. E. (2001). A sacrament of joy the discovery of the Lord's Table as a weekly celebration at the Stanwood Free Methodist Church in Stanwood, Michigan (THES). Northern Baptist Theological Seminary.

Willard, F. B. (1985). Idol of clay. BOOK, Winona Lake, Ind.: Light and Life Press.

Williamson, G. (1972). Frank and Hazel : the Adamsons of Kibogora. BOOK, Winona Lake, IN: Light and Life Press.

Williamson, G. (1976). Gonzalo of Mexican missions. BOOK, Winona Lake, Ind.: Light and Life Press.

Winget, B. (1903). Historical sketch of members of the Free Methodist Church of North America who have gone out to the foreign field of missionaries. BOOK, Chicago, Ill.: Free Methodist Pub. House.

Winslow, C. V. V. (1965). China's four sons. BOOK, Winona Lake, Ind.: Light and Life Pr.

Winslow, C. V. V. (1981). By love compelled : life story. BOOK, Winona Lake, Ind.: Light and Life Press.

Winslow, R. (1984). The mountains sing : God's love revealed to Taiwan tribes. BOOK, Winona Lake, Ind.: Light and Life Press.

Wolfe, K. G. (1999). A history of the founding of the Free Methodist day-schools in Southern California (THES).

Wolfe, M.-E. (2005). A strategy for mobilizing integrated local and global ministry in Free Methodist congregations,with an emphasis on gateway cities (urban hubs for unreached people groups) (THES).

Woods, D. A. (1984). East Michigan's great adventure : a history of the East Michigan Conference of the Free Methodist Church, 1884-1984. BOOK, [Place of publication not identified]: East Michigan Conference of the Free Methodist Church.

Woods, D. A. (1989). Tall timber, deep roots : autobiography of Dale A. Woods. BOOK, Flint, Mich.: D.A. Woods].

Yoder, T., Smidderks, D., Free Methodist Church of North America, Department of Christian Education, Department of World Missions, & Women's Missionary Fellowship International. (1987). The great discovery. BOOK, Winona Lake, Ind.: Light and Life Press.

Your church and education : Christian education handbook of the Free Methodist Church. (1941). BOOK, Winona Lake, Indiana: Commission on Christian Education.

Zahniser, A. D. F., & Easton, J. B. (1932). History of the Pittsburgh Conference of the Free Methodist Church. BOOK, Free Methodist Pub. House.

Free Methodist Church – Biography

Anderson, D. (1989). I have you in my heart : the delights of overseas ministry. BOOK, Indianapolis, Ind.: Wesley Press.

Anderson, M. (1988). Just over the hill : my four-score-plus years under God. BOOK, Gerry, NY: M. Anderson.

Andrews, E. A. (1926). Reminiscent musings. BOOK, Spring Arbor MI: E.A. Andrews.

Archer, A. C. (1930). The man with a thorn in his flesh. BOOK, Medford, Ore.: Schmul Pub. Co.

Arksey, L. (2011). A mission boyhood in Mozambique. BOOK, S.l.: Tornado Creek.

Asher, M. G. (1955). Saints alive! BOOK, New York: Vantage Press.

Babcock, C. A. (1938). Life and labours of Chas. A. Babcock : with a brief sketch of early days in the district in which he was born. BOOK, Brockville, Ont.: Standard Publishing House.

Barnett, L. P. (1965). Yorokobi no otozure. BOOK, Rosanjerusu: Rosanjerusu Furi Mesojisuto Kyokai.

Bates, G. (1981). Soul afire : life of J.W. Haley. BOOK, Winona Lake, Ind.: Light and Life Press.

Beers, A. (1922). The romance of a consecrated life : a biography of Alexander Beers. Chicago: Free Methodist Pub. House.

Black, H. (1932). From newsboy to preacher : the story of my life.

Blews, R. (1939). Master workmen biographies of the deceased bishops of the Free Methodist Church. Winona Lake, Ind.: Light and Life Press.

Blews, R. (1960). Master workmen biographies of the late bishops of the Free Methodist Church during her first century, 1860-1960. Winona Lake, Ind.: Light and Life Press.

Bowell, G. (2014). Reflections and thoughts on a hymnal : The 1910 Free Methodist hymnal. BOOK, Gary E. Bowell.

Brandt, M. E. (1980). Henry and Emma Brandt : memorabelia. BOOK, McPherson, KS: Brandt Family.

Brock, L. W. (1987). The life story of Rev. Lyle and Doris Brock : pioneer pastors of the Free Methodist Church in the West Kansas Conference and the California Conference. BOOK, Stanwood, WA.

Brown, Z. M. (1981). Trailblazers in Livingston country / by Zella M. Brown. BOOK, Winona Lake, Ind.: Light and Life Press.

Chesbrough, S. K. J. (1983). Defence of Rev. B.T. Roberts, A.M., before the Genesee Conference of the Methodist Episcopal Church at Perry, N.Y., Oct. 13-21, 1858. BOOK, Buffalo: Clapp, Matthews & Co's Steam Printing House.

Cook, E. D. (2005). Salt of the sea : a Navy chaplain's experience ashore and at sea. BOOK, Longwood, Fla.: Xulon Press.

Cooke, S. A. B. (1896). The handmaiden of the Lord, or, Wayside sketches. BOOK, Chicago: Shaw Pub. Co.

Cooke, S. A. B. (1983). Wayside sketches (abridged), or, The handmaiden of the Lord. BOOK, Salem, Ohio: Schmul Pub. Co.

Cox, B. E. (1998). Simply following : in all my journeying God went before. BOOK, Spring Arbor, Mich.: Saltbox Press.

Cryderman, L. (1999). Glory land : a memoir of a lifetime in church. BOOK, Grand Rapids, Mich.: Zondervan.

Cryderman, L. (2001). No swimming on Sunday : stories of a lifetime in church. BOOK, Grand Rapids, Mich.: Zondervan.

Damon, C. M. (1900). Sketches and incidents, or reminiscences of interest in the life of the author. BOOK, Chicago: Free Methodist Pub. House.

Davis, R. N. (1954). Redeemed : a remarkable conversion in the heart of India : the story of Moses David, superintendent of the Eastern District, and evangelist, India Free Methodist Church ... BOOK, Winona Lake, Ind.: Woman's Missionary Society, Free Methodist Church.

Dawson, L. (1962). Vital faith. Seattle, WA: Printed by L & H Print. Co.

De Voist, M. (1920). Foot-prints in my life, or, the story told in rhyme. BOOK.

Demaray, D. E. (1978). Near hurting people : the pastoral ministry of Robert Moffat Fine. BOOK, Winona Lake, Ind.: Light and Life Press.

Demaray, D. E. (2000). With His joy : the life and leadership of David McKenna. BOOK, Indianapolis, IN: Light & Life Communications.

DeShazer, J. (2012). Jacob DeShazer's personal testimony. ELEC, Wilmore, Ky.: DQB-LLC for the Marston Memorial Historical Center.

Dolan, T. F. (1880). A bit of experience : showing the dealings of Godmanandthedevil with T.F. Dolan, convert from Romanism ; to which is added a review of the Methodist discipline and selections from Wesley, Clarke, Bramwell, Carvosso, and others. BOOK, Chicago: Baker & Arnold, Printers.

Fairbarn, C. V. (1960). I call to remembrance. BOOK, Winona Lake, Ind.: Light and Life Press.

Fidler, G. (2006). Adventures in India. BOOK, St. Catherines, ON: Cornerstone Research & Pub.

Ford, G. L. (1985). Like a tree planted : the life story of Leslie Ray Marston. BOOK, Winona Lake, Ind.: Light and Life Press.

Goldstein, D. M., & Dixon, C. A. D. (2010). Return of the raider. BOOK, Lake Mary, Fla.: Creation House.

Gramento, J. H. (1992). Those astounding Free Methodist women! a biographical history of Free Methodist women in ministry with an extended bibliography of Free Methodist women's studies : a final document submitted to the Doctoral Studies Committee of United Theological Seminary (THES). United Theological Seminary, Dayton, OH.

Griffith, L. B., & Griffith, G. W. (1937). Living embers : the life and writings of George William Griffith. BOOK, Winona Lake, IN: Light and Life Press.

Hamilton, M. E. (1988). James R. Bishop : God's chosen man : the life story of the founder of South India Biblical Seminary Bangarapet, Karnataka, South India. BOOK, Karnataka, India: South India Biblical Seminary.

Hawke, J. (1999). Hogue. Wilson Thomas. American National Biography., 11. JOUR.

Haywood, A. L. (1942). My life story. ELEC, Stanwood, Mich.: Sanders Print Shop.

Hazzard, A. H., Montmorency County Historical Society, & Tribune., M. C. (1991). Blue Sky Circuit Montmorency County, Michigan, 1922-1926. ELEC, Atlanta, MI: Montmorency County Historical Society: Printed by the Montmorency County Tribune.

Hogue, E. L. (1939). Adella Paulina Carpenter : in memory of a beautiful life. BOOK, Winona Lake, Ind.: Woman's Missionary Society.

Hospital, D. (1975). The Butterfields : 50 years. BOOK, Oklahoma City, Okla.: Deaconess Hospital.

Houser, T., & Houser, G. (2007). Let me tell you : a memoir. BOOK, Charleston, SC: Booksurge.

Ingersol, R. S. (1990). Burden of dissent : Mary Lee Cagle and the Southern Holiness movement. BOOK.

Ivers, K. (1991). Golden memories : God's leading in the lives of His people. BOOK, McPherson, KS.: McPherson Free Methodist Church.

Kelley, A. T., & Kelley, W. W. (1889). Memoirs of Mrs. Augusta Tullis Kelley her experience, labors as evangelist and missionary to Africa, with extracts from her writings. ELEC, Chicago: T.B. Arnold.

Kendall, W. S. (1985). Evangel of the cross : highlights, devotion depths, and bits of humor. BOOK, Stanwood, Wash.: Le Sabre.

Kennedy, J. H. (1954). The Lord shall preserve and Treasures out of the darkness. BOOK, Bern, Ind.: Light and Hope Publications.

Kidney, E. M. (1988). Our Father's care. BOOK, Spring Arbor, MI.: The Author.

Kingsley, C. W. (1990). I stand by the door : the autobiography of Charles W. Kingsley. BOOK, Indianapolis, Ind.: Light and Life Men International.

La Due, J., & La Due, W. K. (1898). The life of Rev. Thomas Scott La Due : with some sketches and other writings. BOOK, Chicago: Free Methodist Pub. House.

Lesalnieks, K. (1970). Unsearchable ways of God : Isaiah 55: 8-9. BOOK, Bicknell, Ind.: Fellowship Promoter Press.

Looman, J. (n.d.). The story of my life. BOOK, Allegan, Mich.: John Looman.

Lyon, D. (1953). My life story. BOOK, D. Lyon.

McChesney, A., & McChesney, B. (1968). Through Congo shadows. BOOK, Salem, Ohio: Convention Book Store Publishers.

McGrew, R. S. (1978). True accounts of divine healing. BOOK, Freeport, Pa.: Fountain Press.

Moore, C. C. (1978). Variety and spice of a minister's life. BOOK, Lakeland, FL: C.C. Moore.

Murphy, M. F. (1921). A memorial to Pauline Fowler Kimball. BOOK, El Paso, Texas: Minnie Ferris Murphy.

Nelson, T. H., & Dake, V. A. (1894). Life and labors of Rev. Vivian A. Dake : organizer and leader of Pentecost Bands : embracing an account of his travels in America, Europe and Africa, with selections from his sketches, poems and songs. BOOK, Chicago: Published for the author by T.B. Arnold ...

Northrup, L. W. (1999). It took a miracle : the life story of L.W. Northrup. BOOK, L.W. Northrup.

Parsons, I. D. (1915). Kindling watch-fires; being a brief sketch of the life of Rev. Vivian A. Dake, together with a compilation of selections from his writings, sermons, and poems, to which is appended a few of his best songs with the music,. BOOK, Chicago, Ill.: Free Methodist Pub. House.

Pauley, R. (1970). DeShazer returns. BOOK, Winona Lake, Ind.: Free Methodist Church of North America, General Missionary Board.

Phillips, H. V. (1987). From the door of an orphanage. BOOK, Sandusky, Mich.: New Creation Ministries.

Rev. Aura Claire Showers : a sketch of his life / by his wife ; together with tributes by ministerial brethren ; to which is added a treatise on the doctrine of eternal punishment and other unpublished manuscripts. (1896). ELEC, Oil City, PA :H.D.W. Showers,1896.

Rhodes, M. L. (1919). Clifford B. Barrett : the "Happy Alleghenian." BOOK, Chicago: W.B. Rose.

Richardson, A. (1998). Maria. BOOK, Indianapolis, IN: Light and Life Communications.

Richardson, A., & Tiedemann, K. (2000). Maria. SOUND, Van Wyck, SC: NorthStar Pub.

Robb, J. A. (1979). Life's golden memories. BOOK, Woodstock, Ont.: Nethercott Press.

Roberts, B. H. B. T., Roberts, A. A. R., Roberts, E. S. E. L. S. E. S., Roberts, G. L., & Division, L. of C. M. (1990). Benjamin T. Roberts family papers. BOOK, Washington, D.C.: Library of Congress, Photoduplication Service.

Root, L. P., & Benson, M. C. (1988). Outflowing love : Auntiebai, Effie Southworth's life of loving service during her more than 50 years in central India. BOOK, Winona Lake, Ind.: Light & Life Communications.

Roper, S. G. (1935). The story of my life from the cradle to now (1859-1935). BOOK, Portland, Or.: Samuel G. Roper.

Sage, C. H., & Olmstead, W. B. (1908). Autobiography of Rev. Charles H. Sage : embracing an account of his pioneer work in Michigan, of the formation of the Canada Conference and of his labors in various states. BOOK, Chicago, Ill.: Free Methodist Pub. House.

Scherer, F. E. (1997). Aunt Edith & Lora. BOOK, Oak Park, Ill.: James A. Scherer.

Sellew, W. A., Hogue, W. T., & America, F. M. C. of N. (1913). Clara Leffingwell, a missionary. BOOK, Chicago: Free Methodist Pub. House.

Shay, E. A. F., America, F. M. C. of N., & Society, W. F. M. (1914). Mariet Hardy Freeland, a faithful witness : a biography. BOOK, Chicago: Woman's Foreign Missionary Society of the Free Methodist Church.

Shelhamer, E. E. (n.d.). A bit of experience. BOOK, Los Angeles, CA.

Shelhamer, E. E. (n.d.). E.E. Shelhamer's life story. SOUND, Knoxville, TN: Evangelist of Truth.

Shelhamer, E. E. (1900). Sixty years of thorns and roses. BOOK, Cincinnati, Ohio: God's Bible School and Revivalist.

Shelhamer, E. E. (1907). Experiences in travel and soul saving : also some of my mistakes and what they have taught me. BOOK, Atlanta, Ga

Shelhamer, E. E. (1991). The ups and downs of a pioneer preacher : also some of my mistakes and what they taught me. BOOK, Salem, Ohio: Allegheny Publications.

Shelhamer, E. E., & Shelhamer, J. A. (n.d.). Ragged Elzie gave hope to the discouraged. BOOK, Winona Lake, IN: Mrs. E.E. Shelhamer.

Showers, H. D. W. (1896). Rev. Aura Claire Showers a sketch of his life. ELEC, Oil City, PA: H.D.W. Showers.

Sims, A. (n.d.). Yet not I, or, A brief sketch of the early life, conversion, call to the ministry, and some of the subsequent labors in the Master's vineyard of A. Sims. BOOK, Toronto.

Sizelove, R. A. H., & Corum, J. F. (2011). A sketch of my life. BOOK, S.l.: s.n.

Smith, B. B., & Shelhamer, J. A. (n.d.). The life story of Minnie B. Shelhamer. BOOK, Atlanta: Repairer Pub. Co.

Smith, B. B., & Shelhamer, J. A. (1904). "A remarkable woman" : the life of Mrs. Minnie B. Shelhamer. BOOK, Atlanta: Repairer Pub. Co.

Smith, B. B., Shelhamer, J. A., Swauger, N. P., & Fero, G. L. (1992). Remarkable women. BOOK, Salem, Ohio: Allegheny Publications.

Smith, E. M. (1943). A child shall lead them. BOOK, Greenville, Ill.: Tower Press.

Snyder, C. A. (2006). Weeping may endure for a night : a spiritual journey. BOOK, Xulon Press.

Snyder, H. A. (1990). Radical holiness evangelism : Vivian Dake and the Pentecost Bands. BOOK, Dayton, OH.

Snyder, H. A. (2006). Populist saints : B.T. and Ellen Roberts and the first Free Methodists. BOOK, Grand Rapids, Mich.: William B. Eerdmans Pub. Co.

Snyder, H. A., Runyon, D. V, & Snyder, H. A. (2011). B. T. and Ellen Roberts and the first Free Methodists. BOOK, Indianapolis, Ind.: Committee on Free Methodist History & Archives.

Snyder, L. E., & Weidman, B. E. (1940). Servant of God : life story and selected articles of Bishop Arthur D. Zahniser. BOOK, Winona Lake, Ind.: Light and Life Press.

Stedwell, A. (1915). Itinerant footprints. BOOK, Shambaugh, Iowa: Stedwell.

Summers, A., & Summers, G. (1952). Sanctified wholly. BOOK, Estevan, Sask.: J. Cowan.

Tapper, R. M., & Young People's Missionary Society of the Free Methodist Church. (1935). Life stories of foreign missionaries of the Free Methodist Church : supported by the Young People's Missionary Society, 1931-1935. BOOK, Winona Lake, Ind.: Y.P.M.S. Council.

Terrill, J. G. (2000). The life of John Wesley Redfield, M.D. BOOK, Salem, Ohio: Allegheny.

Thrall, O. C. (n.d.). From darkness to light and from the power of Satan unto God. BOOK, Titusville, PA: O.C. Thrall.

Trever, R. (1905). Life and labors of Rev. Robert Trever both in England and America also, A sketch of frontier work in connection with the Free Methodist church with an appendix containing temperance and other matter. ELEC, St. Louis: J.H. Flowers.

Tsuchiyama, T., & Olmstead, W. B. (1927). From darkness to light. BOOK, Chicago, IL: Light and Life Press.

Tsuchiyama, T., Richardson, A., & Kaneda, K. (1986). Love shining through : Tsuchiyama. BOOK, Winona Lake, IN: Light and Life Press.

Ward, E. E., America., F. M. C. of N., Free Methodist Church of North America, & America., F. M. C. of N. (1951). Ordered steps, or, The Wards of India : a biography of the lives of Ernest Fremont Ward and Phebe Elizabeth Cox Ward, missionaries to India, 1880-1927. BOOK, Winona Lake, Ind.: Light and Life Press.

Ward, E. F. (1880). Papers. BOOK.

Ward, E. F. (1923). Memory links of "our own Chickabiddie", or, Reminiscences of Mary Louise Vore. BOOK, Chicago: Free Methodist Pub. House.

Watson, C. H. (2002). DeShazer. BOOK.

Watson, C. H., & Fear, L. K. (1972). De Shazer. BOOK, Winona Lake, Ind.: Light and Life Press.

Williamson, G. (1972). Frank and Hazel : the Adamsons of Kibogora. BOOK, Winona Lake, IN: Light and Life Press.

Williamson, G. (1976). Gonzalo of Mexican missions. BOOK, Winona Lake, Ind.: Light and Life Press.

Winslow, C. V. V. (1981). By love compelled : life story. BOOK, Winona Lake, Ind.: Light and Life Press.

Woods, D. A. (1989). Tall timber, deep roots : autobiography of Dale A. Woods. BOOK, Flint, Mich.: D.A. Woods].

Free Methodist Church – Church Growth

America, F. M. C. of N., & Growth, D. of E. and C. (n.d.). Reaching out in love. JFULL, Indianapolis, IN: Free Methodist Church of North America, Dept. of Evangelism and Church Growth.

America, F. M. C. of N., & Outreach, D. of E. (1969). North Michigan Conference survey : requested by the North Michigan Conference and conducted during the conference year 1967-68. BOOK, Winona Lake, Ind.: Dept. of Evangelistic Outreach, Free Methodist Church.

Barnett, L. P. (1965). Yorokobi no otozure. BOOK, Rosanjerusu: Rosanjerusu Furi Mesojisuto Kyokai.

Bastian, D. N. (1978). Cultivating church members : for Free Methodist pastors only. BOOK, Winona Lake, IN: Light and Life Press.

Church, H. G. (2002). Theological education that makes a difference : church growth in the Free Methodist Church in Malawi and Zimbabwe. BOOK, Blantyre, Malawi: Christian Literature Association in Malawi.

Cooper, R. E. (1976). A projected growth strategy for the Madras Free Methodist Church (THES).

Copeland, J. B. (2000). A strategy for relational evangelism at Skyline Family Fellowship (THES).

Cranston, R. J. (1984) A workable program of church growth for the Free Methodist Church of the Philippines (THES).

Crawford, D. L. (1993). Finding small healthy Free Methodist Churches in the state of Illinois (THES). Asbury Theological Seminary. Retrieved from http://place.asburyseminary.edu/ecommonsatsdissertations/75/

Culumber, T. J. (1981). Church growth theology, strategy, and goals for the Department of Evangelism and church growth of the Free Methodist Church of North America (THES).

Davenport, M. S. (1996). Six ministry strategies for planting a seeker sensitive church (THES).

Ellis, R. W. (1993). How to plant a Free Methodist Church : effective models for the 90's. BOOK, Indianapolis, Ind.: Free Methodist Church of N.A.

Gregory, D. T. (2005). From the new day to the new century : Free Methodist strategies for metropolitan church planting in light of 1985-2000 efforts and results (THES).

Harvey, D. (2006). STMO (submission, transformation, multiplication, order) : building a culture of kingdom fruitfulness. BOOK, Indianapolis, IN: Free Methodist Church of North America.

Haskins, A. M. (1997). New life for old churches : a multi-case study of four turnaround small churches (THES).

King, C. W. (1990). Mobilizing the laity : a strategy for obtaining greater numerical growth in the Wilmore Free Methodist Church (THES).

McKenna, D. L. (1955). The Sunday school dropout : the great loss of the church. BOOK, Winona Lake, Ind.: Dept. of Sunday Schools, Free Methodist Headquarters.

Nakajima, M. G. (1983). Growth of Japan Free Methodist Church, 1945-1982 (THES).

Olver, P. S. (1986). A strategy for urban church planting for the Free Methodist Church of North America (THES).

Pierce, M. C. (1998). Developing structures for health and growth for Northgate Free Methodist Church in Batavia, New York (ELEC). Asbury Theological Seminary.

Riggs, D. E. (1981). Make it happen. BOOK, Warsaw, Ind.: LP Products.

Snider, K. L. (1985). Ten more growing churches in Japan today. BOOK, Osaka, Japan: Japan Free Methodist Church.

Snider, K. L., & Nakae, S. (1986). Seicho suru ju kyokai no kiroku : ima, nihon demo ...2. BOOK, Tokyo: Inochi no Kotobasha.

Willard, F. B. (1983). A proposal for the training of lay ministers for Hispanic Free Methodist Churches (THES).

Free Methodist Church – Clergy Biography

Archer, A. C. (1930). The man with a thorn in his flesh. BOOK, Medford, Ore.: Schmul Pub. Co.

Babcock, C. A. (1938). Life and labours of Chas. A. Babcock : with a brief sketch of early days in the district in which he was born. BOOK, Brockville, Ont.: Standard Publishing House.

Beers, A. (1922). The romance of a consecrated life : a biography of Alexander Beers. Chicago: Free Methodist Pub. House.

Black, H. (1932). From newsboy to preacher : the story of my life.

Brandt, M. E. (1980). Henry and Emma Brandt : memorabelia. BOOK, McPherson, KS: Brandt Family.

Brock, L. W. (1987). The life story of Rev. Lyle and Doris Brock : pioneer pastors of the Free Methodist Church in the West Kansas Conference and the California Conference. BOOK, Stanwood, WA.

Cook, E. D. (2005). Salt of the sea : a Navy chaplain's experience ashore and at sea. BOOK, Longwood, Fla.: Xulon Press.

Cryderman, L. (1999). Glory land : a memoir of a lifetime in church. BOOK, Grand Rapids, Mich.: Zondervan.

Cryderman, L. (2001). No swimming on Sunday : stories of a lifetime in church. BOOK, Grand Rapids, Mich.: Zondervan.

Damon, C. M. (1900). Sketches and incidents, or reminiscences of interest in the life of the author. BOOK, Chicago: Free Methodist Pub. House.

Davis, R. N. (1954). Redeemed : a remarkable conversion in the heart of India : the story of Moses David, superintendent of the Eastern District, and evangelist, India Free Methodist Church ... BOOK, Winona Lake, Ind.: Woman's Missionary Society, Free Methodist Church.

Dawson, L. (1962). Vital Faith. Seattle, WA: Printed by L & H Print. Co.

De Voist, M. (1920). Foot-prints in my life, or, the story told in rhyme. BOOK.

Demaray, D. E. (1978). Near hurting people : the pastoral ministry of Robert Moffat Fine. BOOK, Winona Lake, Ind.: Light and Life Press.

Demaray, D. E. (2000). With His joy : the life and leadership of David McKenna. BOOK, Indianapolis, IN: Light & Life Communications.

Fairbarn, C. V. (1960). I call to remembrance. BOOK, Winona Lake, Ind.: Light and Life Press.

Gramento, J. H. (1992). Those astounding Free Methodist women! a biographical history of Free Methodist women in ministry with an extended bibliography of Free Methodist women's studies : a final document submitted to the Doctoral Studies Committee of United Theological Seminary (THES). United Theological Seminary, Dayton, OH.

Hamilton, M. E. (1988). James R. Bishop : God's chosen man : the life story of the founder of South India Biblical Seminary Bangarapet, Karnataka, South India. BOOK, Karnataka, India: South India Biblical Seminary.

Haywood, A. L. (1942). My life story. ELEC, Stanwood, Mich.: Sanders Print Shop.

Hazzard, A. H., Montmorency County Historical Society, & Tribune., M. C. (1991). Blue Sky Circuit Montmorency County, Michigan, 1922-1926. ELEC, Atlanta, MI: Montmorency County Historical Society: Printed by the Montmorency County Tribune.

Hospital, D. (1975). The Butterfields : 50 years. BOOK, Oklahoma City, Okla.: Deaconess Hospital.

Ingersol, R. S. (1990). Burden of dissent : Mary Lee Cagle and the Southern Holiness movement. BOOK.

Kidney, E. M. (1988). Our Father's care. BOOK, Spring Arbor, MI.: The Author.

Kingsley, C. W. (1990). I stand by the door : the autobiography of Charles W. Kingsley. BOOK, Indianapolis, Ind.: Light and Life Men International.

La Due, J., & La Due, W. K. (1898). The life of Rev. Thomas Scott La Due : with some sketches and other writings. BOOK, Chicago: Free Methodist Pub. House.

Lesalnieks, K. (1970). Unsearchable ways of God : Isaiah 55: 8-9. BOOK, Bicknell, Ind.: Fellowship Promoter Press.

Looman, J. (n.d.). The story of my life. BOOK, Allegan, Mich.: John Looman.

Moore, C. C. (1978). Variety and spice of a minister's life. BOOK, Lakeland, FL: C.C. Moore.

Nelson, T. H., & Dake, V. A. (1894). Life and labors of Rev. Vivian A. Dake : organizer and leader of Pentecost Bands : embracing an account of his travels in America, Europe and Africa, with selections from his sketches, poems and songs. BOOK, Chicago: Published for the author by T.B. Arnold ...

Northrup, L. W. (1999). It took a miracle : the life story of L.W. Northrup. BOOK, L.W. Northrup.

Parsons, I. D. (1915). Kindling watch-fires; being a brief sketch of the life of Rev. Vivian A. Dake, together with a compilation of selections from his writings, sermons, and poems, to which is appended a few of his best songs with the music,. BOOK, Chicago, Ill.: Free Methodist Pub. House.

Phillips, H. V. (1987). From the door of an orphanage. BOOK, Sandusky, Mich.: New Creation Ministries.

Rev. Aura Claire Showers : a sketch of his life / by his wife ; together with tributes by ministerial brethren ; to which is added a treatise on the doctrine of eternal punishment and other unpublished manuscripts. (1896). ELEC, Oil City, PA :H.D.W. Showers,1896.

Rhodes, M. L. (1919). Clifford B. Barrett : the "Happy Alleghenian." BOOK, Chicago: W.B. Rose.

Robb, J. A. (1979). Life's golden memories. BOOK, Woodstock, Ont.: Nethercott Press.

Roberts, B. H. B. T., Roberts, A. A. R., Roberts, E. S. E. L. S. E. S., Roberts, G. L., & Division, L. of C. M. (1990). Benjamin T. Roberts family papers. BOOK, Washington, D.C.: Library of Congress, Photoduplication Service.

Sage, C. H., & Olmstead, W. B. (1908). Autobiography of Rev. Charles H. Sage : embracing an account of his pioneer work in Michigan, of the formation of the Canada Conference and of his labors in various states. BOOK, Chicago, Ill.: Free Methodist Pub. House.

Shelhamer, E. E. (n.d.). E.E. Shelhamer's life story. SOUND, Knoxville, TN: Evangelist of Truth.

Shelhamer, E. E. (1900). Sixty years of thorns and roses. BOOK, Cincinnati, Ohio: God's Bible School and Revivalist.

Shelhamer, E. E. (1907). Experiences in travel and soul saving : also some of my mistakes and what they have taught me. BOOK, Atlanta, Ga.

Shelhamer, E. E. (1991). The ups and downs of a pioneer preacher : also some of my mistakes and what they taught me. BOOK, Salem, Ohio: Allegheny Publications.

Shelhamer, E. E., & Shelhamer, J. A. (n.d.). Ragged Elzie gave hope to the discouraged. BOOK, Winona Lake, IN: Mrs. E.E. Shelhamer.

Showers, H. D. W. (1896). Rev. Aura Claire Showers a sketch of his life. ELEC, Oil City, PA: H.D.W. Showers.

Sims, A. (n.d.). Yet not I, or, A brief sketch of the early life, conversion, call to the ministry, and some of the subsequent labors in the Master's vineyard of A. Sims. BOOK, Toronto.

Smith, B. B., & Shelhamer, J. A. (n.d.). The life story of Minnie B. Shelhamer. BOOK, Atlanta: Repairer Pub. Co.

Smith, B. B., & Shelhamer, J. A. (1904). "A remarkable woman" : the life of Mrs. Minnie B. Shelhamer. BOOK, Atlanta: Repairer Pub. Co.

Smith, B. B., Shelhamer, J. A., Swauger, N. P., & Fero, G. L. (1992). Remarkable women. BOOK, Salem, Ohio: Allegheny Publications.

Snyder, C. A. (2006). Weeping may endure for a night : a spiritual journey. BOOK, Xulon Press.

Snyder, H. A. (1990). Radical holiness evangelism : Vivian Dake and the Pentecost Bands. BOOK, Dayton, OH.

Snyder, L. E., & Weidman, B. E. (1940). Servant of God : life story and selected articles of Bishop Arthur D. Zahniser. BOOK, Winona Lake, Ind.: Light and Life Press.

Stedwell, A. (1915). Itinerant footprints. BOOK, Shambaugh, Iowa: Stedwell.

Summers, A., & Summers, G. (1952). Sanctified wholly. BOOK, Estevan, Sask.: J. Cowan.

Terrill, J. G. (2000). The life of John Wesley Redfield, M.D. BOOK, Salem, Ohio: Allegheny.

Thrall, O. C. (n.d.). From darkness to light and from the power of Satan unto God. BOOK, Titusville, PA: O.C. Thrall.

Tsuchiyama, T., & Olmstead, W. B. (1927). From darkness to light. BOOK, Chicago, IL: Light and Life Press.

Tsuchiyama, T., Richardson, A., & Kaneda, K. (1986). Love shining through : Tsuchiyama. BOOK, Winona Lake, IN: Light and Life Press.

Woods, D. A. (1989). Tall timber, deep roots : autobiography of Dale A. Woods. BOOK, Flint, Mich.: D.A. Woods].

Free Methodist Church – Devotional/Christian Life

Andrews, E. A. (2005). Musings on self-deception. BOOK, Chicago, Ill.: Charles Edwin Jones.

Andrews, R. F. (1979). When you need a friend. BOOK, Winona Lake, Ind.: Light and Life Media, Dept. of Communications, Free Methodist Church of North America.

Archer, A. C. (1930). The man with a thorn in his flesh. BOOK, Medford, Ore.: Schmul Pub. Co.

Dake, V. A. (n.d.). Kindling watch-fires : choice extracts. BOOK, Waukesha, WI: Metropolitan Church Association.

Dunn, M. (2000). God's call : from infilling to outpouring. BOOK, Grantham, PA: Wesleyan/Holiness Women Clergy, Inc.

Elder, R. M. (1984). Healing where the hurt is : a new look at some old problems. BOOK, Winona, Minn.: Justin Books.

Ellershaw, J. A. (2005). Apostolic doctrine, practice and experience. BOOK, Fulwood Eng.: Free Methodist Church in the United Kingdom.

Harvey, D. (2006). STMO (submission, transformation, multiplication, order) : building a culture of kingdom fruitfulness. BOOK, Indianapolis, IN: Free Methodist Church of North America.

Humphrey, J. M. (1914). Spiritual lessons from every-day life. BOOK, Lima, Ohio: True Gospel Grain Pub. Co.

Kendall, W. S. (1981). The Holy Spirit in Christian experience. BOOK, Stanwood, Wash.: Warm Beach Printing Services.

Kendall, W. S. (1985). Evangel of the cross : highlights, devotion depths, and bits of humor. BOOK, Stanwood, Wash.: Le Sabre.

Marston, L. R. (1946). "I need a chart." BOOK, Winona Lake, Ind.: Published for The National Association of Evangelicals by courtesy of Light and Life Press.

Marston, L. R. (1950). The spirit and emphasis of Free Methodism. BOOK. Winona Lake, Ind.: Free Methodist Church of North America.

McPeak, R. H. (2001). Earnest Christianity : the practical theology of Benjamin Titus Roberts (THES).

Pelton, H. (1904). The Pilgrim's progress of the twentieth century. BOOK, Chicago, Ill.: Free Methodist Pub.

Roberts, B. T., & Coates, G. W. (2007). Practical piety : daily reflections on Christian virtue. BOOK, Indianapolis, Ind.: Wesleyan Pub. House.

Roberts, B. T., & Demaray, D. E. (1996). The daily Roberts : readings for every day in the year from the writings of B.T. Roberts. BOOK, Indianapolis, IN: Light and Life Press.

Smith, B. B., Shelhamer, J. A., Swauger, N. P., & Fero, G. L. (1992). Remarkable women. BOOK, Salem, Ohio: Allegheny Publications.

Free Methodist Church – Discipline

America., F. M. C. of N. (n.d.). Doutrinas e disciplina da Igreja Metodista Livre da America do Norte. JFULL, S.l.: Free Methodist Church of North America.

America., F. M. C. of N. (1860). Doctrines and discipline. CONF, Winona Lake, Ind.: Free Methodist Pub. House.

America, F. M. C. of N. (1915). Doctrines and discipline of the Free Methodist Church. BOOK, Chicago, Ill.: Free Methodist Pub. House.

America, F. M. C. of N. (1970). Doctrines and discipline of the Free Methodist Church of North America. BOOK, Winona Lake, Ind.: Free Methodist Pub. House.

America, F. M. C. of N. (1990). The book of discipline, 1989. The Book of discipline. BOOK, Winona Lake, Ind.: Free Methodist Pub. House.

America, F. M. C. of N. (2004). 2003 book of discipline. BOOK, Indianapolis, Ind.: Free Methodist Publishing House.

America, F. M. C. of N. (2012). 2011 Book of Discipline. BOOK, Indianapolis, Ind.: Free Methodist Publishing House.

America, F. M. C. of N., & Hart, E. P. (1908). A digest of Free Methodist law : or, Guide in the administration of the discipline of the Free Methodist church. BOOK, Chicago: Free Methodist Pub. House.

Free Methodist Church – Doctrine

America., F. M. C. of N. (n.d.-a). Doctrines et discipline de l'Eglise Méthodiste Libre de l'Amerique du Nord. JFull, Free Methodist Church of North America.

America., F. M. C. of N. (n.d.-b). Doutrinas e disciplina da Igreja Metodista Livre da America do Norte. JFULL, S.l.: Free Methodist Church of North America.

America, F. M. C. of N. (1915). Doctrines and discipline of the Free Methodist Church. BOOK, Chicago, Ill.: Free Methodist Pub. House.

America, F. M. C. of N. (1967). Free Methodist Church, 1860-1978. BOOK, Sun City, Ariz.: Ecumenism Research Agency.

America, F. M. C. of N. (1970). Doctrines and discipline of the Free Methodist Church of North America. BOOK, Winona Lake, Ind.: Free Methodist Pub. House.

America, F. M. C. of N. (1990). The book of discipline, 1989. The Book of discipline. BOOK, Winona Lake, Ind.: Free Methodist Pub. House.

America, F. M. C. of N. (2004). 2003 book of discipline. BOOK, Indianapolis, Ind.: Free Methodist Publishing House.

America, F. M. C. of N.. & Education, D. of C. (1989). What is a Free Methodist? BOOK, Winona Lake, Ind.: Department of Christian Education, Free Methodist Church of North America.

America, F. M. C. of N.. & Kendall, W. S. (1955). From age to age, my church, a living witness. BOOK, Winona Lake, Ind.: Free Methodist Church of North America.

America, F. M. C. of N.. & Mission, G. C. for C. in. (1970). What is a Free Methodist? BOOK, Winona Lake, Ind.: General Council for Church in Mission, Free Methodist Church.

America, R. F. M. C. of N. (1960). Discipline of the Reformed Free Methodist Church. BOOK, Perryopolis, Pa.: Sound of the Trumpet Ministries.

Andrews, E. A. (2005). Musings on self-deception. BOOK, Chicago, Ill.: Charles Edwin Jones.

Andrews, R. F. (1979). When you need a friend. BOOK, Winona Lake, Ind.: Light and Life Media, Dept. of Communications, Free Methodist Church of North America.

Archives, S. P. U. (1950). Free Methodist Church records and publications (UNPB).

Baldwin, H. A. (1987). The coming judgment : general and at the end of time. BOOK, Salem, Ohio: Allegheny Publications.

Bastian, D. N. (1995). Sketches of Free Methodism. BOOK, Indianapolis, Ind.: Light & Life Press.

Bastian, D. N., & Free Methodist Church of North America. (2008). Give it a rest. BOOK, Indianapolis, Ind.: Light and Life Communications.

Boyd, M. F. (1940). Finding, enjoying and retaining God! BOOK, Winona Lake, Ind.: Light and Life Hour.

Christianity, F. for S. (1999). Discovery : basic belief studies for Free Methodists. BOOK, Indianapolis, Ind.: Light and LIfe Communications in cooperation with Bristol House.

College, M. C. of G., & Kline, G. E. (1940). The Wesleyan message, its Scriptures and historical bases : addresses delivered at the 12th Annual Ministers' Conference, Greenville College, April 10-14, 1939. CONF, Winona Lake, IN: Light and Life Press.

Cullum, D. R. (2002). Gospel simplicity : rhythms of faith and life among Free Methodists in Victorian America (THES).

Demaray, D. E. (1958). Basic beliefs : an introductory guide to Christian theology. BOOK, Grand Rapids: Baker Book House.

Demaray, D. E. (1990). An introduction to homiletics. BOOK, Indianapolis, Ind.: Light and Life Press.

Demaray, D. E., Free Methodist Church of North America, & General Leadership and Service Training Council. (1965). Alive to God through prayer : a manual on the practices of prayer. BOOK, Grand Rapids: Baker Book House.

Demaray, D. E., & Sun Liu, Y. (2009). Ji yao zhen li : Jidu jiao Weisili zong shen xue jian jie. BOOK, Gaoxiong Shi: Sheng guang shen xue yuan.

Dolan, T. F. (1880). A bit of experience : showing the dealings of Godmanandthedevil with T.F. Dolan, convert from Romanism ; to which is added a review of the Methodist discipline and selections from Wesley, Clarke, Bramwell, Carvosso, and others. BOOK, Chicago: Baker & Arnold, Printers.

Ellershaw, J. A. (2005). Apostolic doctrine, practice and experience. BOOK, Fulwood Eng.: Free Methodist Church in the United Kingdom.

Fairbairn, C. V. (1957). What we believe : a brief manual of Christian doctrine for young Free Methodists and new converts based upon the catechism and articles of religion of the Free Methodist Church of North America. BOOK, Winona Lake, IN: Light and Life Press.

Free Methodist Church of North America, & Board of Bishops. (1957). Confidentially yours. JFULL, Winona Lake, Ind.: Free Methodist Church of North America.

Free Methodist Church of North America, General Conference, & Study Commission on Doctrine. (1989). Report of the Study Commission on Doctrine : Free Methodist Church of North America, 31st General Conference, August 3-13, 1989, Seattle, Washington. BOOK.

Gagne, R. (1991). The Free Methodist understanding of baptism in the light of John Wesley's teaching and the American Methodist tradition (THES).

Griffith, G. W. (1923). The divine program; an interpretation of the divine method of redemption and of the nature and nurture of the Christian life,. BOOK, Chicago, Ill.: W.B. Rose.

Hitt, R. T., Beltz, R. A., & Watson, C. H. (n.d.). Story of the Light and Life Hour. BOOK, Winona Lake, IN: Forward Movement.

Hogue, W. T. (1916). The Holy Spirit : a study. BOOK, Chicago, Ill.: William B. Rose.

Humphrey, J. M. (1913). Select fruits from the highlands of Beulah. BOOK, Lima, OH: True Gospel Grain Pub. Co.

Humphrey, J. M., & Humphrey, J. M. (2000). The lost soul's first day in eternity. BOOK, Salem, Ohio: Allegheny Publications.

James, J. F., Free Methodist Church of North America, & General Conference. (2008). Our calling to the poor. BOOK, Indianapolis, Ind.: Light and Life Press.

Kaufmann, U. M. (1970). The God who shows himself. BOOK, Winona Lake, Ind.: Free Methodist Church of North America, General Council for Church in Mission.

Kendall, D. W., Winslow, K. S., & Free Methodist Church of North America. (2006). The female pastor : is there room for "she" in shepherd? BOOK, Indianapolis, Ind.: Light and Life Communications.

Knox, L. H. (1970). Security for believers. BOOK, Winona Lake, Ind.: Light and Life Press.

Knox, L. H. (1972). Key to holiness theology : a relational understanding. BOOK, Winona Lake, Ind.: Light and Life Press.

Knox, L. H., Wesley, J., Wesley, C., & Free Methodist Church of North America. (1976). The Faith and life of a Free Methodist. BOOK, Winona Lake, Ind.: Free Methodist Pub. House.

Larm, T. A. (2004). A grammar of conversion (THES).

Livingston, G. H. (1981). Origins of life and faith : Genesis A : study guide. BOOK, Winona Lake, Ind.: Light and Life Press.

Marston, L. R. (n.d.). Thumb-nail sketches of doctrinal patterns : John Calvin, Jacobus Arminius, John Wesley. BOOK, Winona Lake, Ind.: Free Methodist Heaquarters.

McPeak, R. H. (2001). Earnest Christianity : the practical theology of Benjamin Titus Roberts (THES).

Mercer, F. D. (1991). The liturgical and sacramental development of the Free Methodist Church in Canada : with special attention to the rituals of baptism and the Lord's Supper (THES).

Mott, E., & America, F. M. C. of N. (1944). The security of the believers. BOOK, Seattle, Wa.: Board of Aggressive Evangelism, Washington Conference, Free Methodist Church.

Mountcastle, W. D. (2006). Back to the future : evolving the Wesleyan model for renewal and leadership development for the Free Methodist Church (THES). Regent University, Virginia Beach, Va.

Olver, H. L. (1977). Biblical basis for urban ministry : a paper presented at the 1977 Continental Urban Exchange (CUE), Minneapolis, Minnesota. BOOK, Winona Lake, Ind.: Light and Life Men International.

Roberts, B. T., & Coates, G. W. (2007). Practical piety : daily reflections on Christian virtue. BOOK, Indianapolis, Ind.: Wesleyan Pub. House.

Schwanz, K. D. (1991). The "wooden brother" : instrumental music restricted in Free Methodist worship, 1860-1955 (THES).

Snyder, R. D. (2004). Being disciples, making disciples. BOOK, Indianapolis, IN: Free Methodist Church of North America.

The what and the why of Free Methodism. (1927). BOOK, Chicago: Free Methodist Pub. House.

Veldman, R. J. (2006). Classic catechism. BOOK, Indianapolis, Ind.: Light and Life Communications.

Walters, O. S. (1948). The Christian and the movies. BOOK, Winona Lake, Ind.: The Forward Movement, Free Methodist Church of North America.

Watson, C. H. (1950). The Free Methodist Church. BOOK, Winona Lake, Ind.: Free Methodist Church of North America.

We believe! : insights into the beliefs of Free Methodists. (1976). BOOK, Winona Lake, Ind.: Light and Life Press.

Wesley, J. (1940). On dress and evil speaking. BOOK, Winona Lake, Ind.: Free Methodist Publishing House.

Free Methodist Church – Government

America, F. M. C. of N. (1901). A digest of Free Methodist law; or, Guide in the administration of the discipline of the Free Methodist church ... BOOK, Chicago, Ill.: Free Methodist Pub. House.

America, F. M. C. of N. (1915). Doctrines and discipline of the Free Methodist Church. BOOK, Chicago, Ill.: Free Methodist Pub. House.

America, F. M. C. of N. (1970). Doctrines and discipline of the Free Methodist Church of North America. BOOK, Winona Lake, Ind.: Free Methodist Pub. House.

America, F. M. C. of N. (1990). The book of discipline, 1989. The Book of discipline. BOOK, Winona Lake, Ind.: Free Methodist Pub. House.

America, R. F. M. C. of N. (1960). Discipline of the Reformed Free Methodist Church. BOOK, Perryopolis, Pa.: Sound of the Trumpet Ministries.

Mullikin, J. C. (1915). James Clayland Mullikin papers, (UNPB).

Woodruff, D. O., Duncombe, C., Hammond, A. P., Hurd, W., Family., H., O'Callahan, T., ... Family., W. (1836). D.O. Woodruff papers (UNPB).

Free Methodist Church – Handbooks, Manuals, etc.

America., F. M. C. of N., Bishops., B. of, Free Methodist Church of North America, & Board of Bishops. (1998). Pastor's handbook. BOOK, Board of Bishops, Free Methodist Church of North America.

America, F. M. C. of N., & Bishops, B. of. (1980). Lay delegate's handbook. BOOK, Free Methodist Church of North America.

America, F. M. C. of N., & Communication, W. M. (1972). "Communicating our United World Mission for Christ" : minister's manual. BOOK, Winona Lake, Ind.: Free Methodist Church of North America.

America, F. M. C. of N., & Education, C. on C. (1986). Lay leadership training handbook. BOOK, Winona Lake, Ind.: Free Methodist Church of North America.

America, F. M. C. of N., & Van Valin, C. E. (1986). Pastor's handbook of the Free Methodist Church. BOOK, Winona Lake, IN: Light and Life Press.

Brown, A. L., Secord, A. W., & White, E. C. (1946). A handbook for Sunday school workers. BOOK, Winona Lake, Ind.: Department of Sunday Schools, Christian Education Commission : Light and Life Press.

Burritt, C. T., America, F. M. C. of N., & Society, W. M. (1952). A guide for missionary workers. BOOK, Winona Lake, Ind.: Womans' Missionary Society, Free Methodist Church.

Delamarter, G. N. (1985). Pastoral support team manual. BOOK, Winona Lake, Ind.: Free Methodist Church of North America.

Free Methodist Church of North America, & Light and Life Men's Fellowship. (1960). "Break through" : the president's manual. BOOK, Winona Lake, Ind.: Free Methodist Church of North America.

Krober, L. L., & Free Methodist Church of North America Board of Bishops. (2006). Pastors and church leaders manual : resources for leading local churches. BOOK, Indianapolis, Ind.: Light and Life Communications.

Van Valin, C. E. (1991). Pastor's handbook. BOOK, Board of Bishops, Free Methodist Church (USA).

Free Methodist Church – History

Adams, L. J. (2000). Strengthening the vitality of New Hope Free Methodist Church through the natural church development approach (THES). Asbury Theological Seminary.

Babcock, C. A. (1938). Life and labours of Chas. A. Babcock : with a brief sketch of early days in the district in which he was born. BOOK, Brockville, Ont.: Standard Publishing House.

Ballard Free Methodist Church. (1989). Celebrating God's family : August 6, 1989. BOOK, Seattle, Wash.: Ballard Free Methodisct Church.

Barnett, L. P. (1965). Yorokobi no otozure. BOOK, Rosanjerusu: Rosanjerusu Furi Mesojisuto Kyokai.

Bastian, D. N. (1995). Sketches of Free Methodism. BOOK, Indianapolis, Ind.: Light & Life Press.

Bowell, G. (2014). Reflections and thoughts on a hymnal : The 1910 Free Methodist hymnal. BOOK, Gary E. Bowell.

Brito B., I. (1975). Historia de la Iglesia Metodista Libre Dominicana. BOOK, Santo Domingo, D.N.: Editora Educativa Dominicana.

Buchanan, J. (1990). The development of ecclesiastical autonomy for the Free Methodist Chuch in Canada. BOOK, S.l.: s.n.

Chalker, G. I. (1904). Papers (UNPB).

Chauke, H. W. M., & Houser, T. (2009). H.M. Chauke research of African Hlengwe people. BOOK.

Cochrane, R. L. (1960). Years of beginnings : Washinton Conference, 1880-1896 ; outline. BOOK.

Davenport, M. S. (1996). Six ministry strategies for planting a seeker sensitive church (THES).

DeGroot, A. T. (n.d.). American church records. BOOK, United States: Southwest Microfilm.

Denbo, C. T., Schirack, E E., & Schirack, L. (1989). Wabash centennial : together we serve, the history of Wabash conference, Free Methodist Church. BOOK, Greenville, Ohio: E.E. Schirack.

Fidler, G. (2006). Adventures in India. BOOK, St. Catherines, ON: Cornerstone Research & Pub.

Galbreath, M. (1970). 20 centuries of Christianity. Winona Lake IN: Light and Life Press.

Group buys Ottawa County church to save it. (1994). Minor Methodist Sects, Clippings., 1. JOUR.

Hill, C. D., & Archives, S. P. U. (1909). Cyril Hill Papers, (UNPB).

Hospital, D. (1975). The Butterfields : 50 years. BOOK, Oklahoma City, Okla.: Deaconess Hospital.

Howell, R. W., & Jeffery, W. F. (1970). Relections. BOOK, Winona Lake, Ind.: Roy W. Howell.

Iwig-O'Byrne, L. (1993). A Progression of Methodist radicalism : an examination of the history and ethos of the first sixty years of the Nazarites and their heirs (1855-1915) in their social and religious context (THES).

Jacobson, B. (1900). Jacobson, Byron: Papers (UNPB).

Kysor, K. (1976). Benjamin Titus Roberts and the Free Methodist Church. BOOK, Cattaraugus, N.Y.: s.n.

Macy, V. W. (1946). A history of the Free Methodist mission in Portugese East Africa (THES).

Mayer, J. (n.d.). Free methodist churches in Lawrence County. BOOK.

Mercer, F. D. (1991). The liturgical and sacramental development of the Free Methodist Church in Canada : with special attention to the rituals of baptism and the Lord's Supper (THES).

Mullikin, J. C. (1915). James Clayland Mullikin papers, (UNPB).

Murphy, M. F. (1921). A memorial to Pauline Fowler Kimball. BOOK, El Paso, Texas: Minnie Ferris Murphy.

Nazarite review of the pastoral address of the Genesee Conference of the M.E. Church. (1857). BOOK.

Pauley, R. (1970). DeShazer returns. BOOK, Winona Lake, Ind.: Free Methodist Church of North America, General Missionary Board.

Pierce, M. C. (1998). Developing structures for health and growth for Northgate Free Methodist Church in Batavia, New York (ELEC). Asbury Theological Seminary.

Richardson, J. D., Colgate Rochester Divinity School, & Crozer Theological Seminary. (1984). B.T. Roberts and the role of women in ministry in nineteenth-century Free Methodism : by Jack D. Richardson (THES). Colgate Rochester Divinity School/ Bexley Hall/Crozer Theological Seminary, Rochester, NY.

Ryff, F. J. (1954). An examination of the indigenous church principle with special reference to the Free Methodist church in South Africa (THES).

Seattle, F. F. M. C., & Fellowship, M. M. (n.d.). Modern maturity fellowship herald. Modern Maturity Fellowship Herald. JFULL, Seattle, Wash.: First Free Methodist Church.

Shumaker, J. T. (1992). "Having the mind of Christ" presenting christian holiness in the local church : a final document submitted to the Doctoral Studies Committee of United Theological Seminary in partial fulfillment of the requirements for the degree Doctor of Ministry (THES). United Theological Seminary, Dayton, OH.

Snyder, H. A. (1990). Radical holiness evangelism : Vivian Dake and the Pentecostal Bands. BOOK.

Street, N. A. (1983). Zion Chapel, F.M. Church, 1905- : souvenir edition. BOOK, U.S.: s.n.

The Free Methodist Church in postwar Japan. (1971). BOOK.

The what and the why of Free Methodism. (1927). BOOK, Chicago: Free Methodist Pub. House.

Wabash Christian Courier, & Denbo, C. T. (1960). Centennial : "Wabash Conference -- courier to every age" ; Free Methodist Church, 1860-1960 ; Wabash Conference, 1885-1960 ; 100 years of continuous service to the nations. BOOK, Wabash, Ind.: Wabash Christian Courier.

Walton, K. M. (1960). Western convention : "the springboard of Free Methodism." BOOK, S.l.: s.n.

Wesleyan Theological Society. (1963). Wesleyan Theological Society Records (UNPB).

Wolfe, K. G. (1999). A history of the founding of the Free Methodist day-schools in Southern California (THES).

Woodruff, D. O., Duncombe, C., Hammond, A. P., Hurd, W., Family., H., O'Callahan, T., … Family., W. (1836). D.O. Woodruff papers (UNPB).

Free Methodist Church – Holiness

Black, H. (n.d.-a). The Holy Ghost baptism : and seven other sermons on sin, salvation, and holiness. BOOK, Los Angeles, CA.

Black, H. (n.d.-b). The rich man and Lazarus and other sermons. BOOK, Los Angeles, Calif.

College, M. C. of G., & Kline, G. E. (1940). The Wesleyan message, its Scriptures and historical bases : addresses delivered at the 12th Annual Ministers' Conference, Greenville College, April 10-14, 1939. CONF, Winona Lake, IN: Light and Life Press.

College, M. C. of G., & Kline, G. E. (1942). The message bearing fruit. BOOK, Winona Lake, Ind.: Light and life press.

Damon, C. M. (1900). Sketches and incidents, or reminiscences of interest in the life of the author. BOOK, Chicago: Free Methodist Pub. House.

Free Methodist Church of North America. (1959). An Act to incorporate the Free Methodist Chiurch in Canada : assented to 8th July, 1959. BOOK, Ottawa: Queen's printer and controller of stationery.

Free Methodist Church of North America. (2001). Living Holiness: Free Methodist in the Year 2001. VIDEO, New Link Media.

Hill, N. (2007). A brief history of Holiness Movement & Free Methodist missions, Egypt 1899-1986. BOOK, S.l.: s.n.

Hogue, W. (1907). The class-meeting as a means of grace. Chicago: S.K.J. Chesbro.

Ingersol, R. S. (1990). Burden of dissent : Mary Lee Cagle and the Southern Holiness movement. BOOK.

Jones, C. (1974). A guide to the study of the Holiness movement. Metuchen, NJ: Scarecrow Press.

Kline, G. E., College, M. C. of G., & Greenville, I. (1942). The Wesleyan message bearing fruit. BOOK, Winona Lake, Ind.: Light and Life Press.

Knox, L. H. (1972). Key to holiness theology : a relational understanding. BOOK, Winona Lake, Ind.: Light and Life Press.

Lewis, L. G. (1931). Mitama no mi = The Fruite of the Spirit. BOOK, Tokyo-to: Jiyu Mesojisutosha Shuppanbu, dc 1931, Showa 6.

Magida, A. J. (1997). How to be a perfect stranger, vol. 2 : a guide to etiquette in other people's religious ceremonies. BOOK, Woodstock, Vt.: Jewish Lights Publishing.

Nazarene Theological Seminary. (1965). Master bibliography of holiness works. Kansas City, MO: Beacon Hill Press.

Rhoden, M. M. (1956). The recent progress and methods of evangelism of holiness missions in Japan (THES).

Roberts, B. T. (1860). The Earnest Christian. JFULL, Buffalo, N.Y.: B.T. Roberts.

Shumaker, J. T. (1992). "Having the mind of Christ" presenting christian holiness in the local church : a final document submitted to the Doctoral Studies Committee of United Theological Seminary in partial fulfillment of the requirements for the degree Doctor of Ministry (THES). United Theological Seminary, Dayton, OH.

Snyder, H. A. (1990). Radical holiness evangelism : Vivian Dake and the Pentecostal Bands. BOOK.

Van Valin, C. E. (1990). Transforming grace : a biblical guide for holy living. BOOK, Indianapolis, Ind.: Light and Life Press.

Wesleyan Theological Society. (1963). Wesleyan Theological Society Records (UNPB).

Free Methodist Church – Hymns

America., F. M. C. of N. (2011). The Holiness Hymnal. MUSIC, Cooperstown, Pa.: L.W.D. Publishing.

America., F. M. C. of N., America., W. M. C. (or C. of, Free Methodist Church of North America, America., F. M. C. of N., America., W. M. C. (or C. of, Light and Life Press, … Wesleyan Methodist Connection of America. (1951). Hymns of the living faith. MUSIC, Winona Lake, Ind.: Light and Life Press.

America., F. M. C. of N., Conference., G., Free Methodist Church of North America, & General Conference. (1910). Free Methodist hymnal. MUSIC, Chicago: Free Methodist Pub. House.

America, F. M. C. of N., & Cryderman, W. L. (1983). Songs for renewal. MUSIC, Winona Lake, Ind.: Light and Life Press.

America, F. M. C. of N., & Fettke, T. (1989). The hymnal for worship & celebration : containing Scriptures from the New American Standard Bible, Revised Standard Version, the Holy Bible, New International Version, the New King James Version. MUSIC, Irving, Tex.: Word Music.

Archives, S. P. U. (1950). Free Methodist Church records and publications (UNPB).

Beazley, S. W. (1929). Revival gems : number three, a great collection in a modest book. MUSIC, Chicago: Samuel W. Beazley & Son.

Bowell, G. (2014). Reflections and thoughts on a hymnal : The 1910 Free Methodist hymnal. BOOK, Gary E. Bowell.

Boyd, M. F., Andrews, R. F., Choir, S. A. L. and L. S. L. and L., Marston Memorial Historical Center (Winona Lake, I. ., Choir, S. A. L. and L., & Center, M. M. H. (1968). Moments of memory. SOUND, Winona Lake, Ind.: The Center.

Free Methodist Church of North America. (1891). The hymn book of the Free Methodist Church. BOOK, Rochester, N.Y.: B.T. Roberts.

Free Methodist hymnal / Published by authority of the General Conference of the Free Methodist Church of North America. (n.d.). ELEC, Chicago : Free Methodist Pub. House.

Hogue, W. T. (1928). Missionary hymns and responsive scripture readings : for use in missionary meetings. MUSIC, Chicago: Woman's Foreign Missionary Society of the Free Methodist Church.

Hogue, W. T. (1932). Hymns that are immortal : with some account of their authorship, origin, history and influence. BOOK, Chicago, Ill.: Light and Life Press.

McLaren, R. C. (2003). A Wesleyan theology of worship and its development in Free Methodism (THES).

Olmstead, W. B., & Harris, T. (1928). Light and life songs : no. 4, for the Sunday school, social worship, missionary and evangelistic work. MUSIC, Chicago: Light and Life Press.

One way to a whole world sing : the Free Methodist Church 1974 General Conference Official Songbook. (1974). MUSIC, Winona Lake, Ind.

Pearce, W. (1942). Choice hymns : a collection of hymns from the Free Methodist hymnal, especially adapted for revival services. MUSIC, Winona Lake, Ind.: Free Methodist Pub. House.

Smith, A. B., & Rodeheaver, H. A. (1945). Youth rally songs and choruses. MUSIC.

Wesleyan Methodist Church of America, & America. (1951). Hymns of the living faith : official hymnal of the Wesleyan Methodist Church of America. MUSIC, Syracuse, N.Y.: Wesleyan Methodist Pub. Assoc.

Free Methodist Church – Leadership

America, F. M. C. of N., & Conference, O. (1987). Leadership orientation : Septiember 26, 1987, Salem, Oregon ; "planning for 'a new day' in Oregon". BOOK, Turner, Ore.: Oregon Conference, Free Methodist Church of North America.

America, F. M. C. of N., & Education, C. on C. (1986). Lay leadership training handbook. BOOK, Winona Lake, Ind.: Free Methodist Church of North America.

Azusa Pacific University Graduate School of Theology, Free Methodist Center for Transformational Leadership, & Winslow, K. S. (2013). The Free Methodist newsletter. JFULL, Azusa, Calif.: Azusa Pacific University Graduate School of Theology.

Bidwell, D. (1995). Leading lay ministers : a study of the relationship between leadership and factors associated with lay minister job satisfaction in the Fort Worth Free Methodist Church (THES).

Fang, L. L.-H., Theological Research Exchange Network, & Network., T. R. E. (2000). Formative evaluation of a leadership development course in spiritual formation for the China Free Methodist Church in Taiwan. ELEC.

Haskins, A. M. (1997). New life for old churches : a multi-case study of four turnaround small churches (THES).

Houck, L. E. (1988). A descriptive dissertation on trust development between pastor and parish (THES).

King, C. W. (1990). Mobilizing the laity : a strategy for obtaining greater numerical growth in the Wilmore Free Methodist Church (THES).

Kirchhofer, W. (2009). Fire among the stubble : church renewal in the Wesleyan tradition. BOOK.

Lorenz, G. V. (2005). Leading from the margins : recovering the Christian tradition of hospitality in church leadership (THES).

Mountcastle, W. D. (2006). Back to the future : evolving the Wesleyan model for renewal and leadership development for the Free Methodist Church (THES). Regent University, Virginia Beach, Va.

Pierce, M. C. (1998). Developing structures for health and growth for Northgate Free Methodist Church in Batavia, New York (ELEC). Asbury Theological Seminary.

Ward, D. T. (1983). Theological education by extension : a proposal for India's Free Methodist Church (THES).

Ward, D. T., & Theological Research Exchange Network. (2001). Identifying critical areas of need for the future development of teaching lesson plans for the India Free Methodist Church (THES). Trinity Evangelical Divinity School.

Woods, D. A. (1998). Narrative pastoral leadership pastor and people working together (THES). Asbury Theological Seminary.

Free Methodist Church – Missions

America, F. M. C. of N. (1974). One in love and mission : Winona '74, one way to a whole world, General Conference of the Free Methodist Church, June 24-July 1, 1974, Winona Lake, Indiana. CONF.

America, F. M. C. of N., & Board, G. M. (1979). Missions heartbeat, '79. BOOK, Winona Lake, Ind.: Free Methodist Church of North America.

America, F. M. C. of N., & Communication, W. M. (1972). "Communicating our United World Mission for Christ" : minister's manual. BOOK, Winona Lake, Ind.: Free Methodist Church of North America.

America, F. M. C. of N., Conference, P. N., & Board, C. M. (n.d.). On waves of faith. JFULL, Seattle, WA: Conference Mission Board, Pacific Conference of the Free Methodist Church of North America].

America, F. M. C. of N., & Houser, T. (1970). Foreign mission statistical reports of the Free Methodist Church, 1864-1969. BOOK, Winona Lake, IN.: General Missionary Board.

Anderson, D. (1989). I have you in my heart : the delights of overseas ministry. BOOK, Indianapolis, Ind.: Wesley Press.

Arksey, L. (2011). A mission boyhood in Mozambique. BOOK, S.l.: Tornado Creek.

Bastian, D. N. (1995). Sketches of Free Methodism. BOOK, Indianapolis, Ind.: Light & Life Press.

Bates, G. (1981). Soul afire : life of J.W. Haley. BOOK, Winona Lake, Ind.: Light and Life Press.

Betania, R., & America, F. M. C. of N. (1991). Rancho Betania news. JFULL, Nogales, AZ: Free Methodist Mexican Missions.

Brito B., I. (1975). Historia de la Iglesia Metodista Libre Dominicana. BOOK, Santo Domingo, D.N.: Editora Educativa Dominicana.

Brown, Z. M. (1981). Trailblazers in Livingston country / by Zella M. Brown. BOOK, Winona Lake, Ind.: Light and Life Press.

Burritt, C. T., & Hogue, E. L. (1935). The story of fifty years. BOOK, Winona Lake, Ind.: Light and Life Press.

Calkins, P. J. (1968). A comparative investigation of levels of attainment in the development of the indigenous church principle on Latin American Free Methodist mission fields (THES).

Chauke, H. W. M., & Houser, T. (2009). H.M. Chauke research of African Hlengwe people. BOOK.

Cheeseman, S. (1981). Eight Gates Beyond. BOOK, Winona Lake, Ind.: Light and Life Press.

Cheeseman, S. (1984). Wee brown lambs. BOOK, Winona Lake, Ind.; Dept. of Evangelism and Church Growth: Free Methodist Church of North America.

Clyde, A. A. (1954). A study of minimum requirements in religious education for Free Methodist missionaries (THES).

Conference, F. M. W., & Kline, F. J. (1960). Asia Fellowship Conference, April 19-28, Osaka, Japan : a compilation of reports, documents, interpretation. CONF, Winona Lake, Ind.: Continuing Committee of the Free Methodist World Fellowship, North American Division.

Cox, B. E. (1998). Simply following : in all my journeying God went before. BOOK, Spring Arbor, Mich.: Saltbox Press.

Crider, D. W. (1980). Development and rationale of theological education by extension of the Free Methodist Church in South Africa with a programmed text on pastoral theology for Africa (THES).

Damon, C. M. (1900). Sketches and incidents, or reminiscences of interest in the life of the author. BOOK, Chicago: Free Methodist Pub. House.

DeMille, L., Hill, D., Abbott, G., Payne, P., & America, F. M. C. of N. (1984). Stories from Southern Africa. BOOK, Winona lake, Ind.: Light and Life Press.

DeShazer, J. (2012). Jacob DeShazer's personal testimony. ELEC, Wilmore, Ky.: DQB-LLC for the Marston Memorial Historical Center.

Fellowship, F. M. W. (1962). News and views. News and Views. JFULL, Winona Lake, Ind.: Free Methodist Pub. House.

Fidler, G. (2006). Adventures in India. BOOK, St. Catherines, ON: Cornerstone Research & Pub.

Folkestad, R. H. (1969). A historical survey of Free Methodist world missions (THES).

Free Methodist Church of North America, & Department of World Missions. (1989). Across the miles. Across the Miles. JFULL, Winona Lake, IN: Dept. of World Missions, The Free Methodist Church.

Free Methodist Church of North America, & General Missionary Board. (n.d.). Missions perspective. Missions Perspective. JFULL, Winona Lake, IN: General Missionary Board.

Free Methodist Church of North America, & General Missionary Board. (1950). Perspective in missions giving. BOOK, Winona Lake, Ind.: Free Methodist Church of North America, General Missionary Board.

Freeland, M. H., & Her., O. who loved. (1892). Missionary martyrs Mary Louisa Ranf, missionary to India. ELEC, Chicago: T.B. Arnold.

Ghormley, N. B. (1920). The land of the heart of Livingstone; or, The genius of the Bantu. A study of the Bantu tribes of Africa, 100,000,000 souls, with special reference to the agencies which contribute to their civilization. BOOK, Chicago: Published by the author; for sale by the Woman's Foreign Missionary Society of the Free Methodist Church.

Hill, C. D., & Archives, S. P. U. (1909). Cyril Hill Papers, (UNPB).

Hill, N. (2007). A brief history of Holiness Movement & Free Methodist missions, Egypt 1899-1986. BOOK, S.l.: s.n.

Houser, T., & Houser, G. (2007). Let me tell you : a memoir. BOOK, Charleston, SC: Booksurge.

Junker, J. A. (n.d.). Free Methodist missionary work among the Mexicans. BOOK, S.l.: s.n.

Kirkpatrick, C. D., & Church, W. M. S. of the F. M. (1977). Cow in the clinic, and other missionary stories from around the world. BOOK, Winona Lake, Ind.: Light and Life Press.

Kirkpatrick, C. D., & Free Methodist Church of North America. (1971). Profile of missions. BOOK, Winona Lake, Ind.: Light and Life Press.

Macy, V. W. (1946). A history of the Free Methodist mission in Portugese East Africa (THES).

Macy, V. W., & DeMille, L. (1984). Discovery under the Southern Cross : below the equator--missions adventures in Mozambique and South Africa. BOOK, Winona Lake, Ind.: Light and Life Press.

McChesney, A., & McChesney, B. (1968). Through Congo shadows. BOOK, Salem, Ohio Convention Book Store Publishers.

Mission, A. I. B., & America, F. M. C. of N. (1992). Hane' niji'a = It carries the news. Hane' Niji'a = It Carries the News. JFULL, Farmington, NJ: American Indian Bible Mission.

Mylander, R., & Root, H. I. (1944). Japan investment. BOOK, Winona Lake, Ind.: Woman's Missionary Society of the Free Methodist Church of North America.

Pauley, R. (1970). DeShazer returns. BOOK, Winona Lake, Ind.: Free Methodist Church of North America, General Missionary Board.

Pearson, B. H. (1939). Free Methodist Mexican missions. BOOK, Winona Lake, Ind.: Woman's Missionary Society, Free Methodist Church.

Richardson, A. (1988). A heart for God in India. BOOK, Winona Lake, Ind.: Light and Life Press.

Richardson, A., & Secaur, E. (1988). Andrew's secret. BOOK, Winona Lake, Ind.: Light and Life Press.

Roberts, B. H. B. T., Roberts, A. A. R., Roberts, E. S. E. L. S. E. S., Roberts, G. L., & Division, L. of C. M. (1990). Benjamin T. Roberts family papers. BOOK, Washington, D.C.: Library of Congress, Photoduplication Service.

Root, L. P., & Benson, M. C. (1988). Outflowing love : Auntiebai, Effie Southworth's life of loving service during her more than 50 years in central India. BOOK, Winona Lake, Ind.: Light & Life Communications.

Ryff, F. J. (1954). An examination of the indigenous church principle with special reference to the Free Methodist church in South Africa (THES).

Sayre, M. G. (1945). Missionary triumphs in occupied China. BOOK, Winona Lake, Ind.: Woman's Missionary Society of the Free Methodist Church.

Schlosser, F. E. (1940). A Challenge from China. BOOK.

Schlosser, G. (1906). George and Mary Schlosser papers, (UNPB).

Sellew, W. A., Hogue, W. T., & America, F. M. C. of N. (1913). Clara Leffingwell, a missionary. BOOK, Chicago: Free Methodist Pub. House.

Tabor, M., Free Methodist Church of North, & Woman's Missionary Society. (1946). Puss. BOOK, Winona Lake, Ind.: Woman's Missionary Society of the Free Methodist Church.

Tankidaigaku, O. K. (n.d.). Osaka Kirisutokyo Tankidaigaku Kiyo. JFULL, Osaka Shi: Osaka Kirisutokyo Tankidaigaku.

Taylor, E., & Mission, O. B. (1970). The Olive Branch Mission, 1876-1970. BOOK, Chicago, IL: Olive Branch Mission.

The Free Methodist Church in postwar Japan. (1971). BOOK.

Thompson, W. R. (1950a). Factors in the establishing of a Free Methodist mission training school in Paraguay (THES).

Thompson, W. R. (1950b). Factors in the establishment of a Free Methodist mission training school in Paraguay (THES).

Ward, E. E., America., F. M. C. of N., & Free Methodist Church of North America. (1924). Letter links. Letter Links. JFULL, Lucknow: Methodist Pub. House.

Ward, E. E., America., F. M. C. of N., Free Methodist Church of North America, & America., F. M. C. of N. (1951). Ordered steps, or, The Wards of India : a biography of the lives of Ernest Fremont Ward and Phebe Elizabeth Cox Ward, missionaries to India, 1880-1927. BOOK, Winona Lake, Ind.: Light and Life Press.

Ward, E. E., & America, F. M. C. of N. (1937). India letter links. JFULL.

Ward, E. F. (1880). Papers. BOOK.

Ward, E. F., Pyron, D. A., & Ward, P. E. (1878). Papers of this first Free Methodist Church missionary to India. BOOK.

Watson, C. H. (2002). DeShazer. BOOK.

Watson, C. H., & Fear, L. K. (1972). De Shazer. BOOK, Winona Lake, Ind.: Light and Life Press.

Willard, F. B. (1985). Idol of clay. BOOK, Winona Lake, Ind.: Light and Life Press.

Williamson, G. (1972). Frank and Hazel : the Adamsons of Kibogora. BOOK, Winona Lake, IN: Light and Life Press.

Winslow, R. (1984). The mountains sing : God's love revealed to Taiwan tribes. BOOK, Winona Lake, Ind.: Light and Life Press.

Yoder, T., Smidderks, D., Free Methodist Church of North America, Department of Christian Education, Department of World Missions, & Women's Missionary Fellowship International. (1987). The great discovery. BOOK, Winona Lake, Ind.: Light and Life Press.

Free Methodist Church – Sermons

Andrews, R. F. (n.d.). The web of emptiness. BOOK, Winona Lake, IN: Light & Life Hour.

Baker, H. (1945). Sackcloth and purple. Indianapolis, Ind.: Pilgrim Pub. House.

Baker, H. E. (n.d.). Springs of water. BOOK, Freeport, NY: Transylvania Bible School Press.

Baker, H. E. (1944a). Sparks from the anvil of truth. BOOK, East Liverpool, Ohio: The author.

Baker, H. E. (1944b). Travailing for souls. BOOK, Freeport, PA: Transylvania Bible School Press.

Baker, H. E. (1972a). The wardrobe of Christ. BOOK, Olean, N.Y.: H.E. Baker.

Baker, H. E. (1972b). Unlighted glory. BOOK, Freeport, Pa.: Fountain Press.

Baker, H. E. (1978). Degrees of the Spirit. BOOK, Freeport, Pa.: Fountain Press.

Baker, H. E. (1980). Where the corn grows tall. BOOK, Freeport, Pa.: Fountain Press.

Barnett, L. P. (1965). Yorokobi no otozure. BOOK, Rosanjerusu: Rosanjerusu Furi Mesojisuto Kyokai.

Black, H. (n.d.-a). Is the end of the age at hand. BOOK, Los Angeles, CA: H. Black.

Black, H. (n.d.-b). Prophecy sermons by a newsboy preacher. BOOK, Redlands, Calif.: Black.

Black, H. (n.d.-c). Revival sermons on Bible prophecy. BOOK, Los Angeles, CA: Harry Black.

Black, H. (n.d.-d). The Holy Ghost baptism : and seven other sermons on sin, salvation, and holiness. BOOK, Los Angeles, CA.

Black, H. (n.d.-e). The price of a revival and other sermons. BOOK, Los Angeles, CA: Harry Black.

Black, H. (n.d.-f). The rich man and Lazarus and other sermons. BOOK, Los Angeles, Calif.

Black, H. (1900a). Signs of his coming and other sermons. BOOK, Los Angeles, Calif.: Mrs. H. Black.

Black, H. (1900b). Sunday morning (soul food) sermons. BOOK, Los Angeles, Calif.: Black.

Black, H. (1936). Soul food messages. BOOK, Los Angeles, CA: Harry Black.

Black, H. (1952). Tribulation plagues are coming : evangelistic messages on Revelation. BOOK, Los Angeles: Harry Black.

Black, H. (1953a). Satan's masterpiece, the Antichrist : evangelistic messages on Revelation. BOOK, Los Angeles: Harry Black.

Black, H. (1953b). The four horses of the Apocalypse : evangelistic messages on Revelation. BOOK, Los Angeles, CA: Harry Black.

Black, H., & Office, P. N. (1940). The four horses of the Apocalypse : evangelistic messages on Revelation : (an expository and evangelistic message for each chapter in the book of Revelation). Book 1. Messages on Revelation Book 1. Messages on Revelation. BOOK, Los Angeles, Calif.: Prophetic News Office.

Boyd, M. F. (n.d.). A more excellent way : radio messasges on the deeper spiritual life. BOOK, Winona Lake, IN: Light and Life Hour.

Boyd, M. F. (1946). Light and life hour, sixteen radio messages : world-wide gospel broadcast. BOOK, Winona Lake, Ind.: Light and Life Press.

Boyd, M. F. (1953). Honoring the Spirit : 18 radio messages on love and the Holy Spirit. BOOK, Winona Lake, Ind.: Light and Life Hour.

Boyd, M. F., Andrews, R. F., Choir, S. A. L. and L. S. L. and L., Marston Memorial Historical Center (Winona Lake, I. ., Choir, S. A. L. and L., & Center, M. M. H. (1968). Moments of memory. SOUND, Winona Lake, Ind.: The Center.

Boyd, M. F., & Hour, L. and L. (1949). Light and life hour, eighteen radio messages : world-wide gospel broadcast. BOOK, Apollo, Pa.: West Pub. Co.

Coates, G., America, F. M. C. of N., & Conference, G. (2003). Passion of the founders : General Conference 2003. BOOK, Indianapolis, Ind.: Free Methodist Light and Life Communications.

Conference, G. M. (1940). The Wesleyan message : addresses delivered at the 12th-14th sessions of the Ministers' Conference, Greenville College, 1939-1941. CONF, Winona Lake, Ind.: Light and Life P.

Damon, A. J. (1988). A brief history of the Wisconsin Conference of the Free Methodist Church. BOOK.

Dunn, M. (2000). God's call : from infilling to outpouring. BOOK, Grantham, PA: Wesleyan/Holiness Women Clergy, Inc.

Fairbairn, C. V. (1943). "Tarry ye" : with other sermons and studies. BOOK, Winona Lake, Ind.: Light and Life Press.

Griffith, G. W. (1939). Lest we forget : selected messages. BOOK, Los Angeles, CA: Mrs. G.W. Griffith.

Hogue, W. T. (1911). Retrospect and prospect : a semi-centennial sermon preached by Bishop Wilson T. Hogue before the General Conference of the Free Methodist Church, in Chicago, June 18, 1911. BOOK, Chicago, IL: Free Methodist Pub. House.

Hogue, W. T., & Chesbrough, A. E. (1906). A Sermon : preached at the fiftieth anniversary of the marriage of rev. Samuel K.J. and Mrs. Ann E. Chesbrough, February 6, 1898, together with the experience of Mrs. Ann E. Chesbrough, a member of the first class ever formed in the Free Methodist Church. BOOK, Chicago: Free Methodist Pub. House.

Humphrey, J. M. (n.d.). Seven old time gospel sermons. BOOK, Chicago: The Author.

Humphrey, J. M. (1913). Select fruits from the highlands of Beulah. BOOK, Lima, OH: True Gospel Grain Pub. Co.

Humphrey, J. M. (1924). X-ray sermons. BOOK, Omaha, Neb.: "Anywhere" evangelistic workers' Pub. House.

Humphrey, J. M. (2000). Crumbs from Heaven. BOOK, Salem, Ohio: Allegheny.

Humphrey, J. M. (2003). Railroad sermons from railroad stories. BOOK, Salem, OH: Schmul Pub. Co.

James, J. F., Free Methodist Church of North America, & General Conference. (2008). Our calling to the poor. BOOK, Indianapolis, Ind.: Light and Life Press.

Kendall, W. S. (1955). The challenge of this century : a doctrinal emphasis. BOOK, Salem: Free Methodist Church of North America.

Knox, L. H., Martin, C., & Sparrow, R. (1999). Building holy relationships : prayers, sermons, and other writings. BOOK, Indianapolis, IN: Light and Life Communications.

Lamson, B. S. (1987). Greater works than these. BOOK, Winona Lake, Ind.: Light and Life Press.

Lewis, L. G. (1931). Mitama no mi = The Fruite of the Spirit. BOOK, Tokyo-to: Jiyu Mesojisutosha Shuppanbu, dc 1931, Showa 6.

Lincicome, F. (n.d.). The doubles of the Bible. BOOK, Atlanta, GA: Repairer Pub. Co.

Lincicome, F. (1932a). A lot in Sodom. BOOK, Winona Lake, Ind.: Light and Life Press.

Lincicome, F. (1932b). Behold the man! BOOK, Apollo, Pa.: West Pub. Co.

Lincicome, F. (1935). A tribute to mothers. BOOK.

Lincicome, F. (1940). The soul. BOOK, Apollo, Pa.: West Pub. Co.

Marston, L. R. (1946). "I need a chart." BOOK, Winona Lake, Ind.: Published for The National Association of Evangelicals by courtesy of Light and Life Press.

Marston, L. R. (1950). Bring the books. BOOK.

McKenna, D. L. (1993). The works of Dr. David L. McKenna. BOOK, Wilmore, KY: Asbury Theological Seminary.

Oda, K. (1979). Oda Kaneo sekkyoshu. BOOK, Osaka-fu: Seitosha.

Pugerude, D. G. (1987). Preaching from the Old Testament : a study in exegesis and hermeneutics of the Free Methodist Church of North America (THES).

Robb, J. A. (1979). And He said unto me, write. BOOK, Woodstock, Ont.: Nethercott Press.

Shelhamer, E. E. (n.d.). A bit of experience. BOOK, Los Angeles, CA.

Shelhamer, E. E. (1900). Seven searching sermons. BOOK, Cincinnati, Ohio: God's Revivalist.

Shelhamer, E. E. (1920). Searching sermons for saints and sinners. BOOK, Cincinnati, Ohio: God's Bible School.

Shelhamer, E. E. (1926). Sermons that search the soul. BOOK, Kansas City, Mo.: Nazarene Pub. House.

Shelhamer, E. E. (1929). Plain preaching for practical people. BOOK, Cincinnati, Ohio: God's Bible School and Revivalist.

Shelhamer, E. E. (1932). Pointed preaching for practical people. BOOK, Cincinnati, Ohio: God's Bible School and Revivalist.

Taylor, J. P. (1960). Soldiers of Christ. BOOK, Winona Lake, Ind.: Light and Life Press.

Taylor, J. P. (1964). All roads lead to Bethlehem. BOOK, Winona Lake, Ind.: Light and Life Press.

Teed, F. E. S., Rees, P. S., Rees, S. C., Smith, J. H., & Sockman, R. W. (1919). Florence Ernestine Schleicher Teed papers, (UNPB).

Walsh, G., Meeting, B. in C. H. C., & Brethren in Christ Holiness Camp Meeting. (1993). Clearing life's burdens. SOUND, Chambersburg, PA: AV Ministries.

Wesley, J. (1940). On dress and evil speaking. BOOK, Winona Lake, Ind.: Free Methodist Publishing House.

Free Methodist Curriculum

Activity Time. (1969). GEN, Marion Ind.: Wesley Press.

Aldersgate Dialogue Series. (n.d.). GEN, Winona Lake IN: Light and Life Press.

Aldersgate Doctrinal Studies. (n.d.). GEN, Winona Lake, IN: Light and Life Press.

Aldersgate Graded Curriculum. (n.d.). GEN, Winona Lake, IN: Light and Life Press.

All-Bible Graded Series. (n.d.). GEN, Winona Lake, IN: Light and Life Press.

America., F. M. C. of N., Association., A. P., Free Methodist Church of North America, Aldersgate Publications Association, America., F. M. C. of N., & Association., A. P. (1971). Discovery. Discovery. JFULL, Winona Lake, Ind.: Light and Life Press [etc.].

America, F. M. C. of N. (1891). Light and life primary. JFULL, Winona, Lake, Ind.: Light and Life Press.

Association, A. P. (n.d.-a). Junior teacher. JFULL, Winona Lake, Ind.: Light and Life Press.

Association, A. P. (n.d.-b). Young teen teacher. JFULL, Winona Lake, Ind.: Light and Life Press.

Association, A. P. (1975a). Explorer 1. JFULL, Winona Lake, Ind.: Light and Life Press.

Association, A. P. (1975b). Explorer 2. JFULL, Winona Lake, Ind.: Light and Life Press.

Bible Lesson Stories. 1-31, No.4. (1930). GEN, Providence, Rhode Island: Religious Press.

Bible Stories for Threes. (1961). GEN, Kansas City MO: Beacon Hill Press.

Bible Stories for Twos. (1964). GEN, Kansas City MO: Beacon Hill Press.

Christian-Life Graded Bible Lessons. (1948). GEN, Winona Lake, IN: Light and Life Press.

Developing Christian personality. (1970). BOOK, Published for Aldersgate Associates by Beacon Hill Press of Kansas City.

Discover your Bible : a course for persons who believe they should be getting more out of their Bible study. (1970). BOOK, Published for Aldersgate Associates by Beacon Hill Press of Kansas City.

Explore 1-6, No. 3. (1969). GEN, Winona Lake IN: Light and Life.

Holiness alive and well : the meaning of holy living in twentieth-century life. (1970). BOOK, Published for Aldersgate Associates by Beacon Hill Press of Kansas City.

In Touch. (1971). GEN, Winona Lake, IN: Wesley Press.

International Uniform Series. (1885). GEN, Winona Lake, IN: Light and Life Press.

Joy, D. M. (1960). Aldersgate Biblical series. BOOK, Winona Lake, Ind.: Light and Life Press.

Junior's Friend, 1-14, No. 39. (1929). GEN, Winona Lake, IN: Light and Life Press.

Junior Manual, 1-16, No.4. (1953). GEN, Winona Lake, IN: Light and Life Press.

Junior Manual. 1-3, No. 3. (1951). GEN, Winona Lake, IN: Light and Life Press.

Kindergaren Activities. (1969). GEN, Kansas City, MO: Beacon Hill Press.

Kindergarten Activities. (1954). GEN, Winona Lake, IN: Light and Life Press.

Kindergarten Bible Stories, 1-16, No. 4. (1954). GEN, Winona Lake, IN: Light and Life Press.

Kindergarten Stories. 1-16, No. 4. (1954). GEN, Winona Lake, IN.: Light and Life Press.

Kindergarten Teacher. (n.d.). GEN, Kansas City, MO: Beacon Hill Press.

Kindschi, P. (1964). Entire sanctification : studies in Christian holiness. BOOK, Marion, IN: Wesley Press.

Learn and Do. (1969). GEN, Marion, Ind.: Wesley Press.

Light and Life Adult. (1835). GEN, Chicago, IL: Light and Life Press.

Light and Life Beginner Teacher. 1-4, No. 2. (1948). GEN, Winona Lake, IN: Light and Life Press.

Light and Life Evangel. (1912). GEN, Chicago, IL; Winona Lake, IN: Light and Life Press.

Light and Life Graded Series. (n.d.). GEN, Winona Lake, IN: Light and Life Press.

Light and Life Teacher's Quarterly. (1889). GEN, Chicago, IL; Winona Lake, IN: Light and Life Press.

Light and Life Teacher's Quarterly for the Graded Primary Series. 1-9, No. 1. (1941). GEN, Winona Lake, IN: Light and Life Press.

Light and Life Youth. 1-76, No. 3. (1885). GEN, Chicago, IL; Winona Lake, IN: Light and Life Press.

Lily of the Valley. 1-10, No. 12. (1897). GEN, Chicago, IL: W.B. Rose.

Love, marriage - and other hazards. (1970). BOOK, Published for Aldersgate Associates by Beacon Hill Press of Kansas City.

Nursery Activities. (1969). GEN, Winona Lake, IN: Beacon Hill Press.

Nursery Bible Story Cards, 1-12. (1958). GEN, Winona Lake, IN: Light and Life Press.

Nursery Teacher. (n.d.). GEN, Kansas City, MO: Beacon Hill Press.

Our Young Folks. 1-10, No. 12. (1897). GEN, Chicago, IL: W.B. Rose.

Peisker, A. (1969). Peace with God : studies in conversion. BOOK, Marion, IN: Wesley Press.

Peisker, A. (1970). End times : a doctrinal study on the shape of things to come. BOOK.

Prayer that really works. (1970). BOOK, Published for Aldersgate Associates by Beacon Hill Press of Kansas City.

Primary Activities. (1959). GEN, Winona Lake IN: Light and Life Press.

Primary Bible Lesson Stories. 1-17. (1953). GEN, Chicago, IL: W.B. Rose.

Primary Bible Stories. (1969). GEN, Marion, Ind.: Wesley Press.

Primary Days. 17-19, No. 4. (1951). GEN, Chicago, IL: Scripture Press.

Primary Friend. (1969). GEN, Marion, Ind.: Wesley Press.

Primary Teacher. (1969). GEN, Marion, Ind.: Wesley Press.

Primary World. 1-15, No. 3. (1955). GEN, Chicago, IL: Scripture Press.

Probe Student 1-3, No. 4. (1974). GEN, Marion, Ind.: Wesley Press.

Probe Teacher. 1-3, No. 4. (1974). GEN, Marion, Ind.: Wesley Press.

ProTeen. (1971). GEN, Winona Lake, Ind.: Light and Life Press.

Quest Student. (1976). GEN, Winona Lake, Indiana: Light and Life Press.

Quest Teacher. (1976). GEN, Winona Lake, Indiana: Light and Life Press.

Rose of Sharon, 1-10, No. 12. (1897). GEN, Chicago, IL: W.B. Rose.

Senior Teen. 1-14, No.1 (1956). GEN, Winona Lake, IN: Light and Life Press.

Senior Teen Student. (1959). GEN, Marion, Ind.: Wesley Press.

Senior Teen Teacher. (1959). GEN, Marion, Ind.: Wesley Press.

Single in a couples' world. (1970). BOOK, Published for Aldersgate Associates by Beacon Hill Press of Kansas City.

Story Hour. (1885). GEN, Chicago, IL: Light and Life Press.

Story Papers. (n.d.). GEN, Winona Lake, IN: Light and Life Press.

Story Trails. 1-87, No. 8. (1943). GEN, Winona Lake, IN.: Light and Life Press.

Strategies for vital Christian living. (1970). BOOK, Published for Aldersgate Associates by Beacon Hill Press of Kansas City.

Table Talk. (1969). GEN, Winona Lake, IN: Light and Life Press.

Teaching Beginners. 1-3, No. 3. (1951). GEN, Winona Lake, IN: Light and Life Press.

Teaching Juniors, 1-3, No. 3. (1951). GEN, Winona Lake, IN: Light and Life Press.

Teaching Juniors. 1-16, No.4. (1953). GEN, Winona Lake, IN: Light and Life Press.

Teaching Preschool. 1-16, No. 4. (1951). GEN, Winona Lake, IN: Light and Life Press.

Teaching Primaries, 1-3, No. 3. (1951). GEN, Winona Lake, Indiana: Light and Life Press.

Teaching Primaries. 1-16, No.4. (1953). GEN, Winona Lake, IN: Light and Life Press.

Teaching Senior Teens, 1-14, No.1. (1956). GEN, Winona Lake, IN: Light and Life Press.

Teaching Young Teens. 1-16, No.4. (1953). GEN, Winona Lake, IN: Light and Life Press.

The Christian & social problems. (1970). BOOK, Published for Aldersgate Associates by Beacon Hill Press of Kansas City.

The now look of evangelism. (1970). BOOK, Published for Aldersgate Associates by Beacon Hill Press of Kansas City.

The shape of things to come : God's plan for the future. (1970). BOOK, Published for Aldersgate Associates by Beacon Hill Press of Kansas City.

Tracy, W. (Ed.). (n.d.). Dare to Discipline. BOOK, Kansas City, MO: Beacon Hill Press.

Wholesome interpersonal relationships. (1970). BOOK, Published for Aldersgate Associates by Beacon Hill Press of Kansas City.

Why don't you do something, God? (1970). BOOK, Published for Aldersgate Associates by Beacon Hill Press of Kansas City.

Young Teen. 1-16, No. 4 (1953). GEN, Winona Lake IN: Light and Life Press.

Young Teen Student. (1969). GEN, Winona Lake, IN: Light and Life Press.

Free Methodist Periodicals

Free Methodist book bulletin. (Journal, magazine, 1943) [WorldCat.org]. (n.d.). [ICOMM]. Retrieved from http://www.worldcat.org/title/free-methodist-book-bulletin/oclc/28474317&referer=brief_results

Free Methodist Church of North America. (n.d.). General conference daily. ICOMM, Greenville, Ill.: S.K.J. Chesbro.

India letter links (Journal, magazine, 1937). (n.d.). [ICOMM].

Inhambane tidings. (Journal, magazine, 1900s). (n.d.). [ICOMM]. Retrieved from http://www.worldcat.org/title/inhambane-tidings/oclc/14815942&referer=brief_results

Interracial news. (Journal, magazine, 1950). (n.d.). [ICOMM]. Retrieved from http://www.worldcat.org/title/interracial-news/oclc/10917576&referer=brief_results

No. (n.d.). Shortwave, 1-. JOUR.

No Title. (n.d.-a). Sunday School Journal, (1–52). JOUR.

No Title. (n.d.-b). Missions Outlook Leadership Letter, ? JOUR.

No Title. (n.d.-c). Light and Life Hour Transmitter. JOUR.

No Title. (n.d.-d). Encounter. JOUR.

No Title. (n.d.-e). Nzira Iboneye, 1-. JOUR.

No Title. (n.d.-f). The Layman. Voice of the Light and Life Men's Fellowship. JOUR.

No Title. (n.d.-g). Ecos Evangelicos, (1-). JOUR.

No Title. (1962). News and Views, 1-. JOUR.

Press, L. and L. (n.d.). No Title. Just Between Us. JOUR.

Records of the Congo-Nile Mission. (1938). GEN.

The Christian minister. (Journal, magazine, 1949). (n.d.).
    [ICOMM].

The Free Methodist pastor. (Journal, magazine, 1974). (n.d.).
    [ICOMM].

Free Methodist Primary Resources

Allan, D. (1938). "From the lumber camp to the ministry" : the autobiography of Rev. David Allan. Toronto: Evangelical Publishers.

Allen, R. (1911). A century of the Genesee Annual Conference of the Methodist Episcopal Church, 1810--1910. BOOK, Rochester N.Y.: R. Allen.

America, F. M. C. of N. (1970). Doctrines and discipline of the Free Methodist Church of North America. BOOK, Winona Lake, Ind.: Free Methodist Pub. House.

America, F. M. C. of N., & Conference, T. (1960). The Texas Conference of the Free Methodist Church its origin and present churches. BOOK, TX: The Conference.

America, F. M. C. of N., & Education, C. on C. (1961). Let's teach. BOOK, Winona Lake, Ind.: Light and Life Press.

America, F. M. C. of N., & Society, W. M. (1957). The living faith in Japan. BOOK, Winona Lake, Ind.

Anderson, A. (1920). African jungle. BOOK, Anderson Ind.: Gospel Trumpet Co.

Anderson, A. (1931). Ukanya : life story of an African girl. BOOK, Anderson, Ind.: Warner Press.

Anderson, A. (1938). Nkosi : story of an African chief's son. BOOK, Anderson, In.: Warner Press.

Anderson, M. (1985). The school in the vale : a history of Oakdale Christian High School. BOOK.

Arnold, H. (1924). Under southern skies : reminiscences in the life of Mrs. Adelia Arnold. BOOK, Atlanta Ga.: Repairer Pub.

Atkinson, D. (1970). A study of methods used in the establishment and growth of selected churches in the Pacific Northwest Conference of the Free Methodist Church. BOOK.

Backenstoe, M. (1944). Triumphant living. Kutztown Pa.: Kutztown Pub. Co.

Baker, F. (1957). Methodism and the love-feast. BOOK, London: Epworth Press.

Baldwin, H. (1907). Lessons for seekers of holiness : containing numerous quotations from Wesley, Fletcher, and other standard authors, and designed to aid such as are groaning after purity of heart in entering upon the. BOOK, Chicago: W.B. Rose.

Baldwin, H. (1911). Objections to entire sanctification considered. BOOK, Pittsburgh: Published for the author.

Baldwin, H. (1923). The fisherman of Galilee: a devotional study of the Apostle Peter. BOOK, New York; Chicago: Fleming H. Revell Co.

Baldwin, H. A. (1919). Holiness and the human element. BOOK, Chicago: Free Methodist Pub. House.

Barron's profiles of American colleges : an in-depth study. (1971). BOOK, Woodbur, NY: Barrons' Educational Series Inc.

Bartlette, W. (1971). Ethics, real or relative? : an inquiry into the place of Christianity in world ethical philosophies. BOOK, New York: Vantage Press.

Bastian, D. N. (1963). The mature church member. BOOK, Winona Lake, Ind.: Light and Life Press.

Be ye holy : a study of the teaching of Scripture relative to entire sanctification : with a sketch of the history and the literature of the Holiness Movement. (n.d.). [ICOMM].

Binney, A. (1902). Binneys' Theological compend improved : containing a synopsis of the evidences, doctrines, morals and institutions of Christianity. BOOK, New York ; Cincinnati: Methodist Book Concern.

Blackie Buffalo and other stories of North American missions. (1967). BOOK, Winona Lake, Ind.: Light and Life Press.

Bliss, E. (1910). The encyclopedia of missions : descriptive, historical, biographical, statistical. BOOK, New York ; London: Funk & Wagnalls Co.

Bowen, E. (1859). Slavery in the Methodist Episcopal Church. GEN, Auburn, NY: William J. Moses, printer,.

Bownes, L. K. (1962). A study of the Christian day school movement in the Arizona-Southern California conference of the Free Methodist Church (Book, 1962) (ICOMM). Seatlle Pacific University.

Boyd, M. (1958). Flame of a century, what made it burn? : Radio messages on John Wesley and early Methodism. BOOK, Winona Lake, Ind.: World-Wide Gospel Broadcast.

Boyd, M. F. (1964). To tell the world : thirty radio messages. BOOK, Winona Lake, Ind.: Light and Life Hour.

Brauer, J. (1971). The Westminster dictionary of church history. BOOK, Philadelphia: Westminster Press.

Brodhead, C. A. S. (1908). Our Free Methodist missions in Africa, to April, 1907. BOOK, Pittsburgh: Aldine.

Brown, Z. (1977). Aldersgate : the college of the warm heart. BOOK, Moose Jaw, Sask.

Bucke, E. (1964). The History of American Methodism. BOOK, New York: Abingdon Press.

Cameron, R. (1961). Methodism and society in historical perspective. BOOK, New York: Abingdon.

Casberg, J. (1919). Dhatu and his friends. BOOK, Winona Lake, Indiana.

Cattell, J. (1906). American men of science : a biographical directory. BOOK, Lancaster, Pa. ; New York: Science Pr. ; Bowker.

Clark, E. (1949). The small sects in America. BOOK, New York: Abingdon-Cokesbury Press.

Clark, E. (1952a). An album of Methodist history. BOOK, New York: Abingdon-Cokesbury Press.

Clark, E. (1952b). Who's who in methodism. BOOK, Chicago: A.N. Marquis.

Clarke, E. (1915). Mary E. Chynoweth : missionary to India. BOOK, Chicago: Woman's Foreign Missionary Society of the Free Methodist Church.

Conable, F. (1876). History of the Genesee Annual Conference of the Methodist Episcopal Church : from its organization by Bishops Asbury and M'Kendree in 1810, to the year 1872. BOOK, New York: Nelson & Phillips.

Cook, A. W. (1970). An analysis of the responsibilities and training of selected ministers in church business administration (ICOMM). East Tennessee State University.

Cook, T. (1952). New Testament holiness. BOOK, London: Epworth Press.

Coon, A. (1905). Life and labors of Auntie Coon. BOOK, Atlanta: Repairer Office.

Curtiss, G. (1893). Manual of Methodist Episcopal Church history : showing the evolution of Methodism in the United States of America for the use of students and general readers. BOOK, New York: Hunt & Eaton.

Daniels, W. (1880). Illustrated history of Methodism in Great Britain and America, from the days of the Wesleys to the present time. BOOK, New York: Phillips & Hunt.

Davis, R. N. (1954). The Challenge in central India. BOOK, Winona Lake, Ind.: Women's Missionary Society, Free Methodist Church.

De Voist, M. (1925). History of the East Michigan Conference of the Free Methodist Church. BOOK, Owosso, Mich.: Times Print Co.

Deemer, P. (1974). Ecumenical directory of retreat and conference centers. BOOK, Boston: Jarrow Press.

Degen, H. (2013). The guide to holiness. GEN, Wilmore, Ky. : Asbury Theological Seminary,.

Demaray, D. (1958). Loyalty to Christ : sermons with prayers for the Easter season. BOOK, Grand Rapids: Baker Book House.

Demaray, D. (1959). A pulpit manual. BOOK, Grand Rapids: Baker Book House.

Demaray, D. (1964). Bible study source-book. BOOK, Grand Rapids, MI: Zondervan.

Demaray, D. (1972). Preacher aflame. BOOK, Grand Rapids, Mich.: Baker Book House.

Demaray, D. (1973). Pulpit giants : what made them great. BOOK, Chicago: Moody Press.

Demaray, D. (1974). The minister's ministries. BOOK, Winona Lake, Ind.: Light and Life.

Dictionary of American biography. (1943). BOOK, New York: C. Scribner's Sons.

Dieter, M. E. (1973). Revivalism and Holiness (UNPB).

Directory of North American Protestant foreign missionary agencies. (Journal, magazine, 1958) [WorldCat.org]. (n.d.). [ICOMM]. Retrieved from http://www.worldcat.org/title/directory-of-north-american-protestant-foreign-missionary-agencies/oclc/2712345&referer=brief_results

Discipline of the Missionary Bands of the World. (1926). BOOK, Indianapolis, IN: Grace Pub. House.

Dow, L. (1881). The life, travels, labors, and writings of Lorenzo Dow : including his singular and erratic wanderings in Europe and America : to which is added his chain journey from Babylon to Jerusalem dialogue. BOOK, New York: R. Worthington.

Education, U. S. O. of. (n.d.). Education Directory (RPRT).

Embree, E. (1978). Now rings the bell : the story of Ralph Jacobs, missionary pioneer to Africa. BOOK, Winona Lake, IN: Light and Life.

Emerick, S. (1958). Spiritual renewal for Methodism : a discussion of the early Methodist class meeting and the values inherent in personal groups today. BOOK, Nashville: Methodist evangelistic materials.

Fahs, C. (1925). World missionary atlas. BOOK, New York: Institute of social and religious research.

Fairbairn, C. (1929). The secret of the true revival (holiness must be preached). BOOK, Chicago Ill.: Pub. for the author by Free Methodist Pub.c House.

Fairbairn, C. (1930). Purity and power : or the baptism with the Holy Ghost. BOOK, Chicago: Christian Witness Co.

Fairbairn, C. (1946). ... God's plan for world evangelism,. BOOK, Winona Lake Ind.: Light and Life Press.

Fairbairn, C. V. (n.d.). A Primer on Evangelism. BOOK.

Fairbairn, C. V. (1957). What we believe : a brief manual of Christian doctrine for young Free Methodists and new converts based upon the catechism and articles of religion of the Free Methodist Church of North America. BOOK, Winona Lake, IN: Light and Life Press.

Faulkner, J. (1903). ... The Methodists,. BOOK, New York: The Baker & Taylor Co.

Ferguson, C. (1971). Organizing to beat the Devil : Methodists and the making of America. BOOK, Garden City N.Y.: Doubleday.

Ferm, V. (1953). The American church of the Protestant heritage. BOOK, New York: Philosophical Library.

Ferm, V. (1957). Pictorial history of Protestantism a panoramic view of western Europe and the United States. BOOK, New York: Philosophical Library.

Free Methodist Church In Canada, & East Ontario Conference. (1970). 75 years of progress in Canadian Free Methodism, East Ontario Conference : 1895-1970. BOOK, S.l: s.n.

Free Methodist Church of North America. (1959). An Act to incorporate the Free Methodist Chiurch in Canada : assented to 8th July, 1959. BOOK, Ottawa: Queen's printer and controller of stationery.

Free Methodist Church of North America, & Woman's Missionary Society. (1959). Then Jesus came : true stories of African children. BOOK, Winona Lake, Ind.: Free Methodist Church.

Gaddis, V. (1960). The story of Winona Lake : a memory and a vision. BOOK, Winona Lake Ind.: Winona Lake Christian Assembly.

Garber, P. (1939). The Methodists are one people. BOOK, Nashville: Cokesbury Press.

Geiger, K. (1962). Insights into holiness : discussions of holiness by fifteen leading scholars of the Wesleyan persuasion. BOOK, Kansas City, MO: Beacon Hill Press.

Geiger, K. (1963). Further insights into holiness : nineteen leading Wesleyan scholars present various phases of holiness thinking. BOOK, Kansas City, MO: Beacon Hill Press.

General Young People's Missionary Society Council, & Council., G. Y. P. M. S. (1952). It's time you knew ... : the facts about the ministry and operation of the Young People's Missionary Society through the Free Methodist Church around the world. BOOK, Winona Lake, Ind.: Young People's Missionary Society.

Goddard, B. (1967). The Encyclopedia of modern Christian missions the agencies. BOOK, Camden N.J.: T. Nelson.

Goodhew, E. (1960). Echoes from half a century. BOOK, Los Angeles: Los Angeles Pacific College Press.

Griffith, G. (1941). Daily glow. BOOK, Los Angeles, CA.

Grubb, K. (1949). World Christian handbook. BOOK, London: World Dominion Press.

Harmon, N. (1974). The Encyclopedia of world Methodism. BOOK, Nashville: United Methodist Pub. House.

Hart, E. P. (1903). Reminiscences of early Free Methodism. BOOK, Chicago, Ill.: Free Methodist Publ. House.

Harvey, J. (1976). Faith Plus : search for the holy life. BOOK, Winona Lake, IN: Light and Life.

Haviland, E. (1928). Under the Southern Cross : or, a woman's life work for Africa. BOOK, Cincinnati: God's Bible School and Revivalist.

Hawkins, R. (1888). Redemption or the living way : a treatise on the redemption of the body including a doctrinal outline of experimental religion. BOOK, Olean, NY: Herald Publ. House.

Hawkins, R. W. (1880). Life Eternal. BOOK.

Helsel, E. W. (1976). When is Jesus Coming Back? Light and Life, November 9, 6–7,12. JOUR.

Hendrickson, F. (1942). The "Livingstone" of the Orinoco (interior of South America) : the life story of Ford Hendrickson (an autobiography)... BOOK, Wausen, OH.

Herzog, J. (1908). The new Schaff-Herzog encyclopedia of religious knowledge, embracing Biblical, historical, doctrinal, and practical theology and Biblical, theological, and ecclesiastical biography from the earliest. BOOK, New York ;London: Funk and Wagnalls Company.

Historical sketches of the Free Methodist Churches of the East Michigan Conference, 1924-1962. (1963). ELEC, Linden, Mich.: Scottie's Printing.

Hogue, E. (1920). India : a mission study for juniors. BOOK, Chicago: Women's Foreign Missionary Society of the Free Methodist Church.

Hogue, W. (1890). Revivals and revival work. BOOK, Buffalo N.Y.: Published for the author.

Hogue, W. (1915). The believer's personal experience of Christ in the processes of salvation. BOOK, Chicago: W.B. Rose.

Hogue, W. T., & Chesbrough, A. E. (1906). A Sermon : preached at the fiftieth anniversary of the marriage of rev. Samuel K.J. and Mrs. Ann E. Chesbrough, February 6, 1898, together with the experience of Mrs. Ann E. Chesbrough, a member of the first class ever formed in the Free Methodist Church. BOOK, Chicago: Free Methodist Pub. House.

Horner, R. (1891). From the altar to the upper room in four parts. BOOK, Toronto, Montréal: W. Briggs ;;C.W. Coates.

Horner, R. (1908). Bible doctrines. BOOK, Ottawa, Canada: Holiness Movement Pub. House.

Howell, R. (1965). Saved to serve : accent on stewardship. BOOK, Grand Rapids, MI: Baker Book House.

Howland, C. (1913). Manual of missions. BOOK, New York ;Chicago: Fleming H. Revell Co.

Howland, J. (1947). Not mine Steward. BOOK, Winona Lake, IN: Published by Woman's Missionary Society of the Free Methodist Church.

Hudson, W. (1965). Religion in America. BOOK, New York: Scribner.

Hunt, S. (1893). Methodism in Buffalo, from its origin to the close of 1892,. BOOK, Buffalo, NY: H.H. Otis & Sons.

Hurst, J. (1902). The history of Methodism. BOOK, New York: Eaton & Mains.

Hyde, A. (1889). The story of Methodism throughout the world, from the beginning to the present time ... giving an account of its various influences and institutions of to-day. BOOK, Chicago, IL: Johns Publishing House.

Infant baptism in Biblical and Wesleyan theology (Book, 1975). (n.d.). [ICCMM].

Jacquet, C. (1975). Yearbook of American and Canadian churches 1975. BOOK, Nashville, TN: Abingdon Press.

Jernigan, C. (1919). Pioneer days of the Holiness movement in the Southwest. BOOK, Kansas City, MO: Pentecostal Nazarene Pub. House.

Johnston, T. (1974). Yesterday's hate, today's love : the amazing story of Tom & Roberta Johnston. BOOK, Winona Lake, IN: Light & Life Men International.

Joint Commission of the Free Methodist and Wesleyan Methodist Churches on the Matter of Church Union records,. (1944). GEN.

Jones, C. (1974). Perfectionist persuasion: the Holiness movement and American Methodism, 1867-1936. BOOK, Metuchen, NJ: Scarecrow Press.

Joy, D. (1983). Moral development foundations : Judeo-Christian alternatives to Piaget Kohlberg. BOOK, Nashville, TN: Abingdon.

Joy, D. (1985). Bonding : relationships in the image of God. BOOK, Waco, TX: Word Books.

Joy, D. M. (1960). A survey and analysis of the experiences, attitudes and problems of senior high youth of the Free Methodist Church (ICOMM). Southern Methodist University.

Kahl, M. (1970). His guiding hand : an autobiography. BOOK, Overland Park, KS: Herald and Banner Press.

Kelley, D. (1972). Why conservative churches are growing : a study in sociology of religion. BOOK, New York: Harper & Row.

Killion, M. W. (1941). A history of Spring Arbor Seminary and Junior College (ICOMM). University of Michigan. Retrieved from http://www.worldcat.org/title/history-of-spring-arbor-seminary-and-junior-college/oclc/11605017&referer=brief_results

Kingsley, C. (1965). Go! : Revolutionary New Testament Christianity. BOOK, Grand Rapids: Zondervan.

Kingsley, C. (1976). Do : manifesto for concerned Christian community, manual for meaning in mobilization of manpower. BOOK, Winona Lake Ind.: Light and Life Men International.

Klein, M. (1914). By Nippon's lotus ponds pen pictures of real Japan. BOOK, New York ;Chicago: Fleming H. Revell Company.

Knox, L. H. (1976). The Free Methodist minister. BOOK, Winona Lake, Ind.: Light and Life Press.

Lake, C. (1971). Our goodly heritage : a history of the Gerry homes. BOOK, Gerry, NY: Heritage Village; Printed by Falconer Print. and Design Inc.

Latourette, K. (1937). A history of the expansion of Christianity. BOOK, New York; London: Harper & Brothers.

Leaders in education, a biographical dictionary. (Journal, magazine, 1932). (n.d.). [ICOMM].

Lee, J. (1900). The illustrated history of Methodism the story of the origin and progress of the Methodist church, from its foundation by John Wesley to the present day. Written in popular style and illustrated by. BOOK, St Louis, MI: The Methodist Magazine Pub. Co.

Leech, K. (1976). True witness : the amazing story of Detective Leech. BOOK, Winona Lake, IN: Christian Witness Crusades Light and Life Men International.

Leete, F. (1948a). Methodist bishops--personal notes and bibliography : with quotations from unpublished writings and reminiscences. BOOK, Nashville: Parthenon Press.

Leete, F. (1948b). Methodist bishops: personal notes and bibliography. BOOK, Nashville: Printed by the Parthenon Press.

Living hymns of Charles Wesley. The singing saint. (1957). BOOK, Winona Lake, Ind.: Light and Life Press.

Lovejoy, C. (1952). College guide a complete reference book to 2,049 American colleges and universities for use by students, parents, teachers, and guidance counselors. 1953-54. BOOK, New York: Simon and Schuster.

M'Geary, J. S. (1908). The Free Methodist Church : a brief outline history of its origin and development. BOOK, Chicago: W.B. Rose.

Mann, W. (1955). Sect, cult, and church in Alberta. BOOK, Toronto: University of Toronto Press.

Marsh, C. (1936). American universities and colleges. BOOK, Washington, D.C.: American Council on Education.

Marston, L. R. (1939). Youth speaks! BOOK, Winona Lake, Ind.: Light and life Press.

Marston, L. R. (1944). From chaos to character, a study in the stewardship of personality. BOOK, Winona Lake, Ind.: Light and life Press.

Mason, H. (1955). Abiding values in Christian education. BOOK, Westwood, NJ: Fleming H. Revell Co.

Mavis, W. (1963). The psychology of Christian experience. BOOK, Grand Rapids: Zondervan Pub. House.

Mavis, W. (1969). Personal renewal through Christian conversion. BOOK, Kansas City, MO: Beacon Hill Press of Kansas City.

McClintock, J. (1981). Cyclopedia of Biblical, theological, and ecclesiastical literature. BOOK, Grand Rapids, MI: Baker Book House.

McKenna, D. (1986). Renewing our ministry. BOOK, Waco TX: Word Books.

McKenna, D. L. (1967) Free Methodist Education-1992. Free Methodist, October 10, 23. JOUR.

McLeister, I. (1934). History of the Wesleyan Methodist church of America. BOOK, Syracuse, NY: Wesleyan Methodist Pub. Association.

Mead, F. (1970). Handbook of denominations in the United States. BOOK, Nashville: Abingdon Press.

Merrill, A. (1947). Stagecoach towns. BOOK, Rochester, NY: Gannett Co.

Methodist Episcopal Church. (n.d.). Minutes of the annual conferences of the Methodist Episcopal Church. Minutes of the Annual Conferences of the Methodist Episcopal Church. ICOMM.

Miller, D. (1934). History of Greenville College with special reference to the curriculum (ICOMM). New York University.

Miller, D. (1957). The way to Biblical preaching. BOOK, New York: Abingdon Press.

Milner, V. (1871). Religious denominations of the world : comprising a general view of the origin, history and condition of the various sects of Christians, the Jews and Mahometans, as well as the pagan forms of religion existing in the different countries of the earth. BOOK, Philadelphia: William Garretson & Co.

Mission handbook: North American Protestant ministries overseas. (1973). BOOK, Monrovia, Calif.: MARC.

Mission manual. (1966) BOOK, Winona Lake, Ind.: Commission on Missions.

Moore, C. (1976). Hidden strands from the fabric of early Chili. BOOK, Chili, NY: Moore.

Moyer, E. (1962). Who was who in church history. BOOK, Chicago: Moody Press.

Murphy, T. (1941). Religious bodies, 1936. BOOK, Washington: U.S. G.P.O.

Nelson, M. O. (1952). The administration of guidance in colleges related to the Wesleyan and Free Methodist churches (ICOMM). State University of New York at Buffalo.

Noda, S. (1967). A Grain of wheat : memories of a missionary, Eva Bryan Millikan. BOOK, Tokyo, Jap.: Free Methodist Kaganei Church ;Printed by Sanshu Printing Co.

Norbeck, M. (1931). The Lure of the hills a tale of life in the mountains of Kentucky, by Mildred E. Norbeck ... BOOK, Cincinnati, OH: Pub. for the author by the Revivalist Press.

Norbeck, M. (1947). The challenge of the hills. BOOK, Apollo, PA: West Pub. Co.

Norbeck, M. (1964). The Haitian challenge and you. BOOK, Intercession City, Fla.: Great Commission Crusades.

North American Protestant ministries overseas, 1970. (1970). BOOK, Monrovia, Calif.: MARC.

Norwood, F. (1974). The story of American Methodism a history of the United Methodists and their relations. BOOK, Nashville: Abingdon Press.

Nystrom, G. (1960). Mama married me. BOOK.

O'Brien, T. (1970). Corpus dictionary of Western churches. BOOK, Washington: Corpus Publications.

Olmstead, W. (1904). Light and life songs : adapted especially to Sunday schools, prayer meetings and other social services. GEN, Chicago, IL: S.K.J. Chesbro,.

Olmstead, W. (1907). Handbook for Sunday-school workers. BOOK, Chicago: W.B. Rose.

Olmstead, W. (1914). Light and life songs, number two : adapted especially to Sunday schools, social worship, camp meetings and revival services. GEN, Chicago : W.B. Rose,.

Olmstead, W. (1915). Gospel truths in song. GEN, Chicago,: W.B. Rose.

Olmstead, W. (1918). Light and life songs, no. 3 : for Sunday-schools, social worship, camp meetings and revival services. GEN, Chicago, IL : W.B. Rose,.

Olmstead, W. B., & Harris, T. (1928). Light and life songs : no. 4, for the Sunday school, social worship, missionary and evangelistic work. MUSIC, Chicago: Light and Life Press.

Orr, J. (1966). The light of the nations evangelical renewal and advance in the nineteenth century. BOOK, Grand Rapids: W.B. Eerdmans Pub. Co.

Owen, E. (1856). Things new and old. BOOK, Boston: Henry V. Degen.

Owen, E. (1891). Struck by lightning a true and thrilling narrative of one who was struck by lightning : with incidents, experiences, and anecdotes for old and young. BOOK, Otterville, Ont.: A. Sims.

Parker, J. (1938). Interpretative statistical survey of the world mission of the Christian church: summary and detailed statistics of churches and missionary societies, interpretative articles, and indices. BOOK, New York; London: International Missionary Council.

Pearson, B. (1930). Wings to Aztec Land : "things to do" with each chapter : twenty-five attractive patterns for handwork. BOOK, Los Angeles, CA: Harry Harper.

Pearson, B. (1935). Off to Panama : a true adventure story of the opening doors for Christian missions in Panama. BOOK, L.A. Calif.: Free Tract Society.

Pfouts, N. (2000). A history of Roberts Wesleyan College. BOOK, Rochester, NY.

Phillips, P. (1891). Metrical tune book with hymns. GEN, Chicago: T.B. Arnold.

Reed, N. (1936). World treasure trails : Africa. BOOK, Winona Lake, IN: Woman's Missionary Society Free Methodist church of North America.

Reed, N. (1938). World treasure trails II : India. BOOK, Winona Lake, IN: Woman's Missionary Society Free Methodist church of North America.

Rev. Aura Claire Showers : a sketch of his life / by his wife ; together with tributes by ministerial brethren ; to which is added a treatise on the doctrine of eternal punishment and other unpublished manuscripts. (1896). ELEC, Oil City, PA :H.D.W. Showers,1896.

Revell's guide to Christian colleges. (Journal, magazine, 1965). (n.d.). [ICOMM].

Root, H. (1929). An alabaster box : the life story of Grace E. Barnes. BOOK, Chicago, IL: Woman's Missionary Society Free Methodist Church.

Root, H. (1943). A corn of wheat : the life story of Clara Leffingwell. BOOK, Winona Lake, IN: Woman's Missionary Society Free Methodist Church.

Russell, C. (1959). Youth wants to know. BOOK, Winona Lake, IN: Christian Youth Supplies.

Schlosser, J. (n.d.). Church planting in Mindanao. BOOK, Winona Lake, IN: General Missionary Board Free Methodist Church of North America.

Schoenhals, L. R., Lowell, L. M., Schoenhals, L. R., Lowell, L. M., Schoenhals, L. R., & Lowell, L. M. (1950). Choice light and life songs : a collection of the best loved gospel songs and choruses, both old and new for the Sunday School, Young People's meeting, evangelistic service and children's service. MUSIC, Winona Lake, Ind.: Light and Life Press.

Shaw, S. (1893). Touching incidents and remarkable answers to prayer. BOOK, Grand Rapids: S.B. Shaw.

Shaw, S. (1895). Children's edition of touching incidents and remarkable answers to prayer. BOOK, Grand Rapids, MI: S.B. Shaw.

Shaw, S. (1897). God's financial plan, or temporal prosperity the result of faithful stewardship. BOOK, Grand Rapids: S.B. Shaw.

Shaw, S. (1905). The great revival in Wales, also an account of the great revival in Ireland in 1859,. BOOK, Chicago, IL: S.B. Shaw.

Shelhamer, E. (n.d.). False doctrines and fanaticism exposed. BOOK, Atlanta, GA: "The Repairer."

Shelhamer, E. (1900). Pointed Bible readings on various subjects. BOOK, Atlanta, GA.

Shelhamer, E. (1906). Popular and radical holiness contrasted. BOOK, Atlanta.

Shelhamer, E. (1914). Heart searching talks to ministers. BOOK, Louisville, KY: Pentecostal Pub. Co.

Shelhamer, E. (1917). Heart searching sermons and sayings. BOOK, Atlanta, GA: Repairer Pub. Co.

Shelhamer, E. (1919). 5 reasons why I do not seek the gift of tongues. BOOK, Wilmore, KY: Mrs. E.E. Shelhamer.

Shelhamer, J. (n.d.). God, ghosts, and demons, or, A glimpse into the beyond. BOOK, Cincinnati: God's Bible School.

Shelhamer, J. (1900). A message to men. BOOK, Kansas City, MO: Nazarene Pub. House.

Shelhamer, J. (1923). Trials and triumphs of a minister's wife. BOOK, Atlanta: Repairer Pub. Co.

Shumaker, J. T. (1972). Church growth in Paraguay (ICOMM). Fuller Theological Seminary.

Sigsworth, J. (1956). Careers for Christian youth. BOOK, Chicago: Moody Press.

Silver, J. (1914). The Lord's return : seen in history and in Scripture as pre-millennial and imminent. BOOK, New York: F.H. Revell.

Simpson, M. (1878). Cyclopedia of Methodism : embracing sketches of its rise, progress, and present condition. BOOK, Philadelphia: Everts & Stewart.

Simpson, M. (1970). A hundred years of Methodism. BOOK, New York: Phillips & Hunt.

Sims, A. (1886). Bible salvation and popular religion contrasted. BOOK, Kingston Ont.: The Author.

Sims, A. (1886). Helps to Bible study with practical notes on the books of Scripture designed for ministers, local preachers, S.s teachers, and all Christian workers. BOOK, Uxbridge, Ont.

Sims, A. (1896). Remarkable narratives : or, records of powerful revivals, striking providences, wonderful religious experiences, tragic death-bed scenes, and other authentic incidents, to which is added some valuable. BOOK, Kingston, Ont.

Sims, A. (1900a). Beams of light on scripture texts, or, Selected passages of the Word of God illuminated by striking illustrations and choice explanations from eminent writers : also helpful Bible readings and suggestive hints. BOOK, Toronto: A. Sims.

Sims, A. (1900b). Behold the bridegroom cometh : or, Some remarkable and incontrovertible signs which herald the near approach of the Son of Man. BOOK, Kingston, Ont.: A. Sims.

Sims, A. (1900). Grace and glory : or Godly counsel and encouragement for waiting, watching hearts. BOOK, Toronto.

Sims, A. (1902). Valuable bank notes, or, God's immutable promises, searched, tested, and found true. BOOK, Toronto: A. Sims.

Sims, A. (1905). Deepening shadows and coming glories. BOOK, Toronto: A. Sims.

Sing His Praise. (1925). Camp meeting special : a selection of songs specially designed for use in camp meetings and other evangelistic campaigns. MUSIC, Chicago: Light and Life Press.

Smashey, D. (1913). The redeeming purpose of God, including a statement of the Scriptural idea of the doctrine of holiness and its advancement in the church. BOOK, Chicago: Goodspeed Press.

Smith, J. (1961). Religion in American life. BOOK, Princeton, NJ: Princeton University Press.

Smith, R. (1935). Youth's incense, or, Life and writings of Blanche Charlotte Smith. BOOK, Cincinnati: God's Bible School and Revivalist.

Smith, T. (1957). Revivalism and social reform in mid-nineteenth-century America. Chapters I-XI and XIV comprise the Frank S. and Elizabeth D. Brewer prize essay for 1955, the American Society of Church History. BOOK, New York: Abingdon Press.

Snider, K. (1975). Whose ministry? : a group study book on the ministry of every Christian. BOOK, Osaka Japan: Japan Free Methodist Mission.

Stevens, A. (1864). History of the Methodist Episcopal Church in the United States of America. BOOK, New York: Carlton & Porter.

Sweet, W. (1961). Methodism in American history. BOOK, New York; Nashville: Abingdon Press.

Tamblyn, J. (1924). Sweet memories of a trustful life. BOOK, Morristown N.J.: E.A. Smith & Sons Printers.

Tapper, R. (1948). Full years : the life story of Helen I. Root. BOOK, Winona Lake, In.: Young People's Missionary Society.

Tenney, M. (1942). "Still abides the memory." BOOK, Greenville, IL: Tower Press of Greenville College.

The College blue book. (Journal, magazine, 1923). (n.d.). [ICOMM].

The doctrines and discipline of the Methodist Episcopal Church, 1860. With an appendix. (1860). BOOK, New York: Carlton & Porter.

The life and letters of Mrs. Phoebe Palmer (Book, 1984). (n.d.). [ICOMM].

The national faculty directory. (1970). BOOK, Detroit, Mich.: Gale Research.

The Repairer. (Journal, magazine, 1800s). (n.d.). [ICOMM].

The state of the churches in the U.S.A., 1973, as shown in their own official yearbooks : a study resource. (1973). BOOK, Sun City, Ariz.: The Agency.

The World book encyclopedia. (1976). BOOK, Chicago: Field Enterprises Educational Corp.

The young minister's companion : or, A collection of valuable and scarce treatises on the pastoral office. (1813). BOOK, Boston: Printed and sold by Samuel T. Armstrong.

Thomson, F. (1972). The New York Times guide to continuing education in America,. BOOK, New York: Quadrangle Books.

Todd, F. (1963). Camping for Christian youth a guide to methods and principles for evangelical camps. BOOK, New York: Harper & Row.

Townsend, W. (1909). A new history of Methodism. BOOK, London: Hodder and Stoughton.

Tremain, L. C. (1968). An evaluation of the organization and structure of the family camp program of the Pacific Northwest Conference of the Free Methodist Church (ICOMM). Seattle Pacific University.

Turnbull, R. (1974). A history of preaching volume III, from the close of the nineteenth century to the middle of the twentieth century (continuing the work of the volumes I and II by Edwin C. Dargan) and American. BOOK, Grand Rapids Mich.: Baker Book House.

Vincent, B. (1975). "As ye go, preach" : outlines and notes from the papers of Bishop Burton Jones Vincent, 1877-1931. BOOK.

Voices of praise : prepared with especial reference to the needs of the Sunday school, it will also be found suitable for the prayer meeting and other religious gatherings. (1909). GEN, Chicago : W.B. Rose,.

Waller, F. L. (1935). A history of Wessington Springs College. (ICOMM). University of South Dakota.

Walls, A. E., Cochrane, R. L., & Rose, M. L. (1975). Eighty years : historical sketch of thr Woman's Missionary Society of the Free Methodist Church. BOOK, by the Society.

Warner, D. (1914). Glimpses of Palestine and Egypt. BOOK, Chicago: W.B. Rose.

Warner, D. (1921). The book we study : a brief tribute to the Holy Scriptures. BOOK, Chicago: W.B. Rose.

Warren, R. (1955). Spiritual strength for today. BOOK, Toronto ;New York: T. Nelson.

Warren, R. (1960). You can gain spiritual strength. BOOK, New York: Nelson.

Watson, C. (1917). The employer, the wage earner, and the law of love,. BOOK, Lawrence: University of Kansas.

We believe! : insights into the beliefs of Free Methodists. (1976). BOOK, Winona Lake, Ind.: Light and Life Press.

Wesley, J. (1981). John and Charles Wesley : selected prayers, hymns, journal notes, sermons, letters and treatises. BOOK, New York: Paulist Press.

White, C. (1986). The beauty of holiness : Phoebe Palmer as theologian, revivalist, feminist, and humanitarian. BOOK, Grand Rapids, Mich.: F. Asbury Press.

Who's who in America, 1988-1989. (1988). BOOK, Wilmette Ill.: Marquis Who's Who.

Who was who in America : a companion volume to Who's who in America. (1943). BOOK, Chicago: Marquis.

Winslow, C. (1945). Tomorrow. BOOK, Winona Lake, Ind.: Young people's missionary Society.

Winslow, C. (1947). Forward with Christ. BOOK, Winona Lake, Ind.: Young Peoples Missionary Society.

Wiseman, P. (1900). Purity and power, or, Sanctification at Pentecost. BOOK, Chicago: Christian Witness.

Wiseman, P. (1951). Scriptural sanctification. BOOK, Kansas City, MO: Beacon Hill.

Wood, J. (1944). Purity and maturity. BOOK, Kansas City, Mo.: Beacon hill Press.

Wood, J. (1996). Perfect love, or, Plain things for those who need them : concerning the doctrine, experience, profession, and practice of Christian holiness. BOOK, Oceanside, Calif.: Standard of Zion Publications.

Yamada, M. (1966). The Pacific Coast Japanese Conference of the Free Methodist Church. (ICOMM). Fuller Theological Seminary.

Youth in action. (Journal. magazine, 1900s). (n.d.). [ICOMM].

Free Methodist Publishing House

America., F. M. C. of N. (1860). Doctrines and discipline. CONF, Winona Lake, Ind.: Free Methodist Pub. House.

America., F. M. C. of N., Conference., G., Free Methodist Church of North America, & General Conference. (1910). Free Methodist hymnal. MUSIC, Chicago: Free Methodist Pub. House.

America, F. M. C. of N. (1879). The annual minutes. JFULL, Chicago: Free Methodist Pub. House.

America, F. M. C. of N. (1891). Light and life primary. JFULL, Winona, Lake, Ind.: Light and Life Press.

America, F. M. C. of N. (1901). A digest of Free Methodist law; or, Guide in the administration of the discipline of the Free Methodist church ... BOOK, Chicago, Ill.: Free Methodist Pub. House.

America, F. M. C. of N. (1915). Doctrines and discipline of the Free Methodist Church. BOOK, Chicago, Ill.: Free Methodist Pub. House.

America, F. M. C. of N. (1951). Conference minutes of the Free Methodist Church of North America. CONF, Winona Lake, IN: Free Methodist Pub. House.

America, F. M. C. of N. (1956). Records of the Free Methodist Church of North America (JFULL). Winona Lake, Ind: Free Methodist Pub. House.

America, F. M. C. of N. (1960). Yearbook of the Free Methodist Church around the world. JFULL, Winona Lake, Ind: Free Methodist Pub. House.

America, F. M. C. of N. (1970). Doctrines and discipline of the Free Methodist Church of North America. BOOK, Winona Lake, Ind.: Free Methodist Pub. House.

America, F. M. C. of N. (1971). Yearbook. JFULL, Winona Lake, Ind: Free Methodist Pub. House.

America, F. M. C. of N. (1990). The book of discipline, 1989. The Book of discipline. BOOK, Winona Lake, Ind.: Free Methodist Pub. House.

America, F. M. C. of N. (2004). 2003 book of discipline. BOOK, Indianapolis, Ind.: Free Methodist Publishing House.

America, F. M. C. of N., & Conference, G. (1950). A catechism of the Free Methodist Church. BOOK, Winona Lake, Ind.: Free Methodist Pub. House.

Andrews, E. A. (n.d.). A Symposium on instrumental music in public worship. BOOK, Chicago, Ill.: Free Methodist Pub. House.

Baldwin, H. (1926). The carnal mind; a doctrinal and experimental view of the subject. BOOK, Chicago, Ill.: Free Methodist Pub. House.

Baldwin, H. A. (1912). The indwelling Christ. BOOK, Chicago: Free Methodist Pub. House.

Baldwin, H. A. (1919). Holiness and the human element. BOOK, Chicago: Free Methodist Pub. House.

Baldwin, H. A. (1927). The coming judgment, general and at the end of time. BOOK, Chicago, Ill.: Free Methodist Pub. House.

Baym, N. (2011). A History of American Women's Western Books, 1833-1928, 63–80. JOUR.

Beers, A. (1922). The romance of a consecrated life : a biography of Alexander Beers. Chicago: Free Methodist Pub. House.

Branson, W. T. (1892). Hymns and songs of worship. BOOK, Chicago: Free Methodist Pub. House.

Burritt, E. G. (1927). The pupil and how to teach him. BOOK, Chicago: Light and Life Press.

Chesbro, S. K. J. (1900). Reopening the wells, a sermon. BOOK, Chicago, IL: Free Methodist Pub. House.

Cross, W. J. (1939). The great apostle and the great epistles ... BOOK, Winona Lake, Indiana: Free Methodist Pub. House.

Damon, C. M. (1900). Sketches and incidents, or reminiscences of interest in the life of the author. BOOK, Chicago: Free Methodist Pub. House.

Dawson, F. (1929). Life sketch and sermons of Rev. B.C. Dewey. Chicago Ill.: Free Methodist Pub. House.

Fairbairn, C. V. (1900). A Symposium on revivals and the present day need. BOOK, Chicago: Free Methodist Pub. House.

Fellowship, F. M. W. (1962). News and views. News and Views. JFULL, Winona Lake, Ind.: Free Methodist Pub. House.

Free Methodist Church, Church., F. M., Church, F. M., & Church., F. M. (n.d.). Yearbook. BOOK, Winona Lake, Ind.: Free Methodist Publishing House.

Free Methodist Church, & Church, F. M. (1927). Instrumental music in public worship : the position held by the Free Methodist Church. CONF, Chicago, Ill.: Free Methodist Pub. House.

Free Methodist Church of North America. (n.d.). The annual minutes : Free Methodist Church of North America. BOOK, Winona Lake, Ind.: Free Methodist Pub. House.

Free Methodist Church of North America. (1891). The hymn book of the Free Methodist Church. BOOK, Rochester, N.Y.: B.T. Roberts.

Free Methodist Church of North America. (1896). Probationer's guide : instruction to candidates for admission to membership in the Free Methodist Church. BOOK, Chicago, Ill.: Free Methodist Pub. House.

Free Methodist Church of North America. (2008). 2007 Book of Discipline. Book, Indianapolis, Ind.: Free Methodist Publishing House.

Free Methodist Church of North America, Commission on Missions, Woman's Missionary Society, Young People's Missionary Society of the Free Methodist Church, & Junior Missionary Society of the Free Methodist Church. (n.d.). Annual report. In Annual report. CONF, Chicago, Ill.: Free Methodist Pub. House.

Free Methodist Church of North America, General Missionary Board, Woman's Foreign Missionary Society, America., F. M. C. of N., Board., G. M., America., F. M. C. of N., … Woman's Foreign Missionary Society. (1923). Proceedings of the General Missionary Board of the Free Methodist Church of North America. BOOK, Chicago, Ill.

Free Methodist hymnal / Published by authority of the General Conference of the Free Methodist Church of North America. (n.d.). ELEC, Chicago : Free Methodist Pub. House.

Free Methodist Publishing House. (1949). The Christian minister. The Christian Minister. JFULL.

General Council of the Church in Mission of the Free Methodist Church of North America, Free Methodist Church of North America, General Council for the Church in Mission, America., F. M. C. of N., Mission., G. C. of the C. in, Marston, L. R., … Free Methodist Church of North America. (1868). The Free Methodist. The Free Methodist. JFULL, Rochester, N.Y.: Levi Wood.

Greenville College. (n.d.). Annual Register of Greenville College. Annual Register of Greenville College. JFULL, Chicago, IL.: Free Methodist Publishing House.

Haley, J. W., Olmstead, W. B., & America, F. M. C. of N. (1926). Life in Mozambique and South Africa. BOOK, Chicago: Free Methodist Pub. House.

Hart, E. P. (1903). Reminiscences of early Free Methodism. BOOK, Chicago, Ill.: Free Methodist Publ. House.

Hartsough, M. M., Upson, L. E., & Babb, L. W. (1964). A history of the Hartough - Hartsough - Hartsock family. BOOK, Winona Lake, Indiana: The Free Methodist Publishing House.

Hill, D. L., Van Valin, J. E., & Free Methodist Church of North America Board of Bishops. (1988). Membership Care Committee handbook, Free Methodist Church of North America. BOOK, Winona Lake, IN: Free Methodist Pub. House.

Hogg, W. T. (1895). A hand-book of homiletics and pastoral theology. BOOK, Chicago: Free Methodist Pub. House.

Hogg, W. T. (1938). History of the Free Methodist Church of North America. BOOK, Winona Lake, Ind.: Free Methodist Pub. House.

Hogue, W. T. (1905). G. Harry Agnew, a pioneer missionary. BOOK, Chicago: Free Methodist Pub. House.

Hogue, W. T. (1911). Retrospect and prospect : a semi-centennial sermon preached by Bishop Wilson T. Hogue before the General Conference of the Free Methodist Church, in Chicago, June 18, 1911. BOOK, Chicago, IL: Free Methodist Pub. House.

Hogue, W. T. (1915). History of the Free Methodist church of North America. BOOK, Chicago: Free Methodist Pub. House.

Hogue, W. T. (1916). The Holy Spirit : a study. BOOK, Chicago, Ill.: William B. Rose.

Hogue, W. T. (1940). A hand-book of homiletics and pastoral theology. BOOK, Winona Lake, Ind.: Herald and Banner Press.

Hogue, W. T., & Chesbrough, A. E. (1906). A Sermon : preached at the fiftieth anniversary of the marriage of rev. Samuel K.J. and Mrs. Ann E. Chesbrough, February 6, 1898, together with the experience of Mrs. Ann E. Chesbrough, a member of the first class ever formed in the Free Methodist Church. BOOK, Chicago: Free Methodist Pub. House.

Hogue, W. T., & Roberts, B. T. (1896). A Symposium on scriptural holiness. BOOK, Chicago: Free Methodist Pub. House.

Howland, C. L. (1950). Proofs of inspiration : the cumulative proofs of the inspiration of the scriptures. BOOK, Winona Lake, Ind.: Free Methodist Pub. House.

Howland, C. L. (1951). The story of our church : Free Methodism, some facts and some reasons. BOOK, Winona Lake, IN: Free Methodist Pub. House.

Howland, C. L. (1953). A brief story of our church : an historical outline of the origin and growth of the Free Methodist Church of North America. BOOK, Winona Lakes, Ind.: Free Methodist Pub. House.

Jessop, H. E. (1938). Foundations of doctrine in scripture and experience : a students' handbook on holiness. BOOK, Winona Lake, Ind.: Free Methodist Pub. House.

Johnson, H. F. (1900). Handbook of Free Methodist missions. BOOK, Winona Lake, Ind.: Free Methodist Pub. House.

Jones, B. R. (1909). Incidents in the life and labors of Burton Rensselaer Jones, Minister of the Gospel, with extracts from his diary. BOOK, Chicago: Free Methodist Pub. House.

Joy, D. M. (1967). A preliminary report on the Aldersgate Graded Curriculum Project. BOOK, Winona Lake, Ind.: Free Methodist Pub. House.

Knox, L. H., Wesley, J., Wesley, C., & Free Methodist Church of North America. (1976). The Faith and life of a Free Methodist. BOOK, Winona Lake, Ind.: Free Methodist Pub. House.

La Due, J., & La Due, W. K. (1898). The life of Rev. Thomas Scott La Due : with some sketches and other writings. BOOK, Chicago: Free Methodist Pub. House.

Nye, G. A. (1943a). Readings concerning the history of Warsaw. BOOK, Winona Lake, Indiana: Free Methodist Pub. House.

Nye, G. A. (1943b). Readings in early local history. BOOK, Winona Lake, IN.: Free Methodist Pub. House.

Nye, G. A. (1944). Warsaw in 1890's and other stories. BOOK, Winona Lake, IN: Free Methodist Pub. House.

Nye, G. A. (1947). Warsaw in the 1870's and 1880's. BOOK, Winona Lake, IN: Free Methodist Pub. House.

Olmstead, B. L. (n.d.). Serving God and the church : a brief discussion of how to live the Christian life successfully. BOOK, Winona Lake, Ind.: Free Methodist Pub. House.

Olmstead, B. L. (1950). Being a Christian : a guide for early youth. BOOK, Winona Lake, Ind.: Free Methodist Pub. House.

Olmstead, B. L. (1955). Our church at work : a brief manual for the instruction of preparatory members of the Free Methodist Church. BOOK, Winona Lake, Ind.: Free Methodist Pub. House.

Parsons, I. D. (1915). Kindling watch-fires; being a brief sketch of the life of Rev. Vivian A. Dake, together with a compilation of selections from his writings, sermons, and poems, to which is appended a few of his best songs with the music,. BOOK, Chicago, Ill.: Free Methodist Pub. House.

Pearce, W. (1942). Choice hymns : a collection of hymns from the Free Methodist hymnal, especially adapted for revival services. MUSIC, Winona Lake, Ind.: Free Methodist Pub. House.

Phillips, P., Terrill, J. G., Arnold, T. B., & Free Methodist Church of North America. (1906). Metrical tune book : with hymns and supplement. MUSIC, Chicago: Free Methodist Pub. House.

R. B. Spencer papers. (1910). BOOK.

Ray, L. P. (1926). Twice sold, twice ransomed autobiography of Mr. and Mrs. L.P. Ray. BOOK, Chicago, Ill: Free Methodist Pub. House.

Reed, N. A. (1914). Ntombinkulu (Big Girl) : or a Zulu girl in fair View Girls' School, Natal, South Africa. BOOK, New York: Free Methodist Pub. House.

Roberts, B. T. (1948). Fishers of men, or, Practical hints to those who would win souls. BOOK, Winona Lake, Ind.: Light and Life Press.

Roberts, B. T., & Rose, W. B. (1912). Pungent truths : being extracts from the writings of the Rev. Benjamin Titus Roberts ... BOOK, Chicago: Free Methodist Pub. House.

Ronayne, E. (1900). Ronayne's reminiscences: a history of his life and renunciation of Romanism and freemasonry. BOOK, Chicago: Free Methodist Pub. House.

Sage, C. H., & Olmstead, W. B. (1908). Autobiography of Rev. Charles H. Sage : embracing an account of his pioneer work in Michigan, of the formation of the Canada Conference and of his labors in various states. BOOK, Chicago, Ill.: Free Methodist Pub. House.

Sellew, W. A. (1907). Clara Leffingwell, a missionary. BOOK, Chicago: Free Methodist Pub. House.

Sellew, W. A. (1914). Why not? : a plea for the ordination of those women whom God has called to preach the Gospel. BOOK, Chicago, Ill.: Published for the author by the Free Methodist Pub. House.

Shay, E. F. (1913). Mariet Hardy Freeland : a faithful witness : a biography. BOOK, Chicago: Free Methodist Pub. House.

Shelhamer, E. E. (1900). Bible holiness : how obtained and how retained. BOOK, Chicago: Free Methodist Pub. House.

Small Collections. (1870). (UNPB).

Stedwell, A. (1915). Itinerant footprints. BOOK, Shambaugh, Iowa: Stedwell.

Stonehouse, C. (1979). Moral Development: The Process and the Pattern. CVJ Counseling and Values, 24(1), 2–9. JOUR.

Telford, J. (1886). The life of John Wesley. BOOK, Chicago: Free Methodist Pub. House.

Terrill, J. G. (1889). The life of Rev. John Wesley Redfield. BOOK, Chicago: Free Methodist Pub. House.

Terrill, J. G. (2000). The life of John Wesley Redfield, M.D. BOOK, Salem, Ohio: Allegheny.

The what and the why of Free Methodism. (1927). BOOK, Chicago: Free Methodist Pub. House.

Thomson, J. F. (1905). The life and labors of Rev. William Bramwell : a chosen, approved, valiant and successful minister of Christ, 1783-1820. BOOK, Chicago, Ill.: Free Methodist Pub. House.

Upham, T. C. (1907). Inward divine guidance. BOOK, Chicago: Free Methodist Pub. House.

Ward, E. F. (1923). Memory links of "our own Chickabiddie", or, Reminiscences of Mary Louise Vore. BOOK, Chicago: Free Methodist Pub. House.

Ward, E. F., & Ward, P. E. (1908). Echoes from Bharatkhand. BOOK, Chicago, Ill.: Free Methodist Pub. House.

Wesley, J. (n.d.). A plain account of Christian perfection. BOOK, Winona Lake, Ind.: Light and Life Press.

Wesley, J. (1900). On dress. BOOK, Chicago, Ill.: Published by the Free Methodist Pub. House.

Wesley, J. (1902). True holiness as taught by John Wesley : comprising his sermons on Sin in believers, Repentance of believers, Christian perfection. BOOK, Chicago: Free Methodist Pub. House.

Wesley, J. (1940). On dress and evil speaking. BOOK, Winona Lake, Ind.: Free Methodist Publishing House.

Wheatlake, S. K. (1900). The touch of fire : sermons on holiness. BOOK, Chicago: Free Methodist Pub. House.

Wheatlake, S. K. (2006). Casting away our confidence. BOOK, Chicago: Free Methodist Publishing House.

Winget, B. (1903). Historical sketch of members of the Free Methodist Church of North America who have gone out to the foreign field of missionaries. BOOK, Chicago, Ill.: Free Methodist Pub. House.

Winget, B. (1911). Missions and missionaries of the Free Methodist Church. BOOK, Chicago: Free Methodist Pub. House.

Zahniser, A. D. F., & Easton, J. B. (1932). History of the Pittsburgh Conference of the Free Methodist Church. BOOK, Free Methodist Pub. House.

Light and Life Press

Ablard, M., Baker, J., & Club, C. L. (1988). Discovery time : recreation fun, creativity fair, social event ; trailblazer ; grades 3 and 4 ; year one. BOOK, Winona Lake, Ind.: Light and Life Press.

Action. (1981). JFULL, Winona Lake, IN: for Aldersgate Publication Association by Light and Life Press.

Ahern, A. A. (1965). Luke : leader's guide. BOOK, Winona Lake, Ind.: Light and Life Press.

Aldersgate Publications Association. (1938). The Railroad evangelist. JFULL, Winona Lake, Ind.: Light and Life Press.

Aldersgate Publications Association, & Association., A. P. (n.d.). Young teen study guide. JFULL, Winona Lake, Ind.: Light and Life Press.

America., F. M. C. of N. (1964). Hymns of the living faith. MUSIC.

America., F. M. C. of N., America., W. M. C. (or C. of, Free Methodist Church of North America, America., F. M. C. of N., America., W. M. C. (or C. of, Light and Life Press, … Wesleyan Methodist Connection of America. (1951). Hymns of the living faith. MUSIC, Winona Lake, Ind.: Light and Life Press.

America., F. M. C. of N., Association., A. P., Free Methodist Church of North America, Aldersgate Publications Association, America., F. M. C. of N., & Association., A. P. (1971). Discovery. Discovery. JFULL, Winona Lake, Ind.: Light and Life Press [etc.].

America., F. M. C. of N., Bishops., B. of, Free Methodist Church of North America, & Board of Bishops. (1998). Pastor's handbook. BOOK, Board of Bishops, Free Methodist Church of North America.

America, F. M. C. of N. (1891). Light and life primary. JFULL, Winona, Lake, Ind.: Light and Life Press.

America, F. M. C. of N. (1935). The Y.P.M.S. story of Winona Lake. BOOK, Winona Lake, Ind.: Light and Life Press.

America, F. M. C. of N. (1983). Shoes, snakes, and shelves : missionary stories from Asia. BOOK, Winona lake, Ind.: Light and Life Press.

America, F. M. C. of N., & Cryderman, W. L. (1983). Songs for renewal. MUSIC, Winona Lake, Ind.: Light and Life Press.

America, F. M. C. of N., & Education, C. on C. (1961). Let's teach. BOOK, Winona Lake, Ind.: Light and Life Press.

America, F. M. C. of N., Education, D. of C., Board, G. M., & International, W. M. F. (1981). All god's children : stories from Central Africa. BOOK, Winona Lake, Ind.: Light and Life Press.

America, F. M. C. of N., Education, D. of C., Board, G. M., & International, W. M. F. (1982). Island adventures : treasures in Dominican and Pierre, a boy from Haiti. BOOK, Winona Lake, Ind.: Light and Life Press.

America, F. M. C. of N., & Growth, D. of E. and C. (1980). Reach out in love. Winona Lake, Ind.: Light and Life Press.

America, F. M. C. of N., & Van Valin, C. E. (1986). Pastor's handbook of the Free Methodist Church. BOOK, Winona Lake, IN: Light and Life Press.

America, G. C. of the F. M. C. of N., Missions, C. on, & Missions, F. M. W. (1963). Quinquennial report of Free Methodist World Missions. CONF, Winona Lake, Ind.: Light and Life Press.

Andrews, E. A. (2005). Musings on self-deception. BOOK, Chicago, Ill.: Charles Edwin Jones.

Angel, E., & Buswell, R. C. (1982). At ease under pressure : James, I, II Peter leader's guide. BOOK, Winona Lake, IN: Light and Life Press.

Antista, V. J. (1988). So it goes in America. BOOK, Winona Lake, IN: Light and Life Press.

Arnold's commentary : international Sunday school lessons. (1895). JFULL, Winona Lake, Ind: Light and Life Press.

Arnold's practical commentary on the International Sunday School lessons uniform series for 1949 : a practical help for all who use the uniform lessons in the Sunday School, or who desire to do individual Bible study ... (1947). BOOK, Winona Lake, Ind.: Light and Life Press.

Arnold's practical Sabbath school commentary on the international lessons. (1895). JFULL, Winona Lake, Ind.: Light and Life Press.

Arthur, W. (1900). The tongue of fire, or, The true power of Christianity. BOOK, Winona Lake, Ind.: Light and Life Press.

Association, A. P. (n.d.-a). Junior teacher. JFULL, Winona Lake, Ind.: Light and Life Press.

Association, A. P. (n.d.-b). Young teen teacher. JFULL, Winona Lake, Ind.: Light and Life Press.

Association, A. P. (1975a). Explorer 1. JFULL, Winona Lake, Ind.: Light and Life Press.

Association, A. P. (1975b). Explorer 2. JFULL, Winona Lake, Ind.: Light and Life Press.

Bailey, A., Christian Life Club, Boyd, J., Christian Life Club, Club., C. L., Bailey, A., ... Club., C. L. (1988). Trailblazer squadron activities ; year one, grades 3 and 4. BOOK, Winona Lake, Ind.: Light and Life Press.

Bailey, R. Q. (1980). The servant story : Mark : study guide. BOOK, Winona Lake, Ind.: Pub. for Aldersgate Publications by Light and Life Press.

Ballew, J., Sutton, M., & Christian Life Club. (1988). Guide squadron activities , year two, grades 5 and 6. BOOK, Winona Lake, Ind.: Light and Life Press.

Banks, S. (1975). Saints in work clothes. BOOK, Winona Lake, Ind.: Light and Life Press.

Barker, J. H. J. (1975). This is the will of God : a study in the doctrine of entire sanctification as a definite experience. BOOK, Salem, Ohio: Schmul.

Bastian, D. N. (n.d.). Leading the local church : for members of the official board. BOOK, Winona Lake, Ind.: Light and Life Press.

Bastian, D. N. (1963). The mature church member. BOOK, Winona Lake, Ind.: Light and Life Press.

Bastian, D. N. (1964). Galatians : leader's guide. BOOK, Winona Lake, Ind.: Light and Life Press.

Bastian, D. N. (1977). Along the way. BOOK, Winona Lake, Ind.: Light and Life Press.

Bastian, D. N. (1978a). Belonging! : adventures in church membership. BOOK, Winona Lake, Ind.: Light and Life Press.

Bastian, D. N. (1978b). Cultivating church members : for Free Methodist pastors only. BOOK, Winona Lake, IN: Light and Life Press.

Bastian, D. N. (1980). The joy of Christian fathering : five first-person accounts. BOOK, Winona Lake, Ind.: Light and Life Press.

Bastian, D. N. (1986). Managing tainted money. BOOK, Winona Lake, Ind.: Light and Life Press.

Bastian, D. N. (1988). Counterfeit : the lie of living together unmarried. BOOK, Toronto: Light and Life Press Canada.

Bastion, D. N., & Marston, L. R. (1978). Thumb-nail sketches of doctrinal patterns. BOOK, Winona Lake, Ind.: Light and Life Press.

Bates, G. (1981). Soul afire : life of J.W. Haley. BOOK, Winona Lake, Ind.: Light and Life Press.

Bauer, D. R. (1986). Gospel of the king : Matthew study guide. BOOK, Winona Lake, IN: Light and Life Press.

Benson, M. C. (1967). Church library manual,. BOOK, Winona Lake, Ind.: Light and Life Press.

Bilezikian, V. S. (1951). Apraham Hoja of Aintap. BOOK, Winona Lake, IN: Light and Life Press.

Black, J. (1950). "The Word of the Lord came unto me also." BOOK, Winona Lake, Ind.: Light and Life Press.

Blackie Buffalo and other stories of North American missions. (1967). BOOK, Winona Lake, Ind.: Light and Life Press.

Blews, R. (1939). Master workmen biographies of the deceased bishops of the Free Methodist Church. Winona Lake, Ind.: Light and Life Press.

Blews, R. (1960). Master workmen biographies of the late bishops of the Free Methodist Church during her first century, 1860-1960. Winona Lake, Ind.: Light and Life Press.

Book Review Doctors, I Salute . Emilie Conklin. 92 pp. Winona Lake, Indiana. (1939). N Engl J Med New England Journal of Medicine, 221(2), 84. JOUR.

Bounds, E. M. (1946). Preacher and prayer. BOOK, Winona Lake, Ind.: Light and Life Press.

Bowen, B. F. L. (1989). Progressive men and women of Kosciusko County, Indiana and 1903 plat maps. BOOK, Winona Lake, Ind.: Light and Life Press.

Boyd, M. F. (1946). Light and life hour, sixteen radio messages : world-wide gospel broadcast. BOOK, Winona Lake, Ind.: Light and Life Press.

Brause, D. (1979). Expanded ministry to adults : program guidelines. BOOK, Winona Lake, Ind.: Light and Life Press.

Bready, J. W. (1952). Faith and freedom : the roots of democracy. BOOK, Winona Lake, Ind.: Light and Life Press.

Bready, J. W., & American Tract Society. (1950). This freedom - whence? BOOK, Winona Lake, Ind.: Light and Life Press.

Brown, A. L., Secord, A. W., & White, E. C. (1946). A handbook for Sunday school workers. BOOK, Winona Lake, Ind.: Department of Sunday Schools, Christian Education Commission : Light and Life Press.

Brown, Z. M. (1981a). Trail-blazers in Livingstone country : the story of Ronald and Margaret Collett. BOOK, Winona Lake, Ind.: Light and Life Press.

Brown, Z. M. (1981b). Trailblazers in Livingston country / by Zella M. Brown. BOOK, Winona Lake, Ind.: Light and Life Press.

Burgess, R. J. (1900). Winning others : studies in evangelism for everyone. BOOK, Winona Lake, Ind.: Light and Life Press.

Burritt, C. T., & Hogue, E. L. (1935). The story of fifty years. BOOK, Winona Lake, Ind.: Light and Life Press.

Burritt, E. G. (1927). The pupil and how to teach him. BOOK, Chicago: Light and Life Press.

Buswell, R. C. (1982). At ease under pressure : James, I, II Peter study guide. BOOK, Winona Lake, IN: Light and Life Press.

Canada, F. M. C. I., & Free Methodist Church. (1990). The Book of discipline. JFULL, Mississauga, Ont.: Light and Life Press Canada.

Centz, H. B. (1951). Prelude to Armageddon : shadows on the sundial. BOOK, Winona Lake, Ind.: Light and Life Press.

Cheeseman, S. (1981). Eight Gates Beyond. BOOK, Winona Lake, Ind.: Light and Life Press.

Church, H. (1987). Light is shining in the Africa I know. BOOK, Winona Lake, Ind.: Light and Life Press.

Church, W., & Crusaders, C. Y. (1969). Crusaders guide for young teens. BOOK, Winona Lake, Ind.: Light and Life Press.

Church, W., & Crusaders, C. Y. (1970). God and church -- doctrine : for young teens in all local churches. BOOK, Winona Lake, Ind.: Light and Life Press.

Clem, M., & Bailey, R. Q. (1980). The servant story : the Gospel of Mark : leader's guide. BOOK, Winona Lake, Ind.: Published for the Aldersgate Publications Association by Light and Life Press.

Clyde, A. A., America, F. M. C. of N., & Society, W. M. (1979). International cookbook. BOOK, Winona Lake, Ind.: Light and Life Press.

Cockroft, B., Club, C. L., Staneart, F., & Christian Life Club. (1988). Guide chapel plans ; year one. BOOK, Winona Lake, Ind.: Light and Life Press.

Cockroft, M., & Cottrill, K. (1984). Expanded ministry to children : program guidelines. BOOK, Winona Lake, Ind.: Light and Life Press.

College, M. C. of G., & Kline, G. E. (1940). The Wesleyan message, its Scriptures and historical bases : addresses delivered at the 12th Annual Ministers' Conference, Greenville College, April 10-14, 1939. CONF, Winona Lake, IN: Light and Life Press.

College, M. C. of G., & Kline, G. E. (1942). The message bearing fruit. BOOK, Winona Lake, Ind.: Light and life press.

Compton, H. (1988). Through eyes of love : ventures of faith in India. BOOK, Winona Lake, Ind.

Conklin, E. (1938a). Doctors, I salute. BOOK, Winona Lake, Ind.: Light and Life Press.

Conklin, E. (1938b). Songs in the night. BOOK, Winona Lake, Ind.: Light and Life Press.

Conklin, E. C. (1939). Religion marches. BOOK, Winona Lake, Ind.: Printed for the author by Light and Life Press.

Cordell, B. (1948). Precious Pearl. BOOK, Winona Lake, Ind.: Light and Life Press.

Cordell, B. B. (1949). Blossoms from the flowery kingdom. BOOK, Winona Lake, Ind.: Light and Life Press.

Cox, B. E. (1963). Mwene of the Congo. BOOK, Winona Lake, Ind.: Light and Life Press.

Crandall, R. A. (1981). Ministry to persons : organization and administration. BOOK, Winona Lake, IN: Light and Life Press.

Cranston, R., & Cranston, C. (1983). Stars for the baliti tree : the story of Free Methodist missions in the Philippines. BOOK, Winona lake, Ind.: Published for Women's Missionary Fellowship International by Light and Life Press.

Davis, J. L., & rtMyette, F. E. (1960). Official Bible quiz text : the Gospel of Mark. BOOK, Winona Lake, Ind.: Light and Life Press.

Davis, J. L., & Taylor, W. H. (1960). Let's learn Mark. BOOK, Winona Lake, IN: Light and Life Press.

Day, B., Wesleyan Methodist Church of America, Christian Youth Crusaders, Church, W., America, W. M. C. of, & Crusaders, C. Y. (1970). Cadet trails. BOOK, Winona Lake, Ind.: Printed by Light and Life Press.

Dayton, W. T. (1960). Romans : leader's guide. BOOK, Winona Lake, Ind.: Light and Life Press.

Demaray, D. E. (1958a). "Amazing grace!" BOOK, Winona Lake, Ind.: Light and Life Press.

Demaray, D. E. (1958b). Basic beliefs : an introductory guide to Christian theology. BOOK, Grand Rapids: Baker Book House.

Demaray, D. E. (1961). Acts : leader's guide. BOOK, Winona Lake, Ind.: Light and Life Press.

Demaray, D. E. (1976). Alive to God through praise. BOOK, Winona Lake, Ind.: Light and Life Press.

Demaray, D. E. (1978). Near hurting people : the pastoral ministry of Robert Moffat Fine. BOOK, Winona Lake, Ind.: Light and Life Press.

Demaray, D. E. (1985). The people called Free Methodist : snapshots. BOOK, Winona Lake, Ind.: Light and Life Press.

Demaray, D. E. (1990). An introduction to homiletics. BOOK, Indianapolis, Ind.: Light and Life Press.

Demaray, D. E. (1995). Laughter, joy and healing. BOOK, Indianapolis, Ind.: Light and Life Press.

Demaray, D. E., & Sun Liu, Y. (2009). Ji yao zhen li : Jidu jiao Weisili zong shen xue jian jie. BOOK, Gaoxiong Shi: Sheng guang shen xue yuan.

Demaray, K. (1965). Train up a child. BOOK, Winona Lake, IN: Light and Life Press.

DeMille, L. (1966). Black Gold : a story of Mozambique and Transvaal. BOOK, Winona Lake, Ind.: Light and Life Press.

DeMille, L. (1987). Prairie rose. BOOK, Winona Lake, IN: Light and Life Press.

DeMille, L., Hill, D., Abbott, G., Payne, P., & America, F. M. C. of N. (1984). Stories from Southern Africa. BOOK, Winona lake, Ind.: Light and Life Press.

Deratany, E. (1988). When God calls you. BOOK, Winona Lake, Ind.: Light and Life Press.

Deratany, E. (2007). Why fear? freedom from fear in the secret place. SOUND, Winona Lake, IN: Light and Life Press.

Drury, K. W., & Drury, S. (1979). Children as learners. BOOK, Winona Lake, Ind.: Light and Life Press.

Duewel, W. L. (1974). The Holy Spirit and tongues. BOOK, Winona Lake, Ind.: Light and Life Press.

Earle, R. (1961). Matthew : leader's guide. BOOK, Winona Lake, Ind.: Light and Life Press.

Earle, R. (1965a). Ezekial, Haggai, Zechariah : leader's guide. BOOK, Winona Lake, Ind.: Light and Life Press.

Earle, R. (1965b). Ezekiel, Haggai, Zechariah : study guide. BOOK, Winona Lake, Ind.: Light and Life Press.

Easton, J. B. (n.d.). The baptism and indwelling of the Holy Ghost,. BOOK, Chicago: Light and life Press.

Embree, E. (1973). Chikombedzi : a missionary wife writes home. BOOK, Winona Lake, Ind.: Light and Life Press.

Evangel. (n.d.). JFULL, Winona Lake, IN: Light and Life Press.

Evangelicals, N. A. of, & Commission, E. E. (1957). New churches for a new America. BOOK, Winona Lake, Ind.: Light and Life Press.

Failing, G. E. (1963). I Corinthians : leader's guide. BOOK, Winona Lake, Ind.: Light and Life Press.

Fairbairn, C. (1946). ... God's plan for world evangelism,. BOOK, Winona Lake Ind.: Light and Life Press.

Fairbairn, C. V. (1947). A primer in evangelism : new "Secret of true revival", specially revised, rechaptered and rewritten by the author for service training course 134A, "Evangelism in the local church." BOOK, Winona Lake, Ind.: Light and Life Press.

Fairbairn, C. V. (1943). "Tarry ye" : with other sermons and studies. BOOK, Winona Lake, Ind.: Light and Life Press.

Fairbairn, C. V. (1957). What we believe : a brief manual of Christian doctrine for young Free Methodists and new converts based upon the catechism and articles of religion of the Free Methodist Church of North America. BOOK, Winona Lake, IN: Light and Life Press.

Fairbarn, C. V. (1960). I call to remembrance. BOOK, Winona Lake, Ind.: Light and Life Press.

Fear, L. K. (1979). New ventures : Free Methodist missions, 1960-1979. BOOK, Winona Lake, Ind.: Light and Life Press.

Fields, W. W. (1973). Unformed and unfilled : a critique of the gap theory of Genesis 1:1,2 (THES). Light and Life Press, Winona Lake, Ind.

Fine, R. M. (1976). Great todays, better tomorrows. BOOK, Winona Lake, Ind.: Light and Life Press.

Fink, N. W., Lutz, J. B., & Rose, W. B. (1924). Inspirational songs for the Sunday school, social worship, missionary and evangelistic work. MUSIC, Chicago: Light and Life Press.

Finley, H. E. (1961). I and II Samuel (and related Chronicles passages) : leader's guide. BOOK, Winona Lake, Ind.: Light and Life Press.

Finley, H. E. (1964). Zephaniah, Nahum, Habakkuk, Obadiah, Daniel : leader's guide. BOOK, Winona Lake, Ind.: Light and Life Press.

Ford, G. L. (1976). All the money you need. BOOK, Winona Lake, Ind.: Light and Life Press.

Ford, G. L. (1985). Like a tree planted : the life story of Leslie Ray Marston. BOOK, Winona Lake, Ind.: Light and Life Press.

Free Methodist Church of North America. (n.d.). Free Methodist ministries today. JFULL, Indianapolis, IN: Light and Life Press.

Free Methodist Church of North America. (1960). God made a colorful world. BOOK, Winona Lake, Ind.: Light and Life Press.

Free Methodist Church of North America, & Commission on Christian Education. (n.d.). Concepts in Christian education. BOOK, Winona Lake, Ind.: Light and Life Press.

Free Methodist Church of North America, & General Conference. (n.d.). General Conference today. JFULL, Winona Lake, IN: Light and Life Press.

Free Methodist Church of North America, & General Missionary Board. (1974). Missions quinquennial report. JFULL, Winona Lake, Ind.: Light and Life Press.

Free Methodist Church of North America, & Home Ministries. (n.d.). Free Methodist ministries update. JFULL, Indianapolis, IN: Light and Life Press.

Galbreath, M. (1970). 20 centuries of Christianity. Winona Lake IN: Light and Life Press.

Galbreath, M. L. (1962). James and Peter : leader's guide. BOOK, Winona Lake, Ind.: Light and Life Press.

Gaylord, M. L. (1976). Tender heart. BOOK, Winona Lake, In.: Light and Life Press.

Gear, F. B. (1955). Book Review: Peloubet's Select Notes on the International Bible Lessons for Christian Teaching, Uniform Series, 1955, by Wilbur M. Smith. W. A. Wilde Co., Boston. 473; The Douglass Sunday School Lessons, 1955, by Earl L. Douglass. The Macmillan. Interpretation: A Journal of Bible and Theology Interpretation: A Journal of Bible and Theology, 9(2), 235–236. JOUR.

Gilmore, A. (1964). Treasure in the Dominican. BOOK, Winona Lake, IN: Light and Life Press.

Godfroy, C., & McClurg, M. U. (1961). Miami Indian stories. BOOK, Winona Lake, Ind.: Light and Life Press.

Griffith, L. B., & Griffith, G. W. (1937). Living embers : the life and writings of George William Griffith. BOOK, Winona Lake, IN: Light and Life Press.

Hall, B. H. (1962). Job : leader's guide. BOOK, Winona Lake, Ind.: Light and Life Press.

Harvey, J. D. (1973). Dimensions in Christian living. BOOK, Winona Lake, Ind.: Light and Life Press.

Harvey, J. D. (1979). The Wesleyan way today. BOOK, Winona Lake, Ind.: Light and Life Press.

Haslam, R. B. (1977). Peepholes on life : 44 fun looks at the serious side of life. BOOK, Winona Lake, Ind.: Light and Life Press.

Hawley, D., & Hardy, J. (1980). Living water, living letter : Free Methodist missions in Egypt and India. BOOK, Winona Lake, IN: Light and Life Press.

Heer, K., Hubbard, M., & Dymale, M. (1980). Open letters from a Roman prison : Philippians/Colossians/Philemon : study guide. BOOK, Winona Lake, Ind.: Published for the Aldersgate Publications Association by Light and Life Press.

Helms, E. E. (1923). God in history. BOOK, Chicago, IL: Light and Life Press.

Helsel, E. W. (1965). Timothy, Titus : leader's guide. BOOK, Winona Lake, Ind.: Light and Life Press.

Hilson, J. B. (1950). History of the South Carolina Conference of Wesleyan Methodist Church of America; fifty-five years of Wesleyan Methodism in South Carolina. BOOK, Winona Lake, Indiana: Light and life Press.

Hockett, B., & Abbott, G. (1977). Life changing learning for children : resources that work. BOOK, Winona Lake, Ind.: Light and Life Press.

Hodson, O., America., F. M. C. of N., & International., W. M. (1990). Free to choose : lessons from the Gospel of John. BOOK, Winona Lake, Ind.: printed for Women's Ministries International by Light and Life Press.

Hoffer, M. (1982). George Poore (1723-1810) and descendants. BOOK, Winona Lake, IN: Light and Life Press.

Hogue, W. T. (1932). Hymns that are immortal : with some account of their authorship, origin, history and influence. BOOK, Chicago, Ill.: Light and Life Press.

Holdren, D. W. (1986). The power to become : I, II, III John, Jude ; study guide. BOOK, Winona Lake, Ind.: Published for Aldersgate Publications by Light and Life Press.

Horton, C. A. (1980). Money counts : a handbook on local church finance. BOOK, Winona Lake, IN: Light and Life Press.

Houser, G. (1969). Boadi and Tembi of Africa's grasslands. BOOK, Winona Lake, Ind.: Light and Life Press.

Houser, G., Johnson, J., & Church, H. (1978). Adventures in Africa's grasslands : stories from Southern Africa. BOOK, Winona Lake, Ind.: Light and Life Press.

Howell, R. W. (1965). Christian family : a symposium. BOOK, Winona Lake, Ind.: Light and Life Press.

Hoyer, J. (1984). Life-changing learning for adults : resources that work. BOOK, Winona Lake, Ind.: Light and Life Press.

Huffman, J. A. (1939). The Messianic hope in both Testaments. BOOK, Winona Lake, IN: Light and Life Press.

Huffman, J. A. (1944). The Holy Spirit. BOOK, Butler, Ind.: Higley Press.

Huffman, J. A. (1948). The stones cry out. BOOK, Winona Lake, Ind.: Light and Life Press.

Huffman, J. A. (1951a). Building the home Christian. BOOK, Winona Lake, Ind.: Light and Life Press.

Huffman, J. A. (1951b). Golden treasures from the Greek New Testament for English readers. BOOK, Winona Lake, IN: Light and Life Press.

James, J. F. (1987). On the front lines : a guide to Church planting. BOOK, Winona Lake, Ind.: Light and Life Press.

James, J. F., Free Methodist Church of North America, & General Conference. (2008). Our calling to the poor. BOOK, Indianapolis, Ind.: Light and Life Press.

Jessop, H. E. (1942). That burning question of final perseverance. BOOK, Winona Lake, Ind.: Light and Life Press.

Jessop, H. E. (1956). I met a man with a shining face : an autobiography in the things of God. BOOK, Winona Lake, Ind.: Light and Life Press.

Johnson, C. E. (1969). How in the world? BOOK, Winona Lake, Ind.: Light and Life Press.

Johnson, H. F. (1939). Heroes of other lands. BOOK, Winona Lake, IN: Light and Life Press.

Joy, D. M. (1960). Aldersgate Biblical series. BOOK, Winona Lake, Ind.: Light and Life Press.

Joy, D. M. (1962). Psalms : leader's guide. BOOK, Winona Lake, Ind.: Light and Life Press.

Joy, D. M. (1965). The Holy Spirit and you : leadership and service training/series. BOOK, Winona Lake, Ind.: Light and Life Press.

Joy, D. M., & Association, A. P. (1969). Meaningful learning in the church. BOOK, Winona Lake, Ind.: Light and Life Press.

Kaub, V. P. (1946). Collectivism challenges Christianity. BOOK, Winona Lake, Ind.: Light and Life Press.

Kaufmann, U. M. (1981). Heaven : a future finer than dreams. BOOK, Winona Lake, Ind.: Light and Life Press.

Kendall, W. S. (1964). That the world may know. BOOK, Winona Lake, Ind.: Light and Life Press.

Kerby, R. A. (1949). A shuffling theology. BOOK, Winona Lake, IN: Light and Life Press.

Kettinger, L., & Stonehouse, C. (1983). Youth as learners. BOOK, Winona Lake, Ind.: Light and Life Press.

Keys, C. E., & Todd, P. H. (1965). Christian youth looks at evolution : ... Bible exploration guide of the Christian youth camper curriculum. BOOK. Winona Lake, In.: Light and life Press.

King, W. (1977). The joy of ministry : my role in Christian education. BOOK, Winona Lake, Ind.: Light and Life Press.

Kirkpatrick, C. D., & Church, W. M. S. of the F. M. (1977). Cow in the clinic, and other missionary stories from around the world. BOOK, Winona Lake, Ind.: Light and Life Press.

Kirkpatrick, C. D., & Free Methodist Church of North America. (1971). Profile of missions. BOOK, Winona Lake, Ind.: Light and Life Press.

Kleinsteuber, R. W. (1980). Coming of age : the making of a Canadian Free Methodist Church. BOOK, Hamilton, Ont.: Light and Life Press, Canada.

Kleinsteuber, R. W. (1984). More than a memory : the renewal of Methodism in Canada. BOOK, Mississauga, Ont.: Light and Life Press Canada.

Kline, G. E., College, M. C. of G., & Greenville, I. (1942). The Wesleyan message bearing fruit. BOOK, Winona Lake, Ind.: Light and Life Press.

Knox, L. H. (1963). Philippians and Thessalonians : leader's guide. BOOK, Winona Lake, Ind.: Light and Life Press.

Knox, L. H. (1970). Security for believers. BOOK, Winona Lake, Ind.: Light and Life Press.

Knox, L. H. (1972). Key to holiness theology : a relational understanding. BOOK, Winona Lake, Ind.: Light and Life Press.

Knox, L. H. (1974). Key Biblical perspectives on tongues. BOOK, Winona Lake, Ind.: Light and Life Press.

Knox, L. H. (1976a). Everybody wants your money : how to be generous, not gullible. BOOK, Winona Lake, Ind.: Light and Life Press.

Knox, L. H. (1976b). The Free Methodist minister. BOOK, Winona Lake, Ind.: Light and Life Press.

Knox, L. H. (1977). A faith to grow. BOOK, Winona Lake, IN: Light and Life Press.

Kuhn, H. B. (1966). Colossians, Philemon : leader's guide. BOOK, Winona Lake, Ind.: Light and Life Press.

Lamb, E. W., & Shultz, L. W. (1964). Indian lore. BOOK, Winona Lake, Ind.: Light and Life Press.

Lamson, B. S. (1950). The holiness teachings of New Testament literature : part I: the teachings of Jesus. BOOK, Winona Lake, Ind.: Light and Life Press.

Lamson, B. S. (1960). Venture! : the frontiers of Free Methodism. BOOK, Winona Lake, Ind.: Light and Life Press.

Lamson, B. S. (1987). Greater works than these. BOOK, Winona Lake, Ind.: Light and Life Press.

Leech, K. (1995). Dark providence, bright promise. BOOK, Indianapolis: Light and Life Press.

Lewis, M. E. (1900). The invisible railway. BOOK, Winona Lake, Ind.: Light and Life Press.

Lieby, R. J. (1960). Here's your answer! BOOK, Winona Lake, Ind.: Published by Light and Life Press for the Forward Movement of the Free Methodist Church.

Light and life junior. (n.d.). Light and Life Junior. JFULL, Winona, Lake, Ind.: Light and Life Press.

Light and Life Press. (n.d.). The Junior's friend. The Junior's Friend. JFULL, Chicago, IL: Light and Life Press.

Lincicome, F. (n.d.). The doubles of the Bible. BOOK, Atlanta, GA: Repairer Pub. Co.

Lincicome, F. (1932a). A lot in Sodom. BOOK, Winona Lake, Ind.: Light and Life Press.

Lincicome, F. (1932b). The three D's of the sanctified. BOOK, Winona Lake, Ind.: Light and life Press.

Lincicome, F. (1933). What is your life? BOOK, Chicago, Ill.: Light and life Press.

Lincicome, F. (1934). Enemies of the home. BOOK, Winona Lake, IN: Light and Life Press.

Lincicome, F. (1935). A tribute to mothers. BOOK.

Lincicome, F. (1936). Prayer. BOOK, Winona Lake, Ind.: Light and Life Press.

Linton, J. (1947a). From coalpit to pulpit : an informal autobiography. BOOK, NI: Light and Life Press.

Linton, J. (1947b). Tears in heaven : and other sermons. BOOK, SI: Light and Life Press.

Livermore, H. E. (1962). Psalms. BOOK, Winona Lake, Ind.: Light and Life Press.

Livermore, P. (1982). Resources for renewal : Romans study guide. BOOK, Winona Lake, IN: Light and Life Press.

Livermore, P. (1995). The God of our salvation : Christian theology from the Wesleyan perspective. BOOK, Indianapolis, IN: Light and Life Press.

Living hymns of Charles Wesley. The singing saint. (1957). BOOK, Winona Lake, Ind.: Light and Life Press.

Livingston, G. H. (1960a). Genesis. BOOK, Winona Lake, Ind.: Light and Life Press.

Livingston, G. H. (1960b). God's spokesman. BOOK, Winona Lake, IN: Light and Life Press.

Livingston, G. H. (1960c). Roots of the Church in the Old Testament. BOOK, Winona Lake, IN: Light and Life Press.

Livingston, G. H. (1971). Genesis : leader's guide. BOOK, Winona Lake, Ind.: Light and Life Press.

Livingston, G. H. (1981a). Origins of life and faith : Genesis A : study guide. BOOK. Winona Lake, Ind.: Light and Life Press.

Livingston, G. H. (1981b). Trial and triumph : Genesis B, study guide. BOOK, Winona Lake, Ind.: Light and Life Press.

Livingstone, G. H. (1963). Jeremiah, Lamentations : leader's guide. BOOK, Winona Lake, Ind.: Light and Life Press.

Livingstone, G. H. (1964). Jeremiah-B and Lamentations. BOOK, Winona Lake, Ind.: Light and Life Press.

Lois Evelyn Worbois. (n.d.).

Loss, M. (1983). Culture shock : dealing with stress in cross-cultural living. BOOK, Winona Lake, Ind.: Light and Life Press.

Lovell, O. D. (1962). Ephesians : leader's guide. BOOK, Winona Lake, Ind.: Light and Life Press.

Lowell, L. M. (1939). Building the house beautiful : a study in personal religious living. BOOK, Winona Lake, Ind.: Light and Life Press.

Macy, V. W., & DeMille, L. (1984). Discovery under the Southern Cross : below the equator--missions adventures in Mozambique and South Africa. BOOK, Winona Lake, Ind.: Light and Life Press.

Mannoia, F., & Huston, L. (1979). Amigos. BOOK, Winona Lake, Ind.: Light and Life Press.

Mannoia, K. W. (1994). Church planting : the next generation : introducing the Century 21 Church Planting System. BOOK, Indianapolis, IN: Light and Life Press.

Mannoia, K. W. (1996). Church planting : the next generation : Century 21 Network, leader's manual. BOOK, Indianapolis, IN: Light and Life Press.

Markell, D. (1981). Expanded ministry to youth : program guidelines. BOOK, Winona Lake, IN: Light and Life Press.

Markell, D. (1981). Origins of life and faith : Genesis a leader's guide. BOOK, Winona Lake, Ind.: Light and Life Press.

Markell, D., Cleveland, A., & America, F. M. C. of N. (1978). Young teen organizational manual. BOOK, Winona Lake, Ind.: Light and Life Press.

Markell, D., Cleveland, A., Free Methodist Church of North America, & America., F. M. C. of N. (1977). FMY organizational manual. BOOK, Winona Lake, Ind.: Light and Life Press.

Markley, R., Vandenberg, J., & Yoder, G. (1986). Ancestors and descendants of Thomas Bays Nelson and Frances Miller. BOOK, Winona Lake, Ind.: Light and Life Press.

Marston, C. D. (1940). Life is for that. BOOK, Winona Lake, In.: Printed for the author by Light and Life Press.

Marston, L. R. (1939). Youth speaks! BOOK, Winona Lake, Ind.: Light and life Press.

Marston, L. R. (1944). From chaos to character, a study in the stewardship of personality. BOOK, Winona Lake, Ind.: Light and life Press.

Marston, L. R. (1946). "I need a chart." BOOK, Winona Lake, Ind.: Published for The National Association of Evangelicals by courtesy of Light and Life Press.

Marston, L. R. (1960). From age to age a living witness; a historical interpretation of Free Methodism's first century. BOOK, Winona Lake, Ind.: Light and Life Press.

Marston, L. R. (1965). The river of spiritual life. BOOK, Winona Lake, Ind.: Light and Life Press.

Marston, L. R. (1979). He lived on our street : enduring words for today. BOOK, Winona Lake, Ind.: Light and Life Press.

Marston, L. R., & Free Methodist Church of North America. (1949). Your bishops speak. BOOK, Winona Lake, IN: Light and Life Press.

Martin, C., & Hoyer, J. (1987). Guidelines for service : I, II Timothy Titus study guide. BOOK, Winona Lake, Indiana: Light and Life Press.

Mason, H. C. (1960). The teaching task of the local church. BOOK, Winona Lake, Ind.: Light and Life Press.

Mason, H. C., & National Sunday School Association. (1946). Reclaiming the Sunday school. The Sunday school. JFULL, Winona Lake, Ind.: Light and Life Press.

Mavis, W. C. (1957). Advancing the smaller local church. BOOK, Winona Lake, Ind.: Light and Life Press.

Mavis, W. C. (1958). Beyond conformity. BOOK, Winona Lake, Ind.: Light and life Press.

Mavis, W. C. (1977). The Holy Spirit in the Christian life. BOOK, Winona Lake, Ind.: Light and Life Press.

Mayse, P. T. (1987). Confronting in love : I and II Corinthians ; study guide. BOOK, Winona Lake, Ind.: Published for Aldersgate Publications by Light and Life Press.

McAllaster, E. (1954). My heart hears heaven's reveille. BOOK, Winona Lake, Ind.: Light and Life Press.

McConnell, L. G. (1946). Faith victorious in the Kentucky mountains : the story of twenty-two years of spirit-filled ministry. BOOK, Winona Lake, Ind.: Printed for the author by Light and Life Press.

McCutchen, R. (1986). Be strong and courageous : Joshua study guide. BOOK, Winona Lake, Ind.: Light and Life Press.

McDowell, A. (1940). The passion of our Lord : six service outlines and poster suggestions. BOOK, Winona Lake, Ind.: Light and Life Press.

McElhinney, R. S., & Smith, H. L. (1942). Personality and character building,. BOOK, Winona Lake, Ind.: Light and life Press.

McGhie, A. E. (1942). Loving talks to young Christians. BOOK, Winona Lake, Ind.: Printed by Light and Life Press for the author Anna E. McGhie.

McGhie, A. E. (1947). The miracle hand around the world. BOOK, Ft. Valley, Ga.: Printed for the author.

McKenna, D. L. (1977). Awake, my conscience. BOOK, Winona Lake, Ind.: Light and Life Press.

McKenna, D. L. (1995). A future with a history : the Wesleyan witness of the Free Methodist Church, 1960-1995. BOOK, Indianapolis, IN: Light and Life Press.

McKeown, M. E. (1962). This is how to teach. BOOK, Winona Lake, Ind.: Light and Life Press.

Miles, M. L. (1957). Quiet moments with God. BOOK, Winona Lake, IN: Light and Life Press.

Mortenson, A. H. (1954). Knee-deep in snow and other poems. BOOK, Winona Lake, In.: Light and Life Press.

Mottweiler, J. H. (1984). Adults as learners. BOOK, Winona Lake, Ind.: Light and Life Press.

Munn, N. P., & Perkins, N. (1982). Dear folks : letters from Nahum Perkins, missionary to the Caribbean. BOOK, Winona Lake, Ind.: Light and Life Press.

Nelson, R. S., America, F. M. C. of N., & Education, C. on C. (1963). Here's the answer : a handbook for Sunday-school workers. BOOK, Winona Lake, IN: Light and Life Press.

Northrup, L. W. (1973). Ancient mirrors for modern churches : a study of the seven churches of the book of Revelation relating them to the church in modern society. BOOK, Winona Lake, IN: Light and Life Press.

Northrup, L. W. (1988). Ambassadors for Christ : the story of Free Methodism in Northern Ireland. BOOK.

Olmstead, B. L. (1938). A brief life of Paul, with a chart and six maps. BOOK, Winona Lake, Ind.: Light and Life Press.

Olmstead, B. L. (1942). Three types of eternal security : a simple and clear discussion of a doctrine which, in various forms, is being widely propagated at the present time. BOOK, Winona Lake, Ind.: Light and Life Press.

Olmstead, B. L. (1951). Arnold's practical commentary on the International Sunday school lessons, improved uniform series. JFULL, Winona Lake, Ind.: Light and Life Press.

Olmstead, B. L. (1960). Arnold's practical commentary on the International Sunday School lessons uniform series for 1952 : a practical help for all who use the unform lesson in the Sunday School, or who desire to do individual Bible study. There are ample explanatory notes ... BOOK, Winona Lake, Ind. Light and Life Press.

Olmstead, W. B., & Harris, T. (1928). Light and life songs : no. 4, for the Sunday school, social worship, missionary and evangelistic work. MUSIC, Chicago: Light and Life Press.

Olver, P. S. (1986). A strategy for urban church planting for the Free Methodist Church of North America (THES).

Parsons, E. E. (1967). Witness to the resurrection. BOOK, Winona Lake, Ind.: Light and Life Press.

Parsons, E. E., & Oswalt, J. N. (1990). Living the holy life today. BOOK, Indianapolis, Ind.: Light and Life Press.

Payne, P. (1984). Teaching for life-changing learning. BOOK, Winona Lake, Ind.: Light and Life Press.

Pearce, B. W. (1900). Our incarnate Lord. BOOK, Chicago, Ill.: Light and Life Press.

Pearce, W. (1935). Worship in song : an all purpose song book for use in the church but especially adapted for use in the Sunday school, missionary, young people's & evangelistic services. MUSIC, Winona Lake, Ind.: Light and Life Press.

Pearce, W. (1945). The preacher and his reading. BOOK, Winona Lake, Ind.: Light and Life Press.

Pearson, B. H. (1937). The lost generation returns. BOOK, Winona Lake, Ind.: Light and Life Press.

Pearson, B. H. (1940). Next! Our Sunday-School quest in South America : a "Caleb-Joshua" story of the expedition of "The spies" sent forth by the "Birthday pennies for South America fund" into the lands "Beyond the Amazon." BOOK, Winona Lake, Ind.: Light and life Press.

Pearson, B. H. (1940). The monk who lived again; a tale of South America. BOOK, Winona Lake, Ind.: Light and Life Press.

Pearson, B. H., Howland, J. H., Harper, M. W., & Root, H. I. (1938). Sunday evenings with Jesus : volume II. BOOK, Winona Lake, Ind.: Light and Life Press.

Phillips, R. M. (1940). Bird against the wind. BOOK, Winona Lake, Ind.: Light and Life Press.

Phillips, R. M. (1950). Journey by night. [Poems]. BOOK, Winona Lake, Ind.: Light and Life Press.

Pirie, M. (1955). The inseparables. BOOK, Wimona Lake, Ind.: Light and Life Press.

Press., L. and L. (1954). Hymns of the living faith. MUSIC, Winona Lake, Ind.: Light and Life Press.

Progressive men and women of Kosciusko County, Indiana and 1903 plat maps : illustrated, portraits of many well-known residents of Kosciusko County, Indiana. (1989). BOOK, Winona Lake, Ind.: Light and Life Press.

Purkiser, W. T. (1961). Leviticus, Deuteronomy : leader's guide. BOOK, Winona Lake, Ind.: Light and Life Press.

Purkiser, W. T. (1963). Joel, Jonah, Amos, Hosea, and Micah : leader's guide. BOOK, Winona Lake, Ind.: Light and Life Press.

R. B. Spencer papers. (1910). BOOK.

Rader, L. (1965). The Book of Books. BOOK, Winona Lake, Ind.: Light and Life Press.

Reynolds, M., & Abbott, G. (1978). Life changing learning for youth : resources that work. BOOK, Winona Lake, Ind.: Light and Life Press.

Reynolds, W. C. (1941). A flaming cross : a story of first century Christians. BOOK, Winona Lake, Ind.: Light and Life Press.

Rich, M. (1980). Hidden treasure : a missionary story from Haiti. BOOK, Winona Lake, Ind.: Light and Life Press.

Richardson, A. (1988). A heart for God in India. BOOK, Winona Lake, Ind.: Light and Life Press.

Richardson, A., & Leder, D. (2004). In grandma's attic. BOOK, Colorado Springs, CO: David C. Cook.

Richardson, A., & Secaur, E. (1988). Andrew's secret. BOOK, Winona Lake, Ind.: Light and Life Press.

Roberts, B. T. (1948). Fishers of men, or, Practical hints to those who would win souls. BOOK, Winona Lake, Ind.: Light and Life Press.

Roberts, B. T. (1960). Living truths. BOOK, Winona Lake, Ind.: Light and Life Press.

Roberts, B. T. (1992). Ordaining women. BOOK, Indianapolis, IN: Light and Life Press.

Roberts, B. T., & Demaray, D. E. (1996). The daily Roberts : readings for every day in the year from the writings of B.T. Roberts. BOOK, Indianapolis, IN: Light and Life Press.

Roberts, E. M. (1962). The bishop and his lady. BOOK, Winona Lake, Ind.: Light and Life Press.

Roller, D. T., Parker, J., & America, F. M. C. of N. (1985). Journey to Mexico. BOOK, Winona lake, Ind.: Light and Life Press.

Root, L. P. (1938). Patches : missionary life in India as seen by drawing of the dog Patches. BOOK, Winona Lake, Ind.: Light and Life Press.

Root, L. P., & Zahniser, A. (1971). Friends from the East. BOOK, Winona Lake, Ind.: Light and Life Press.

Rose, D. R. (1961). Hebrews : leader's guide. BOOK, Winona Lake, Ind.: Light and Life Press.

Rose, D. R. (1964). Epistles of John and Jude : leader's guide. BOOK, Winona Lake, Ind.: Light and Life Press.

Rose, D. R. (1967). Hebrews : study guide. BOOK, Winona Lake, Ind.: Light and Life Press.

Ross, I. M. (1984). Golden bells : poems and songs. BOOK, Winona Lake, Ind.: Light and Life Press.

Rowe, A. T. (1927). Ideals for earnest youth. BOOK, Chicago: Light and Life Press.

Russell, C. M. (1960). Giving our young people evangelism know how. BOOK, Winona Lake, Ind.: Light and Life Press.

Ryckman, L. D. (1979) Paid in full : the story of Harold Ryckman, missionary pioneer to Paraguay and Brazil. BOOK, Winona Lake, Ind.: Light and Life Press.

Sayre, G., & Williamson, G. (1974). On the brink. BOOK, Winona Lake, Ind.: Light and Life Press.

Scearce, M. (1988). Bless this house. BOOK, Winona Lake, IN: Light and Life Press.

Scherer, F. S. (1976). George and Mary Schlosser : ambassadors for Christ in China. BOOK, Winona Lake, Ind.: Light and Life Press.

Schlosser, R., & Groesbeck, G. H. (1956). Lighting the Philippine Frontier. BOOK, Winona Lake, Ind.: Light and Life Press.

Schoenhals, G. R. (1978). When trouble comes : How to find God's help in difficult times. BOOK, Winona Lake, Ind.: Light and Life Press.

Schoenhals, L. R. (1960). Light and Life choral arrangements. MUSIC, Winona Lake, IN: Light and Life Press.

Schoenhals, L. R., America., F. M. C. of N., & Church., W. (1980). Companion to hymns of faith and life. BOOK, Winona lake, Ind.: Light and Life Press.

Schoenhals, L. R., Church, W., & America, F. M. C. of N. (1976). Hymns of faith and life. BOOK, Winona Lake, Ind.; Marion, Ind.: Light and Life Press ; Wesley Press.

Schoenhals, L. R., Lowell, L. M., Schoenhals, L. R., Lowell, L. M., Schoenhals, L. R., & Lowell, L. M. (1950). Choice light and life songs : a collection of the best loved gospel songs and choruses, both old and new for the Sunday School, Young People's meeting, evangelistic service and children's service. MUSIC, Winona Lake, Ind.: Light and Life Press.

Sellew, W. A. (1928). Obligations of civilization to Christianity; or, The influence of Christianity upon civilization. BOOK, Chicago, Ill.: Light and Life Press.

Shelhamer, E. E., & Shelhamer, J. A. (1951). A spartan evangel : life story of E.E. Shelhamer. BOOK, Winona Lake, Ind.: Light and Life Press.

Shepherd, V. A. (1993). So great a cloud of witnesses. BOOK, Mississagua, Ont.: Light and Life Press Canada.

Shepherd, V. A., Canada, U. C. of, & Canada, D. of M. in. (1993). Ponder and pray : seven weeks of meditations and prayers for personal enrichment during any season of the year. BOOK, Mississauga: Light and Life Press.

Shultz, L. W. (1954). Schwarzenau yesterday and today : where the brethren began in Europe ; told in picture and story. BOOK, Winona Lake, Indiana: Light and Life Press.

Shultz, L. W. (1963). Paul family record, 1763-1963. BOOK, Winona Lake, Ind.: Printed by the Light and Life Press.

Shultz, L. W. (1966). Shultz family record, 1716-1966 : from Hesse-Darmstadt to Huntingdon and Hagerstown. BOOK, North Manchester, Ind.: Lawrence W. Shultz.

Shultz, L. W., & Taylor, H. E. (1963). Paul family records 1763-1963 ... including the 1917 record. BOOK, Winona Lake, Ind.: Printed by the Light and Life Press.

Sing His Praise. (1925). Camp meeting special : a selection of songs specially designed for use in camp meetings and other evangelistic campaigns. MUSIC, Chicago: Light and Life Press.

Sloan, H. P. (1942). He is risen. BOOK, Winona Lake, IN: Light and Life Press.

Smith, W. M. (1961). The incomparable Book : to guide you as you read it through. BOOK, Winona Lake, Ind.: Light and Life Press.

Snider, L. (1968). Snow Pearl, a girl of Japan. BOOK, Winona Lake, IN: Light and Life Press.

Snyder, H. A. (1981). Under construction : Ephesians study guide. BOOK, Indianapolis, IN: Light and Life Press.

Snyder, L. E., & Weidman, B. E. (1940). Servant of God : life story and selected articles of Bishop Arthur D. Zahniser. BOOK, Winona Lake, Ind.: Light and Life Press.

Spears, A. K., & Hinton, L. (2010). Languages and Speakers: An Introduction to African American English and Native American Languages. TRAA Transforming Anthropology, 18(1), 3–14. JOUR.

Stewart, E. E. (1961). Joshua, Judges, Ruth : leader's guide. BOOK, Winona Lake, Ind.: Light and Life Press.

Stonehouse, C. (1980). Adventures in Belonging : membership labs for young churchmen ; leader's guide. BOOK, Winona Lake, Ind.: Light and Life Press.

Stonehouse, C., & Joy, D. M. (1969). Leader's discussion guide. BOOK, Winona Lake, IN: Light and Life Press.

Stratton-Porter, G., Liechty, R., Cornwell, D., & Press, L. and L. (1986). Euphorbia. BOOK, Berne, IN: Liechty.

Suderman, J. P., Church, G. C. M., & Missions, C. on H. (1972). Hopi gospel songs; for church and street services in Hopi-Land. BOOK, Winona Lake, IN: Light and Life Press.

Sung, F., & Bastian, D. N. (1993). In the church and in Christ Jesus : essays in honour of Donald N. Bastian. BOOK, Mississauga, Ont.: Light and Life Press Canada.

Taylor, A. H. (1982). Rescued from the dragon : true accounts from China. BOOK, Winona Lake, Ind.: Light and Life Press.

Taylor, J. P. (1951). The music of Pentecost. BOOK, Winona Lake, Ind.: Light and life Press.

Taylor, J. P. (1960). Goodly heritage. BOOK, Winona Lake, Ind.: Light and Life Press.

Taylor, J. P. (1960). Soldiers of Christ. BOOK, Winona Lake, Ind.: Light and Life Press.

Taylor, J. P. (1963). Holiness, the finished foundation. BOOK, Winona Lake, Ind.: Light and Life Press.

Taylor, J. P. (1964). All roads lead to Bethlehem. BOOK, Winona Lake, Ind.: Light and Life Press.

Taylor, W. H. (1963). II Corinthians : leader's guide. BOOK, Winona Lake, Ind.: Light and Life Press.

Teaching beginners. (1953). JFULL, Winona Lake, Ind.: Light and Life Press.

Teaching juniors. (1953). JFULL, Winona, Lake, Ind.: Light and Life Press.

Teaching primaries. (1953). Teaching Primaries. JFULL, Winona Lake, Ind.: Light and Life Press.

Tenney, M. A. (1953). Blueprint for a Christian world; an analysis of the Wesleyan way. BOOK, Winona Lake, Indiana: Light and Life Press.

Tenney, M. A. (1958). Living in two worlds; how a Christian does it! BOOK, Winona Lake, Ind.: Light and Life Press.

Tenney, M. A. (1964). Adventures in Christian love. BOOK, Winona Lake, Ind.: Light and Life Press.

Thompson, F. H. (1963). Proverbs, Ecclesiastes, Song of Solomon : leader's guide. BOOK, Winona Lake, Ind.: Light and Life Press.

Thompson, W. R. (1961). The Gospel of John : book of proofs of the deity of Christ ; official Bible quiz text. BOOK, Winona Lake, Ind.: Light and Life Press.

Thompson, W. R. (1967). John : official quiz text. BOOK, Winona Lake, Ind.: Light and Life Press.

Thompson, W. R. (1992). The road to heaven : the way of holiness. BOOK, Indianapolis, IN: Light and Life Press.

Todd, P. H. (1961). Truth in action. BOOK, Winona Lake, Ind.: Light and Life Press.

Todd, P. H. (1963). Becoming a Christian : the beginning of a happy life. BOOK, Winona Lake, Ind.: Light and Life Press.

Tongue-speaking in historical perspective. (1990). BOOK, Indianapolis, IN: Light and Life Press.

Toole, I. N. (1939). Living or dead. BOOK, Winona Lake, IN: Light and Life Press

Tsuchiyama, T. (n.d.). Victory of the cross, or, An account of my trip in China. BOOK, Winona Lake, IN: Light and Life Press.

Tsuchiyama, T., & Olmstead, W. B. (1927). From darkness to light. BOOK, Chicago, IL: Light and Life Press.

Tsuchiyama, T., Richardson, A., & Kaneda, K. (1986). Love shining through : Tsuchiyama. BOOK, Winona Lake, IN: Light and Life Press.

Turner, G. A. (1952). The more excellent way : the Scriptural basis of the Wesleyan message (THES). Light and Life Press, Winona Lake, Ind.

Turner, G. A. (1959). Uesure shingaku no chushin mondai (THES).

Turner, G. A. (1962). John : study guide. BOOK, Winona Lake, Ind.: Light and Life Press.

Turner, G. A. (1964). Revelation : leader's guide. BOOK, Winona Lake, Ind.: Light and Life Press.

Turner, G. A. (1966a). Ezra, Nehemiah, Esther, Malachi. BOOK, Winona Lake, Ind.: Light and Life Press.

Turner, G. A. (1966b). Isaiah : leader's guide. BOOK, Winona Lake, Ind.: Light and Life Press.

Turner, G. A. (1966c). Isaiah -- A : first of two units. BOOK, Winona Lake, Ind.: Light and Life Press.

Van Valin, C. E. (1990a). Tithing : God's plan for the church. BOOK, Indianapolis, IN.: Light and Life Press.

Van Valin, C. E. (1990b). Transforming grace : a biblical guide for holy living. BOOK, Indianapolis, Ind.: Light and Life Press.

Van Valin, C. E. (1991). Pastor's handbook. BOOK, Board of Bishops, Free Methodist Church (USA).

Van Valin, F. (1963). Mark : leader's guide. BOOK, Winona Lake, Ind.: Light and Life Press.

Van Valin, W. B. (1913). Little white girl in Eskimo land. BOOK, Winona Lake, Ind.: Light and Life Press.

Vore, E. (1972). Mud pies. BOOK, Winona Lake, Ind.: Light and Life Press.

Walls, F. E. (1980). The church library workbook : how to start and maintain the church library. BOOK, Winona Lake, Ind.: Light and Life Press.

Walters, O. S. (1939). Christian education in the local church. BOOK, Winona Lake, IN: Light and Life Press.

Walters, O. S. (1951). You can win others; how to adventure in sharing the good news. BOOK, Winona Lake, Ind.: Light and Life Press.

Walters, S. D. (1961a). Exodus, Numbers : leader's guide. BOOK, Winona Lake, Ind.: Light and Life Press.

Walters, S. D. (1961b). Exodus - Numbers : study guide. BOOK, Winona Lake, Ind.: Light and Life Press.

Ward, E. E., America., F. M. C. of N., Free Methodist Church of North America, & America., F. M. C. of N. (1951). Ordered steps, or, The Wards of India : a biography of the lives of Ernest Fremont Ward and Phebe Elizabeth Cox Ward, missionaries to India, 1880-1927. BOOK, Winona Lake, Ind.: Light and Life Press.

Warner, D. S. (1925). The anointing of the Holy Spirit. BOOK, Chicago, Ill.: Light and Life Press.

Warrington, J. M. (1981). The Humpty Dumpty syndrome. BOOK, Winona Lake, Ind.: Light and Life Press.

Watson, C. A. (1945). Repeal has succeeded,. BOOK, Winona Lake, Ind.: Pub. by Light and life Press.

Watson, C. A. (1946). God's plan for civil government. BOOK, Winona Lake, Ind.: Light and Life Press.

Watson, C. H. (1946a). Light and Life Scripture memory plan for Christian workers. BOOK, Winona Lake, IN: Light and Life Press.

Watson, C. H. (1946b). Light and Life scripture memory plan for Christian workers : a series of pocket-kits of selected scripture verses chosen to be hidden in the heart for ready use. BOOK, Winona Lake, Ind.: Light and Life Press.

Watson, C. H. (1950). De Shazer : Doolittle Raider Turned Missionary. BOOK, The Light and Life Press.

Watson, C. H. (1950). De Shazer : the Doolittle raider who turned missionary. BOOK, Winona Lake, Ind.: Light and Life Press.

Watson, C. H. (1950). De Shazer, the Doolittle raider who turned missionary : a true and thrilling story of how the practical demonstration of the law of love is bringing international understanding and the spirit of Christ to Japan. BOOK, Winona Lake, Ind.: Light and Life Press.

Watson, C. H. (1998). DeShazer. BOOK, Coquitlam, B.C., Canada: Galaxy Communications.

Watson, C. H., & Fear, L. K. (1972). De Shazer. BOOK, Winona Lake, Ind.: Light and Life Press.

Watson, C. H., & Howell, R. W. (1964a). Advancing in church membership : Pastor's instruction series, youth division. BOOK, Winona Lake, Ind.: Light and Life Press.

Watson, C. H., & Howell, R. W. (1964b). Exploring church membership : pastor's instruction series, junior division. BOOK, Winona Lake Indiana: Light and Life Press.

We believe! : insights into the beliefs of Free Methodists. (1976). BOOK, Winona Lake, Ind.: Light and Life Press.

Welliver, D. (1975). I need you now, God, while the grape juice is running all over the floor. BOOK, Winona Lake, Ind.: Light and Life Press.

Welliver, D. (1976). Thank you, God, for ninety-five pounds of peanut butter. BOOK, Winona Lake, Ind.: Light and Life Press.

Welliver, D. (1978). Some of God's miracles wear cowlicks. BOOK, Winona Lake, In.: Warner Press; Light and Life Press.

Welliver, D. (1979). Dorsey's diary : her daze ["X"-figure marked through word] days and yours. BOOK, Winona Lake, Ind.: Light and Life Press.

Wesley, J. (n.d.). A plain account of Christian perfection. BOOK, Winona Lake, Ind.: Light and Life Press.

Wesleyan Church, & Crusaders, C. Y. (1970). Herald highways. BOOK, Winona Lake, Ind.: Light and Life Press.

Wesleyan Church Department of Youth, & Youth. (1969). First studies in Christian teachings. BOOK, Winona Lake, Ind.: Light and Life Press.

Whitcomb, A. L. (1900). Emmanuel and stepping stones to union with God. BOOK, Winona Lake, Ind.: Light and Life Press.

Whiteman, J. H. (1920). Amen hallelujah. BOOK, Winona Lake, Ind.: Light and Life Press.

Wilder, J. E. (1974). The descendants of Harvey Wilder and his ancestors to 1485 in England : with a history of the Wilder name and related families of Warner, Barnhard, Benedict, Hepworth, Poore, Crocker, and Newman. BOOK, Winona Lake, Ind.: Printed by Light and Life Press.

Willard, F. B. (1985). Idol of clay. BOOK, Winona Lake, Ind.: Light and Life Press.

Williamson, G. (1969). Julia : giantess in generosity ; the story of Julia Arnold Shelhamer. BOOK, Winona Lake, Ind.: Light and Life Press.

Williamson, G. (1972). Frank and Hazel : the Adamsons of Kibogora. BOOK, Winona Lake, IN: Light and Life Press.

Williamson, G. (1974). Geneva : the fascinating story of Geneva Sayre, missionary to the Chinese. BOOK, Winona Lake, Ind.: Light and Life Press.

Williamson, G. (1976). Gonzalo of Mexican missions. BOOK, Winona Lake, Ind.: Light and Life Press.

Williamson, G. (1977). Brother Kawabe. BOOK, Winona Lake, Ind.: Light and Life Press.

Winslow, C. V. V. (1981). By love compelled : life story. BOOK, Winona Lake, Ind.: Light and Life Press.

Winslow, R. (1984). The mountains sing : God's love revealed to Taiwan tribes. BOOK, Winona Lake, Ind.: Light and Life Press.

Winters, P. (1954). Lab brevities. BOOK, Winona Lake, Ind.: Light and Life Press.

Wood, J. A., & Adell, W. R. (1927). El perfecto amor : una explicaciÃ3n de la doctrina, la experienca, la profesiÃ3n y la practica de la santidid Cristiana. BOOK, Chiquimula, Guatemala: Mision de Los Amigos.

Woods, D. A. (1984). East Michigan's great adventure : a history of the East Michigan Conference of the Free Methodist Church, 1884-1984. BOOK, [Place of publication not identified]: East Michigan Conference of the Free Methodist Church.

Woodworth, R. (1978). Light in a dark place : the story of Chicago's oldest rescue mission. BOOK, Winona Lake, Ind.: Light and Life Press.

Worbois, L. E. (1977). The thorn. BOOK, Winona Lake, Ind.: Light and Life Press.

Yoder, T., Smidderks, D., Free Methodist Church of North America, Department of Christian Education, Department of World Missions, & Women's Missionary Fellowship International. (1987). The great discovery. BOOK, Winona Lake, Ind.: Light and Life Press.

Young, C. (1991). Seeds for life: a guide for new believers, leaders guide. BOOK, Winona Lake, IN: Light and Life Press.

Recent Publications (Last 10 Years)

Adams, P. L. (2014). The lessons I've learned in politics. ELEC. Retrieved from http://place.asburyseminary.edu/ecommonsatschapelservices/

Andrews, E. A. (1926). Reminiscent musings. BOOK, Spring Arbor MI: E.A. Andrews.

Andrews, E. A. (2005). Musings on self-deception. BOOK, Chicago, Ill.: Charles Edwin Jones.

Arksey, L. (2011). A mission boyhood in Mozambique. BOOK, S.l.: Tornado Creek.

Azusa Pacific University Graduate School of Theology, Free Methodist Center for Transformational Leadership, & Winslow, K. S. (2013). The Free Methodist newsletter. JFULL, Azusa, Calif.: Azusa Pacific University Graduate School of Theology.

Bai, Z. (2005). Ran dian yi sheng : zhang zhe shi feng shi kuang yu xin dong xiang, Xianggang Xun li hui zhang zhe shi gong yan jiu. BOOK, Xianggang: Jidu jiao zhuo yue shi tuan.

Bastian, D. N., & Free Methodist Church of North America. (2008). Give it a rest. BOOK, Indianapolis, Ind.: Light and Life Communications.

Bates, G., Snyder, H. A., & Marston Memorial Historic Center. (2007). Soul searching the church : Free Methodism at 150 years. BOOK, Indianapolis, Ind.: Light & Life Communications.

Baym, N. (2011). A History of American Women's Western Books, 1833-1928, 63–80. JOUR.

Bowell, G. (2014). Reflections and thoughts on a hymnal : The 1910 Free Methodist hymnal. BOOK, Gary E. Bowell.

Chauke, H. W. M., & Houser, T. (2009). H.M. Chauke research of African Hlengwe people. BOOK.

Climenhaga, G. G., & Mercer, J. (2010). The call was clear : superintendents of the Free Methodist Church in the Canadian prairie provinces, 1901-1995. BOOK, Canada.

Coates, G. R. (2015). Politics strangely warmed : political theology in the Wesleyan spirit. BOOK, Eugene, Ore.: Wipf & Stock Publishers.

Cook, E. D. (2005). Salt of the sea : a Navy chaplain's experience ashore and at sea. BOOK, Longwood, Fla.: Xulon Press.

Cook, E. D. (2010). Chaplaincy : being God's presence in closed communities : a Free Methodist history 1935-2010. BOOK, Bloomington, IN: AuthorHouse.

Coolen, J., & Thunder Bay Branch of Ontario Genealogical Society. (2009). O'Connor Free Methodist Cemetery : grave marker transcriptions, OGS #5737, O'Connor Township, Thunder Bay District, Ontario. BOOK, Thunder Bay, Ont.: Ontario Genealogical Society, Thunder Bay Branch.

Degen, H. (2013). The guide to holiness. GEN, Wilmore, Ky. : Asbury Theological Seminary,.

Demaray, D. E. (1990). An introduction to homiletics. BOOK, Indianapolis, Ind.: Light and Life Press.

Demaray, D. E., & Sun Liu, Y. (2009). Ji yao zhen li : Jidu jiao Weisili zong shen xue jian jie. BOOK, Gaoxiong Shi: Sheng guang shen xue yuan.

Deratany, E. (2007). Why fear? freedom from fear in the secret place. SOUND, Winona Lake, IN: Light and Life Press.

Derr, M. K. (2006). Suggs, Eliza G. Oxford: Oxford University Press.

DeShazer, J. (2012). Jacob DeShazer's personal testimony. ELEC, Wilmore, Ky.: DQB-LLC for the Marston Memorial Historical Center.

Ellershaw, J. A. (2005). Apostolic doctrine, practice and experience. BOOK, Fulwood Eng.: Free Methodist Church in the United Kingdom.

Ferndale Free Methodist Church. (2010). Ferndale Free Methodist Church, a place for you, Ferndale, Michigan. BOOK, Chattanooga, TN: Olan Mills.

Fidler, G. (2006). Adventures in India. BOOK, St. Catherines, ON: Cornerstone Research & Pub.

Fletcher, C. (2011). Sacramental discipleship as a pathway to ecclesial reformation in the Free Methodist Church in Canada (THES). Gordon-Conwell Theological Seminary.

Free Methodist Bradbury Chun Lei Primary School. (2013). Li qing 30 : Xun li jian zheng ji. BOOK.

Goldstein, D. M., & Dixon, C. A. D. (2010). Return of the raider. BOOK, Lake Mary, Fla.: Creation House.

Gregory, D. T. (2005). From the new day to the new century : Free Methodist strategies for metropolitan church planting in light of 1985-2000 efforts and results (THES).

Harvey, D. (2006). STMO (submission, transformation, multiplication, order) : building a culture of kingdom fruitfulness. BOOK, Indianapolis, IN: Free Methodist Church of North America.

Hill, N. (2007). A brief history of Holiness Movement & Free Methodist missions, Egypt 1899-1986. BOOK, S.l.: s.n.

Houser, T., & Houser, G. (2007). Let me tell you : a memoir. BOOK, Charleston, SC: Booksurge.

James, G. (2012). The sanctified way of life. ELEC, Wilmore, Ky.: DQB-LLC for Asbury Theological Seminary.

James, J. F., Free Methodist Church of North America, & General Conference. (2008). Our calling to the poor. BOOK, Indianapolis, Ind.: Light and Life Press.

Kendall, D. W., Winslow, K. S., & Free Methodist Church of North America. (2006). The female pastor : is there room for "she" in shepherd? BOOK, Indianapolis, Ind.: Light and Life Communications.

Killingray, D. (2005). Soga, Tiyo. Oxford: Oxford University Press.

Kirchhofer, W. (2009). Fire among the stubble : church renewal in the Wesleyan tradition. BOOK.

Krober, L. L., & Free Methodist Church of North America Board of Bishops. (2006). Pastors and church leaders manual : resources for leading local churches. BOOK, Indianapolis, Ind.: Light and Life Communications.

Kulaga, J. S. (2007). Edward Payson Hart : the second man of Free Methodism. BOOK, Spring Arbor, Mich.: Spring Arbor University Press.

Lorenz, G. V. (2005). Leading from the margins : recovering the Christian tradition of hospitality in church leadership (THES).

Mahoney, M. A., & Theological Research Exchange Network. (2007). The impact of formational prayer upon spiritual vitality (THES). Ashland Theological Seminary.

Mountcastle, W. D. (2005). Back to the future : evolving the Wesleyan model for renewal and leadership development for the Free Methodist Church (THES). Regent University, Virginia Beach, Va.

Ongley, M. L., & Theological Research Exchange Network. (2005). The impact of training in inner healing for sexual brokenness upon attitudes toward homosexuals (THES). Ashland Theological Seminary.

Oral Hisotory Interview: David Black. (2011). ELEC. Retrieved from http://digital.library.wisc.edu/1793/55519

Roberts, B. T. (2013). Why another sect containing a review of articles by bishop simpson. BOOK, SI: Book On Demand Ltd.

Roberts, B. T., & Coates, G. W. (2007). Practical piety : daily reflections on Christian virtue. BOOK, Indianapolis, Ind.: Wesleyan Pub. House.

Sizelove, R. A. H., & Corum, J. F. (2011). A sketch of my life. BOOK, S.l.: s.n.

Snyder, C. A. (2006). Weeping may endure for a night : a spiritual journey. BOOK, Xulon Press.

Snyder, H. A. (2006). Populist saints : B.T. and Ellen Roberts and the first Free Methodists. BOOK, Grand Rapids, Mich.: William B. Eerdmans Pub. Co.

Snyder, H. A. (2008). Concept and commitment : a history of Spring Arbor University, 1873-2007. BOOK, Spring Arbor, MI: Spring Arbor University Press.

Snyder, H. A., Runyon, D. V, & Snyder, H. A. (2011). B. T. and Ellen Roberts and the first Free Methodists. BOOK, Indianapolis, Ind.: Committee on Free Methodist History & Archives.

Spears, A. K., & Hinton, L. (2010). Languages and Speakers: An Introduction to African American English and Native American Languages. TRAA Transforming Anthropology, 18(1), 3–14. JOUR.

Terhune, C. P. (2006). McCray, Mary F. Oxford: Oxford University Press.

Veldman, R. J. (2006). Classic catechism. BOOK, Indianapolis, Ind.: Light and Life Communications.

Wheatlake, S. K. (2006). Casting away our confidence. BOOK, Chicago: Free Methodist Publishing House.

Wolfe, M.-E. (2005). A strategy for mobilizing integrated local and global ministry in Free Methodist congregations, with an emphasis on gateway cities (urban hubs for unreached people groups) (THES).

Woods, D. A. (1998). Narrative pastoral leadership pastor and people working together (THES). Asbury Theological Seminary.

World Book Inc. (2014). Free Methodist Church.

Roberts, Benjamin Titus, 1823-1893

Bowen, E. (1871). History of the origin of the Free Methodist Church. BOOK, Rochester, N.Y.: B.T. Roberts.

Chesbrough, S. K. J. (1983). Defence of Rev. B.T. Roberts, A.M., before the Genesee Conference of the Methodist Episcopal Church at Perry, N.Y., Oct. 13-21, 1858. BOOK, Buffalo: Clapp, Matthews & Co's Steam Printing House.

Coates, G. R. (2015). Politics strangely warmed : political theology in the Wesleyan spirit. BOOK, Eugene, Ore.: Wipf & Stock Publishers.

Dunning, J., Platt, S. H., & Roberts, B. T. (1877). Brands from the burning : an account of a work among the sick and destitute in connection with Providence Mission, New York City. BOOK, New York.

Hogue, W. T., & Roberts, B. T. (1896). A Symposium on scriptural holiness. BOOK, Chicago: Free Methodist Pub. House.

Iwig-O'Byrne, L. (1993). A Progression of Methodist radicalism : an examination of the history and ethos of the first sixty years of the Nazarites and their heirs (1855-1915) in their social and religious context (THES).

Kysor, K. (1976a). Benjamin Titus Roberts and the Free Methodist Church. BOOK, Cattaraugus, N.Y.: s.n.

Kysor, K. (1976b). The wonderful ways and works of God. BOOK, Cattaraugus, NY.

Lee, L., & Roberts, B. T. (1985). Holiness tracts defending the ministry of women. BOOK, New York: Garland Publ.

McPeak, R. H. (2001). Earnest Christianity : the practical theology of Benjamin Titus Roberts (THES).

Palmer, A. C., & Roberts, B. T. (1875). Lay aside every weight. BOOK, Yarmouth, Me.: I.C. Wellcome.

Priset, D. W., & Herringshaw, T. W. (1999). Roberts, Benjamin Titus. Herringshaw's National Library of American Biography : Contains Thirty-Five Thousand Biographies of the Acknowledged Leaders of Life and Thought of the United States; Illustrated with Three Thousand Vignette Portraits., 18. JOUR.

Reber, C. E. (1985). The doctrine of holiness as taught by B.T. Roberts (THES).

Richardson, J. D., Colgate Rochester Divinity School, & Crozer Theological Seminary. (1984). B.T. Roberts and the role of women in ministry in nineteenth-century Free Methodism : by Jack D. Richardson (THES). Colgate Rochester Divinity School/Bexley Hall/Crozer Theological Seminary, Rochester, NY.

Roberts, B. (1879). Why another sect: containing a review of articles by Bishop Simpson and others on the Free Methodist church,. Rochester, NY: "The Earnest Christian" Pub. House.

Roberts, B. (1984). Why another sect. New York: Garland Pub.

Roberts, B. H. (1900). Benjamin Titus Roberts : a biography. BOOK, North Chili, N.Y.: "The Earnest Christian" Office.

Roberts, B. H. B. T., Roberts, A. A. R., Roberts, E. S. E. L. S. E. S., & Roberts, G. L. (1832). Family papers. (UNPB).

Roberts, B. H. B. T., Roberts, A. A. R., Roberts, E. S. E. L. S. E. S., Roberts, G. L., & Division, L. of C. M. (1990). Benjamin T. Roberts family papers. BOOK, Washington, D.C.: Library of Congress, Photoduplication Service.

Roberts, B. T. (n.d.-a). The holiness teachings. ELEC, Grand Rapids, Mich.: Christian Classics Ethereal Library.

Roberts, B. T. (n.d.-b). The right of women to preach the gospel. BOOK, Rochester, N.Y.

Roberts, B. T. (1860). The Earnest Christian. JFULL, Buffalo, N.Y.: B.T. Roberts.

Roberts, B. T. (1862). The Earnest Christian and golden rule. JFULL, Buffalo, N.Y.: Benjamin T. Roberts.

Roberts, B. T. (1878). Spiritual songs and hymns for pilgrims. BOOK, Rochester, N.Y.: B.T. Roberts.

Roberts, B. T. (1886). First lessons on money. ELEC, Rochester, N.Y.: Christian Classics Ethereal Library.

Roberts, B. T. (1948). Fishers of men, or, Practical hints to those who would win souls. BOOK, Winona Lake, Ind.: Light and Life Press.

Roberts, B. T. (1960). Living truths. BOOK, Winona Lake, Ind.: Light and Life Press.

Roberts, B. T. (1992). Ordaining women. BOOK, Indianapolis, IN: Light and Life Press.

Roberts, B. T. (1997). Fishers of men. BOOK, Indianapolis, IN: Light and Life Communications.

Roberts, B. T. (2013). Why another sect containing a review of articles by bishop simpson. BOOK, SI: Book On Demand Ltd.

Roberts, B. T., & Coates, G. W. (2007). Practical piety : daily reflections on Christian virtue. BOOK, Indianapolis, Ind.: Wesleyan Pub. House.

Roberts, B. T., & Demaray, D. E. (1996). The daily Roberts : readings for every day in the year from the writings of B.T. Roberts. BOOK, Indianapolis, IN: Light and Life Press.

Roberts, B. T., & Rose, W. B. (1912). Pungent truths : being extracts from the writings of the Rev. Benjamin Titus Roberts ... BOOK, Chicago: Free Methodist Pub. House.

Roberts, B. T., Thornton, W. O., Clarke, A., Hills, A. M., & Godbey, W. B. (2001). Chained by a leaf : the use and abuse of tobacco. BOOK, Salem, Ohio: Schmul Pub. Co.

Roberts, E. M. (1962). The bishop and his lady. BOOK, Winona Lake, Ind.: Light and Life Press.

Snyder, H. A. (2006). Populist saints : B.T. and Ellen Roberts and the first Free Methodists. BOOK, Grand Rapids, Mich.: William B. Eerdmans Pub. Co.

Snyder, H. A., Pickerill, K. W., Century, L. of J. W. for the T., & Legacy of John Wesley for the Twenty-first Century. (2003). B.T. Roberts, the Farmers' Alliance and the rise of American populism. SOUND, Wilmore, KY: Asbury College Tape Ministry.

Snyder, H. A., Runyon, D. V, & Snyder, H. A. (2011). B. T. and Ellen Roberts and the first Free Methodists. BOOK, Indianapolis, Ind.: Committee on Free Methodist History & Archives.

Zahniser, C. H. (1957). Earnest Christian; life and works of Benjamin Titus Roberts. BOOK.

Roberts, Ellen Lois Stowe

Carpenter, A. (1926). Ellen Lois Roberts, Life and writings. A sketch. Chicago: Woman's Missionary Society.

Roberts, B. H. B. T., Roberts, A. A. R., Roberts, E. S. E. L. S. E. S., & Roberts, G. L. (1832). Family papers. (UNPB).

Roberts, E. M. (1962). The bishop and his lady. BOOK, Winona Lake, Ind.: Light and Life Press.

Snyder, H. A. (2006). Populist saints : B.T. and Ellen Roberts and the first Free Methodists. BOOK, Grand Rapids, Mich.: William B. Eerdmans Pub. Co.

Snyder, H. A., Runyon, D. V, & Snyder, H. A. (2011). B. T. and Ellen Roberts and the first Free Methodists. BOOK, Indianapolis, Ind.: Committee on Free Methodist History & Archives.

www.ingramcontent.com/pod-product-compliance
Lightning Source LLC
Chambersburg PA
CBHW060448090426
42735CB00011B/1944